MW00444469

Reshaping Our National Parks
and Their Guardians

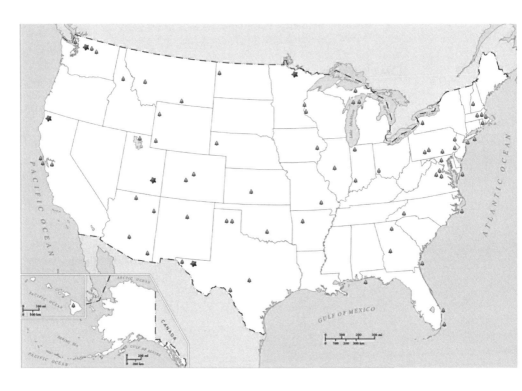

Map 1: During Hartzog's almost nine-year tenure, a record seventy-two parks spread across the country were added to the National Park System. The stars represent "national parks" (Guadalupe Mountains, Canyonlands, Redwood, and North Cascades), while the arrowheads stand for other types of park units. Courtesy of Bob King.

Reshaping
Our National Parks
and Their Guardians

The Legacy of
George B. Hartzog Jr.

KATHY MENGAK

FOREWORD BY
Robert M. Utley

University of New Mexico Press | Albuquerque

LIBRARY OF CONGRESS CATALOGING-IN-PUBLICATION DATA

Mengak, Kathy, 1956–

  Reshaping our national parks and their guardians : the legacy of George B. Hartzog Jr. / Kathy Mengak ; foreword by Robert M. Utley.

    p. cm.

Includes bibliographical references and index.

ISBN 978-0-8263-5108-1 (cloth : alk. paper) — ISBN 978-0-8263-5110-4 (electronic)

1. Hartzog, George B. 2. United States. National Park Service—Officials and employees—Biography. 3. United States. National Park Service—History. 4. National parks and reserves—United States—History. I. Title.

SB481.6.H37M46 2012

333.78´4—dc23

2011041935

DESIGN AND LAYOUT: Melissa Tandysh

Composed in 11/14 Dante MT Std

Display type is Berliner Grotesk Light

Contents

Illustrations and Maps

Illustrations

Maps

Foreword

ROBERT M. UTLEY

George B. Hartzog Jr. served as seventh director of the National Park Service for nine years, from 1964 to 1972. As an outsized personality who studded his career with outsized achievements, he has long deserved a biography. Kathy Mengak has filled that need admirably. She came to know both George and Helen Hartzog intimately when she began to interview him in 1996. In a succession of interviews that continued virtually to the day of his death in 2008, she drew from him a body of priceless oral history. He spoke in colorful, graphic, and emphatic language, so eminently quotable that deciding what to exclude proved a challenge. Relying on many other interviews with knowledgeable people and on her wide-ranging research in Hartzog's papers and other primary sources, she crafted the excellent biography that follows. It not only portrays an extraordinary man but offers a valuable contribution to the history of the national parks and the National Park Service.

I view George Hartzog from the perspective of both historian and participant in his administration. As participant, I served as chief historian of the National Park Service through his entire directorate. As historian, I have had more than three decades to study and reflect on those frantic, momentous years.

I remember George Hartzog as an administrator of rare ability. He was a workaholic who drove his staff at his pace. He not only managed, he ruled. He could be deeply caring, friendly, and sentimental with everyone in the service. He could also be nearly tyrannical in his demands for instant, superior performance. He entertained a broad vision of what the national parks should be and should mean to the American people, and he pursued his vision relentlessly. Above all, both with the executive branch and with Congress, he possessed political cunning, insight, and mastery almost nonexistent among federal agency heads. He employed these talents to the great benefit of the National Park Service and the environmental movement launched by his chief, secretary of the interior Stewart Udall.

As historian rather than as participant in the Hartzog directorate and his friend, I appraise him and his career from a more detached point of view.

Most important, he led the largest expansion of the National Park System in history. During his nine-year tenure, the system grew by seventy-two units totaling 2.7 million acres—he didn't add just national parks but also historical and archaeological monuments and sites, recreation areas, seashores, riverways, memorials, and cultural units celebrating minority experiences in America.

Working closely with subcommittee chairman Senator Alan Bible in 1971, he laid the legislative basis for the expansion of the National Park System in Alaska. When Congress in 1980 finally acted on this provision of law, it doubled the acreage of the National Park System.

Determined that the National Park Service reflect the growing national concern for minorities, Hartzog developed programs that gave the service a different complexion. He took charge of a largely white-male organization steeped in tradition. It did not readily accept change. Even so, women and minorities of different color and ethnicity began to appear in its ranks. When he left the directorate in 1972, the promotion of women and minorities was firmly established procedure, and the number of women and minorities advancing in the ranks has steadily expanded over the years since.

Hartzog persuaded Congress to authorize a program for citizens to volunteer their time and talents to both parks and park visitors. The Volunteers-in-Parks program has flourished as budgetary shortfalls have increasingly overburdened permanent employees.

Beyond the parks themselves, Hartzog pursued outreach programs. Examples are the first environmental education curriculum in kindergarten through the twelfth grade. Complementing this initiative, he inaugurated study areas in a system of national education and development landmarks, christened NEED. He also put into effect programs to make national parks relevant to an urban society, such as Summer in the Parks, Parks for All Seasons, and Living History—two urban parks, in New York and San Francisco, are testimony to his dedication to urban needs. He pushed legislation that created the National Park Foundation, which summoned philanthropic contributions to projects not funded by Congress.

Vastly expanding the reach of historic preservation to the nation as a whole, the National Historic Preservation Act of 1966 would not have passed but for George Hartzog. Many people worked hard on this initiative, but without Hartzog's largely hidden political labors on Capitol Hill with congressional staff as well as members, the law would not have been enacted. He not only brought his legendary political skills to bear, but he also ensured that the entire program would rest with the National Park Service. This I know because I witnessed it as participant.

George Hartzog made great things happen. He benefited from a rare combination of circumstances that favored his vision. It fit neatly into Lyndon Johnson's Great Society and into Stewart Udall's robust environmentalism. The secretary, moreover, not only selected Hartzog for the directorship but gave him full rein and support in pursuing his vision. A Democratic Congress receptive to the Great Society favored the measures Hartzog promoted. Members discovered that voters concerned for their national parks and the environment in which they lived were ready for the laws he sought.

Together with many peers, I look back on the Hartzog years as the "glory years."

I am familiar with the record of every director since the creation of the National Park Service in 1916. Excepting the cofounders, Stephen Mather and Horace Albright, I have no hesitation in pronouncing George Hartzog the greatest director in the entire history of the service.

All these initiatives and more Kathy Mengak chronicles and interprets in this biography, larding the text with compelling quotations from her many interviews. She adds substantially to the lengthening shelf of books about national parks and the National Park Service. At a time when Americans increasingly value their national parks, they should welcome her illumination of this significant man.

(Before his retirement from federal service in 1980, Robert M. Utley served not only as chief historian of the National Park Service but as director of the Office of Archeology and Historic Preservation, assistant director of the Service for Park Historic Preservation, and deputy director of the President's Advisory Council on Historic Preservation. He is the author of sixteen books on the history of the American West.)

Acknowledgments

When someone first suggested I write a book about George Hartzog I thought they were crazy. Sure Hartzog was a fascinating person who left his indelible mark on the National Park System and warranted a book—but me an author! Over time I came to believe it possible. So I send my heartfelt thanks to the many people who believed in me and made this book possible.

Chief among those to acknowledge would be George Hartzog, who along with his gracious wife, Helen, welcomed me into their home. Patiently George answered my many questions, walked me through the inner workings of the National Park Service, told stories of what happened behind the scenes, and explained his actions and decisions as director. In March 2003, he wrote that he felt "deeply humbled that a perfect stranger would devote so much time and attention as to how I got to be who I am." He went on to say that "I suspect except for my bride that you know more about me than any other person alive." He exaggerated but I was touched by his words.

I simply could not have turned a rambling 493-page dissertation into something readable without the guidance of Robert M. Utley. Patiently, he read draft after draft, trying to mold me into a writer. I marveled at the effortlessness with which he turned my unintelligible passages into something that sparkled with clarity. Despite a full schedule of his own research and writing projects, he somehow found the time to promptly answer e-mail questions or read chapters. Since he experienced the Hartzog years as chief historian, he proved to be the ideal mentor. He wanted no special recognition for his efforts and volunteered to lend his name to the effort by writing the foreword. I learned so much from him and am forever in his debt. His wife, fellow writer and former long-time Park Service employee, Melody Webb, likewise provided invaluable writing suggestions and insights.

I would also like to thank the many people who agreed to be taped and interviewed for their perspectives of the Hartzog years. Bill Everhart came to many of my interviews with Hartzog and provided his candid perspectives. Others include Stewart L. Udall, Nathaniel Reed, Robert Stanton, Bill Brown, George Hartzog III, Howard Chapman, Phyllis Shaw, Lorraine Mintzmyer Denning, Ira Hutchinson, Flip Hagood, Doris Osmundson Bowen, Bob Barbee, and Brett Wright. Bill Everhart, Bill Brown, and Frank Norris went a step further by reviewing chapters and providing valuable suggestions. Thanks also to the many other current and former Park Service employees, too numerous to name, who helped with this project.

Thanks to Clemson University's Parks, Recreation, and Tourism Management Department and former Clemson faculty Wesley Burnett, Gina McLellan, Richard Conover, and William F. Stierer Jr., who helped direct initial research and writing. Thanks also to Clemson Library's Special Collections, especially to Laurie Varenhorst, who spent countless hours cataloging Hartzog's papers, and to Michael Kohl, who first suggested Hartzog as a research topic. I am also indebted to the members of the University of New Mexico Press for their efforts in turning the work into a polished book.

Finally thanks to my family for their continued support over the many years it took to bring this effort to fruition. My children, Chris and Lara, grew from children to adults over the course of the research and writing. And my husband, Mike, remained forever supportive and never questioned the time invested.

Introduction

While much has been written about Stephen T. Mather and Horace M. Albright, the founding fathers of the National Park Service, subsequent directors who shaped the agency's vision and direction remain less studied. Among these, George B. Hartzog Jr., the seventh director, was one of the most colorful, powerful, and politically astute. Selected for the top post by Stewart L. Udall, secretary of the interior, in 1964 and dismissed by President Richard M. Nixon in 1972, George Hartzog led the National Park Service for nearly nine years during an exciting and volatile era in our country's history.

Hartzog directed the Park Service during prosperous times when people spent money and enjoyed their leisure as never before. During Hartzog's first five years, Democrat Lyndon B. Johnson occupied the White House and drew powerful support from a Democratic Congress that shared his vision of expanding the federal government's role in improving people's lives. When *Apollo 8* beamed back images of our fragile world spinning in space, we were amazed and humbled. A year and a half later we marveled as Neil Armstrong took the spellbinding first steps on the moon. These triumphs in space helped counterbalance the many problems at home—the Vietnam War, explosive race relations, urban decay, rising inflation, deepening unemployment, and environmental degradation. But at last environmental degradation captured the attention of Congress and led to a series of landmark laws: the Wilderness Act (1964), the Land and Water Conservation Fund Act (1965), the Water Quality Act (1965), the Endangered Species Act (1966 and 1969), the Air Quality Act (1967), the Wild and Scenic Rivers Act (1968), the

1

National Trails System Act (1968), the National Environmental Policy Act (1969), the Environmental Education Act (1970), the Clean Air Act (1970), and the Water Pollution Control Act (1972).

Against this backdrop, George Hartzog sought to make national parks relevant and responsive to the nation's changing needs. The most urgent matter he had to confront was the growing numbers of park visitors who expected unprecedented facilities and services, and he had to balance their wants against the legislative mandate to preserve park resources for the benefit of future generations. He also had to merge a backlog of proposals for new parks with his own agenda for expansion of the National Park System.

Dynamic, aggressive, and exuding certitude, he aroused a range of emotions in contemporaries. At one pole, he could be seen as one "who refreshed the outlook of a tradition loving organization, with a stream of fresh ideas. Perhaps more important, he knew how to make the ideas work."[1] At the other pole, critics could accuse him of having "little personal grasp of natural values, resisting wilderness designations, consistently erring on the side of use over preservation, vindictive toward Park Service employees who did not toe the line and a poor administrator."[2] The truth lies somewhere between these two poles.

❧

My interest in telling George Hartzog's story evolved over a number of years. Like many, I harbor fond memories of family vacations to national parks. Who can easily forget the first view of the rugged Grand Tetons rising dramatically almost a mile and a half above the valley floor? Or the indelible picture of the Great Smokies at dusk when undulating, cloud-shrouded mountains appear to a small child's imagination as sleeping giants? Mammoth Cave, Everglades, Rocky Mountain, and other national parks evoke feelings of wonder, beauty, and adventure. National parks hold the power to inspire yet humble both children and adults.

I experienced George Hartzog for the first time in 1985, when he and former interior secretary Stewart Udall delivered the annual Hartzog Lecture at Clemson University, where I was a graduate student. Departing from the traditional lecture format, they captivated the audience with informal bantering and even told a few whoppers about their adventures in managing and expanding the National Park System. As a prologue to what would unfold some ten years later, I wrote an article about their visit entitled "Hartzog and Udall Reminisce," which appeared in the May 1986 issue of the National Park Service newsletter *Courier*.[3]

In the fall of 1994, after teaching at Ferrum College, a small liberal arts college in Virginia, I returned to Clemson University to work on a doctorate. Following that fall's Hartzog Lecture, a librarian in special collections stated his belief that George Hartzog would provide an ideal masters or doctoral research project. Hartzog had donated personal papers to Clemson to start what he hoped would become a major research collection for studying the National Park Service.

Despite a limited background in history, I felt drawn to such a project. I knew and understood survey research methods but had little grasp of historical methods. With coursework and the guidance of sympathetic historians, I would learn. As one recreation researcher said, "historical research in the recreation field is relatively rare." He stressed the importance of undertaking historical studies that explored the evolution of the park and recreation field before key players were gone. "The need is urgent," he wrote, "for many legends and their contemporaries in the first half of the twentieth century are dying of old age and few written records exist."[4]

In 1995, when my doctoral project was materializing, George Hartzog was seventy-five years old and, because of advanced age, a relentless work schedule, and years of heavy smoking and drinking, in failing health. Many of his contemporaries had passed away or were also experiencing health problems. When I contacted him, he agreed to be interviewed and subsequently gave generously of his time even as his health continued to deteriorate.

Following his directorate, Hartzog maintained close connections with the National Park Service for numerous reasons—he was personally interested in the organization, he had many friends there, and the connections benefited his law practice, which often involved park concessions work. Despite his strong feelings about the National Park System, he tried to avoid criticizing or commenting on how his successors ran the agency. As he said, "I've had my inning and I'm in no position to evaluate . . . today."[5] He also did little to promote his own record, although he had written a book. In a folksy, story-telling manner, *Battling for the National Parks*, published in 1988, shed some light on his tenure. But as Robert M. Utley, his chief historian, later wrote to me, "I leaned heavily on him to share himself and his accomplishments with the world, but he would not do it. Now as he winds down, he wants to leave a legacy and you are the chosen instrument . . . and you must not let him down."[6] From all indications, it seemed that George Hartzog had a worthwhile story to tell, and if I did not tell it, possibly no one would.

In carrying out the research for this work, I interviewed Hartzog, examined his personal papers housed at Clemson University as well as newspaper and magazine accounts of him and books about national parks, and corresponded with friends and coworkers. Because of Hartzog's age, I put considerable emphasis on interviewing him. Over a period of twelve years, I conducted numerous interviews in person and over the phone.

All personal interviews took place at Hartzog's remodeled farmhouse in McLean, Virginia, just outside Washington, D.C. Purchased in 1963 in what was at the time the rural outskirts of the capital, his house in the mid-1990s lay surprisingly close to a heavily traveled road but was protected by large evergreens that maintained privacy and blocked road noises. He had donated additional pine trees to an adjacent park. Once they were planted along the road leading to his house, they further muffled noise and screened the development closing in around him. He owned several acres, which included a house next door that he had originally bought for his mother to live in but that he now rented. A small stream ran along the back of the property. At one time, he raised chickens, pigs, and other farm animals because he wanted his youngest son, Edward, to have a taste of farm life. George and Helen Hartzog had once grown a large garden in their backyard and kept a burro with a two-wheel cart for Edward to ride. No longer able to keep up with a garden, they substituted a variety of flowering plants.

Behind the main house sat two outbuildings. One had been used for Helen's antique business and for storage. The other had been converted into guest quarters and a law office. Here we met for our first interview on March 23, 1996. An Ansel Adams print adorned one wall of his simple, uncluttered office, which contained a desk, filing cabinet, small refrigerator, several chairs, and a coffee table in the shape of the National Park Service arrowhead. Throughout early interviews, Hartzog sipped coffee and chain-smoked, lighting a new cigarette as the previous one dwindled.

Later health problems prompted Helen to get rid of all his cigarettes, cigars, and alcoholic beverages. After an especially traumatic visit to the hospital, this and all other impediments to health were removed. As he explained, "When I got back all my booze and tobacco were gone. I told somebody the other day that I'm reapplying for my Methodist preacher's license. I told them I got one leg so I can't chase women. Helen threw out my booze and tobacco, and I only eat what the doctor prescribes and she fixes. She puts me to bed at 8:30 at night. So I'm better than half of those bastards that are out preaching."[7] Despite his salty language, he held deep-seated religious beliefs.

Health problems eventually forced Hartzog to move his office to the main house in a large airy room with many windows at the back of the house. The room was filled with antique furniture, bookshelves, office work-space, comfortable chairs and a couch, and years of accumulated memen-tos. The few rooms between his office and the bathroom were likewise crammed with memorabilia and family keepsakes given to him or acquired during his travels. One of the most intriguing was what he and his wife called the "Indian room." In it hung an Indian rug given to the Hartzogs by Grace and Horace Albright, who had bought it during their honeymoon. A large Navajo rug covered another wall and antique Indian baskets and other Native crafts were scattered around. A small painting by Arthur Demaray, the Park Service's fifth director, hung next to Helen's museum-quality collec-tion of more than twenty-five hundred stereoscopic cards of national park scenes, which she intends to donate to the Park Service.

All face-to-face interviews were tape-recorded. Bill Everhart, formerly a high-ranking Park Service official who lived nearby in Reston, Virginia, came to many of our interviews. As a close friend and confidante of Hartzog's, Bill could elaborate and prompt Hartzog on certain issues. He felt more com-fortable than Hartzog in committing his own comments to tape. At times, Hartzog deferred to Bill, looking to him to supply his impressions and to handle more sensitive issues. Everhart remained respectful of his former boss, but he was also willing to disagree with him on occasion. Generally, very little prompting was needed to get Hartzog or Everhart started on a lengthy discussion. Hartzog had eloquently demonstrated in congressional testimony that he was a master of redirecting questions he preferred not to answer, and he hadn't changed. Typically, he would restate a question into something he wanted to talk about, tell a few humorous stories to lighten the mood, and then proceed to move the conversation far enough away from the original question that you forgot what you wanted to know. He was so good at this that it often took reading the interview transcripts to understand how effectively he had controlled the discussion.

Hartzog remained conscious of the fact that he was being tape-recorded but would sometimes say things he regretted and then would point out that he trusted me to delete any inappropriate remarks. Since I found it difficult to second guess what he thought inappropriate, I gave him tape transcripts to edit before they became part of his collection at Clemson University. He suggested few deletions; generally these were comments about people. Several times during an interview, he asked to turn the tape recorder off when he was going to launch into a story he did not want on the record. Over the years, Hartzog grew more comfortable during our interviews and revealed some information he had closely guarded at first. For example, he shared little at first about the rocky transition between himself and his predecessor, Conrad L. Wirth, but eventually he let tidbits slip out, generally off the record.

Most of the interviews took place on weekends and lasted from two to five hours. These in-person interviews combined with taped phone interviews yielded typed transcripts of over six hundred pages. Weekend interviews were scheduled around Sunday's *Meet the Press*, which he watched regularly. Hartzog remained amazingly patient with questions and only displayed hints of his legendary temper when a sensitive or controversial topic was broached. George and Helen treated me as a valued friend, offering drinks, snacks, and even lunch on occasion. One time, I arrived for an interview I had neglected to confirm and caught George unprepared. I was embarrassed, but he warmly welcomed me and rearranged his schedule to spend most of the day answering questions. Helen fixed lunch for us all.

I grew very fond of George and Helen Hartzog. Initially, Hartzog started and ended our interviews with his characteristic warm handshake, practiced and engaging smile, and a positive remark for some relatively insignificant thing I had done. Several years into our interviews, the handshakes became hugs. While I personally disagreed with some of his actions and his tipping the balance toward use over preservation, I chose to concentrate on understanding the man, what he did, how he did it, and why he might have done it that way in the context of the times.

Having Hartzog clarify or elaborate on past decisions and events proved invaluable. Such insights into his character, personality, interests, and reasons for his actions I could have gotten nowhere else. However, the downside of the emphasis on interviews was that the information he was supplying came from his memory of things that happened sometimes more than thirty years earlier. Although he remained mentally alert and could respond with surprising clarity and detail to questions, some of his attitudes and opinions had probably changed over the years. In many respects though, his current views compared well with those in earlier interviews, with media accounts during his directorate, and with data found in his papers. Even so, he understood the dangers of recounting events that occurred so long ago, admitting that "recollection is a bad witness to the truth."[8]

Hartzog's memories were corroborated by a number of Park Service contemporaries. These included such people as Stewart Udall, former secretary of the interior; Robert Stanton, the first black director of the service, who served from 1997 to 2001; Nathaniel Reed, assistant secretary of the interior during the Nixon administration; Lorraine Mintzmyer (now

Denning), an early woman pioneer who became regional director; and long-time Park Service employees Howard Chapman, William E. Brown, and Robert D. Barbee. Some, such as Robert Utley, former chief historian, chose to respond to my questions in writing rather than participate in taped interviews. Through e-mail correspondence with a number of people, I was able to clarify data, get additional sources of information, and solicit constructive criticism. Most interviews and e-mail correspondence were conducted with those who worked with Hartzog and respected him, even when they disagreed with him. As Utley admitted, affection for Hartzog came only toward the end of his tenure and "has deepened as nostalgia for the old days takes over, and as comparisons become more evident between him and those who followed him."[9] My contact with Hartzog's critics was limited and would have provided a better balance. Most criticism came from newspaper accounts, magazine articles, letters, and books related to national parks.

Hartzog's collection of personal papers also provided a valuable source of information. Begun in 1984, his Clemson University collection grew to more than 180 boxes and 45 oversized folders. As Hartzog admitted, there were a few things he should have saved that he did not, but in general, he made it a practice to save everything he signed while in office. Prior to donating them, he went through his papers and occasionally destroyed items that he felt uncomfortable including in the public record—especially those reflecting on particular people. He kept a small number of personal papers and left instructions for his children to sort through them upon his death.

Even though Hartzog left a substantial body of papers, as Bill Everhart admitted, "Most of the important things are never written down" and could not be found in Hartzog's papers. As an example, he told the story of the Gettysburg Tower, the looming monster that, although erected on private land, could only be accessed by crossing land within Gettysburg National Military Park.

Everhart recalled a meeting in which the tower's builder, a politically powerful developer, informed Hartzog that he had already been to the secretary of the interior and Senator Hugh Scott, Pennsylvania Republican and Senate minority leader, and implied that it was a done deal. As Everhart remembered, Hartzog responded: "In the history of Gettysburg, there have been a lot of mistakes made. Some of them by local people and many of them by the Park Service. Apparently, there's one mistake that hasn't been made and you want to make it, and I'm telling you I'm going to fight you with everything I have."[10]

No written documents exist that support these objections, and Hartzog took severe criticism for not blocking such an eyesore. But Nathaniel Reed, the assistant secretary, explained how he and Hartzog had battled the proposal. "We fought that bloody tower from one side of the park to the other side of the park. . . . Finally, George and I got a memorandum from John Ehrlichman saying that enough was enough. 'We can't stand it any longer. Let him build his friggin' tower on the least conspicuous piece of land.' It was one of our great losses."[11]

Hartzog's personal papers might also have gaps because, like many government officials, he learned to be careful about what went into the file. For example, the orange interoffice memos clearly stated that they were not to be copied or filed. Also, Hartzog periodically shredded pages from his daily log. He knew that any investigations of park business might bring a subpoena for his and other files, and he wanted them free of misleading or controversial correspondence. During our interviews, Hartzog related the story of how assistant secretary of the interior Stanley Cain (1965–1968) had naively saved personal interoffice correspondence and had to explain in a congressional hearing what he meant when he wrote to Secretary Udall that he supported a controversial decision "for political reasons." "Congress absolutely gave him the burn treatment," Hartzog recalled. "He had to have new skin put all over his back trying to explain what he meant by 'political considerations.'"[12]

Hartzog's donated papers cover a wide variety of topics; they include files on specific parks, memos, press releases, speeches given by Hartzog and others, congressional testimony, media accounts of the Park Service and national parks, letters and other correspondence, and Park Service policies and programs. Some topics, such as National Park Service policies, are represented by considerable holdings, while others, like enhancing workplace diversity, are not. Material used in his book, *Battling for the National Parks*, is also part of the collection. Very few documents survive that relate to his early life and early career with the Park Service. He lamented the loss of these early records, which had been destroyed after a flooded basement dampened beyond repair papers stored in a footlocker. Among other things, he lost his clergyman's license, which he said he earned at the age of seventeen.

There are few secondary sources that deal specifically with George Hartzog. John McPhee wrote the most intriguing account, a long article that appeared in the *New Yorker* issue of September 11, 1971. Hartzog's less flamboyant superiors in the Nixon administration were not amused.[13] In another significant account, Frank Sherwood profiled Hartzog in the 1992 book

Exemplary Public Administrators: Character and Leadership in Government.[14] Additional sources include the many books, articles, and newspaper reports written about national parks and the Park Service, which proved useful in understanding park history, Park Service culture, and the context of Hartzog's times.

The Hartzog years could have been approached from a number of different perspectives, but it was Hartzog himself who helped shape the direction of this work. According to his vitae, he accomplished much over his career. During my first interview with Hartzog in March 1996, I asked him what accomplishments he was the proudest of, and he named three. He said, "We opened up the system to women and minorities. . . . We appointed the first woman superintendent, first black superintendent, and the first Indian superintendent." Secondly, "I brought parks to people with this urban program." Finally, "we enlarged the system to try to preserve the best that was left, including the lands in Alaska."[15] Later, he would add to his accomplishments, noting how he helped expand the Park Service's research capabilities and played a major role in getting legislation passed for the National Park Foundation, Volunteers-in-Parks program, and the National Historic Preservation Act of 1966. These plus chapters describing his early life, career, and post–Park Service years became the framework for what follows.

CHAPTER ONE

The Early Years

For years an old stone fireplace stood near the crossroads village of Smoaks in rural South Carolina. Before crumbling into rubble, it bore the tiny ink-and-soot imprint of an infant's foot. The footprint had been placed there on March 17, 1920, by a proud father celebrating the birth of his first male child. The child bore the father's name, George, and with Abraham Lincoln as his idol, George Sr. may have hoped his son would also rise above his station as a southern farmer to a position of national importance. Although his father did not live to see it, George B. Hartzog Jr. did transcend his station. But he occasionally went back to search for the fireplace with his imprint—perhaps to remember the happy, carefree days of his youth, to soften the painful memories of later family hardships, and to get back in touch with his roots.

☙

The Hartzogs descended from a long line of dirt farmers. Hartzog's father worked 150 acres in a rural farming community 5 miles from Smoaks, South Carolina. The house was unpainted and weathered. A large porch wrapped around the front corner, and another porch lay off the kitchen in back. Water came from a pump in the yard amid smokehouses, chicken coops, and other outbuildings. George's mother cooked on a large black stove that "devoured wood" and kept George busy filling the woodbin.[1]

With most others in the Smoaks area, the Hartzogs relied almost entirely on cotton. They also grew black-eyed peas, green beans, and other vegetables for food and for barter. Corn was served whole-kernel at the dinner table and was also taken to a nearby mill to be ground into cornmeal and grits. There was always a hog or two being fattened in the surrounding woods, a milk cow or two, and occasionally a bull calf for slaughter, as well as plenty of chickens for eggs and meat. Like other farm women, Hartzog's mother spent many hours during late summer canning fruits and vegetables. The land had been intensively farmed, and not always wisely, yet it yielded a modest livelihood for the Hartzogs and their neighbors.

Life in the Smoaks community went on pretty much as it always had. To outsiders, this bucolic existence doubtless seemed "hayseed" and "hillbilly," narrow minded and provincial, but those who populated Colleton County staunchly defended their way of life, gladly prized their exclusion from urban dens of iniquity, and stubbornly held their Bible-based morality and what they perceived as common-sense values.

With its cotton gin, feed mill, bank, barbershop, and hardware store, Smoaks indeed lay well off main-traveled roads. A branch railway line meandered through the area, but the community was not on a main line to anywhere. Crops, weather, the agricultural market, births, deaths, and church activities dominated thought and conversation. People often lived and died in the area without ever leaving its coarse roads and dusty farm lanes. Smoaks experienced barely a hint of the roaring twenties.

Farm life placed constant work demands on the Hartzogs and other farm families. Even young children did their share. Farmers planted cotton in March and vegetables in April. In May, June, and July they hoed, sprayed, and plowed. From sunup to sundown, Hartzog recalled "pickin' cotton and pullin' cotton, spraying boll weevils, and plowing with a mule." When the cotton crop was "layed by," or plowed for the last time in August, families enjoyed a short period of idleness, relaxing, hunting, fishing, organizing family reunions, and attending church-camp meetings.[2]

August and September turned the entire community back to the fields, broiling under a sun that often sent temperatures above one hundred. Young and old joined with neighbors in the exhausting labor of picking cotton and filling the sacks slung over their shoulders. A full sack held upward of one hundred pounds, and the best trailed two sacks behind as they worked. The young Hartzog gloried in the time he finally picked one hundred pounds in a day. "When you pick a hundred pounds of cotton, old friend, I got news for you," he reminisced. "You're really pickin' cotton." It was a "tough, tough life."[3]

Farm families usually had money only at harvest time—if it had been a good year. Barter substituted. The doctor accepted produce, while the barber charged ten cents for a haircut but also took goods in trade. If people wanted something, Hartzog learned, they had to give something up to get it.[4] The few frills families like the Hartzogs indulged in depended on the year's crops. More often than not the dreams of a year faded as the limited cash disappeared to pay bills, purchase next year's seed, and buy necessities such as clothes and shoes. Little money remained to run the household until the next harvest. In a particularly good year, enough might be left over for a radio, new church clothes, or curtains to brighten the home. In lean years, farmers lived on the dream that next year would be better.

⁂

According to Hartzog, religion played a "paramount" role in his early life. Both parents immersed themselves in the Green Pond Methodist Church. For hardworking farm families, religion provided comfort, camaraderie, and hope of better times. Hartzog recalled that between twelve and fifteen families composed the Green Pond congregation. He remembered the church as a quaint clapboard building set in a grove of large trees with enough surrounding land for a small cemetery. Later he grew incensed when the congregation "modernized" it. "Those idiots!" he exclaimed. "That was one of the most beautiful clapboard churches . . . and they were going to modernize it and improve it, so the idiots built a brick veneer over the whole thing and reduced it to nothing."[5]

It was hard to find ministers for the numerous rural churches, and so many were forced to share preachers. Green Pond's minister lived in Smoaks but preached at three or four other churches. He made the rounds two Sundays a month. Elders gave Sunday school lessons on alternate Sundays.[6]

Churches not only nourished the soul but also offered a social outlet for the isolated families. The church hosted "the central event to the social life of the community."[7] Many churches such as Green Pond maintained church camps where days-long camp meetings and revivals took place—generally in August to accommodate planting and harvesting schedules. The Green Pond meetings were held on the banks of the Edisto River and drew families from miles around.

Typically, a well-known evangelist joined the local preachers in leading highly charged, emotional meetings. They pounded the pulpit and raged against modern-day sins. Hartzog remembered a strict church that condoned "no smoking, no drinking, no card playing, no dancing. These were cardinal sins."[8]

Parishioners ate communally and used free time to visit with friends and neighbors. Farmers talked about the weather, crop prices, and the expected

harvest. Women discussed their children, cooking, and community happenings. The young people played, socialized, and courted. Hartzog fondly
recalled church services in the mornings and evenings and afternoons spent
fishing, hiking, or playing ball.[9]

Church was where you "learned everything from manners to ethics,"
according to Hartzog. Youngsters received sharp reprimands if they were
caught misbehaving, and "it didn't take long to understand what manners
were about and it didn't necessarily have to be your mom or dad."[10] Rearing
good children was the job of the entire community.

In Hartzog's view, the church strengthened community ties as well as
religious beliefs. Contemporary society, he contended, had lost the sense
of community he felt as a child.[11] Hartzog's later push for urban parks was
motivated in part by his desire to help restore this lost connection among
city dwellers.

In his youth, religion became such a pervasive influence that he resolved
to become a minister. At the age of seventeen, he recounted, he became the
state's youngest licensed Methodist minister.[12]

⁂

Other than church activities, farmers had little opportunity for leisure pursuits, but they showed their practical side by being both useful and helpful
to others in their community. Hartzog remembered times when neighbors
moved from one farm to the next helping with the fall harvest and social-
izing over shared meals. Families also gathered during butchering time
because the work was so heavy. Hartzog recalled loving the liver pudding
and cracklings made from pork skins. At other times, women socialized over
quilting frames or in sewing circles while men hunted and fished, usually
eating what they killed for dinner. "There'd be a half dozen people hunt
a deer," Hartzog recalled, "and whoever shot the deer got first pick of the
dressed-out meat and then everybody else drew lots. So everybody got some
who was on that particular hunt if they got a deer." Deer were scarce, however, and provided only a small portion of the family's diet. Most meat came
from hogs and chickens.[13]

While Hartzog lacked the temperament to enjoy hunting, he acquired
his grandfather's passion for fishing. Hartzog's eyes sparkled when he
spoke of the catalpa worms that "red breasts just went bananas" over. On
those rare occasions when he and his grandfather were able to sneak away
to a nearby sinkhole lake or the Edisto River, they would catch perch, flat
fish, and catfish. His father disapproved of shirking farm chores, but his

grandfather would always remind Hartzog's father that "the Lord does not count time against you when fishing." Hartzog's father himself loved shad fishing, which was a dusk-till-midnight activity. Hartzog fondly recalled his mother cooking the fish in such a way that the bones just seemed to melt away. He had less fond memories of his maternal grandfather's turtle soup. His grandfather stored the severed turtle heads in the barn loft, and according to Hartzog, "those damn heads would open and close for two or three days at a time." No amount of explaining could convince the horrified youth that those heads were dead. Afterward he always avoided turtle soup.[14]

In later years, Hartzog would find that fishing made a fine bridge between himself and influential fishing buddies he cultivated in and out of Congress.

⚡

Young George's education began in a one-room schoolhouse about a mile from his house, where a local farmer's wife taught first through seventh grade. George, a cousin, and the teacher's son made up the entire first-grade class.[15] By his second year, South Carolina had begun consolidating area elementary schools, so he rode a bus the 5 miles to Smoaks. Because of a poor financial base, southern schools often struggled to provide a quality education. Frequently schooling consisted of only the basics of reading, writing, spelling, and math. School attendance was not mandatory, so many failed to attend regularly, particularly if their help was needed at the farm. Many never made it past seventh grade. During the Depression increasing numbers, especially boys, dropped out—as did Hartzog temporarily—to help support their families.

Although Hartzog claimed he was not a scholar, he did gain effective communication skills. Under the guidance of a special second-grade teacher who believed children should be able to speak in public, he spent considerable time writing and delivering speeches. In fact, he wore his first pair of long pants at a speech he and other second graders gave during high school graduation ceremonies. George went on to enter a number of area speaking contests, including a national contest sponsored by the American Legion that he made it to the regional level in. Hartzog credited speaking contests, involvement in a debate club, and church preaching with enabling him to think and talk on his feet. So he would not "stand up there like a dummy," he learned to grasp the essential facts of an issue and respond quickly and intelligently.[16]

From his father, Hartzog acquired the gift of storytelling. His father was extraordinarily articulate, and he could keep a crowd entertained all evening with his immense repertoire of stories that spoke to the everyday and humorous sides of life. Effective speaking and the ability to spin a good yarn were skills that served Hartzog well later in life.[17]

While sheltered as a child from many of the changes sweeping the country, Hartzog would soon see his world turn upside down. As a market crop, cotton was doomed. Caught in the national mood of prosperity of the 1920s, however, many cotton farmers spent more than they made. Bolstered by a few good cotton crops, even the Hartzogs succumbed by indulging in a new Model T Ford. As one of the first in the neighborhood, the new Hartzog car was undoubtedly a great source of family pride. Hartzog delighted in telling the story of his father's first experience in learning to drive a car. Long used to his horses and wagon, the elder Hartzog drove the car to church, and as he drew near, he shouted "WHOA, WHOA" without putting his foot on the brake. While "WHOA" had always stopped his team of horses, it took two large pine trees to stop the Model T Ford.[18]

As early as 1925, farmers began to fail, and one after another they went bankrupt. Even before the crash that launched the Great Depression of the 1930s, the Hartzogs joined many of their neighbors in bankruptcy. "When you went bankrupt," Hartzog recalled, "it was when the price of cotton dropped to five cents a pound after ginning. It just didn't pay to pick it and you just left it in the field." In his last year as a farmer, Hartzog's father turned the cows into the unpicked fields so at least some good could come from the crop. Hartzog vividly remembered the pain of standing by his "bewildered and distraught father and grandfather when the farm was sold to pay the mortgage."[19]

This devastating experience left an enduring memory of the preciousness of land that would powerfully influence Hartzog's thinking in later years.

After they lost their farm, the Hartzogs moved into George's grandfather's house. For the young Hartzog it marked the end of relatively carefree, happy childhood days. Worse was to come. What lay ahead would push the family to their limit and test their belief in God. Soon after losing the family farm, George came home from school to see his grandfather's house engulfed in flames, leaving the Hartzogs nothing but the clothes they were wearing. They moved into a rented house and continued to farm his grandfather's land. Desperate, they and some of their neighbors switched to truck farming and grew perishables. When George Sr. shipped a load of watermelons to New York, the railroad sent him a bill for freight costs instead of a check for produce, which had found no market.[20] With the failure of that venture, Hartzog and other truck farmers were left with crops they could not sell and mortgages they could not pay. The Great Depression that began in 1929 all but destroyed the already embattled farmers.

If the loss of his family's farm and his grandparents' home had not stripped the last vestiges of childhood innocence from the young Hartzog, then surely the Great Depression did. The Hartzogs had difficulty making ends meet. Slowly the government responded with food and, eventually, jobs for those in need. Hartzog's father walked to Smoaks for government handouts of butt meat, sugar, flour, and cornmeal, and for that night the family had biscuits. The 5-mile walk for free food dealt a severe blow to the dignity and self-respect of the man who had once driven a new Model T Ford to Smoaks.[21]

Many thought that the hard times were temporary and that conditions would improve as President Hoover promised, but the Depression continued and deepened. As Hartzog put it, "Poverty clung to us like a sweat-soaked shirt."[22]

The Hartzogs had lost almost everything. In addition, George's father suffered from severe asthma and his mother from a debilitating form of arthritis that left her often bedridden and with a permanent limp.[23] The family had hit bottom. With misted eyes, Hartzog recalled the strength and determination of his mother as she forced herself from bed to pull the family together toward some semblance of recovery and stability. In 1933, she moved the family to Walterboro, the county seat, where she found work as a seamstress. Thirteen-year-old George remained behind to work for Arthur Thomas, a farmer and principal of the Sunday school class at Green Pond Church. Without George, his mother had one less mouth to feed, and George could earn his own keep.

George rejoined the family a year later, at which point he was diagnosed with pellagra, a widespread nutritional condition caused by a poorly balanced diet and an overdependence on corn products. The condition left him feeling as if he had no energy.[24] Untreated, his pellagra could have resulted in mental problems, general debilitation, and eventually death. Fortunately, however, health officials mounted a balanced-diet campaign that encouraged people to keep a cow and grow home gardens to put fresh vegetables on their plates. Once George's problem was identified and he ate a proper diet, his health and energy levels rebounded.

George's mother steadfastly refused to let the family lose hope and faith. She "kept that vision there all the time 'cause she refused to believe that things could happen the way they happened to us. At one point, to be the wife of a very successful farmer and then wind up with not a damn thing to eat and not a house to live in. That almost killed her, but she got up and out of her sick bed . . . and went on to keep that family together for the many years my father was incapacitated and that was it."[25] Hartzog's mother served as a valuable role model for him in later years as he confronted societal problems of gender and of the place of women in a man's world.

Hartzog's relationship with his father is harder to discern, for he discussed it reluctantly. In happier times, George Sr. was a hardworking farmer who loved to tell a good story. Then health problems, loss of his farm, and ensuing hardships left him a broken man. Respect lavished on his mother did not appear to extend to his father. One can imagine the emotional difficulties the family would have faced each day when Hartzog and his mother left for work, and his ailing father stayed behind with his two sisters.

An accomplished seamstress, George's mother eventually became supervisor for the county's Works Progress Administration sewing room, which made clothes for the poor. Work relief often stigmatized a family, but it provided a way for people to survive with dignity, and relief workers received twice the support of basic welfare. Typically, the government paid women less than men even if they were their family's main financial provider and doing comparable work. The Works Progress Administration, for example, paid men $5 a day and women only $3.[26] Popular attitudes held that men were the breadwinners and women merely supplemented their income.

The Depression robbed many children of a carefree adolescence filled with simple pleasures. As the oldest and only male child, George felt the pressure to assume some of the family responsibilities, especially since his father could not. George worked a variety of part-time jobs during high school and turned his wages over to his mother. "You didn't feel deprived or unique or any of those things," he said. "What you were expected to do was to work and try to take care of your family."[27]

Many children who grew up during the Depression were left with what has been called an "invisible scar."[28] For some, that scar shaped and molded the adults they became. According to one researcher, "Some lives were cut short or stunted while others found purpose and opportunity to achieve beyond all imagining."[29] George Hartzog developed the resourcefulness, resilience, and drive to become one of the latter. And like many of his generation, making money and living frugally became a way of life.[30]

❧

To help support his family, the teenage Hartzog took a series of after-school jobs, working at an icehouse, delivering papers, cutting grass, and washing clothes in a laundry. These did not bring enough money, so he quit school and worked both a day and a night job. At first, he worked days at an Amoco filling station and nights as a desk clerk at the Lady Lafayette Hotel, where he registered guests, carried luggage to rooms, and listened for the teletype that might bring a telegram for someone in the hotel. In between duties, he would catch some sleep on the couch in the lobby.

A high school diploma seemed increasingly beyond reach. Then, an old friend of his mother's intervened. Colonel James Risher, owner and head-master of Carlisle Military Academy, persuaded the family to let George attend the remaining six weeks of the academy's semester. If he could pass the final exam, Risher would grant him a high school diploma. Although the family needed George's salary of a dollar a day, they agreed. Six weeks later he passed the final exam and received his diploma.[31]

Seeing a similar promise in the young Hartzog, local businessmen asso-ciated with his church paid his tuition at Wofford College in Spartanburg, South Carolina. They wanted him to keep working toward his dream of becoming a practicing Methodist preacher.[32] Bethel Methodist Church, sev-eral miles from the college, also helped out by giving him a student pastor's appointment. After one semester, however, the donations ran out, his father became totally incapacitated, and the family needed his income. He had to drop out of college.

Hartzog found work at Beckers Bakery in Gaffney, South Carolina, where each night he packed bread into boxes. Soon he was promoted to the higher-paying job of a "jumper," a person who stands poised, ready to leap from the delivery truck the moment it stops at a country store. With the grin of a gifted storyteller, Hartzog told how in an explosion of activity, he would quickly "take every damn piece of bread that's on those upper shelves and put it to the bottom in order to get a more favorable space for your bread." And if by "accident" you happened "to stick your thumb through the [com-petitor's] wrapper that's all right too." Hartzog knew that any subsequent jumper would do the same to his bread.[33]

Next, Hartzog parlayed typing and shorthand skills gained in high school into a better paying secretarial job that was federally funded by the National Youth Association.[34] Although he only stayed in this job a short while, this work later provided a topic of conversation with Lyndon B. Johnson, who administered the Texas National Youth Association program at the start of his political career.

Before long, Hartzog switched jobs again and began work with a timber cruiser in Brunswick, Georgia. The crew consisted of the timber cruiser, who marked and evaluated the land for sale; Hartzog, who held one end of the chain while the timber cruiser did his calculations; and a black man about Hartzog's age, who chopped through the thick undergrowth.

In the spring of 1939, Hartzog secured his future by winning a secretarial position in the office of Joe Moorer, a prominent Walterboro lawyer. Under Moorer's tutelage, Hartzog embarked on a rigorous program of "reading law." South Carolina permitted high school graduates to pursue this route in the office of a practicing attorney through a three-year curriculum prescribed by the state supreme court. His motives were largely pragmatic. The law offered a path to a higher standard of living, and the fact that Walterboro's finest homes belonged to lawyers was not lost on the young Hartzog. "I didn't want to be a ditch digger," he explained. "That was your alternative. . . . It was all financial necessity. I wouldn't say there was a lot of philosophical or aesthetic ambition involved in it."[35]

Even so, legal training imparted insights beyond the purely legal, such as the importance of getting all the facts and knowing where your support lies. "You want to be sure that when you have finished with a subject and are ready to make a decision on it, you've got a better case against yourself than the other fellow has. . . . You want to make sure you research the cases for the opposition as well as for your own, so that you understand what the issue is."[36]

To increase his salary of $10 a week, Hartzog joined the South Carolina National Guard. In September 1940, little more than a year into his legal program, he was called to active duty. After a year at Camp Jackson, near Columbia, South Carolina, family hardship gained him an early discharge.

Back in Walterboro, Hartzog resumed his secretarial job and law studies. To supplement his income, he also sold insurance and worked as a stenographer, transcribing political speeches and reporting them for the county newspaper. From local politicians, he learned the importance of "pressing the flesh," a technique he would later use to solidify his allies and disarm his adversaries.[37]

In December 1942, after two unsuccessful attempts, Hartzog passed the South Carolina bar exam. Now a credentialed lawyer, he could launch a career as a practicing attorney. More than two years after Pearl Harbor, he remained a civilian. In March 1943, the day after his twenty-third birthday, however, his call finally came to report for active duty. His legal background landed him a position as a clerk in the judge advocate's office of the Seventy-Fifth Infantry Division at Fort Leonard Wood in Missouri.[38]

Here Hartzog made friends with a fellow clerk, destined to exert a major influence on his career. A Jewish refugee from Austria, Paul Gantt, mesmerized Hartzog with personal stories of German atrocities. While Gantt managed to escape the Nazis by bribing a Gestapo officer, his mother and father were both incarcerated, and his father ultimately perished in prison. Gantt eventually made his way to the United States. Although trained as a lawyer, he sold brushes for a living while he learned English and completed enough courses at the College of William and Mary to pass the Virginia bar. Because of a severe asthmatic condition, he received a disability discharge, but he and Hartzog kept in touch, and after the war Gantt steered Hartzog toward government work.[39]

While stationed at Fort Leonard Wood, Hartzog applied for a number of jobs that offered higher rank and thus more money. His first opportunity came when he was accepted as a navigator at flight school in Galesburg, Illinois, but the Air Corps scaled back the program, and Hartzog was reassigned to Biloxi, Mississippi. Soon afterward, another opportunity came through, and he entered Officer Candidate School. Commissioned a second lieutenant, he was assigned to the military police and sent to work at the Port of Embarkation in Boston, Massachusetts.

During his infantry training, Hartzog learned judo (what he called "dirty fighting"). In confrontations with infantrymen who let off too much steam at the bars, brothels, and tattoo parlors near the base, the military police officers where he was assigned had been "getting the living hell beat out of them" and were being hauled off in greater numbers than those they were trying to police. The base's commanding officer wanted Hartzog to help reverse the trend, so he taught the men judo and how to use their pistols and nightsticks effectively. During one of these physically demanding training exercises, he slipped a disk in his back, which later led to severe back problems. Eventually his back was operated on, but he dealt with persistent pain ever after.

Although Hartzog disliked military service, he later came to appreciate it as "one of the great experiences of my life." His work exposed him to a range of human behaviors from heroism to debauchery and led him not to be "generally surprised by human disappointment."[40] He also used the military's educational benefits to begin college at American University in Washington, D.C.

For a small-town boy, the military opened Hartzog's eyes to a world of opportunities lying beyond Colleton County, South Carolina. By the time Hartzog finished his military service in March 1946, Joe Moorer had hired a new law clerk, and Hartzog had lost many of the local contacts necessary for a successful law practice. Additionally, he was not anxious to return to a place where he had experienced so much hardship and heartbreak. So he concentrated his job search around the Washington, D.C., area.

⚜

Hartzog's interest in the Washington area was also influenced by Helen Carlson, a young woman he had met while serving in Boston. Helen's brother had been stationed at a small air base in Walterboro, South Carolina, where both of Hartzog's sisters worked as secretaries. They befriended the young man from Massachusetts and invited him over for home-cooked meals. When Hartzog was later sent to the Boston Port of Embarkation, Helen's family reciprocated by inviting him to dinner. Since he was new to Boston, he had arranged to meet Helen at the Statler Hotel, where he would identify her as a blond in a green fur-trimmed coat. Amid the hustle and bustle of the Statler, he finally spotted his attractive dinner escort.

Over time, Hartzog fell for the lively young woman and asked her to marry him. He was devastated when she declined, but when she called to wish him a happy twenty-sixth birthday, he thought he might still have a chance. As the avid fisherman observed years later, "I've been playing with a bass for a long time. I know when I got one. I just got to let the rascal play his way out. I knew then [with her call] that I was in pretty good shape."[41] Although Hartzog was enchanted with Helen's good looks, vivacious nature, and gracious manners, his mother never completely warmed to the northern woman, and the two never became close. Nevertheless, George and Helen were married in June 1947. Helen became a staunch national park advocate, a charming hostess for official functions, the mother of his three children, and a lifetime partner to whom he credited much of his success. Hartzog dedicated his book, *Battling for the National Parks*, to Helen: "Marrying her was the smartest thing I ever did."[42]

⚜

Hartzog's early years were difficult, but they molded him into the man he became. He grew up in a southern agrarian environment where traditional values predominated. Hard work, faith in God, and a strong sense of community held the rural neighborhood together. People went to church, worked their farms, and enjoyed the few leisure opportunities available. Bartering and helping neighbors substituted for cash money.

Farming the worn-out soil in a fading cotton economy kept the Hartzog's family in a cycle of indebtedness until conditions beyond their control took away their livelihood. The Depression managed to heap misery on top of heartache as the Hartzogs struggled to survive with the federal government's assistance. Hartzog learned how difficult conditions could become, and he was determined that such hardships would never return. So when the door to the ministry closed, law practice became infinitely preferable to digging ditches. He sought opportunity behind every door as he studied law, did secretarial work, sold insurance at night, and transcribed political speeches. Throughout his life, he skillfully cultivated influential mentors and friends who helped advance his career. The intervening World War II redirected and matured him, opening his eyes to the possibilities beyond Colleton County, South Carolina. Connections, and a bigger paycheck, would bring the ambitious Hartzog to the National Park Service, where he would remain for twenty-six years, eventually rising to the agency's highest rank.

The National Park Service

In October 1946, at age twenty-six, George Hartzog joined the National Park Service—an agency only slightly older than he was. Despite its youth, the Park Service already possessed a strong sense of mission and a body of rich traditions. Although officially established in the Department of the Interior in 1916, its roots lay in the government's much earlier role in setting aside parcels of the public domain as national parks.

Americans did not come easily to the idea of their government managing lands set aside for enjoyment and edification rather than economic exploitation. Only because the remote Yellowstone highlands seemed to have little economic potential did Congress in 1872 bow to the appeals to declare it a national park. Yellowstone set the precedent, and other national parks followed: Yosemite (1890), Sequoia (1890), Mount Rainier (1899), and Crater Lake (1902).[1]

These first parks showcased the country's natural wonders, but interest started to grow in protecting prehistoric Indian ruins. Looting of invaluable cultural artifacts from the cliff dwellings of southwestern Colorado led to the establishment of Mesa Verde National Park in 1906. That same year, Congress passed the Antiquities Act, which gave the president executive authority to set aside as national monuments sites on the public domain containing scientific, historic, and scenic treasures. In the remaining three years of his administration, President Theodore Roosevelt, a staunch outdoorsman and conservationist, exercised this power to proclaim eighteen national monuments.[2]

By 1915 thirteen national parks and eighteen national monuments had been established. Most fell under the jurisdiction of the Department of the Interior, but some fell to the Forest Service in the Department of Agriculture and to the War Department. Regardless of administering agency, all lacked consistent and uniform management. On behalf of Interior, the U.S. Army guarded big national parks like Yellowstone, Yosemite, Sequoia, and General Grant. Civilian appointees of the Interior Department, rarely more than political hacks, held responsibility for others like Mount Rainier and Crater Lake. Funding was always inadequate and almost nonexistent for the national monuments.

Early in the twentieth century, the compelling need for management consistency gave birth to a movement to create a separate bureau to care for national parks and monuments. Franklin K. Lane, secretary of the interior in the Woodrow Wilson administration (1913–1921), recognized the need and sought a strong proponent to bring the idea to fruition. He turned to Stephen T. Mather, a self-made borax millionaire interested in national parks and deeply concerned for their future. Mather agreed to serve as Lane's assistant and to take charge of the department's responsibility for parks and to promote a parks bureau. Horace M. Albright, a newly recruited young lawyer from California, agreed to serve as Mather's assistant. An instant chemistry and symbiotic relationship developed between the twenty-four-year-old Albright and Stephen Mather, a man twice his age.[3]

Mather and Albright—these were the founding fathers of the National Park Service. As Albright accurately noted, Mather was "an experienced public relations man, created instant rapport with strangers, had a personality that radiated poise, friendliness and charm, could talk easily with anyone he met, confidently instilling perfect strangers with his enthusiasm." Albright described himself as "knowledgeable about Washington, the Interior Department, and the Congress," as being "quite good at detail and administrative work, which he [Mather] obviously hated," as able to "help with legal problems," and as, above all, "loyal and conscientious." Both would leave a powerful legacy; it was this heritage that made the National Park Service so appealing to George Hartzog.[4]

A talented promoter, Mather felt that success in establishing a parks bureau lay in making people aware of the parks and encouraging as many as possible to visit them. Drawing on his own fortune, he launched a massive publicity campaign and turned his charm on key members of Congress. One of his promotional strategies included hosting "mountain parties" in the Sierra Nevada for influential congressmen, publishers, businessmen, writers, and conservationists. Not a minimalist by nature, Mather treated his guests to luxuries not associated with wilderness camping experiences. "Roughing it was not a term used for our dining," admitted Albright. "As it was every night on our trip, the table was set with snowy white linen table-cloths and napkins, silverware and china." A chef accompanied the group, baking bread daily, fixing fresh trout, and feeding the group from his store of specialties.[5] By the trip's end, Mather had turned the group into enthusiastic park supporters.[6]

Legislation to establish a national parks bureau had come before Congress many times, but in 1916, largely because of Mather's promotional activities, it gave promise of passage. In an election year, however, even supportive congressmen working on various drafts of the bills proved difficult to corral. Mather and Albright persisted, and the publicity campaign kept the subject alive across the nation. Finally, on the eve of adjournment, Congress passed the National Park Service Enabling Act, and on August 25, 1916, President Wilson signed it. An excited Albright sent Mather, who was off on another mountain party, a telegram saying, "Park Service bill signed nine o'clock last night. Have pen used in signing for you."[7] On May 16, 1917, Secretary Lane appointed Stephen Mather the first director of the National Park Service and Horace Albright his assistant director.

The heart of the 1916 act lay in a mission statement composed by Frederick Law Olmsted Jr., son of the famous landscape architect. It charged the National Park Service to "conserve the scenery and the natural and historic objects and the wild life therein and to provide for the enjoyment of the same in such a manner and by such means as will leave them unimpaired for the enjoyment of future generations."

The law thus imposed a dilemma on the new agency: preservation versus use. The resources that justified a national park must be made available for the enjoyment of the present generation but also passed on intact to future generations. As Albright conceded years later, he and Mather recognized the paradox, but the acts creating Yellowstone, Yosemite, and other parks had also contained these opposing edicts. Public opinion embraced Theodore Roosevelt's concept of conservation as combining protection with use. "We felt it was understood to be standing policy," recalled Albright. Not only Mather and Albright but all their successors sought a balance between these conflicting components of their legislative mandate. Administrative interpretations and preferences, often influenced by politics, determined whether the balance leaned more heavily toward preservation or use. It could never be purely one or the other.

With the fight to establish the National Park Service over, Albright and Mather struggled to turn the disorganized conglomeration of parks into a uniformly managed system and to further develop a guiding philosophy. Some park enthusiasts pressed for more hotels, roads, and other amenities, while others wanted strict limits on development. Appropriations seemed to depend more on how many voters visited the parks than on how well they were cared for.

Aware that they could not please all their constituents, Mather and Albright tried to chart a middle ground between preservation and use. "It is a lofty but erroneous belief that Stephen Mather and I were great idealists," recalled Albright, "that we indulged in philosophical discussions and charted the ways we would carry out our dreams for the reservations under our control. There wasn't any magnificent plan, only a series of problems that had to be solved as they arose. We improvised as we went along."[8]

During these early years, Secretary Lane left Mather and Albright to run the parks as they saw fit. Both knew that the agency would endure only if the cause of national parks gained vigorous champions in congressional appropriations committees, which meant that the base of public support had to be enlarged and energized. Albright saw the answer largely in establishing more parks and thus gaining more park visitors. Mather, however, assigned top priority to consolidating and improving existing parks. New parks meant more work, and they usually came without the money to staff them. Both approaches, however, would help boost public awareness of parks and attract more visitors, and throughout the Mather-Albright era, the Park Service adopted both.

Significant in this effort were railroads and automobiles. The rail companies launched "See America First" campaigns that drew on wartime patriotism to persuade Americans to turn their backs on ocean liners bound for Europe and instead ride passenger coaches bound for the parks. Automobiles, increasingly affordable, allowed owners the freedom to ignore railroad timetables and visit and tour parks on their own timetable. Mather worked closely with railroad companies and local and national automobile associations to promote park visitation.

Without more and better facilities and services, the parks would not lure more visitors. Dissatisfied tourists did not make enthusiastic supporters on Capitol Hill. Trapped from the beginning in the quandary of preservation versus use, Mather and Albright therefore pushed the balance toward use. To accommodate the influx of cars, roads designed for stagecoaches were upgraded and more miles built. Foot and horse trails encouraged people to leave their cars and more fully experience the parks. During the Mather years, the Park Service built some 1,300 miles of roads and 4,000 miles of trails. Accommodations ranging from luxurious to rustic took shape. Railroad companies continued their practice of constructing and promoting grandiose hotels. Campgrounds proliferated. Sewer and water systems, power plants, and communication lines supported the expanding facilities.

Later critics charged Mather and Albright with sacrificing preservation to use and, worse yet, laying the groundwork for a lasting partiality toward development within the Park Service. Confronted with political reality, however, the founders understood that only happy users could assure an enduring National Park Service. They rationalized the pragmatically essential development by representing it as confined to small islands amid a vast park wilderness.

To protect the parks and visitors, the Park Service had to improve and increase staffing. This became especially important once the big parks were no longer being overseen by the military. As opportunities allowed, Mather and Albright also replaced the ineffectual political appointees who were serving as civilian superintendents. As a professional Park Service took shape, two major centers of influence emerged. On the one hand were the engineers and landscape architects who designed and developed park facilities and on the other the managers, rangers, and naturalists who guided the park's daily operations. The two groups formed the organization's foundation and instilled it with a strong sense of mission and identity. They helped define the values and principles and established lasting traditions. They also coalesced into a close-knit family. This was especially true of the superintendents, rangers, and naturalists, who wore forest green uniforms and broad-brimmed Stetson hats. They became the visible expression of agency customs and traditions and the first embodiment of later generations of proud "green bloods."

Later a third group emerged: the natural scientists and foresters who fought for the management of park flora and fauna according to scientific principles rather than managerial whim. They often found themselves at serious odds with the other two elements of leadership and suffered many frustrating defeats.[9]

To enhance camaraderie and seek opinions on management problems, Mather held superintendents' meetings. After lively discussions of park issues, the director hosted elaborate dinners accompanied by singing, practical jokes, and horseplay. These meetings helped to establish loyalty and develop lifelong friendships. Esprit de corps and strength of purpose fostered from the beginning would later bind George Hartzog to the National Park Service.

⁑

Late in 1916, Albright noticed an alarming shift in Mather's behavior, and in January 1917, Mather suffered a severe mental breakdown. This left Albright to direct the National Park Service, an awesome responsibility for a young man not quite twenty-seven years old. During the next two years, Mather faded in and out of park business as his health improved only to worsen again. Acting as he believed Mather would, Albright worked to develop consistency in such matters as uniforms, policies, and park manager qualifications. He understood the importance of guiding principles, but this was the task that tormented him most. "The thing that weighs the heaviest on me is policy making," he confessed to a friend. "Organizing this new Service with few precedents to go by and no one but myself to make decisions is a terrible burden."[10]

Even so, Albright strongly felt the need for a "creed" set to paper that would provide guidance for all managers. On May 13, 1918, Secretary Lane himself issued just such a doctrinal manifesto to Director Mather. It elaborated the mandates of both preservation and use and spelled out other principles, such as regulation of concessions, a ban on hunting, and elimination of private inholdings, that would provide a basis for managing the parks and building the park system. Lane's directive spelled out the "creed" and earned a hallowed place in the history of the National Park Service. Not until 1964 did Albright admit that he, not Lane, had authored this document and persuaded the secretary to sign it.

To add to Director Albright's difficulties, on April 6, 1917, the United States declared war on Germany. The war left few competent men to run the parks, seriously limited budgets, and tested the Park Service's ability to protect the parks. Under the guise of patriotism, commercial interests made repeated efforts to open the parks to exploitation—to cattle grazing, to hunting of wildlife for food, to felling forests for timber, and to other profitable concessions. During the next two years, Albright managed to deflect most of the inappropriate proposals but found that Secretary Lane had boxed him into a compromise permitting the grazing of sheep, or "hoofed locusts" as John Muir called them, in some areas. Albright learned, as did his successors, that compromise went with the job, but the difficulty lay in determining when and to what extent compromise was acceptable.

In 1919, Mather's health recovered enough to allow him to return to the directorship. Albright redefined his position, assuming the superintendency of Yellowstone National Park, while at the same time acting as Mather's field assistant. The two continued to function as a team in leading the Park Service. They worked toward refining policies, adding to the park system, battling an aggressive Forest Service that wanted to run the parks, and seeking ways to expand into the East.

Eastern expansion presented a formidable challenge. The western parks had all been carved out of the public domain. No such lands existed in the East; there parklands would have to be purchased from private owners. In 1926, Congress authorized the establishment of Shenandoah National Park in Virginia, Great Smoky Mountains National Park in Tennessee and North Carolina, and Mammoth Cave National Park in Kentucky but stipulated that they could be established only after the necessary lands had been acquired. Mather and Albright turned successfully to philanthropy. The pennies of schoolchildren added to the millions donated by John D. Rockefeller Jr. eventually brought these parks into the system, but not until after the Mather-Albright era.

In 1928, Mather suffered a debilitating stroke, the complications from which would lead to his death in 1932. In 1929, Albright doffed his green uniform and moved from Yellowstone to Washington, D.C., to become second director of the National Park Service. As the nation plunged into the Great Depression, he remained essentially true to the policies developed during the 1920s. In one way, however, he leaped ahead of Mather. Albright had long loved history and wanted to include more historic places in the system, even the battlefields and forts of the War Department and the national monuments of the Forest Service. Mather had had little interest in this course. Shortly after Franklin D. Roosevelt won the White House in the election of 1932, he named Harold Ickes as secretary of the interior. Albright presented his new boss with a briefing book that included the goal of consolidating all the battlefields and historical monuments in the National Park System. On April 9, 1933, he got a chance to pitch this scheme directly to the new president. After Albright showed him a potential retreat in Shenandoah National Park, Roosevelt invited him to ride with him back to Washington. En route they passed the Civil War battlefield of Manassas. Knowing the president's similar love of history, Albright pointed out the salient features.

He then went on to propose that all battlefields be transferred from the War Department to the Park Service.

Albright felt that Roosevelt was receptive, but he was stunned by the scope of the government-wide reorganization that the president announced on June 10, 1933. More than fulfilling the proposal Albright had put forth during the ride back from Shenandoah, it consolidated all national parks and monuments, all national military parks, all national memorials, eleven national cemeteries, and all the parks of the national capital into a single system to be administered by the National Park Service.[11]

The reorganization made the park system truly "national." It gained twelve natural areas in nine western states and Alaska, fifty-seven historical areas in seventeen mostly eastern states, and the parks and memorials of the District of Columbia.[12] The number of park units more than doubled, from 67 to 137. For the first time, historical areas outnumbered natural areas. The administration of so many parks and monuments demanded that the tightly knit cadre of "Mather men" be expanded into a much larger and thus more unwieldy bureaucracy. The 1933 reorganization would forever change the character of the National Park System and those who managed it.

With Park Service's future secure from a Forest Service takeover and the historic monuments safely tucked under its protective wing, on July 5, 1933, Albright resigned as director to pursue a career in private business. No person left a more powerful stamp on the Park Service than Horace Albright. His legacy still defined the agency when George Hartzog joined it in 1946.[13]

From private life, Albright continued to exert a strong influence on the Park Service and never hesitated to make suggestions on how the parks should be run. Subsequent directors, including George Hartzog, would seek his counsel and often receive it whether they wanted or not.

❧

Albright's departure left Arno Cammerer as the third director of the National Park Service. "Cam" had joined "Mather's men" in 1919 as an assistant director. Over the years, he had worked closely with top management, advancing to associate director under Albright in 1929 before assuming the directorship in 1933. While Mather and Albright had built a solid foundation for the Park Service, much still needed to be done, and the agency would find itself pulled in new directions. Arno Cammerer was competent and well liked but lacked the dynamism of his predecessors.[14]

In addition to reigning over a park system that had doubled in size under the reorganization of 1933, the new director had to deal with the

Park Service's new responsibilities with the Civilian Conservation Corps (CCC), one of many government relief programs. As a further complication, the irascible secretary of the interior, Harold Ickes, did not like Cammerer and seemed to take particular delight in harassing him.

Foreseeing the benefits of the coming relief programs, the departing Albright had tried to prepare and strategically position the Park Service by calling for lists of system-wide conservation needs along with estimated costs. Nevertheless, the CCC program, described as the largest peacetime mobilization of men ever, tremendously strained the Park Service, which was not equipped to handle the staggering number of enrollees employed in six-month time blocks. Anxious to provide relief to the unemployed, President Franklin Roosevelt hoped to have 250,000 men working nationwide in parks and forests by July 1, 1933, a mere three months after signing the bill. Some Park Service staff worked sixteen-hour days seven days a week to meet the president's deadline. By July 1 the Park Service had found work for thirty-four thousand men in 172 camps in thirty-five states. The Park Service administered conservation work not only in the national parks but on state and local parklands as well.[15]

Cammerer had to double the Park Service workforce so that there would be enough supervisors for the influx of CCC workers. At the program's height in 1935, the agency needed 6,000 employees to oversee 120,000 enrollees located in some 600 camps. Of these, 112 were located in national park areas and 482 in state parks. The state park branch, directed by Conrad L. Wirth, helped state agencies organize and develop programs modeled on those of the Park Service. Under Wirth's supervision, the CCC helped establish the first state parks in Virginia, West Virginia, South Carolina, Mississippi, and New Mexico as well as upgrading systems in other states. Wirth's employees provided crucial aid to 711 new state parks.[16]

By 1937 Roosevelt had begun to cut back CCC numbers, and by 1942 World War II had brought the program to an end altogether. It had been an enormous success, and the National Park Service had contributed vitally. During its nine-year lifetime, the CCC had enrolled some two million men in 198 camps located in 94 national parks and 697 state and local sites, leaving as visible evidence new trails, bridges, roads, campgrounds, and visitor facilities. The Park Service had also hired unemployed professionals such as historians, archaeologists, and museum curators. Afterward, many remained as career employees, steering the Park Service towards increasing specialization. The organizational needs of the massive CCC program also led to decentralization, with a field office administering programs in each of five geographical regions.[17]

Although the Depression and its relief programs dominated Cammerer's directorship, he managed to expand the park system somewhat. In 1934, he added Florida's Everglades and in 1935 the Texas Big Bend.

Under Cammerer, furthermore, the Park Service moved aggressively into historic preservation and recreation. The Historic Sites Act of 1935 charged the agency to identify, catalog, and protect significant historic sites, buildings, and objects. The Park, Parkway, and Recreational Area Study Act of 1936 assigned the agency a prominent role in planning for the country's park and recreation needs. Under these laws, the Park Service became the lead federal agency for both historic preservation and recreation and the channel through which federal aid flowed to lower levels of government.

In 1936, the Park Service launched the Historic Sites Survey and also assumed responsibility for all recreational activities at Lake Mead, whose waters backed up 115 miles behind Nevada's Hoover Dam. The following year, Cape Hatteras, North Carolina, became the first national seashore.

With his health broken by years of exhausting work, a hostile Harold Ickes, and finally a heart attack, Arno Cammerer stepped down in 1940 to become regional director in Richmond, Virginia. He died a year later. Although unpretentious and soft spoken, he had ruled with a firm and experienced hand. Under his oversight, the Park Service had moved from a small agency that managed western natural areas to a large agency that also protected the nation's historical treasures and provided for its recreational enjoyment.

※

In 1940, Newton B. Drury succeeded Arno Cammerer, the first director drawn from outside the Park Service. An articulate environmentalist and head of California's Save the Redwoods League, he brought a conservative philosophy to the directorate. He thought that the Park Service, spurred by New Deal programs, had strayed too far from its roots as "the custodian of the masterpieces of nature and sites that are of great historical worth because they are significant examples of the greatness of America."[18] It had become a "Super-Department of Recreation" and a "glorified playground commission."[19] Indiscriminate park additions diluted the high standards of an earlier time, and these additions, he maintained, ought to be managed by state systems. He opposed the emphasis on recreation and favored minimal development of visitor facilities. As director, he sought to tip the balance of the dual mission back toward preservation. The budgetary constraints imposed by World War II helped by limiting development. His principal duty lay in protecting the parks from the same kind of commercial interests that Albright had fought off in World War I.

To free office space in Washington, D.C., Drury had to move the Park Service headquarters to the Merchandise Mart in Chicago, leaving only a skeletal crew behind in the nation's capital. This loss of proximity to the policy makers and appropriations committees hurt the Park System, as did Drury's lack of experience and contacts in Washington. While his predecessors had been opportunistic and aggressive, Drury favored a more conciliatory, less confrontational style. Conflicts could be resolved amicably through compromise and gentlemanly discussions. He found the Washington political scene distasteful and felt out of his element when testifying before appropriations committees.[20]

As once-abundant relief funding dried up and the New Deal relief programs ended, appropriations dropped from $21 million in 1940 to just $5 million in 1943. As staff headed off to war and funding diminished, full-time employees fell from 3,500 in 1941 to less than 2,000 the following year. With gasoline rationing, visitation to the parks plummeted. Although Drury had inherited a park system in good shape due largely to Civilian Conservation Corps efforts, the war choked off funds necessary to maintain even minimum standards. And Drury worked hard but not always successfully to defend the parks against a barrage of military and commercial interests that sought special uses for "patriotic" purposes.

After years of austere spending and a battle simply to hold onto what it had, the Park Service found itself ill prepared for the war's aftermath. Lacking proper funding, roads, trails, and buildings had deteriorated and only skeletal staff remained to care for them. At war's end, however, people flooded into the parks. Between 1945 and 1947, the Park Service saw visitation jump from 11.7 million to 25.5 million. As the country dealt with its huge war debts, austere park budgets failed to recover. To make matters worse, the unassertive Drury, inhibited by his opposition to development, did not push aggressively for more.

At this stage in its evolution a young George Hartzog, fresh from military service, entered the Park Service, still headquartered in Chicago, remote from the centers of power. Despite the director's conservatism, both the new recruit and the agency brimmed with a youthful enthusiasm accompanied by a feeling of urgency to accomplish great things. The dedicated, close-knit family of park employees, infused with an almost missionary zeal for their work, provided a comfortable fit for a man who once aspired to the ministry. The Park Service Hartzog joined was evolving, just as it had done since its inception. It would continue to be an agency assailed by a multitude of threats and pressured by many diverse interests to alter its balance of use and preservation.

Journey to the Directorate

Hartzog left the military in 1946 in search of a career path. With his South Carolina contacts largely dried up, he decided to look in the Washington area, which also brought him closer to Helen Carlson. Paul Gantt, a military buddy, helped get him interviews with two federal agencies. They were the General Land Office (later Bureau of Land Management) in the Department of the Interior and the Office of the Solicitor of the Interior Department. The solicitor's office offered work in public land law, the land office work in oil and gas leases. Because he believed oil and gas work would benefit his career, he chose the General Land Office. Within six months, he grew frustrated with government bureaucracy and joined a private law firm that provided counsel for such companies as Phillips Oil.[1]

Several weeks later, Hartzog got a call from Jackson Price, chief counsel for the National Park Service, another Interior Department bureau. Price had seen Hartzog's credentials when he was processed out of the General Land Office. Impressed, Price offered him a job that paid more than his first government position and even his present private position. For financial reasons, Hartzog accepted. As he later admitted, he knew so little about the National Park Service that he thought he was being interviewed for a position in the U.S. Forest Service. "We didn't know the Park Service in South Carolina. All we knew was the Forest Service from Francis Marion [National Forest]."[2] In fact, he had visited only one national park in his life, Mount Rainier, while he was at Fort Lewis, Washington, awaiting a discharge from the army.[3]

George Hartzog quickly gained an appreciation of national parks. He had joined a small agency, set in its ways but steeped in tradition and intensely proud of its mission. "You felt as though you had the opportunity for individual growth and achievement. Whereas in the General Land Office at that time you were a lawyer handling oil and gas leases and that was it and stay out of anything else, you know. And so I felt a sense of freedom and an opportunity for growth in the Park Service that I had not known in the General Land Office, and I think that persisted throughout that agency for many, many years."[4]

In October 1946, George Hartzog moved to National Park Service headquarters, temporarily housed in Chicago, where he rented a room until he married Helen in 1947. Due to a severe housing shortage, the newlyweds were forced to live in hotel rooms. City ordinances outlawed people from occupying a room for more than a week, so at the week's close the couple packed up and moved to a new location. Finally, they managed to move into the apartment of a friend on temporary assignment.

Because of his prior experience in the military police, one of Hartzog's first tasks was to develop a law enforcement handbook outlining procedures for dealing with common ranger problems. Lacking park experience, he attended a park operations conference for chief rangers and clerks. Here the twenty-six-year-old Hartzog got to know men from parks he had read about but never seen and found himself impressed with their knowledge and love of their parks. They were "individualistic, tough, self-reliant men bound to a common code above service."[5] Holding them in awe, he wanted to become a part of this cadre of spirited, dedicated people.

In October 1947, the National Park Service headquarters moved back to its home in the Interior Department building in Washington. Here Hartzog learned he would have to give up his position to a senior employee "riffed" from another federal agency. He had sufficiently impressed his supervisors, however, that they wanted to retain him, and so they created a temporary position for him in Region III and stationed him at Lake Texoma, Oklahoma. There, as regional attorney, he used his legal expertise to work out business and agricultural lease agreements for land around the lake.[6] Just as he was completing this work in 1948, a position in Washington opened, and he transferred back to work with the legal and contract aspects of concessions management. In August 1950, his division chief died in an accident, leaving Hartzog the acting chief.

Part of the driving force behind Hartzog's move to concessions and his appointment was Arthur Demaray, a highly respected Park Service icon. Demaray had worked with Stephen Mather and was one of the original three employees hired in 1916 to staff the Park Service. Preparing for retirement, Demaray was honored with an eighteen-month appointment as the agency's fifth director while Conrad L. Wirth prepared to take the helm. Although Hartzog had known Demaray at work, it was not until they became neighbors that their friendship blossomed. The Demarays took a special interest in the young Hartzog couple. The new director's support smoothed the way for Hartzog to become acting chief of concessions. He learned much from the benefactor he described as a "master of legislative programs" with unexcelled human skills. Demaray "could be tough when he wanted to be tough and part of human skills is to know when to draw the line and where to draw it," and, according to Hartzog, he did know. "He could be testy for you when you crossed his lines."[7] It was a style Hartzog cultivated.

Hartzog applied to become permanent chief of concessions, but he failed to qualify for the position's GS-13 grade because of insufficient administrative experience. After a new chief was named, Hartzog returned to his role as assistant and worked to complete administrative manuals on concessions and land management.[8]

While in Washington, Hartzog applied for admission to the bar of the U.S. Supreme Court. This required a lawyer to have passed the bar in at least one state and to be of good character. According to custom, the Interior solicitor moved for the admission for all the department's lawyers. To get better acquainted, Solicitor Mastin White asked Hartzog to join him for the short ride to the Supreme Court building. En route, White learned that Hartzog had simply read law to pass the bar and had not earned a college degree. A graduate of the University of Texas Law School and a Harvard PhD, White lapsed into silence. At the Supreme Court, he duly moved Hartzog's nomination. Shortly afterward, however, a memorandum circulated through the Department of Interior stating that only graduates of reputable law schools would be hired as lawyers. "Overnight I improved the level of legal talent in the Department of the Interior," Hartzog quipped. White "didn't think much of my legal education." In the Park Service, however, Hartzog was a "comer," one who moved swiftly up the ranks. Between October 1949 and April 1951, he rose from GS-11 to GS-13 and brought home 26 percent more pay.[9]

Although Hartzog never attended law school, he attended night school at American University and in June 1954 earned a BS in business administration. His heavily business-oriented coursework included such classes as public administration, business forecasting, industrial relations, and supervision in industry. He continued his studies, reportedly falling three hours short of an MBA before transferring to his first field position.[10] Hartzog later found the training helpful because he came to believe that "big government and big business have a great deal in common."[11]

⚜

To Hartzog, "it was perfectly obvious . . . that the people that were going to lead were people who had served in parks." To move into higher echelons, he requested a field assignment, even though it meant a lateral move at his current GS-13 grade.[12] After ten years with the Park Service, he understood the agency, had cultivated important friends, and knew what it took to rise in the hierarchy.

In August 1955, Hartzog accepted his first field position in Rocky Mountain National Park as assistant superintendent. A former boss, James Lloyd, had recently been made superintendent. Over the next two years, Hartzog learned much about park operations from Lloyd, who was a stickler for such details as clean restrooms, smooth entrance station operations, and friendly rangers who personally greeted visitors. As Hartzog described him, Lloyd "was a resourceful, tough—sometimes tyrannical—boss who worked interminably long hours to perfect the new ranger organization and demanded that his rangers do likewise."[13]

As the park's assistant superintendent, Hartzog's duties were largely administrative, but he loved telling stories about how the rangers indoctrinated the "Washington bureaucrat" who had taken a job one of them should have gotten. As part of his field initiation, he recalled being invited to go fishing at Bierstadt Lake with one of the rangers. Although a determined Hartzog fished the beautiful mountain lake for hours, he never caught anything—did not even get a bite. The following day, he complained to Lloyd that the "damn fish . . . don't like to bite a Southerner's hook." The amused superintendent informed him that the lake never had any fish. It was sterile. The Washington man had been duped.[14]

Hartzog soon recognized that Rocky Mountain had created a better permit form for saddle-horse operations than the one he had put into the concessions manual he had written in the Washington office. Since permits were shipped to the regional office, the different form prompted a regional memo inquiring why the correct form had not been used. Since Hartzog had created what he now saw as an inferior form, he and the superintendent chose to ignore the memo, and nothing more was ever mentioned.

After a little over two years, Hartzog received one of eight government-wide scholarships for a management course given by the American Management Association. He was also offered the assistant superintendent's position at Great Smoky Mountains National Park, a large park bordering Tennessee and North Carolina. Soon after moving his family to housing near the park's western entrance at Gatlinburg, Tennessee, Hartzog was detailed to the Washington office to complete his last manual. Despite his waning belief in the value of such manuals, he completed one on land acquisition policies in several weeks and rejoined his family.[15]

From his superintendent at Great Smoky Mountains, Edward A. Hummel, Hartzog learned the importance of joining such organizations as the Rotary Club, the PTA, and local church. In that way park personnel and their families became recognizable members of the community, which helped smooth over the adversarial mentality that could prevail in gateway communities. Locals could attach a face to those who made decisions that affected their community.

Hartzog took Hummel's advice and joined the local Rotary Club, which sponsored a number of projects, including athletic programs for children. Since his twins were eight, it fell to him to organize a baseball program for seven- to ten-year-olds. With only enough local boys to make up one team, he formed another team from local girls, including his own daughter, who was a tomboy and skilled player. Gentleman that he was, he encouraged the boys to let the girls bat first. For a number of innings, the girls lobbed balls over the boy's heads for home runs until the flustered boys managed to get them out. When the boys came to bat it was "three boys up and three boys down." Only by talking the victorious girls into evenly matched coed teams could the season continue. The girl's victory had left him and the boys "mystified" about the "weaker sex." Fortunately before the next season he was transferred to St. Louis.[16]

※

In 1959, after less than a year and a half in the Smokies, Hartzog was offered the superintendency of Jefferson National Expansion Memorial, an aging and neglected park on the St. Louis waterfront. Centered on the old courthouse, scene of the historic Dred Scott decision of 1857, the park had long been mired in controversy over a proposal to erect a memorial to westward expansion on the waterfront. The project seemed destined to remain in limbo, and park management looked on the memorial as an undesirable assignment.

Not Hartzog. He had been a GS-13 for almost eight years. The park meant promotion to GS-14 and a daunting challenge to give new life to the memorial project. He knew the risk to his career if he failed, but he did not expect to fail. Complex coordination, agreement among diverse organizations, and staying just inside legal limits would become his trademarks at Jefferson National Expansion Memorial.[17]

"I got a promotion to a [GS-]14 when I went to St. Louis," Hartzog said. "It cost me $190 because St. Louis had the commuter tax. If you lived outside the city you still had to pay city income tax. So I had to pay city income taxes. I lost $190 and I got a promotion to a GS-14."[18]

The memorial idea had originated in the 1930s to commemorate the nation's territorial expansion and as a means to rejuvenate the Mississippi River waterfront, which had deteriorated into an eyesore. Initially, President Franklin Roosevelt was not enthusiastic about funding such a memorial, but he changed his mind as elections neared and the importance of carrying Missouri was brought to his attention. The recently enacted Historic Sites Act of 1935 gave the federal government a way to fund the project on a cost-share basis. For every $1 of city money, the government would provide $3 of federal money.

In preparation for the memorial, buildings were torn down and land cleared, but World War II put the project on hold. In 1947, reinvigorated city leaders sponsored a design competition. Architect Eero Saarinen won, beating out his own well-known father. Saarinen's major purpose was "to create a monument which would have lasting significance and would be a landmark of our times." He ruled out an obelisk, a rectangular box, and a dome on the grounds that none of those matched the monument's purpose or the site. What did seem right was a great arch—the "gateway to the west" that would appear to be "leaping up" out of the ground rather than squatting down.[19]

In 1956, Congress appropriated funds to begin construction. During the first phase, railroad tracks were to be relocated to an underground tunnel. There were delays in bid preparation, however, which angered the St. Louis mayor Raymond Tucker, who then elicited a promise from Conrad Wirth, director of the Park Service, that track relocation would commence before July 1, 1959. This deadline put incredible pressure on the new superintendent, who arrived in St. Louis in January 1959. Additionally, he had to gain citywide support for a project that the city's media lukewarmly labeled the "wicket." Superintendent Hartzog knew that without widespread popular backing his chances for success would be seriously diminished, so he directed part of his effort toward convincing the media and citizens that they truly wanted a memorial arch.[20]

Instrumental in moving forward was Mayor Tucker. Hartzog told Tucker that he had "come out of a small community background, I'd never been in a big city in my whole life. I knew nothing about big city politics . . . because I'd been involved with the federal government and its legislative programs." Since Tucker knew politics and had public support, he agreed to handle the politics while Hartzog dealt with the paperwork.[21]

Hartzog had less than six months to work a bureaucratic miracle. He had to solicit relocation plans, share them in a preliminary review with multiple parties, revise them accordingly, advertise for bids, obtain signed contracts, and begin work before his July 1 deadline. When preliminary relocation plans were finally completed in March, he insisted on further shortcuts. Rather than conducting a series of plan reviews, he held a daylong plan review that attracted more than a hundred engineers, architects, estimators, construction superintendents, union representatives, and state, city, and railroad officials.[22] To further speed the process, he solicited bids with a unit pricing structure that enticed companies to bid the unit cost of doing, for example, a yard of excavation work or pouring a yard of concrete. Hartzog had a signed contract by June 18 and broke ground on June 23, a week before the mayor's deadline.

Next on the schedule were the huge overlooks and retaining walls essential to completion of the railroad relocation. Emboldened, Hartzog proposed bypassing normal contracting procedures and instead wrote a change order for the new work so MacDonald Construction Company, which had won the original contract, could continue. Hartzog reasoned that keeping the same contractor would save time, eliminate coordination difficulties if another contractor were to step in, and ultimately save taxpayer money. MacDonald agreed to extend the contract for the same unit prices despite price increases in concrete and steel.

While small change orders were common government practice, the magnitude of Hartzog's change order of $2.5 million threw Park Service officials into an uproar, especially since the change order was larger than the original contract by $106,000. As Bill Everhart explained, Hartzog is a "kind of person who looks at things in a different way than everybody else, which was always one of his great traits, and he didn't react instinctively, the way he'd been trained. He didn't think in straight lines. Linear thinking wasn't his bag."[23]

Despite strong objections from every Park Service official, including Director Wirth, Hartzog persisted. Eventually the unusual measure was arbitrated by the comptroller general of the General Accounting Office in Washington, D.C. He sided with Hartzog and allowed the original contractor to continue to work uninterrupted.

The next major phase involved excavation and preparation for the arch footings estimated to cost $3.5 million, even though the budget allocated only $1.65 million. With Hartzog's blessing, St. Louis media and influential citizens campaigned to get additional funding. The efforts focused on Clarence Cannon, a Missourian who chaired the House Appropriations Committee. Sensitive to allegations of Democratic overspending and cognizant of the fact that St. Louis fell outside his district, he stubbornly refused to intervene. Instead, he suggested that President Eisenhower request the funds. Finally, Tom Curtis, a Republican representative from south of St. Louis, forwarded the necessary legislation through.

Meanwhile, Eero Saarinen was still working on the height of the catenary curve, which takes the shape of a heavy chain hanging freely from two points. Because the placement of the footings and surrounding construction depended on the height, any changes in the height caused problems. As Saarinen continued to contemplate the "right shape of the curve," the arch's height of 590 feet rose to 600 feet, peaked at 640 feet, and finally settled at 630 feet. Each change required a redesign of construction plans.[24]

As trucks from every cement plant in St. Louis lined up and began pouring concrete for the park's overlook, Saarinen realized as he walked around the project that the overlook walls had to curve rather than go straight up as planned. He insisted that the plans be redrawn—before any more concrete was poured. Much to the outrage of MacDonald's general superintendent, the trucks turned back, leaving Hartzog and others to deal with the aftermath.[25]

Tragically, Eero Saarinen died in 1961, before seeing his project completed. According to original estimates, the $9 million federal and $3 million city funds should have completed Saarinen's vision for the arch, visitor center, site landscaping, and Museum of Westward Expansion tucked under the arch. Revised bids made Hartzog realize that the transportation system inside the arch, the museum, and site landscaping were doomed unless creative solutions could be found. He solved the problem of how to move visitors inside the arch by using regional transportation development funds. While transporting people within a catenary curve hardly matched the fund's intent, few could deny that it fit the legal guidelines. Since the unique tram system moved people from one place to another, it qualified as a fundable "transportation system." Had it been classed as an elevator or escalator, it would have been ineligible.

As for the proposed underground Museum of Westward Expansion, Hartzog knew if the acre of space for the museum were not excavated as the arch went in, no one would ever go back and add it. So even though he could not finish the museum, he argued successfully that the site be prepared for its addition and finally sold Wirth on the need to find the funding.[26]

Hartzog had evolved into a bold, innovative, and resourceful leader. Performance ratings from 1951, when he worked in concessions, showed high marks for "work habits" and "work attitude," but his overall rating was "satisfactory." By 1955, at Rocky Mountain National Park, he was "excellent" in all categories. Several years into his superintendency at Jefferson National Expansion Memorial, the "excellent" rankings were all replaced with all "outstanding," the highest rating possible.[27] By accomplishing the nearly impossible in St. Louis, he solidified his reputation as a "comer" in the Park Service. Experience had taught him that "no" did not necessarily mean that something could not be done; it simply meant that you had to approach the problem from a different angle, that you might have to alter the rule book, and that you had to be willing to push the limits. At Jefferson National Expansion Memorial, Hartzog fine-tuned his people skills through complex negotiations involving a variety of interdependent agencies that had to agree before work progressed. By working closely with political leaders at all levels of government, he honed his natural affinity and flair for politics that stemmed from his background as a preacher, lawyer, and former associate of South Carolina political figures. His success also encouraged his later movement into urban recreation areas as director.

Hartzog's extraordinary achievement in getting the arch construction underway had impressed the St. Louis political and business establishment. Early in 1962, Mayor Tucker urged him to leave the Park Service and become executive director of Downtown St. Louis, a city agency charged with revitalizing the downtown. If he made the move, his salary would increase substantially, but he preferred to move up in the Park Service. On three occasions, however, he had approached Director Wirth about transferring to a higher position, only to be told to stand in line and wait his turn. Despairing of a promotion during the Wirth regime, in July 1962, Hartzog resigned from the Park Service and accepted the position as head of Downtown St. Louis. Although he had spent fifteen years with the Park Service, which he called a family, he resigned himself to watch from the sidelines as pieces of the arch were lifted into place.

Meanwhile, the retirement of Eivind Scoyen had left the associate directorate of the Park Service vacant. Scoyen himself headed a committee charged with compiling a short list of five candidates for the position. As Hartzog later learned, his name was not only on the list but at the top. Even so, Wirth had pointed out that Hartzog had no regional office experience to qualify him for a Washington assignment (Wirth himself had no field experience at all). To Hartzog, "It was perfectly clear that I was not his [Wirth's] choice."[28]

⁂

While Hartzog's resignation seemed to close the chapter on his Park Service career, an earlier fortuitous meeting would reopen it. In 1960, Hartzog had been chosen to develop local support for the proposed Ozark National Scenic Riverways in Missouri. For several months on weekends, he traveled 300 miles to southeastern Missouri to develop a constituency. If a park lacked significant local support, the area congressmen would not champion the cause in Washington.

By the fall of 1961, Hartzog had generated enough support to warrant a visit from the new secretary of the interior appointed by President Kennedy, Stewart L. Udall. According to Udall, Hartzog had "formulated a political game-plan to turn the Show Me State's rivers into a new kind of national park," which would mark the first protected river in the park system, predating the 1968 Wild and Scenic Rivers Act.[29] Hartzog knew the park's supporters and detractors, and he shared with the secretary his insights on how to make the park appealing to the "hillbillies" who lived along its banks. Udall was impressed with Hartzog's preparations and recalled seeing "him immediately as a good leader, a driving type, full of enthusiasm and interest."

During the two-day trip an almost brotherly relationship developed as the two floated down the Current River. Less than three months separated them in age. Both were from small towns, had lived through the Depression, and had served in the military. Although of different faiths, both were reared with strong religious values, and both had law backgrounds. Udall recalled the Ozarks trip as "a situation of utter informality, heightened communications. We went skinny-dipping at night. It was September, and chilly. But this was a group of outdoor people, who were in their element. The Current was going to be the first national river. We hadn't done anything like this before."[30]

Even at that time, Udall had thought that the Park Service needed a new director. From the beginning, his relationship with the older Wirth had been rocky. As writer Mike Frome saw it, Wirth "wanted to be left alone to run his own show. . . . He didn't take direction well from the top. Connie was a good man and a good manager, but when we got into this whole expansion program, a park director had to . . . be a politician and help sell the park. Connie couldn't do that. He set Sleeping Bear Dunes back for years. He went to an angry citizens meeting, tried to reason with them, and then told them, 'Well, there's going to be a national lakeshore whether you people like it or not.' And he stomped out."[31] If Udall needed a more politically adept director willing to sell the idea of parks, he had found the right person in George Hartzog.

Visiting St. Louis in September 1962, Udall discovered that Hartzog had quit the Park Service. Asked why, Hartzog explained that he saw no future in it. "Would director be enough future?" Udall asked. "Mr. Secretary, it sure would," responded Hartzog.[32]

And there the enigmatic exchange rested for several months, until the Hartzogs journeyed to Washington for a ceremony in which George received the Department of Interior Distinguished Service Award. Afterward, summoned to the secretary's ornate office, he joined Udall and assistant secretary John Carver. Wirth would retire soon, Udall said—although Hartzog had the impression that Wirth did not know it yet—whereupon Udall would offer the directorship to Hartzog. "I want that job more than anything in the world," Hartzog declared. But he did not want to be seen pushing Wirth out and thus making enemies of Wirth's friends. With Carver, he worked out a strategy that Udall accepted. Wirth would select Hartzog for the vacant associate directorship and later in 1963 announce his retirement. Udall would then name Hartzog director. In February 1963, after only seven months with Downtown St. Louis, Hartzog moved his family to Washington and became associate director of the National Park Service.[33]

The transitional period through 1963 was rough for both Hartzog and Wirth. Bill Everhart recalled that Wirth "really gave George some bad times."[34] Later, in one of the drafts of his book, Hartzog wrote about this period and mentioned a number of intentional slights. During his first six weeks as associate director, for example, his new office "was crammed to the walls with accounting and budgeting equipment." Very slowly his office was "cleared of its contents." Everhart, however, urged Hartzog not to disparage anyone's good name, and he deleted the criticism in the final version.[35]

Hartzog's tireless work ethic coupled with his ambition, resourcefulness, and people skills had led to his rapid rise through the ranks. Although he entered as a lawyer working in concessions and other legal areas, he realized that promotions depended on field experience. So he requested moves that took him to Rocky Mountain and Great Smoky Mountains national parks. In a career gamble, he accepted the superintendency at Jefferson National Expansion Memorial, where he grew as an administrator and honed his talents for building political support among diverse groups. His ability to get things done, even though it meant pushing the limits of acceptable practices and procedures, brought him to the attention of high departmental officials. Secretary of the Interior Stewart Udall would find in Hartzog a younger, more progressive director not entrenched in what his assistant secretary felt was an "insular, rigidly bureaucratic, and politically unresponsive" agency and someone who could actively support the secretary's agenda and pursue new, innovative directions.[36]

Figure 1:
Hartzog entered active service in March 1943, just after his twenty-third birthday. Military service exposed him to job possibilities beyond rural South Carolina and brought him in contact with his future bride, Helen. Courtesy of the Hartzog family.

Figure 2: The happy couple departs for their honeymoon on Martha's Vineyard, June 28, 1947. Helen became an important partner throughout her husband's career. Courtesy of the Hartzog family.

Figure 3:
George and Helen at Vanderbilt Mansion in Hyde Park, New York, with their twins, Nancy and George, in 1950. At the time, Hartzog was using his law background to work on legal and contract issues involving Park Service concessions operations. Courtesy of the Department of the Interior. National Park Service Historic Photograph Collection, HPC-001117, Harpers Ferry Center, WV. W. Ray Scott, photographer.

Figure 4:
Assistant superintendent Hartzog working at his desk in Rocky Mountain National Park, 1957. He accepted a lateral move to the field from his Washington, D.C., position so he could move up in the agency ranks. Courtesy of the National Park Service. Rocky Mountain National Park, Estes Park, CO.

Figure 5: Superintendent Hartzog pointing out features on an architectural model of the proposed Jefferson National Expansion Memorial to Vice President Richard Nixon and others, 1960. Hartzog had been warned against taking the superintendency, since the complexities of getting the Gateway Arch built seemed overwhelming and failure would hurt his career. Courtesy of the Department of the Interior. National Park Service Historic Photograph Collection, HPC-001116, Harpers Ferry Center, WV. Harold Ferman, photographer.

Figure 6: Superintendent Hartzog surveying the construction site for the Gateway Arch with its architect, Eero Saarinen (far right) and his wife, Aline, while business associate John Dinkeloo, looks on, ca. 1961. Saarinen died before seeing his project to completion. Courtesy of the Hartzog family.

Figure 7:
Associate director Hartzog
at his desk in 1963. Behind
him rests a model of the
Gateway Arch and pictures
of his family. To his right,
on the upper left hangs a
picture of Conrad Wirth,
the man he would soon
replace as director. Courtesy
of the Department of the Interior.
National Park Service Historic
Photograph Collection, Harpers
Ferry Center, WV.

Figure 8: Hartzog is sworn in as the seventh director of the National Park
Service along with associate director A. Clark Stratton, while secretary of
the interior Stewart Udall looks on, in 1964. A youthful Hartzog would bring
change and innovation to an agency content with the status quo. Courtesy of
the Department of the Interior. National Park Service Historic Photograph Collection,
Harpers Ferry Center, WV.

The Hartzog Directorate

The assassination of President Kennedy on November 22, 1963, threw George Hartzog's appointment as director into question. Wirth was not retiring by choice, Hartzog believed, and he reasoned that if Lyndon Johnson selected another secretary of the interior, Conrad Wirth might keep his position. But when Johnson retained Udall, Wirth retired. On January 4, 1964, Hartzog became director. He had leapfrogged many more senior employees and, as a result, would be under critical scrutiny. According to Robert Utley, chief historian during Hartzog's tenure:

> The career service resented the way Wirth was booted out and greeted Hartzog with apprehension, anxiety, and a wait-and-see resignation. Hartzog had held two assistant superintendencies before taking over JNEM, and he had been a lawyer before that. But I don't think the fraternity of superintendents ever thought of him as one of them. He just wasn't the orthodox gray-and-green, as he swiftly demonstrated on becoming director.[1]

Hartzog knew of the widespread opposition to his selection but hoped he could eventually convince the skeptics that Udall had made a wise choice. Acceptance did come, not only because of vigorous and effective leadership but also owing to the rapid turnover in personnel as the 1930s generation reached retirement age. Some of the old guard retired willingly, some with a push from the new director. As a friend pointed out, "You are really shaking the tree! Overripe fruit will surely fall!"[2] As the fruit fell, Hartzog appointed people he trusted or in whom he saw potential, thus increasingly gaining the allegiance of key personnel.

Young and energetic, Hartzog "hit the ground running," according to Utley, and "launched all sorts of non-traditional initiatives." His unorthodox style appalled many, especially the more traditional veterans. A nearly constant stream of reorganization schemes kept old and new employees "constantly off balance and scared for their jobs and programs and staff." Whether he reorganized through genuine interest in organizational excellence or used it as an "FDR-like ploy for keeping people alert and competitive," or both, is open to question. Regardless, reorganization was "a constant fact of life that kept everyone in turmoil and diverted much time and energy to efforts to defend what one had or grab what someone else had."

No one questioned that Hartzog was totally in charge of the Park Service and very much a hands-on director. As Utley described him, he was a micromanager who "professed to delegate freely . . . but everyone knew the delegation to be heavily qualified by the imperative to exercise it as the chief wanted and to cross him at your peril."[3] Those who served during the Hartzog years remember him as harshly demanding, but they also nostalgically recall the creativity, innovation, and excitement. They remember that things got done, and they believe he was the last director to exercise power effectively. At the same time, years did not dull the impression that he was "a demanding taskmaster with high standards," "sure as hell not the easiest guy to work for," "very hard on his people, and equipped with 'a short fuse.'"[4]

Stories abound of Hartzog's thoughtfulness and thoughtlessness. He could be utterly charming and make employees feel valued or he could just as easily tear them to shreds. As retired superintendent Forrest Benson wrote to him:

> You gave me an unheard of three-hour lead time to provide you with a briefing statement on the Ozette Indians. With considerable frantic search I learned they once existed on the Olympic Peninsula. . . . Have you ever tried to go through 16 file drawers searching for what you know not what with the boss's secretary calling every ten minutes asking where the statement was? I was wound tighter than a two dollar clock by the time I got something on paper.

Benson also recalled the time he and another employee worked until midnight getting information together for a Great Basin proposal. As Benson remembered:

> I made the mistake of volunteering to bring it in the following morning to one of your infamous 7 am sessions. What we put together was not what you wanted, you had an accident coming to work that morning, and were in a vile temper and yours truly was the first pigeon to enter the inner sanctum. You had me for breakfast—in spades. Helen Saults [Hartzog's appointment secretary] kidded me for months about how upon her leaving the elevator and rounding the corner to the "Hall of Heroes" she could hear you reaming me up one side and down the other. It was really a top flight tail chewing.[5]

Hartzog insisted that he "tried to maintain their respect but didn't go out there seeking their love."[6] He admitted that he had a temper and came to regret what one called his "brutal treatment of subordinates, sometimes in publicly humiliating situations."[7] As assistant secretary Nathaniel Reed saw it, Hartzog got angry over "stupidity, lack of vision, lack of supervision, or a personnel failure." Reed never saw his anger "directed at anything that wasn't an appropriate anger maker. Hartzog demanded perfection and reacted when he did not get a person's best effort."[8] Bill Everhart reasoned that Hartzog probably felt that "this week I've got to be a son-of-a-bitch and have to kick ass." Everhart went on to say that "if somebody wasn't cutting it, they were going to hear from George. I heard from him myself."[9] Hartzog explained that he "tried to be tolerant of mistakes but I was impatient. There is no question about that. When I wanted it done, I wanted it done."[10]

Although he could be tough on employees, Hartzog could also be considerate; he could lavish praise, extend comfort during times of sorrow, and when necessary go to bat for them. Robert Utley observed Hartzog's congratulatory telephone call to Senator Strom Thurmond of South Carolina just after his young wife had a baby.[11] Superintendent William (Joe) Kennedy remembered Hartzog's call during a serious illness and said, "Hearing from you always gave me a big lift." He went on to declare that "when you were director we superintendents always knew you were in our corners fighting for us. There was nothing wishy washy about you."[12] Lorraine Mintzmyer added that employees given tough assignments in which they had to "take a strong stand on behalf of a park area or to make certain our policies were carried out" would be taken care of "when the political heat got so bad that you just had to be moved out."[13]

Hartzog declared that, "the surest way for a superintendent to be secure in his job was for a congressman to get on his back. . . . I never in all of the time I was director ever moved a superintendent under political pressure." "Now when it was all over," he added, "I moved some of them, but it was with their consent." He maintained that the worst thing he could have done under political assault was to run. It was like facing a bear. If you run, "I guarantee ya they'll eat ya and if you panic when a politician gets after you, I'll guarantee you you're dead. . . . Once they figure they can make you run, you're runnin' the rest of your life."

Bowing to such pressures also would have undermined the support he needed from the superintendents. As he liked to say, "Every superintendent in the National Park Service has a knife in his hand and could cut my throat any day he wanted to."[14] Often his biggest headaches were local issues that escalated into national problems because of the way superintendents handled them at the local level. "I got two senators and a congressman in Washington and in comes a letter," he said. "Now when it gets to Washington on that congressman's desk or that senator's desk, it's a national problem. It's not local anymore even though the solution to it is right there in the park, but it's a national problem because those guys can kill ya up there."[15] Therefore, he handpicked every superintendent. That ensured a degree of loyalty, but he was also quick to move them if they failed to perform according to his standards.[16]

Hartzog felt one of his most difficult jobs as director involved hard personnel decisions, especially when they upset families. He liked to make tough calls first thing in the morning and tried to remain focused on what was best for the parks and the public they served rather than on the inconvenience to the family.[17] Due to the park system's expansion, promotions and the resulting moves became commonplace. Unlike today, when employees more or less move themselves by applying for vacant positions, at that time they had little choice but to go where Hartzog directed. As Nathaniel Reed described it, if George thought a new superintendent was not doing the job after six months, he would move him, and of course that required that someone else be moved. Reed reasoned that Hartzog was "only concerned that he had the right body at the right place. . . . These people were like the Marine Corps. . . . These people belonged to him and the National Park Service, and they moved at his pleasure."[18] At the same time, and not inconsistently, Robert Stanton, who was director of the Park Service from 1997 to 2001, gave

Hartzog high marks for "unwavering care for the people of the National Park Service and their families."[19]

Hartzog oversaw a multidimensional agency with a range of professional staff spanning the natural, historical, and recreational fields. Unlike the Forest Service, which employed mostly foresters with similar backgrounds, the Park Service hired a diverse staff that gave the agency a certain vibrancy but created dissension as well. For instance, some associated with historical areas felt like second-class citizens in comparison to their counterparts in large natural areas. Many had difficulty adjusting to the growing emphasis on urban recreation, which required different qualifications. The addition of women, ethnic minorities, research scientists, and those who had not come up through the ranks added yet another disquieting dimension.

Hartzog recognized the great talent and commitment of those already in the agency, and he knew that throngs of idealistic people were competing for vacancies. Expansion of the park system presented exciting opportunities for promotions and created vacancies as the director shuffled people to fill them. Often employees had barely learned their jobs before being moved elsewhere or further up the career ladder. Despite the turmoil, a strong esprit de corps marked the Park Service, and many looked on themselves as part of an extended family.

Hartzog said he relied on the advice of the "able and talented people" he worked with. He personally met with his principal staff on a weekly basis, his regional directors quarterly, and with all his superintendents yearly in small groups.[20] As John McPhee noticed of his meetings, "There is much laughter around his conference table, shot through with moments of high-pitched intensity. The men seem to care a great deal about what they are saying." McPhee added that Hartzog was a "master of transitions from subject to subject or meeting to meeting" as long as he felt it productive. When it ceased to be productive he stopped it.[21] Hartzog also constantly talked on the phone with people inside and outside the Park Service.

George Hartzog accomplished much in part because he had what Everhart referred to as a "furious work ethic." As Lorraine Mintzmyer, a pioneering female in Park Service management, described it, "The man worked twenty-four hours a day and expected everybody that worked under him to do the same." He would frequently call meetings on nights and weekends and even during holidays. Mintzmyer recalled one scheduled for Thanksgiving Day until Bill Everhart, one of the few people who could stand up to Hartzog, said, "I'm going to spend Thanksgiving with my family, and I would expect you to do the same."[22] Hartzog knew he pushed himself and his staff hard but justified it by saying, "I felt I was the public's last defense against irresponsibility and that meant you had to be on top of your job. . . . That meant more than eight hours a day. . . . If you're going to represent the public, that is the highest responsibility that a man or woman can have and I took that seriously."[23]

While an admitted workaholic, Hartzog was a people person, a hand shaker, and a consummate politician. Unlike most of his predecessors, he loved the challenge and the excitement of the political process, and as a result he thrived in the political arena. Mingling with politicians and other powerful people proved enjoyable. "They were gregarious people, otherwise they wouldn't be in politics. So it's not all that difficult to get along with them . . . be friendly with 'em. And to like them. I never did meet any of them that I didn't like. You know, you meet a lot of people that didn't necessarily agree with you, but they weren't your enemies."[24]

⁂

Of all the Park Service directors, Hartzog perhaps best understood the importance of Congress to accomplishing the agency's goals. While the president and secretary of the interior furnished the policy framework, Congress provided authorizing legislation and money. As Hartzog said, "I believed very strongly in the role of Congress in shaping the public land policy of America, and I had to have their support if I was going to get my legislation and my money. I did what I thought was appropriate to cultivate that with information, friendship, and whatever it took to get those objectives."[25]

Hartzog spent considerable time and energy cultivating friends and influence on the Hill. One of the first things he did as director was to make every member of Congress aware of his programs. When he arrived in 1963 as associate director, he knew nine members of Congress. By the time he left, he knew at least three hundred and was on a "howdying" basis with the rest.[26] He reportedly wore out a pair of shoes every three months traveling around the halls of Congress, paying particular attention to influential committee and subcommittee members. Hartzog kept files on key members of Congress and made frequent courtesy calls. When calling at an office, if the member was unavailable, he left his card and followed up with a letter expressing his respect and desire to serve the member's constituents. As Nat Reed said, "He knew every single dime that had been spent in each one of those congressmen's districts."[27] In his travels, he courted local congressional staff because they supplied key information and gave advice to their boss.

When superintendents came to Washington, he made sure they visited their congressional delegation—a sharp change from past practice.[28]

Hartzog also built support by establishing "VIP" retreats for members of Congress and key staff as well as White House and departmental officials. These were elaborate houses or modest cabins that fell under Park Service jurisdiction as part of the park. For Senator Alan Bible, chairman of the National Park Service legislative subcommittee, he specially outfitted a gun casement at Fort Jefferson National Monument, in the waters off the Florida Keys where the senator loved to fish. Each guest facility had an established rental rate visitors were expected to pay. If they failed to pay after a follow-up reminder, Hartzog paid it out of his own pocket.[29] Later administrations discontinued this practice after adverse publicity questioned the preferential treatment and the extremely low rates charged for the accommodations.[30]

One of Hartzog's greatest talents was his ability to perform as a witness before congressional committees. As Everhart said, it was "like a curtain went up on a production."[31] Hartzog was poised, confident, and well pre-pared but displayed an appropriate level of deference and respect. Accord-ing to Julia Butler Hansen, chair of the House Subcommittee on Interior Appropriations, Hartzog "demonstrated creativity and near genius when appearing before Congressional Committees and because of this we looked forward to his appearance."[32] When asked particularly sensitive questions, he would graciously thank the questioner and proceed to redirect the ques-tion to one he preferred answering. If reeled back to the original ques-tion, he would politely extend thanks again and invent another question to answer. All but the junior committee members knew of Hartzog's tac-tics. To some, it became a game to ask questions they knew he would not respond to directly just "for the fun of seeing me squirm. They had no belief whatsoever that they were going to get any damn answer out of me."[33]

But as John McPhee wrote, "What he says is clear and is obviously well prepared, and this, among other things, has earned him the high regard of the men on the platform." Moreover, observed McPhee, Congress knew that when "he speaks he always knows what he is talking about and that puts him in something of a minority among bureaucrats making appearances on the Hill."[34]

According to Bill Everhart, Hartzog's efforts paid off, since legislators recognized the director almost as a peer.[35] He gained the attention, trust, and support of many in Congress. He claimed that to help gain that trust, he never lied to anyone on the Hill. In tight Washington circles, once labeled a liar, a person's credibility was forever tarnished and his or her effectiveness undermined. As Hartzog knew, "You can get into his office and he'll listen to you and shake hands with you and smile at you, but you're dead. You're never going to get a thing. So you don't lie. Absolutely, you don't lie." He believed it better to tell the truth and prepare for a fight than to tell a lie.[36]

Hartzog took great pains to keep members of Congress informed of any changes that might affect parks in their districts and upset constituents. For example, he decided to stop the firefall of burning red-cedar bark pushed off the 3,500-foot Glacier Point in Yosemite National Park, a popular spectacle. First, however, he informed the California congressmen of the environmental damage caused by scouring the park for red cedar, thus preparing them for the vociferous outbursts of concessioners and visitors.[37] (He also told them there were two other projects he wanted to discontinue, but he did not in fact intend to drop them; he backed off on them as a show of concession to get the one dropped that he wanted dropped.)[38]

Hartzog also actively courted the media to keep the public informed. He tried to be open with them and thought he maintained a good relationship with most. He purposely invited members of the press on his show-me tours, which used Washington area parks to present a microcosm of the park system. He met with his critics and employed an old Methodist philosophy of "converting them one at a time" to his way of thinking. With some, such as the outspoken critic Michael Frome, Hartzog laughingly admitted he "didn't always win."[39]

What Hartzog refused to do was get into public debates over what he called misinformation about himself or his policies that appeared in the press. To vent his frustration, however, he often wrote rebuttals but never sent them. The only response his critics received was a polite letter thanking them for their input and his assurance that their views would be taken into consideration. Hartzog's attitude was that it is useless

to argue with people who don't know what they're talking about. . . . Let them say what they want to say. If they are right then pay attention to it. If they aren't . . . so be it. You enjoy reading it. . . . So that's why I would always write those letters 'cause they wrote some terrible things about me when I was Director and they never got a letter. But I wrote them, and I mean I drove my secretary, Helen, crazy typin' 'em, but we always tore them up in very small pieces and threw them into the trash can because I didn't want anybody reading them except Helen and me. She used to say to me, "Not another one of those!" and I said, "Tonight we're writin' a good one."

Unlike his predecessor, Conrad Wirth, Hartzog refused to provide ammunition that his critics could manage to turn against him. Apparently, Wirth spent hours drafting just the right response only to have the media attack his view, forcing him the next week to admit "how stupid he was for saying those things."[40]

§

While Hartzog developed strong allies on and off the Hill, he had mixed success with the executive branch. As director, he served first under President Lyndon B. Johnson, with whom he was politically and ideologically well aligned, and then under Richard Nixon, who wanted Hartzog dismissed from the very beginning.

Lyndon Johnson had won a landslide victory in 1964 on the promise of stemming Communism and creating a "Great Society." Coming from an impoverished background himself, the newly elected president declared war on poverty, envisioned a country where old injustices were eliminated, and sought equal educational and job opportunities.[41] What unfolded was one of the greatest outpourings of social legislation in the country's history. Johnson felt federal solutions to the country's social problems were integral to creating a Great Society, so federal involvement and spending spiraled ever higher. While Johnson supported national park programs, especially when they dovetailed with Great Society initiatives, the Park Service got its best backing from the president's wife, Lady Bird Johnson, who became active in beautification efforts and a strong advocate for national parks. Hartzog relied on her to relay national park information to the president.

Johnson's secretary of the interior, Stewart Udall, said that the president "wanted new programs. He wanted to be innovative. His ideal was Franklin D. Roosevelt."[42] In response to this vision, the National Park Service operated "like a mini–Great Society in its frantic pace and search for new ideas and programs," according to Robert Utley.[43] Park Service confidante Bill Everhart described how Hartzog liked to pounce on innovative ideas, leading Everhart to exclaim, "George, it was only an idea. Now listen. Think it through!" When George wanted something done, "boom and it's there."[44]

Although he met with President Johnson on occasion, Hartzog got to know him on a more personal level only after he left office and had used his tremendous energy to get his birthplace, boyhood home, and ranch set aside as a national historical park. During this process, Johnson never hesitated to request Director Hartzog personally to address any problems encountered, and the two men developed a friendship. They had similar personalities and much in common, prompting Mrs. Johnson to remark that Hartzog reminded her so much of her husband.[45]

As Bill Everhart suggested, they were both "poor boys from the South who had a natural affinity for politics, ambition, energy and so forth."[46] Both men kept murderous work schedules, and they both expected the same dedication from their coworkers. Both could be tough on staffers they felt had stepped out of line. As one relayed, "God, he [Johnson] could rip a man up and down."[47]

While both were demanding, they also inspired their staff with a missionary zeal about the important work they were doing. Hartzog emphasized the urgency of saving parklands and meeting urban recreation needs, while Johnson talked about rescuing the downtrodden. And as one Johnson staffer said, Johnson "gave you enthusiasm for the work that you were doing, and he set some kind of vision and objective ahead of you that made you want to work just as hard as he worked."[48]

Robert Utley recalled Hartzog being visibly shaken when, in January 1973, the TV news in the lobby where they were having dinner announced Johnson's death at his ranch in Texas. That night, Hartzog relayed to his dinner companions the story of his last visit with LBJ on the front porch of the ranch house. The former president had leaned over and slapped George on the knee and said, "George, I wish the hell I had known you when I was president because between the two of us we could have remade the f—— world."[49]

As Richard Nixon came into office, the nation was divided over turbulence in its cities, the war in Vietnam, and a large budget deficit. Soon after his 1968 victory, he offered the Park Service directorate to William Penn Mott, then director of California State Parks, but Mott declined, saying that Hartzog should be kept on.[50] Nixon extended a similar offer to Nathaniel Reed, who refused but two years later accepted a position as assistant secretary of the interior. In January 1969, Reed recalled being approached by John Erlichman, Nixon's chief domestic advisor, with a message from Nixon asking him to serve as director. "I wasn't ready for it," recalled Reed, who had recently begun his public service in Florida and felt ill equipped to take on the incredible variety of problems that faced a director. "I mentioned that I thought that George Hartzog was one of the most interesting public servants in government, and I strongly recommended nose to nose to Erlichman that Hartzog not be removed [and] that the administration attempt to work with him."[51]

Although Nixon was touted as an environmentalist and park supporter, Hartzog felt that he could never "bring himself to embrace parks as

Kennedy and Johnson had done." Hartzog could not recall one instance in which Nixon arranged a ceremony for signing a park bill.[52] With Johnson, on the other hand, "you could hardly get a bill through without having a ceremony and passing out pens to everybody there."[53] According to Reed, Nixon "didn't give a damn [about parks and the environment]. He just wanted good news and to be looked well upon, but he was uninterested in the details."[54]

⁂

During his directorate, Hartzog served under three secretaries of the interior—Stewart Udall, Walter Hickel, and Rogers Morton. As environmentalist Michael Frome points out, secretaries of the interior are not chosen for their strong environmental stands. They are "good politicians, party regulars worthy of reward who come from the right part of the country and have the ability to make deals and accept deals." The president's first consideration for secretary of the interior is never who is the "best qualified."[55] In Udall's case, he was rewarded with the position for his efforts to secure John F. Kennedy's presidential nomination. Udall also came from the West, which was typical of secretaries of the interior, and since Kennedy lacked strong support in that region, he felt Udall might boost his standings. Other possible choices, such as Senator Henry "Scoop" Jackson of Washington, held seniority in Congress, so the prospect of being a cabinet member lacked appeal. Since there were no other westerners to whom Kennedy owed greater debts, Udall became the logical choice for secretary.[56]

While Hartzog claimed to have worked well with all the secretaries, he formed the best relationship with Udall, the man who hand picked him. Close in age and with commonalities of background, the two forged a strong and mutually beneficial relationship. Unlike many secretaries who fade nearly to obscurity, the energetic Udall became a visible component of both the Kennedy and Johnson administrations. While Department of the Interior secretaries usually had tenures of four years or less, Udall served eight. Only two served longer—Harold Ickes for almost thirteen (1933–1949) and Ethan Allen Hitchcock (1899–1907) for only two weeks longer than Udall. As an Arizona congressman, Udall had served on the House Interior and Insular Affairs Committee, so he brought familiarity with resource-managing agencies to the job.[57] During his eight years, he had time to formulate a vision, select supportive agency leadership that he brought together on a regular basis, and exert significant influence over a department with seventeen agencies and some fifty-five thousand employees.[58]

Although Udall felt that it took several years to get rolling as secretary of the interior, he grew comfortable in the position and began to press his "new conservation" message.[59] In President Kennedy's cabinet, only Udall had served in Congress. This, he believed, gave him a freer hand in running his department since Kennedy, and later Johnson, trusted him to know how best to deal with Congress. In practice, Udall left most of the national parks work on the Hill to Hartzog. As Everhart said, Udall "preferred going out and speaking on behalf of parks and environmental concerns . . . so that George then had to do much of the work in the Congress."[60] According to Hartzog, Udall gave him a lot of latitude in running the National Park Service and working the Hill. Hartzog had great access to Udall both because of Udall's interest in the Park System and because the secretary's office lacked burdensome layers of administrators. By the time Hartzog left, the secretary's personal staff seemed to have swelled tenfold, and, as Hartzog said, "the director could no longer pick up the phone and ask to speak to the secretary."[61]

Although Hartzog never experienced the close bond with Walter Hickel that he did with Stewart Udall, the two worked well together. One of ten children of a Kansas tenant farmer, Hickel had gone to Alaska and made a fortune in construction, real estate, and hotels. Before becoming secretary of the interior, he had served as governor of Alaska and was seen as development oriented and antienvironment, which drew sharp opposition from many environmental groups. Hartzog recalled being the only bureau head to visit Hickel when he was governor and explain his programs in Alaska. When Hickel became secretary, Hartzog felt the attention he had paid Hickel served him well.[62]

When Hickel arrived in Washington, Hartzog presented him with a draft of proposed Park Service policies and objectives. Hartzog hoped Hickel would adopt the draft as his official position. Hickel read the policy draft, made a few minor changes, and on June 19, 1969, issued it as his policy for the National Park Service.[63] Pleased with Hartzog's approach, Hickel instructed his other agency heads to prepare similar documents for his perusal.[64] Hickel lasted only twenty-two months before being fired by Nixon after a letter critical of the president's policies on Vietnam was leaked to the press. During Hickel's brief tenure, Hartzog felt that Hickel was largely concerned with trying to get a handle on the large department and to establish his credentials as a conservationist.[65] But when he returned to Alaska, he became a strong opponent of Alaska national parks, wildlife refuges, and wilderness areas.[66]

On January 30, 1971, Nixon replaced Hickel with Rogers Morton, a conservative Republican who supported parks but had a reputation for being development oriented.[67] He came from a wealthy Kentucky family, had attended Yale, and got into politics after moving to the Chesapeake Bay area in Maryland. Morton had served as chairman of the Republican National Committee.[68] Fortunately, he had also served on the National Park Subcommittee of the House Interior and Insular Affairs Committee and so was familiar with the park system. Hartzog and Morton had become acquainted as they worked closely on legislation to protect Assateague Island National Seashore off the Maryland and Virginia coasts.[69]

Morton had wanted Hartzog to move over to assistant secretary, but Hartzog told him he preferred continuing as director unless ordered to do otherwise. As far as Hartzog was concerned, an assistant secretary had no program, no people, and no money, so therefore no real power. After Hartzog refused the position, Morton selected Floridian Nathaniel P. Reed, who had taken over his family's development of Hobe Sound, Florida, and gone on to become special assistant to the governor of Florida for environmental issues.[70] While Secretary Morton was a "softy" who "hated controversy and confrontation" and liked to smooth over conflicts, both Reed and Hartzog had volcanic tempers that could erupt with little warning, and they often had words.[71] These conflicts resulted, in Harztog's opinion, from what he saw as Reed's interference in daily park management issues. As Hartzog explained, "They put assistant secretaries in to help the secretary develop policy. Well there's very little damn activity in policy, but there's a lot of activity in running a park or a fish and wildlife refuge, so they got nothing to do, so now they want to become park superintendents and if you let them they will. My problem was like that, and why I had difficulty was I wouldn't let them." According to Hartzog,

> They used to call up my superintendents—Nat Reed and some of his staff that had been out in the park—and told them to do this and do that and I found out about it because they called to tell me. So I went down to the end of the hall and talked with him and said, "You know you can't run an outfit like this. If you see something in the park you want done you come back and tell me and if I got the budget to do it and you want it done I'll do it. But you mess up that superintendent something fierce because you go out and scare the hell out of him in the first place and tell him to do it and he drops whatever he's doing and does it and that's how we lose control of the operation." "Oh, we won't do that anymore." Well, it didn't stop. It kept on, and sometimes I would get a report back that even

one of his underlings . . . would make the call. So I just simply had a conference call to my regional directors and I said, "You get on the phone to all your superintendents and tell them anytime they get a call from the assistant secretary's office or the assistant secretary telling them to do something it's perfectly agreeable to me to do it. I just want a report from them as to how much it costs because that's how much money I'm taking out of their [park] budget next year." Man, oh, man alive! All hell broke loose. But you know something—it stopped. It stopped because the way you deal with the superintendent is just tell him he's going to get more money or less money, and I tell you he shapes up immediately.[72]

With his wry sense of humor, Everhart recalled that Reed would send out "tiny little notepads" that were no "bigger than a playing card in a little envelope," and that "became known as 'Nat-o-grams.'" Everhart concurred that Reed "wanted to be the director of the Park Service."[73] As director, Hartzog managed to keep control of the Park Service, but once he left, Nat Reed became de facto director since Ronald Walker was ill-equipped for the post.

While he worked well with Morton, Hartzog was extremely disappointed in the secretary's handling of proposed Alaska park additions when federal lands Hartzog felt belonged in the park system were shifted to the Forest Service and Fish and Wildlife Service. Part of the problem might have been the devastating blow Morton received when he found out he had prostate cancer. After that, Hartzog felt, Morton lost interest in park programs and turned over much of his responsibilities to what Hartzog called a "bunch of bureaucrats."[74]

In his observations, Nat Reed agreed that Hartzog and Morton seemed "extremely friendly on the outside" toward each other. However, Reed felt Morton was convinced that "George had to be supervised and watched like a hawk. That he knew more about how to get money, manpower from the Democratic Congress than any man alive and that we [the secretary of the interior's office] would only get in trouble with the president if George was left as a free running back."[75]

Hartzog came under increasing scrutiny by the Nixon administration. Due to his bipartisan support on the Hill, however, he managed to hang on long after most bureau heads had been replaced. Hartzog believed it was an administrative faux pas that eventually cost him his job.

Opening the Door to Workforce Diversity

At forty-three, George Hartzog brought youth, vigor, and change to a largely white male organization that promoted from within its ranks and understood that a reasonably good performance would eventually be rewarded by promotion. When he became director of the National Park Service in 1964, pressures were mounting to include women and members of ethnic groups in professional positions. He could have either ignored these pressures or pushed aggressively for change. What transpired during his tenure was that women and minorities joined the Park Service in unprecedented numbers.

To exert leadership in this time of changing attitudes, Hartzog had to transcend stereotypes about women and blacks prevalent during his youth. Although immersed in southern culture, his experiences of family, community, and church belied a number of these stereotypes and opened his mind to the sweeping social movements of the 1960s. Church taught compassion, brotherly love, and the virtues of living a righteous life. Honor, trust, loyalty, and integrity inculcated in the youth provided a moral anchor for the adult.

Hartzog's upbringing brought him face-to-face with blacks' social standing in southern society. As a child, he grew close to the black family that lived on his father's farm and helped in the kitchen and fields. That he referred to the big black woman as "Aunt" Lula attests to their close bond. He fondly remembered Aunt Lula coming to his rescue after his angered mother discovered that he had dirtied his newly laundered clothes in a water puddle. He recalled her "big bosoms and holding me with my mother standing there with that switch while she talked her out of beating my behind." Because blacks lived nearest his rural home, Hartzog played with a lot of black children. Aunt Lula's son Harrison was about his age, and they became constant companions.

Despite these bonds, young George undoubtedly grew up knowing that blacks had their place. As he reached his teenage years, societal norms forced a separation between the races. Adolescents seldom socialized with someone from another race.[1] In a particularly revealing story, Hartzog recalled one of his first jobs at a dry cleaners that accepted clothes from both whites and blacks. As part of his training, he was instructed to use one washboard for clothes from white families and another one for clothes from black families.[2]

The young Hartzog learned that blacks seldom held professional positions. Many people believed that blacks lacked the intelligence and "gumption" for professional positions. Countering that notion was the black electrician he knew in Walterboro. He was the area's best tradesman, but he still had to come in the back door and address the teenager as "Mr. George."[3]

Through his later work on a timber crew, Hartzog came to learn firsthand that the lower-paying menial positions characteristically went to blacks. In his three-man crew, he held one end of the timber cruiser's chain while the cruiser calculated the amount of timber in an area and the black man hacked through the dense understory. Hartzog's job required no special skills and could have just as easily been done by the black man, but in all likelihood he received more money to do less work. Also, the white crewmen had to drop off their black coworker at a black boarding house before returning to their own quarters. Hartzog remembered that working with that "awfully nice guy" for the summer prompted him to examine more closely the treatment of blacks. He recognized "that something was wrong with a society in which you could work with black people all day, but they had to go to a black boarding house to spend the night."[4] While the young Hartzog may have recognized the inequities, like most good Christians he simply accepted discrimination as the way things were done.

If blacks faced an unyielding color bar, the southern women of Hartzog's youth enjoyed only slightly more latitude. Men's power and influence extended beyond the family farm to neighboring communities and politics, while women's centered on home, family, and the church. Not just in the South, but elsewhere in America, a woman's appearance in the workplace outside the home often signified meager family revenue, or worse, the inability of the man of the house to provide adequately for his family, a failing likely to diminish his reputation among his male peers.

When the depression of the 1930s deepened, more women moved into the workplace. They drew criticism for displacing men who needed jobs to support their families. Often, however, women held jobs that men did not want, such as the low-paying sewing job Hartzog's mother and other hard-pressed women took. And many women, such as Hartzog's mother, became the family's primary breadwinner.[5]

Experiencing the hardship, discouragement, and social upheaval of the Depression as he did, George Hartzog learned firsthand that women were hardly the frail and helpless "weaker sex" of social convention and male egotism. By witnessing his mother's struggles, he discovered that women possessed far more talent, strength, and determination than many real-ized. He watched as his mother took control of family life as her husband's health failed. To Hartzog's mind, "The women saved the South during the Depression."[6]

Even though he knew firsthand how capable women were, his southern upbringing and the prevailing view of man's responsibility also imposed on him the belief that he needed to take care of women and shelter them from working outside the home. He wished that he could have done more to ease his mother's burden and lamented that she had to work to support the fam-ily when she preferred staying at home.

In his own marriage, Hartzog became the traditional breadwinner, while his wife, Helen, took care of the house and children and sold antiques and real estate. With a degree of remorse, Hartzog explained that Helen did not purposely seek a career outside the home but "had" to go to work to help pay the bills. Often the Hartzogs incurred expenses related to his job that were not reimbursable. They made a point of going to parties where important people might be, and they hosted a lot of parties. No budget line supported that type of entertaining, so he paid for it out of his own salary. He felt such social occasions were important for advancing his agenda, and they were also fun. These and other family expenses prompted Helen to work and bring in additional income.[7]

Hartzog had been reared in a world of inflexible racial discrimination and of less fixed attitudes toward women's place in society. Successful white men served as his mentors, and career-oriented women and blacks were rare. At the same time, from his earliest years, observation and experience had led him to question if not openly reject many of the norms of society. In World War II, he confronted segregation as the army separated blacks into units commanded by white officers. He recalled bunking in a building with white military police at one end and black at the other. But since no wall separated the two, Hartzog defied convention and frequently wandered over to interact with his black counterparts.[8]

Hartzog came to realize that he "never found that the color of a man's skin had a hell of a lot to do with his character. I reckon I've seen as many scoundrels that are white as anybody ever needs to see." To him, treating all people like human beings was just the right thing to do. While conceding that his own positive associations with blacks hardly provided the basis for later Park Service policies, he maintained that they gave him a "sensitivity for the goodness of black people."[9] His childhood poverty also led him to feel empathy for the downtrodden.

Although he would bring to the directorate a southern race-and-gender heritage, he also brought an open mind that, drawing on doubts about the world in which he grew up, made him receptive to the momentous social changes sweeping the nation. Hartzog's predecessor, Conrad L. Wirth, resisted hiring women and to a lesser extent minorities in professional positions. While Wirth was clearly part of the old guard, Hartzog was comparatively young and politically astute, and he had been purposely brought in to bring a more contemporary approach to parks and their management. Workforce change, however, would require him and other government bureaucrats to abandon old ideas of what kinds of jobs women and minorities wanted and could do. This was not an instant revelation but a slow realization of equity and fairness.

Rather than ignoring the government policy with respect to diversity, as many executives did, Hartzog chose the more difficult path of pushing an organization that liked things the way they were. In the process, he discovered that inequities hundreds of years in the making could not be solved easily or overnight. In looking back at his administration's record, he would rank opening the National Park Service to workplace diversity as one of his proudest achievements.

⁂

As Hartzog ascended to the directorate, mounting racial tensions were gripping the country. The irony of fighting a war against Nazi racism abroad while flagrant discrimination occurred at home had not been lost on blacks and other ethnic groups. Serving in the military had broadened their horizons and heightened their expectations, but they returned to an America little changed. Jim Crow laws ruled below the Mason-Dixon line, while less formal kinds of racism existed above it. Blacks still faced separate restrooms, drinking fountains, and eating facilities. Inequity in the workplace persisted despite halfhearted attempts by government boards and commissions to correct problems. Even once laws had been passed, organizations found loopholes or paid no attention because they knew enforcement lagged far behind enactment. Circumstances propelled underprivileged groups toward the realization that if they wanted to see change, they would have to lead the fight. While the charismatic Martin Luther King Jr. advocated a dynamic, nonviolent protest movement, other "black power" groups pressed for more rapid change, not always with the proviso of nonviolence.[10]

Although he received two-thirds of the black vote, President John F. Kennedy was not initially a strong civil rights advocate.[11] That changed as the civil rights movement intensified and the media showed such unsettling images as Alabama's governor refusing two blacks admission to the University of Alabama and Birmingham's police force unmercifully using hoses and biting police dogs against peaceful demonstrators. Kennedy responded in June 1963 with one of the strongest civil rights addresses ever made by an American president. He reminded Americans that "this nation was founded by men of many nations and backgrounds. It was founded on the principle that all men are created equal, and that the rights of every man are diminished when the rights of one man are threatened."[12]

That August, close to 250,000 people rallied in Washington, D.C., and heard Martin Luther King Jr. deliver his famous "I Have a Dream" speech, in which he envisioned a nation where his children would not "be judged by the color of their skin but by the content of their character."[13] As King held his audience spellbound outside, associate director Hartzog dealt with crowd management and watched the speech on television. Since the event took place on the National Mall and other lands managed by the Park Service, it was the U.S. Park Police's job to keep order. To the end of his life, Hartzog got emotional every time he heard King's speech replayed.[14]

After Kennedy's death in November 1963, it fell to Lyndon Johnson to lead the country toward greater racial equity. From his work as chair of the Committee on Equal Employment Opportunity while vice president, Johnson knew of problems in government employment practices. The committee had evaluated compliance with the 1961 Executive Order 10925, which required the federal government to promote and ensure equal employment opportunities "for all qualified persons, without regard to race, creed, color, or national origin, employed or seeking employment with the Federal Government and on government contracts."[15] In the interim report, the committee found blacks to be seriously underrepresented in skilled government jobs. Blacks constituted only 1 percent of the GS-12 through GS-18 professional positions, while 72 percent of all blacks fell into the unskilled GS-1 through GS-4 ranks.[16]

Government solutions would prove difficult, as Johnson told a graduating class of blacks at Howard University. "You do not take a person who for years has been hobbled by chains and liberate him, bring him up to the starting line of a race and then say, 'You are free to compete with all the others' and still justly believe you have been completely fair. . . . We need not just freedom but opportunity . . . not just equality as a right and a theory but equality as a fact and as a result."[17] Blacks and other ethnic groups would need special government help to receive equitable job opportunities.

⁂

As director, Hartzog would also experience pressures to broaden the historically limited roles women had played within the Park Service. The agency had a history of hiring tough, rugged outdoorsmen who were expected to put in long, hard days and be jacks-of-all-trades.[18] Ranger positions, therefore, were filled by white males. Since many rangers were former soldiers, a strong sense of military decorum and an up-through-the-ranks mentality pervaded the organization.

Since the inception of the National Park Service, only a limited number of women managed to break the gender barrier.[19] They experienced their greatest inroads in the interpretive field, where teaching duties appeared more socially acceptable. Two sisters, with advanced degrees and a passion for the outdoors, led trips as early as 1917 in the Rocky Mountains. The following year, several women were hired as replacements for men who had left to serve in World War I. In the 1920s, Superintendent Horace M. Albright hired several women naturalists at Yellowstone. Even though amply qualified for her position, one cautioned the others "not to stress the outside work too much—many still think that women's work should be inside."[20]

As more women sought entry into the Park Service, opposition rose. Male administrators worried about suitable housing arrangements, keeping women safe and virtuous, and whether women's presence would hurt the credibility of the newly created Park Service. Albright countered by saying that "in certain places of our educational work women can do just as well or better than men." But as progressive as he was, even he admitted that "there is a certain romance and glamour to the 'title' ranger which seems to be lost when a woman accepts the position."[21]

In 1931, the first woman was selected from the civil service register for the National Park Service, but as custom dictated, she quit when she married.

Work relief programs of the 1930s had limited openings for women, and while World War II created jobs for many, few opened in the parks. Funds flowed to the war effort, and due to gas rationing, few visited the parks. But even as the war ended and visitation soared, returning veterans got preference.

If a woman wanted to be a part of the Park Service, her best chance was often to "marry a ranger." Before visitor centers became common, wives "filled the role of helpmate, offering information, first aid, meals and comfort to visitors and staff and served as centers of communications."[22] Until the parks built visitor centers, the park ranger's home functioned as the informal greeting and information center. Many wives assisted their husbands in the daily park operations and often took over in their absence. As Helen Hartzog later said, "We always did things to support the men, and when the men went to town to take care of business they [the wives] would take care of the operations. Nobody ever mentioned that this was illegal. Women just worked."[23] Although unpaid, their efforts helped pave the way for later paid employment.

Throughout his career, Hartzog relied heavily on the considerable social talents of Helen, who regularly helped entertain important guests. More than once he called and said something to the effect of, "Dear, I'm leaving Van Buren, and we will be home soon. I got the secretary and two congressmen, and we're going to need dinner. Why don't you fry up some chicken by the time we get there?" And with three children under foot it was done.[24]

Although Helen provided essential support to her husband, she and other wives faced limitations on their involvement in official park business. As stated in an orientation booklet, park wives were not to intrude into their spouse's official duties. They were to keep their husbands' uniforms washed and ironed and be cognizant that any impression they made in the community was reflected on the agency.[25]

At the time George Hartzog became associate director of the National Park Service in February 1963, increasing numbers of women had begun working and seeking careers outside the home. World War II had compelled many to join the workforce for patriotic reasons. In addition to taking traditionally male jobs in factories, mills, and rail yards, women moved into professional positions in business, medicine, the sciences, engineering, law, and the press corps. After the war ended, many continued working despite pay cuts, demotions, and shifts to more gender-appropriate jobs. Others returned to their traditional roles as homemakers, but some grew increasingly restless.

Feminists such as Betty Friedan would challenge the popular notion that women could be fulfilled solely by being wives and mothers. More and more, women sought the intellectual stimulation, expanded friendships, and sense of independence the workplace offered.[26] At the same time, the civil rights movement had raised the public's sensitivity to social inequity, and for women it suggested organizational models and modes of protest that could be directed toward their issues.[27] Elected officials knew women's discontent could not be ignored if they hoped to remain in office.

Responding to such social changes, President John F. Kennedy had created a Commission on the Status of Women, with Eleanor Roosevelt as chair.[28] The commission's 1963 report documented discrimination against working women. Kennedy asked the commission to review hiring practices to "assure that selection for any career positions hereafter [be] made solely on the basis of individual merit and fitness without regard to sex." The president urged that the government, the largest employer of women, become "a showcase . . . of equality of opportunity" and base hiring decisions on individual merit and not sex.[29] The Civil Rights Act of 1964 went further by prohibiting workplace discrimination based on race, religion, national origin, or sex. The act also created the Equal Employment Opportunity Commission to implement and enforce the Civil Rights Act.

While not opposed to workplace diversity, Hartzog did not come to the directorate as a strong proponent of hiring minorities or women. When he became superintendent at Jefferson National Expansion Memorial in 1959, he had his first opportunity to advance minorities and women. He made little effort. Yet Interior secretary Stewart L. Udall expected him to lead the Park Service in new directions, and diversity was one of them. Hartzog, therefore, made it one of his new directions. In part he would be nudged by Udall's early initiatives with blacks. Perhaps the lawyer in him also worried about the legal ramifications of the Equal Pay Act and Civil Rights Act, which made it illegal and potentially costly to discriminate. The growing militancy and political power of ethnic groups and women would undoubtedly have registered with his political instincts as they did with his superiors. The Great Society mentality combined with his own youthful struggles helped Hartzog see the importance of giving disadvantaged groups a leg up. He was pushed to act, and act he did. According to those around him, he moved decisively and effectively.[30]

When Hartzog became director in 1964, women largely occupied clerical and housekeeping positions while minority males commonly worked in maintenance or as custodians. The prevailing attitude was "you didn't need 'em" in professional positions. Despite managing sites such as George Washington Carver and Booker T. Washington, which commemorated black achievements, the National Park Service did not have a single black superintendent. A few American Indians had worked as rangers, but none had become superintendents. One woman, Wilhemina Harris, had served as superintendent. She had been live-in secretary to Brook Adams and his wife, the last family to occupy the Adams house in Quincy, Massachusetts. With three sons to support, the recently widowed Harris had been urged by the Adamses to help interpret the house. In effect, she came with the property.[31] To enhance diversity, the Park Service would have to change its tradition of hiring white males from "ranger factories" and overcome the significant societal and agency barriers to hiring woman and ethnic minorities.

⁑

Although new rulings would forbid the hiring of only men into ranger positions, in practice these positions remained closed to women. The Park Service interpretive and historical units were the most receptive to women. These positions seemed acceptable for women, who were often stereotyped as adept social hostesses who were comfortable with repetitive tasks common in housekeeping and liked to talk and share information. Park officials even conceded that they could be capable leaders of children's programs, an arena in which they could be "even more effective than men."[32]

Park Service men believed, however, that women lacked the strength, endurance, and mental toughness to become U.S. Park Police officers, rangers, or maintenance workers. Protective legislation put limits on heavy lifting by women and on how late they could work into the night and allowed job descriptions to be written in such a way as to exclude women. Women also had difficulty combating the long-standing Western belief that they lacked powers of reason and were overly emotional.[33] As a former superintendent said, "Women probably could work on the protective force, but we have found that they seem to adapt better to a routine job in a confined area. The gals we have are well adapted to the entrance station."[34]

In the U.S. Park Police, men reasoned that women could not handle difficult situations encountered by police without becoming emotionally distraught and that they could never physically subdue a male suspect. Furthermore, they believed that women should be protected from life's seamier side of law enforcement work. In explaining to one young woman who had accused his department of being prejudiced, Secretary Udall said it was "our concern and affection for girls that prevents us from saddling them with the full load of ranger duties," which he called "law enforcement, use of firearms, night patrol, and . . . the need for sheer muscle power in possibly ugly situations." Instead, she was encouraged to apply for a park naturalist or historian position.[35]

Men argued that women lacked the background, necessary skills, physical strength, and aptitude for such jobs and that the workplace would be unsuitable for ladies. Men claimed that women could never handle the necessary tools and equipment. As one ranger declared, "Women will never make it in the woods. Can you see me say to a fellow female ranger, 'Now you take that trail and remove the 50 trees that have fallen across it and I'll take this one. What do you mean you don't know how to sharpen the saw blade?'" One spirited female ranger responded to these kinds of accusations by saying that "I think I can learn anything they can teach me."[36]

Her retort proved correct. With minimal training, women could master a variety of tools and equipment, although they struggled with equipment sized for large men and performed better when the tools were refitted for their smaller frames. Lighter weight and better-proportioned tools significantly dropped the accident rates for women.[37] In cases where brute strength was thought to be essential, women proved to be creative thinkers who might use a hoist rather than muscle a heavy load as men were more likely to do.

Hartzog struggled with allowing women to work in nontraditional areas. He admittedly had difficulty picturing women with a pistol strapped to their hip and with a laugh exclaimed that he would "rather just see the hip." He knew better than to think women could not do ranger work or serve with the U.S. Park Police, but he "wasn't prepared for it" when he became director in 1964. The change came as a result of an evolution of thought and what he called a "growing up." And even though his revelation may have taken longer than he liked to admit, he said he arrived there with an open mind. His challenge then became to drag the rest of the Park Service along with him to accept women in traditionally male jobs.[38]

Hartzog had to overcome the fact that the Park Service found it easier to hire one of the many interested, college-educated white males or military veterans receiving preferential ratings on their applications. Recruiting systems frequently depended on referrals from men already employed, who not surprisingly recommended their male friends. Resource management programs typically had male professors who taught male students. The entrance of women upset the comfortable brotherhood that had developed over the years.

Many worried that hiring women to work alongside men might lead to unseemly behaviors and place both in awkward situations. As a result, the Park Service refused to consider a woman for jobs that required quartering her with men. For assignments in the remote backcountry, one superintendent worried that "it would be too difficult to mix the sexes back there." Employers pictured affairs blossoming between male and female coworkers that would destroy families.[39]

Even if concerns were not voiced aloud, some men were reluctant to hire women or serve as their mentors for fear of what their wives or coworkers might think. Working alongside or being supervised by women presented special challenges for men. Some responded with cat calls, sexual innuendos, or open hostility. Others used to male supervisors were uncomfortable with the idea of taking orders from a female boss.

Surprisingly, women did not always support others of their gender rising in the ranks. Some pioneers faced hostile attitudes from other women, who, like men, had a hard time adjusting to their new positions of power.[40] Lorraine Mintzmyer recalled the jealous reactions she received as she advanced through the ranks and was no longer "one of the girls." Perplexed and dismayed at first, she concentrated on doing her job well, and eventually the other women came to admire her and become her strongest supporters. For Mintzmyer, being a woman in a largely man's world was "a very lonely existence." Whenever "I was anyplace in a meeting I was always the only female."[41] For women searching for female friendship and camaraderie in the workplace, the Park Service presented an inhospitable environment.

After being told for so long they could not do men's work and were not welcome in those fields, women had to convince themselves that they had a place in the Park Service and could do the work. Until the word circulated that the Park Service was actively seeking females, few thought of seeking positions typically held by men. According to a superintendent at Mesa Verde National Park, "Women don't want that kind of work. In fact, they don't even apply."[42]

Doris Osmundson Bowen needed a gentle push to apply. She had never regarded it as a career option until friends encouraged her to seek a seasonal position at Point Reyes National Seashore in California. Following Grand Canyon's successful experiment with women seasonals, Point Reyes followed suit by hiring Bowen for the summers of 1967 and 1968. Pleased with her work, the park employed her full time as a clerk-typist although she ended up doing largely what she had been doing as a seasonal, visitor information and interpretive work. Even when promoted to superintendent, she continued to question her abilities, explaining that she had "never been so scared because I have never been involved with anything at this level before." Since she was one of the first women superintendents, there were few role models to help guide her, but she felt male mentoring and hard work enabled her to minimize problems of gender.[43]

Like women, members of ethnic groups faced employment barriers that kept them from entering a Park Service filled with white males. Some were simply long-seated prejudices. As former director Russell Dickenson has candidly said, "Some prejudiced members of the Service have been resistant to Indian employment."[44] Acceptance of stereotypes added support to this resistance by keeping certain groups from moving beyond the unskilled positions seen as their place. Since the races remained largely segregated, little opportunity arose to dispel such stereotypes. Even those within the Park Service who were not openly prejudiced worried about how well minorities in professional positions would mesh with other park employees, whether park visitors would feel comfortable with nonwhite faces, and whether they would be accepted and safe within the park and local communities.

Former National Park Service director Robert Stanton believes that not having a diverse population of national park visitors affects the diversity of its employees.[45] Park visitors fail to mirror the country's diversity for reasons incompletely understood.[46] One veteran black told of a black family that traveled through some of the better-known western national parks in the early 1960s. While the family experienced little open hostility, many white faces registered surprise and even shock at seeing a black face in a national park.[47] Stanton confirms that experience by recalling that few black families passed the Grand Teton entrance station where he worked during the summers of 1962 and 1963. If blacks or other ethnic groups do not visit national parks, Stanton reasons, they will be less likely to look to the Park Service as a desirable career option.[48]

Some minorities were reluctant to associate with government agencies and authority figures such as law enforcement personnel since they represented a strong-armed white government that habitually harassed and arrested them. For example, many American Indians disliked anything having to do with a federal government they felt had mistreated them and stolen their native lands. As a result, "It is not easy for some Indians to work for the United States, and doubly hard if it means wearing a federal uniform among their people."[49] A black ranger who had avoided Washington, D.C., parks as a kid said, "We were turned off by the ranger uniform. In Yellowstone people respect it. . . . In Washington the uniform signifies authority. The black community didn't see the guy wearing it as a friend. They saw him as The Man, who is out to get you, and that made him bad news."[50]

To some, becoming a uniformed park ranger symbolized selling out to the Establishment they were supposed to resent and despise. During the Vietnam War, anyone wearing any type of uniform faced potential harassment. Hartzog remembered even whites feeling nervous about wearing their uniforms in volatile settings such as inner cities.[51]

Additionally, most minorities lacked the standard training, education, and experience to move into professional Park Service positions. Many did not finish high school, let alone attend college.[52] Few traditionally black schools had courses directly related to resource management, and minorities attending other predominately white schools typically opted for more lucrative fields. Clemson University, the land grant university in Hartzog's home state of South Carolina, for example, did not graduate its first African American in its resource management track until 1978.[53]

As a result, minorities, like women, lacked the required credentials to compete for entry-level park ranger positions. A catch-22 arose whereby minorities and women failed to see the Park Service as a career option and so did not seek specialized training, and the Park Service failed to hire them because they either did not apply or lacked the necessary credentials. Park Service employers typically wanted to hire people who looked, talked, and appeared to be like them.

Even though legislation such as the Civil Rights Act of 1964 forbade discriminatory practices in hiring, in reality, prohibiting discrimination was much easier to mandate than to achieve. Astute employers lacking adequate oversight knew they could easily get around such laws. While the Equal Employment Opportunity Commission eventually became an avenue for redress, it was soon overloaded and found that although everyone knew job discrimination existed, proving it was difficult.

Perhaps the biggest barrier to workforce diversity was an overabundance of appropriately credentialed white males eager to join the Park Service in the 1960s and 1970s. The agency could more than fill its job vacancies with this pool and so was inclined to avoid the added complications of hiring women or minorities. Only as pressure mounted to diversify did the Park Service actively seek minority and women candidates and provide them with the training needed to be competitive with the many white men trying to join the agency.

Such an effort began in 1962 under the leadership of Secretary Stewart Udall. President Kennedy had been lukewarm to minorities, but his cabinet had been publicly encouraged to examine their hiring practices. Udall recalled Park Service director Conrad Wirth telling him that the Virgin Islands had recently hired a black park ranger, the first in Park Service history. While Wirth suggested making this a newsworthy event, Udall felt it highlighted the Park Service's dismal hiring record and instead decided to take steps to improve the situation. He pulled together a cadre of recruiters to target historically black colleges and universities for seasonal employees, but when summer came, only about half of those recruited actually showed up at their assigned parks.[54] To a young black in the early 1960s, traveling to a national park in a distant part of the country must have been a daunting prospect.

Robert Stanton, one of the gutsy recruits who showed up as a 1962 seasonal ranger, remembered being one of perhaps forty or fifty black seasonals hired to work in one of Interior's agencies. The young Stanton spent two summers at Grand Teton National Park in Wyoming and came away impressed with the comfortable work environment and professionalism, which helped convince him the Park Service was the type of career agency he was looking for.[55] He went on to become the agency's first black director.

Secretary Udall's diversification efforts of the early 1960s were initiated and run from his office. Director Wirth did not propose or encourage them. The concerted drive Udall intended would depend on the more progressive Hartzog. In retrospect, Hartzog remembered little pressure from the president and Congress to diversify his workforce. Instead, in his view, he received "support" for his own efforts. But he could not have been oblivious to the media emphasis on the issue, nor of the rising pressures on Interior and other agencies to demonstrate advances in diversity recruiting.

In the 1960s and early 1970s, minority hiring efforts centered on blacks and, to a lesser extent, Native Americans. As Hartzog admitted, there "wasn't any real push for women." Women had a longer history in the Park Service, he explained, and boasted some early success stories.[56] Indeed, the agency did employ a host of women, but they were underemployed, trapped at lower wage grades, and largely in traditionally female positions. The Park Service proved slow to exploit this potential.

Hartzog knew the Park Service lacked a similar pool of blacks and therefore had to pursue them actively.[57] The agency did in fact employ a number of blacks, Indians, and Hispanics at low wage grades, so Hartzog's emphasis on black recruiting probably reflected the active and, at times, volatile civil rights movement as well as Secretary Udall's priorities. Asked about his recruiting efforts for Hispanics, Hartzog replied that not much attention was directed to this quarter because the agency employed them in the Southwest, although he conceded that they usually worked in the nonprofessional ranks.[58] The push for more Hispanics, Pacific Islanders, and other underrepresented ethnic groups would come during later directorates.

As Hartzog became increasingly committed to diversifying his workforce, he applied pressure to his subordinates. Park Service regional directors and superintendents knew to take any directives from Hartzog's office seriously; if you didn't, then, as former regional director Howard Chapman declared, "YOU DID NOT REMAIN IN YOUR POSITION VERY LONG!"[59]

In August 1969, Hartzog sent a memo to all superintendents. In it, he forcefully shared the secretary's commitment to Equal Employment Opportunity programs and charged each to become "personally involved in seeing that the EEO program in Interior becomes a successful program." He extracted quotations from a secretarial speech that included such declarations as "[Discrimination] is unacceptable to me," "I am not looking for tokenism. I am looking for results," and "This is not a situation to be proud of—and I expect it to be changed—promptly." Hartzog expressed particular concern about permanent professional positions, of which minorities held only 8 percent.[60]

Strongly worded memos like this, in addition to service-wide Equal Employment Opportunity presentations and superintendents' meetings where hiring practices were commonly discussed, left no doubt about Hartzog's determination to diversify the Park Service. According to one of his regional directors, every meeting during the latter part of Hartzog's tenure included an EEO presentation. Following a 1971 EEO meeting in the Pacific Northwest region, regional director John A. Rutter assured Hartzog that participants had gained a new "awareness of the pressure of the program" and Hartzog's "personal interest in it."[61]

Hartzog conceded that diversifying the agency's workforce did not come easily.[62] To build a workforce more reflective of the country's population, he pursued such measures as seeking fresh talent outside the Park Service, recruiting at minority colleges and universities, searching for trainable talent within the agency, launching a new park technician series through which employees could cross over to the professional ranks, and expanding training for and special assistance to disadvantaged groups.

By recruiting outside the agency, Hartzog found fresh talent, advanced diversity, and addressed the complaints of assistant secretary John A. Carver, who had labeled the Park Service an "insular, rigidly bureaucratic, and politically unresponsive organization."[63] Although Hartzog considered himself a career employee, he agreed that the agency had become too inbred and that employees expected to move in a "lockstep" from ranger to assistant superintendent to superintendent. He challenged that assumption and asserted that he was "going to promote to the best of my abilities on merit and talent and contribution."[64] He himself had leaped over many senior employees, and he wanted to provide others the same chance.

Hartzog recalled telling Horace Albright that "I thought we needed some outside people and that I had in mind a certain number. And he said to me, 'I agree with you. . . . Don't tell anybody what your number is. At the end of every year make the personnel department tell you how many came in from outside and then open your desk drawer and compare it to see how you did.' And I did that. In my first year, I doubled my estimate. And in nine years it was never less than what I estimated." In the first year, Hartzog secretly set a quota of 10 percent and finished the year with 11 percent of vacancies going to outsiders. As he contended, he always exceeded his yearly goal for new hires from outside the agency.[65] The new hires blended into the Park Service with mixed success. Bill Everhart recalled the office joke that "every time George rode with somebody in an airplane he hired him and there he was for work on Monday morning."[66] According to former chief historian Robert Utley, Hartzog "brought in people almost off the street with no National Park Service background that he thought would inject new thinking and fresh blood. . . . Many of these bombed."[67] The new hires had difficulty meshing with the close brotherhood and long-standing traditions of the Park Service, and career employees for their part resented newcomers who often came in at higher wages without putting in their time.

Women and minorities drove an even larger and more decisive wedge between the old line and the new. In an attempt to diversify different wage grades, the Hartzog administration hired minorities for middle management positions. To find good candidates, his personnel officers raided other organizations.

An especially rich source was the Job Corps. Patterned after the 1930s Civil Conservation Corps, the Job Corps, which was administered by existing agencies, targeted poor, undereducated young men and provided them with training programs at resident conservation camps, usually located in urban areas. At the height of the program, the Park Service administered nine Job Corps centers, all east of the Mississippi River. Minorities frequently served as center directors, counselors, and teachers and provided an easily accessible source of talent for the Park Service. According to Robert Stanton, many of the professional staff moved out of the Job Corps into the traditional Park Service as supervisors and superintendents.[68]

Black middle managers helped demonstrate diversity, but their addition created problems. Part of the problem undoubtedly lay with prejudice, but another part related to the organizational structure of the Park Service, which clearly delineated the new employees as not "one of us." To many, the women and minorities who were hired were not "green bloods." According to Reginald "Flip" Hagood, a former director of education and training, who began his career in 1970, the good-ol'-boy network "resented the fact they hadn't been seasonals. They resented . . . that they had not come up through the ranks and paid their dues. . . . These are our jobs. We've worked for them. We've paid our dues. You're not going to come in here and take the easy route and get to the best." According to Hagood, within several years a large number of the middle management hires quit to take positions in more hospitable environments.[69]

Following the lead of Secretary Udall, the Hartzog administration continued to seek minority candidates for seasonal positions by recruiting at a number of the country's predominately black colleges and universities. Recruiting efforts centered largely on those in the sciences for resource management positions and those in business and related fields for administrative positions. Hartzog hoped a seasonal experience would draw blacks into a career with the Park Service, as it did Robert Stanton.

Stanton recalled from his seasonal work in the early 1960s that he stood "in awe of the beauty of Grand Teton National Park, but really what impressed me as a youngster coming from Texas . . . out of a segregated social environment was the quality of the permanent staff." As a seasonal, Stanton worked with a number of Park Service icons, including Harthon "Spud" Bill (superintendent and later deputy director under Hartzog), Russell E. Dickenson (chief ranger and later director), and Jack Davis (who became associate director for operations). "That gives you some idea of the kind of top-notch career people that I met during my first assignment," Stanton said, "and that has always had a lasting impression."[70]

Gentry Davis, studying at Grambling University in Louisiana, was the kind of prize government recruiters sought. Graduating with a high grade point average in recreation, he admitted to having "quite a few job offers" from organizations such as the Forest Service, Bureau of Land Management, and others. He had always pictured himself as a park ranger. No ranger intake-training session was scheduled at the time he graduated, so in the meantime, he was hired as group leader at Harper's Ferry Job Corps Center in Harper's Ferry, West Virginia.[71]

Although not actively recruited in 1970 from Howard University in Washington, D.C., Hagood remembered being very aware of the Park Service's minority recruiting efforts and as a result applied to the U.S. Park Police. His 1970 training class had the highest percentage of minority hires of any previous one.[72]

While Hartzog sought outside talent, he also recognized that underused talent lay within the agency. A notable example was a young security guard, Sylvester Putnam, whom Hartzog met when he was superintendent at Jefferson National Expansion Memorial. In July 1971, Putnam moved quickly in one step from a guard to superintendent of Fort Union Trading Post National Historic Site.[73]

Women employees also benefited as more opportunities became available. For example, Lorraine Mintzmyer started as a GS-4 clerk-stenographer before moving up to a secretarial position in the regional office. Marked as a "comer," she eventually became chief of programming and budgeting in the Omaha office, an appointment that Hartzog had to approve personally. To advance, Mintzmyer closely studied the upper echelons of the organization because she realized that women "would have to do a lot more than any man ever had to." Her preparation paid off when regional director Len Volz recommended her for superintendent of Herbert Hoover National Historic Site in Iowa. Later she rose to superintendent of Buffalo National River in Arkansas before becoming the first woman deputy regional director and then first regional director of the Southwest Region in Santa Fe.[74]

In 1965, the Civil Service Commission requested that all agencies review their classification series for federal employment. Under its maximum utilization of skills and training program, the commission required agencies to look at separating nonprofessional from professional duties and skill requirements. In part, the commission wanted to provide greater opportunities for minorities who might not qualify for professional positions.[75] Hartzog responded by assembling a field operations study team, made up of rotating superintendents, to study the issues and make recommendations. Ideally, Hartzog wanted to professionalize the ranger series while at the same time expanding job opportunities for minorities, women, and locals living near the parks.

With input from the field operations study team, Hartzog created a new park technician series (026) to add to the existing park ranger series (025). He reasoned that the technical series could provide opportunities for "the less educated local population" living near national parks, thereby helping local economies and improving the Park Service's image in the community. He also envisioned the technical series as a new route for minorities and women to get into the professional ranks. Under the new 026 series, employees lacking the educational requirements necessary for the ranger ranks could enter at GS-4 and, after gaining work experience for several years, advance to GS-7 and become eligible to cross over to the professional 025 series. In time, he thought he could move more women and minorities into the professional mainstream, thereby improving his workplace diversity.

Hartzog believed the new technical series would further professionalize the existing 025 series since the new park aids and technicians would support the professional staff in routine duties and thereby free them up so they could focus on more complex activities. Technical work is "essential and fulfilling work," Hartzog admitted, "but it just doesn't require an academic degree to be a good guard or to watch over the fire tower."[76]

Hartzog believed this plan should have benefited everyone. In reality, it ended in failure. He tried to convince the Civil Service Commission to restrict the park technical series to those lacking a college education, thereby giving minorities and women a chance. Not accustomed to penalizing applicants for having too much education, the commission refused. Hartzog then tried to pressure superintendents into hiring less educated women, minorities, and locals for the technical series to help meet service-wide goals for diversity. They balked. Hordes of idealistic people with college and advanced degrees wanted to get into the Park Service. When faced with a white PhD or an undereducated black or woman, superintendents made an obvious choice, despite Hartzog's wishes. They "filled up every cotton pickin' technician job with college-educated, professionally qualified interpreters and natural scientists." He felt they ended up "hogging" the technical series.[77]

Often the new park technicians were better qualified, certainly by education, than the professionals they supported, many of whom had not been to college at all. Some, such as Doris Osmundson Bowen, joined the technical series, crossed over, and advanced to superintendency, but most failed to advance fast enough or at all.[78] Not surprisingly, the park techs began "raising hell because they want to be promoted like the professional people."[79] Morale plummeted, and many gave up in disgust and left.

What Hartzog had hoped would be yet another means to increase diversity had failed. "I broke my back trying to resolve that controversy . . . but nothing satisfied them."[80] With Hartzog's departure in 1972, the Civil Service Commission abolished the tech series by combining it with the ranger series, which he thought only "deprofessionalized" the ranger and reduced opportunities for disadvantaged persons.[81]

To improve conditions for what Stewart Udall had called the "most impoverished minority in America," Hartzog sought ways to hire more Native Americans. Under the Indian Resources Development Act, the Department of the Interior tried to encourage the development of Indian lands, increase training opportunities, and provide advice and assistance.[82] Walter Hickel, who followed Udall as secretary of the interior, encouraged these efforts by directing the Park Service in his policy guidelines to "take the lead in working cooperatively with the Bureau of Indians Affairs and Bureau of Outdoor Recreation . . . to plan programs for developing the recreational and cultural resources of the Indian people, thus enhancing the economy of our Indian reservations."[83]

These efforts represented a shift in the government's policy toward Indians from paternalism to assistance in achieving self-sufficiency. One means the Park Service adopted was employing Indians as cultural demonstrators. In 1967, for example, the superintendent at Nez Perce National Historical Park in Idaho hired local Nez Perce tribe members to demonstrate cornhusk weaving, buckskin tanning, dances, and food preparation, all of which proved popular with visitors.[84]

Encouraging the development of Indian lands for such recreational uses as ski resorts, campgrounds, and cultural sites was another way to help Indians secure greater self-sufficiency. Proper training, however, was critical. Cecil D. Lewis Jr., the Park Service's Indian liaison and superintendent of Badlands National Park in South Dakota, wrote in 1970 that "there is not an area I've visited or have arrangements to visit, where the Indian isn't undertrained in resource management, wildlife management, and interpretation." Lewis, himself an Indian, felt the Park Service had an opportunity to provide specialized training and planning assistance. For example, it could arrange with the Fish and Wildlife Service to set up seasonal employment for tribal members at one of the bison-management areas so that similar herds could be established in their historic range.

Lewis wrote that Indians were not yet ready to attend Park Service training sessions because of expense and the tribes' inability to identify people interested and available. Meantime, he suggested that a certain number of seasonal positions be reserved for Native Americans.[85] In addition, through an Indian youth summer program, the Park Service attempted to interest young Indians in park and recreation careers.[86]

To provide greater assistance, Hartzog lured retired Congressman Ben Reifel, a Native American and former Bureau of Indian Affairs regional director with a Harvard doctorate, out of retirement to develop an Office of Indian Programs. One program under Reifel's direction brought Indians to Albright Training Center at Grand Canyon, where they learned about the financial and technical aspects of running campgrounds on reservation lands. For the public such campgrounds provided unique opportunities to experience private tribal lands, while for the Indians it could mean jobs and economic self-sufficiency.[87] In 1972, the Park Service reported providing additional types of recreation planning and development assistance to Crow, Northern Cheyenne, Blackfeet, Shoshone, Arapahoe, Navajo, Hopi, Apache, Havasupai, Choctaw, and Cheyenne-Arapahoe tribes.[88]

Another initiative aimed at establishing a Zuni-Cibola National Historical Park to interpret tribal culture and preserve native artifacts at Zuni Pueblo in New Mexico. Hartzog argued that protection of the country's nationally significant resources was his primary concern, but the Park Service need not manage them all. Sometimes it made sense to enter into cooperative agreements so more areas could be protected. He also knew that Indian activists would aggressively fight any attempt to acquire any more tribal lands, so a partnership remained his best approach for park expansion. He proposed a joint management arrangement in which the Park Service would appoint its own superintendent who would work closely with an Indian superintendent. When both parties felt the tribe was ready to run the park alone, the Park Service would remove its superintendent. In that way, the Indians could ease into the park business while taking advantage of the Park Service's expertise in interpretation, resource management, and artifact preservation and curatorship. Congress would later authorize such a park, but the Zuni-Cibola proposal would fail when the Indians decided they did not want a partnership with the National Park Service.[89] The area was deauthorized in 1994.

Hartzog also supported the idea of a federally financed Indian national park system for which the Park Service would provide the training and technical help to ensure its success.[90] That idea likewise never came to fruition.

Hartzog understood that increasing workforce diversity depended on expanding training opportunities. The Park Service took a tentative step for women in 1964 by allowing two women to attend the twelve-week intake training session at Albright Training Center at Grand Canyon. The two un-married women joined some forty men, many of them married and with a military background.[91] Reaction to the women varied from acceptance to intolerance even though one already possessed outdoor skills comparable to many of the men.[92] During the session, the attendees went hiking and camping, learned fire control, did target practice, and practiced search and rescue techniques, including rappelling over canyon rims—all of which was foreign to many men as well as women. Although many believed women incapable of successfully participating in these kinds of field activities, a later female trainee said "most of those things done at the canyon were things I was very comfortable doing, more so than the guys that came from the National Capital Park units."[93]

Of Albright's first two women recruits, the larger and more outspoken Barbara Lund, dubbed "tall by tough," earned more respect from the men than the smaller "short by sweet," soft-spoken Barbara Sorrill, a historian at Colonial National Historical Park. The two Barbaras were followed by two older women, Glennie Murray and Betty T. Gentry, who were both single parents. Gentry, a former U.S. Marine and historian at Vicksburg National Military Park, Mississippi, eventually rose to the superintendency at Pea Ridge National Military Park in Arkansas.[94] Despite the single program for men and women, Albright's first women trainees bore titles of historian or interpreter instead of park ranger like their male counterparts. As regional director Howard Chapman said, the Park Service projected a strong macho persona, and had women "been identified as a 'ranger' their lives would have been difficult—to say the least." Chapman felt that the very idea of women rangers could offend men's masculinity and bring out their protec-tive instincts. "What self-respecting ranger would send a woman out to fight a forest fire?" he asked. "[What] self-respecting park policeman would dis-patch a woman to make an arrest of a drunken man?"[95] Many in the Park Service failed to recognize that competency had more to do with training and experience than gender or ethnic background.

Although in 1962 U.S. attorney general Robert Kennedy invalidated, except in the case of extenuating circumstances, an 1870 regulation that allowed the government to specify "male only," many jobs remained closed to women. Kennedy discovered that half of the positions above a GS-4 had requested male applicants. In the three highest federal grades, 94 percent specified "men only."[96] During Hartzog's early directorate, ranger positions remained closed to women owing to, as a 1965 NPS statement declared, "the rugged, and sometimes hazardous, nature of the duties."[97]

In other areas, such as history, women found professional job opportunities largely because of the 1966 National Historic Preservation Act, although rarely in the parks.[98] The act required the Park Service to maintain a National Register of Historic Places, evaluate potential sites for inclusion, administer matching grants to states, and advise states on their preservation programs. The Park Service, therefore, had to hire professionals in the architectural and art history fields, nearly all of whom were from academia. They were lodged in a newly created Office of Archeology and Historic Preservation, which was separate from the uniformed service and dealt with subjects foreign to park personnel. Almost never did they cross to the traditional service. As Robert Utley claimed, "We never practiced any sexual discrimination in that office, so they were hired simply on their merits. Many offices, especially the National Register, may have had more women than men on the professional level. . . . But the women in OAHP *led the way and penetrated this previously all-male bastion.*" Utley felt that Hartzog actively encouraged this influx of women but was not sure whether to attribute it to a "genuine conviction or because he saw it as a sign of the times." While the new archaeology and historic preservation office succeeded in hiring women, it had little success with blacks, who according to Utley were not interested in working for the National Park Service.[99]

By the spring of 1969, the requirements for Albright Training Center's ranger intake class had eased. For the first time, nonprofessionals such as clerk-typists, park guides, and fire control technicians were admitted.[100] Of the forty or so trainees, about a quarter were from ethnic minority groups, nine were women, and several were close to sixty years old, making it an entirely different group than had ever gone through Albright.[101] The face of the National Park Service was slowly transforming.

From 1964 to early 1969, women made up 9 percent of the total ranger intakes at the Albright Center. In fall of 1969, the Office of Personnel Management loosened standards for ranger-intake positions that required specific outdoor and maintenance skills, which many women and minorities lacked. These requirements had unduly restricted positions and were skills that could be taught.[102] With the new standards, women could now qualify as rangers and escape the hybrid status of earlier years.

In 1969, the Civil Service Commission also made it clear that federal agencies could no longer request men only for law enforcement positions. Although women like Betty Knight had been doing law enforcement work for several years, the first woman to take law enforcement training at the

U.S. Park Police Academy in Washington, D.C., was Helen Mullins Lindsay. This was in 1971, the same year women were permitted to wear firearms.[103]

⁂

During his last three years in office, Hartzog made notable progress in advancing women and minorities to management positions. He appointed the first Native Americans, first blacks, and the first women to park superintendencies, a record of which he was justly proud. In June 1970, he promoted Carl Lewis and Clarence Gorman, both of Navajo descent, to the superintendencies of Badlands National Park and Pipestone National Monument, respectively. On August 23, 1970, Hartzog promoted the first black, Robert Stanton, to the superintendency of National Capital Parks—East. Sylvester Putnam and Eugene Colbert followed in 1971. Colbert took over George Washington Carver National Monument as the first black to supervise a park dedicated to the life of a famous black man.

Although he greatly respected Superintendent Wilhelmina Harris at Adams National Historic Site, as Hartzog noted, the Park Service "had to take her [in 1950] with the property."[104] She was not selected from a civil service register. Therefore, Hartzog takes credit for personally appointing Carol Martin in April 1971 as the agency's first female superintendent. Although her appointment to Tuzigoot National Monument marked a step forward for women, many in the Park Service would consider it a less than desirable position. Even Hartzog in casual conversation referred to Tuzigoot as a place where recalcitrant superintendents who needed some "reconditioning" were sent. With such a placement, however, he could promote a woman to a superintendency while minimizing objections from men who had their eyes on more prestigious parks.[105]

In 1971, achieving increased diversity appeared prominently in Hartzog's written goals for the year. He set a goal to "obtain a new plateau in seeking out, employing, training, and providing promotional opportunities for disadvantaged groups including affirmative action plans by concessioners."[106] Meanwhile, the federal government had begun linking government contracts to requirements that companies take serious steps toward employing minority groups. By 1972, President Richard Nixon was pushing for more affirmative action measures, to which Hartzog responded by ordering that 150 ranger-intake positions be set aside for minorities and women who met the Office of Personnel Management standards and agreed to relocate. Restricting the ranger-intake slots angered qualified white males who coveted the positions.[107]

Nixon's affirmative action emphasis came at a time when the economy had slowed, the Vietnam War was winding down, and unemployment had risen, pitting minorities and women against white males for fewer jobs.[108] To make himself more appealing to voters for a second term, Nixon ordered severe cutbacks in government spending and jobs. The Park Service lost 375 permanent and 350 seasonal positions. Management of the park system grew correspondingly more difficult, and efforts at workplace diversity suffered.[109]

Against a background of civil unrest, shifting attitudes, and change in the 1960s, regional director John Rutter said after an EEO workshop in 1971 that "we visualize that the hiring of the disadvantaged will be a continuing and unsatisfactory problem until we have minority people entering into employment with the Park Service through the normal channels and growing into their jobs just like the rest of us."[110]

The Park Service lacked the time. As Bill Everhart explained, meeting the requirements for a Park Service job took a number of years. Just to prepare for a full-time career, most applicants should have attended four years of college and worked summers in the parks. Most men would have started at GS-5, but most women typically started lower in rank. It would take several years to advance from an entry-level grade to GS-7 and then to GS-9, GS-11, and on up. So, "to be minimally prepared for a GS-12 or 13 superintendent position, you needed to have been in the pipeline for ten years."

In the 1970s, someone looking at the roster of eligible applicants would have been lucky to find even one female or minority on it. Park Service upper management was thus "faced with a difficult decision"—whether or not to eliminate "the merit system and start picking women, blacks, and giving them a chance . . . which was done and I'm sure done in every organization and in a way needed to be done. But for every push there is a shove. I mean the people who are passed over felt, you know, 'I deserved the job.'" Occasionally an ethnic minority or female candidate was promoted without regard to the traditional system, thus angering those waiting patiently for such an opportunity. But as Everhart also admitted, you have to ignore the merit system "because you can't wait that ten years until you get these people in."[111]

Meanwhile, the president, secretary, civil rights groups, and others pushed hard to see tangible results. Hartzog had to bring in women and minorities and compress advancement into fewer years. For example, Robert Stanton admitted that "he moved fairly rapidly into the management ranks."[112] He was recruited for full-time work with the Park Service in 1966 as a public information specialist. Within four years and after only one career move, he jumped to management assistant. He gained Hartzog's nod for superintendent at National Capital Parks—East, a first for blacks. After only a year, Hartzog promoted Stanton to Virgin Islands, where he became another first as a black superintendent of a "national" park. When questioned, Hartzog admitted Stanton and others were "targeted." That Stanton was talented, articulate, and genuinely likeable only added to his appeal and the speed with which he advanced.[113]

Pioneering women and minorities faced racial and sexual discrimination as they infiltrated the Park Service. Blacks carried the added burden of worrying for their personal safety. Betty Knight recalled the seasonal black recruits she worked with in 1967 in Yellowstone. They got along well with the staff and had a penchant for instigating Friday night parties. But they also knew they were not as warmly welcomed in the local community.[114] Stanton experienced that prejudice his first summer in Grand Teton, when a bartender in Jackson, Wyoming, refused to serve him and another black.[115] Gentry Davis worked in law enforcement at Grand Canyon and invariably drew the toughest details and the night shifts and had to endure racist remarks from visitors.[116] To Flip Hagood, another black who started in law enforcement, there was a general "lack of acceptance" and "no efforts of communication." Often Hagood and other minority pioneers were the only persons of color in meetings or in travels around the park system and "had to put up with a lot of crap because of it."[117] Some expected this type of reception and coped well with it, but others found the sometimes hostile environments daunting.

Mary Meagher, with a masters in wildlife biology and a desire to research bison, first applied to the Park Service in 1959 but was offered a typist position only if she could improve her skills. For years she floated to various jobs until she completed her dissertation under A. Starker Leopold. This made her eligible in the agency's eyes to head the division of wildlife biology, but at a lower grade than the man who previously held the job. Dr. Meagher said, "The reason I sound warped is that I was treated, like shabby, for so long. Things have improved, but the Park Service still isn't there yet when it comes to equal opportunity for women. Now I'm being used as an example of what women can achieve! I wasted so much time surviving. That's what I resent the most."[118]

Flip Hagood resented the constant questions about his qualifications. Since these kinds of questions were not asked of white counterparts, the implication was that he had gotten the position because of the color of his skin. Women expressed the same frustration about the constant review of their background. Lorraine Mintzmyer accepted several lateral assignments at the same rank so she could get the necessary credentials to move up, but she felt these were moves a man would not have had to make. As she moved into regional management positions, she had to defend her qualifications with each successive administration.[119]

In addition to resistance from within the Park Service, women and minorities in uniform faced unfavorable reactions from outside the agency. As Celia Suggs suggested, sometimes negative reactions were unconscious and subtle. For example, visitors stopping by an information desk would invariably select a white Park Service employee over an equally unoccupied minority. Persons coming into park offices searching for someone in charge would automatically assume that the white male employee outranked any minority or woman present.[120]

Other times the reactions were stronger, such as from the local Arkansas congressman who learned that Lorraine Mintzmyer was to be the next superintendent at the controversial Buffalo National River in his district. After he called the Park Service and complained, Mintzmyer had to visit the man personally to convince him she was up to the job. After she started, a local newspaper ran a prominent story about the new superintendent who was a "woman!" As superintendent, she later hired the park's first black ranger and recalled having to build a support system around him to protect him from discrimination that was "absolutely flagrant."[121] Even superintendents who sought diversity in their ranks had to think twice about subjecting minority employees to the reception they would receive in some areas, and those employees themselves would likewise be reluctant to step into such potentially hostile environments.

Despite the problems, Mintzmyer and others found pockets of support from persons within the Park Service who had confidence in their abilities.[122] She recalled receiving great encouragement from her regional director, J. Leonard (Len) Volz, who gave her well-directed pushes that allowed her to grow professionally. Mintzmyer related one particularly intimidating experience when she walked into a meeting as the only woman among some fifty men, a situation that, in itself, was not unusual. The problem arose when she found herself the only person on one side of an issue she felt very strongly about. Volz withheld support and told her that because she felt that strongly she would have to sell her position by herself. By the session's end, she had mustered enough nerve to convince the room to move in her direction.[123]

Women recalled some men showing protective feelings much like those they would have shown toward a sister or mother. One woman cited an early law enforcement training session in which an FBI speaker blatantly remarked that he did not understand why the Park Service hired women law enforcement officers. The agent said that anything he needed done by a woman, he would simply ask his secretary to do. Not only did the women protest, but many of the men voiced strong objections to his attitude and rose to the women's defense.[124]

Racial resentment did not necessarily surprise minorities. Flip Hagood, for example, expected it. He had grown up in the segregated South, lived in Washington, D.C., as a youth, and had graduated from the historically black Howard University during the height of the civil rights movement. Hagood understood the difficulties he might face but accepted them as a challenge and part of the price he was willing to pay to work for the Park Service, especially since he knew blacks all over the country were facing similar difficulties.

Early black pioneers had to push themselves beyond the deferential role they had grown up with. As one said, "When you've been a female or minority in a subservient role, your inclination is to stay there and just stay behind the umbrella of someone who is used to being a decision maker."[125] Hagood said he felt the "extra need to prove oneself and an extra sense of making sure that you were one cut above."[126] Pioneering women and minorities felt pressured to excel to quell speculation that they were given special consideration. They felt the need to be better than their white male counterparts so they could justify their positions and pave the way for those that would hopefully follow them. As Gentry Davis said, "I knew that if I as an Afro-American didn't shine . . . if I didn't step up to the plate, then it was going to be very difficult for someone to come up behind me—another Afro-American."[127]

Mentoring relationships might have helped these new employees, but there was no strong support system in place composed of persons of their own gender or race. Although women found support among some men, their mentors could not fully relate to the difficulties of being a woman in a man's organization. The same could be said for minorities, who faced their own sets of problems. Lorraine Mintzmyer remembered her upward climb as a "very lonely existence." Although she might have been accepted on one level, she realized she "wasn't one of the good ol' boys and never would be," so at times she found herself shut out of the informal discussions in which decisions were frequently made. She found it especially frustrating when decisions were made in places like urinals in restrooms. So she had to develop new ways to make sure that important discussions took place in her presence. At meetings, she would pointedly invite key players to her room for an after-work informal cocktail hour so she could be a part of any after-hours business.[128]

Some supervisors used the fact that women might quit their jobs after marrying or having children to avoid hiring or selecting them for advancement. Some women responded by putting children on hold until they had progressed further in their career, while others opted not to have children. Working mothers faced the added difficulty of reliable childcare that would allow them the flexibility to travel and attend additional training sessions often necessary for advancement. Dual-career families faced the tough decision of what to do about transfers, since they were key to career advancement, but they put strains on marriages and children, who had to adjust to a new home.[129]

Often women or ethnic minorities seemed to track into stereotyped positions. Women, particularly as they became superintendents, seemed more likely to be sent to small- or medium-sized historical parks, where their presumed skills as hostesses and educators would be an asset. Later, women superintendents experienced difficulties moving up to a higher-graded park superintendency.[130] Minorities were characteristically placed in urban settings or, if black, assigned to parks such as Booker T. Washington National Monument or Maggie Walker National Historic Site. Hartzog strongly believed that the "opportunities for your women and minorities are in the urban population."[131] He and other administrators thought that most blacks would be uncomfortable in rural settings and face stronger prejudices in heavily segregated areas. As one regional director put it, "Blacks are not mountain or country oriented. They are simply city oriented."[132] In sending blacks to urban locations, Hartzog faced less opposition from those whose vision of an ideal park setting was one of the large western crown jewels—not one in the heart of New York City or Washington, D.C.

⁂

Despite a southern upbringing that encouraged negative stereotyping of women and blacks, Hartzog was ahead of his times in bringing diversity to the National Park Service. Perhaps the poverty he experienced as a youth allowed him more easily to understand the frustrations of other disadvantaged groups. Maybe his strong-willed mother showed him that people could move beyond their expected role in society. Possibly the pressures on government officials for change spurred him to turn the rhetoric of equity into reality. Whatever combination of factors contributed to his actions,

Hartzog can be credited with expanding the idea of what a Park Service employee should be. He could have dragged his feet on integration, but he chose to push change on an organization that disliked change. He "took a lot of heat" for his efforts, but he purposely sought workforce diversity for an organization that already had an ample supply of white male recruits.[133]

To say, however, that Hartzog did not share any of the prevailing attitudes about women and minorities would be inaccurate. Like many others, he felt a protectiveness toward women and came gradually toward accepting them in certain types of positions—what he called "an evolution of thought." He did not fully understand equality. For example, at a 1968 superintendents' meeting, he reportedly favored hiring lower-paid female cashiers rather than rangers because using women would save money and "in some cases girls do a much better job."[134] He also supported the feminine uniforms fashioned after airline stewardess dresses that proved a disaster everywhere. Hartzog liked and admired talented women, but he wanted them to be ladies. He, like other men, wanted to shelter them from the more physically challenging and dangerous work, and he was not convinced women were capable of doing it. Without consulting women, the Park Service decided what was best for them.

Hartzog's attitudes about minorities is less clear. Whether he occasionally fell prey to derogatory thoughts, remarks, and actions is unknown. Like any other white person who grew up amid the negative stereotyping of blacks prevalent in the South of his childhood, Hartzog had to discover for himself the lies and indecency of this racist perspective. By his conduct, he demonstrated that he had shed the negative attitudes that might have lingered when he began his career with the Park Service.

Hartzog came willingly to the decision to seek diversity within the ranks. Without a nudge from above, however, other Park Service concerns would have taken precedent. As an energetic director hired to make progressive changes, he desperately wanted the agency to excel at all it did. As a lawyer, he understood the legal ramifications and costs of not showing effort toward promoting diversity. He set high standards, worked extraordinarily hard, and expected everyone to do the same. After deciding that he wanted more women and minorities in the Park Service, he exhorted and sometimes relentlessly bullied his agency and used a variety of means to achieve his objectives. During Hartzog's tenure, diversity meant enhanced opportunities for blacks and women, and to a lesser extent Native Americans. Although Hispanics, Asian Americans, and other groups were not purposely excluded, neither were they actively targeted.[135]

Hartzog knew where he wanted to go, but he also came to realize that no matter how strongly and autocratically he ruled, he could only move the organization so far and so fast. He understood that change could not occur overnight and that many in the Park Service, including those he affectionately called "the old stags," did not favor women and minorities in professional positions. Competition for the limited positions was stiff, and park managers wanted the best-qualified candidates. Managers also wanted people they could work with comfortably. Hiring women in traditionally male fields, they reasoned, might create tension within the ranks and "feminize" masculine occupations. People of color had conventionally been segregated from whites in social and work environments, so integration would create difficulties in the Park Service as it did elsewhere.

As director, Hartzog felt he could not move too quickly to assimilate women and minorities into the professional ranks. He compared diversifying the system with crossing the Grand Canyon. A backpacker could not jump the 10-mile distance from the south to the north rim but instead had to descend to the Colorado River, cross it, and slowly head back up the other side. Hartzog felt that you "can only do what you'd like to do with the permission of the organization. That's the hardest lesson I had to learn."[136]

In hindsight, one can ask whether Hartzog could have cracked the door a little wider. Probably yes. Throughout his tenure, he skillfully balanced his convictions about the worth and desirability of women and minorities against Park Service traditions and political realities. He was not ready in 1964 to accept many women or minorities, but he was by 1972. Could he have moved the Park Service farther? Probably, but diversity was only one among a host of issues that constantly crossed his desk. Was enhancing diversity one of his top priorities? Probably not. He does not appear to have approached enhancing diversity with the same zeal as other interests such as expanding the park system. Hartzog's extensive collection of personal papers contains little information related to diversity, and fellow Park Service employees do not seem to automatically associate the concept with him. His primary responsibility was to carry out the Park Service mission of resource protection and visitor enjoyment, not advance job opportunities for disadvantaged groups. Nevertheless, he personally selected it as one of his three proudest achievements as director

As testimony to this achievement, Hartzog recalled returning to Harper's Ferry, West Virginia, for a speech in the early 1990s. When he had first spoken at Harper's Ferry to a group of Park Service employees some thirty years earlier, only one woman sat in the audience, and she was someone's secretary getting coffee for the group. Thirty years later, he was amazed to see the large number of women. Quick with a joke, he remarked to the audience that for a brief moment he thought he was addressing a National Organization for Women convention instead of the National Park Service.[137] To George Hartzog, the evidence of his success was in that room.

Urban Recreation Programs and Areas

When George Hartzog became director of the Park Service in 1964, many American cities lacked adequate outdoor spaces that provided opportunities for recreation. In a rush to grow, America's quaint old towns had given way to an ever-widening circle of homes, businesses, roads, and parking lots. Government officials and planners had not assured a sustainable balance between development and open spaces.[1] At the same time, an increasingly industrialized and urban society had rewarded people with more free time to pursue the good life. They traveled in record numbers and sought places they could go to enjoy the outdoors. Unfortunately, ugly, polluted, and congested cities afforded few natural areas for escape. Furthermore, a healthy economy ignited a development spree that gobbled up accessible resources suitable for outdoor recreation.

Due to limited budgets, the Park Service struggled to meet the heightened demand for outdoor recreation that taxed even the ability of the ambitious Mission 66, the ten-year capital-improvement program initiated during Wirth's directorate, to keep up. "There are millions of young people that are being reared in asphalt and concrete jungles completely isolated from their natural and cultural inheritance," Hartzog emphatically told Congress, "and they are growing up with no appreciation of the important values that undergird our Republic."[2]

As President Lyndon B. Johnson fought to build a Great Society, concern about the lack of accessible outdoor spaces reached the national level. The National Park Service, under Hartzog's leadership, became one of many agencies that stepped forward to enhance programming efforts and add urban recreation areas. Hartzog was sensitive to the winds of change and to the interests of those above him.[3] His own socioeconomic background combined with his interest in the ministry gave him a special empathy for the underprivileged. During his superintendency of Jefferson National Expansion Memorial in downtown St. Louis, he had witnessed how that park just "rejuvenated that whole city."[4] He could easily envision parks and special programs doing the same for other cities. He knew his agency could lead in this effort, and he recognized the potential political benefits. His gravitation toward urban programs and areas seemed almost predetermined.

The addition of urban recreation areas to the National Park System, however, stirred strong emotions both within and outside the agency. As historian Ronald Foresta observes, "No question has been so debated within the National Park Service as that of the appropriateness of urban parks in the National Park System. Aside from the use versus preservation question, no issue has been its equal in forcing the agency to ask itself questions about its basic mission or in involving it in controversy."[5]

Traditionally, Americans associated national parks with great scenic wonders like Yellowstone, Yosemite, and Grand Canyon. They could easily imagine a ruggedly handsome ranger silhouetted against a backdrop of remote mountain peaks, but they had difficulty picturing one leading an interpretive walk along a beach in the shadow of skyscrapers with jets flying overhead. Many struggled with accepting a new type of park that emphasized mass recreation over resource protection.

Few questioned the merits of providing recreational opportunities for city dwellers, but many debated whether the Park Service should be the agency to provide it on a large scale. Some thought the Park Service was trying on a new pair of shoes. Whether the discomfort arose from newness or just a poor fit was not apparent. That the shoes were ever allowed to be tried on, however, pointed to strong support for the Park Service's involvement. Even as powerful as he became, Hartzog could not have made such a move alone. An influential mixture of presidential, congressional, departmental, and private interests pushed at the same time that Hartzog aggressively pulled his agency toward accepting urban parks and programs.

In reflecting on his career, Hartzog pointed to his urban initiative as one of his proudest accomplishments as director. "I brought parks to the people," he declared, "[and] made them relevant to a changing urban population."[6]

At first glance, Hartzog's focus on urban parks and programs seemed a major departure for the Park Service. In reality, it was not. The National Park System has always been an ever-changing entity. Since their creation, national parks have evolved to reflect the country's changing interests, needs, and values. They are made to embody what Americans and their congressional representatives deem important at a given time. With each addition, the kaleidoscope that has become the National Park System changes in a subtle or more noticeable way.

From the beginning, proposals to set aside lands for parks have generated debate—often quite heated. To many, dispensing public land for homesteads, schools, timber harvest, mines, and railroads seemed like an appropriate government function. Protecting parklands for recreational use did not. Acceptance of the idea that the government had a responsibility to protect the land would require a gradual shift in thinking about the role of government and the value of the country's resources. From a need to subdue it and profit from its resources had to come respect and a sense of stewardship. Two hundred sixty-five years would pass between the settling of Jamestown and the establishment in 1872 of Yellowstone, the country's first national park. But even with Yellowstone's unrivaled geologic wonders, the park initially lacked widespread support in Congress and among private citizens. "The best thing the Government could do with the Yellowstone National Park," declared a Kansas senator in 1883, "is to survey it and sell it as other public lands are sold."[7]

Fortunately that never happened, but after Yellowstone, park additions grew slowly as the country struggled to determine what type of resources warranted federal protection and what responsibilities the government had in facilitating visitors' use of them. Most early additions, such as Yosemite in California, Grand Canyon in Arizona, and Glacier in Montana, followed the mold of having magnificent scenery, sublime vistas, and unique geologic features.

Founding fathers Stephen Mather and Horace Albright continually struggled with the extent and types of development appropriate for the variety of park units they managed. They recognized that "no sharp line between necessary, proper development and harmful over-development" existed. Initially, they built basic accommodations, including roads, trails, bridges, public campgrounds, and water and sewer systems. At times, however, they proposed moving beyond these basics in an effort to attract more visitors and keep them longer. They believed, as would Hartzog, that connecting people with the parks was key to the system's survival. To that end, they proposed more elaborate projects such as building golf courses in several parks, spanning the Grand Canyon with a cable-car tram, and even making the extensive changes to Yosemite Valley that would have been necessary for it to host the 1932 Winter Olympics (which ultimately went to Lake Placid). Although most of their resort-oriented ideas failed to gain enough support, they could have led the National Park Service down a very different path during these formative years.[8]

Until the mid-1920s, the Park System had a strong western orientation; the only park that lay east of the Mississippi was Acadia National Park in Maine. Mather and Albright recognized the need to make the system more representative of the entire country and pushed for such parks in the Shenandoah Mountains in Virginia and the Great Smoky Mountains in Tennessee and North Carolina. They knew that failure to make a strong presence in the East might allow recreation to fall to rival agencies such as the Forest Service. They also understood that national parks needed to be relevant to a growing urban population, a belief that Hartzog likewise shared. As they searched for suitable parklands, however, Mather and Albright found the East lacking in large tracts of public domain lands similar to what was used to carve out western parks. As a result, donations or costly and complicated private land purchases often became necessary, unless existing lands could be transferred from other agencies.[9]

In 1933, a government reorganization shifted many predominately historical and often eastern areas to the Park Service. This not only greatly expanded and diversified the National Park System; it also threw the Park Service firmly into the urban park business by giving it jurisdiction over the parks and memorials of Washington, D.C. Added were Rock Creek Park; Potomac Park, which was an artificial area created by fill dredge from the Potomac River that became the site for the Lincoln, Jefferson, and Roosevelt memorials; and the George Washington Parkway on the Virginia shore of the Potomac River.[10]

While there was support for the 1933 reorganization, such departures from tradition stirred strong emotions. Critics charged the Park Service with straying too far from its conventional course and lamented what they saw as a shift away from protecting the large, scenic wonderlands in the West. As James Foote of the National Audubon Society wrote in a 1937 letter to Interior secretary Harold Ickes, "The National Park Service has been expanding in recent years—so rapidly that the original precepts and ideals on which the Service was founded appear to have become lost or forgotten. State parks, recreational areas, national parks and primeval national parks have been shuffled and jumbled until today a confused American public scarcely knows which is which."[11] Similar charges would be leveled against Hartzog thirty years later as he steered the Park Service toward greater involvement in urban parks and programs.

To the public and Park Service alike, capital parklands seemed unrelated to traditional national parks. As one administrator observed, "The Service felt that the capital parks were a horse of a different color, separate from the rest of the System. Even the personnel were different."[12] According to Hartzog, many thought "national capital parks were a joke. . . . Nobody paid a lot of attention. They were independent."[13]

To Hartzog, capital parks came to represent a "microcosm of the National Park System." There were historical areas like the Washington Monument; natural areas like Rock Creek Park, a parkway that exhibited the scenic Virginia shore all the way to Mount Vernon; and recreational areas like the Potomac River, where multitudes of rowing teams practiced and used Park Service boathouses. Rather than ignore these parks, Hartzog used them to showcase the entire system as a means of gaining public support.[14] Without strong support, he knew he had little chance of advancing his programs.

Between the reorganization of 1933 and the start of the Hartzog directorate in 1964, the National Park System continued to grow and diversify. The addition of 102 new units brought the total to 239. Historical additions outnumbered natural ones by a large margin. Due to the country's increased appetite for recreational pursuits, parks with a major recreation component took on a new importance. In response, the system acquired parkways (Skyline Drive, Blue Ridge, Natchez Trace), reservoir playgrounds (Lake Mead, Grand Coulee, Shadow Mountain, Glen Canyon, Whiskeytown-Shasta-Trinity), and seashores (Cape Hatteras, Cape Cod).

Not surprisingly, the emphasis on such nontraditional areas and use of resources provoked purists. They objected to the visual and environmental intrusions of reservoirs, parkways, and roads into wild areas. They objected to the lax standards of recreation areas that allowed hunting and trapping and placed special emphasis on use-oriented activities. Because of the ocean's popularity and the scarcity of public access, however, seashore parks with a strong recreation component met little opposition. Two entered the system before Hartzog's time and pressure mounted to add more. As it had been required to do previously for new types of additions, the Park Service had to determine standards for inclusion. Often they made them up as they went. When Bill Everhart began work on locating possible seashore parks, he asked about the criteria for national seashores, thinking there would be some sort of manual on the topic. Instead, his boss's response was "you will recognize it when you see it."[15]

During the Hartzog years, the park system continued to evolve, with urban recreation areas becoming one area of logical expansion. The Park Service was responding to a perceived need, just as it had done with natural areas, historical areas, parkways, seashores, and recreation lands surrounding reservoirs. As Hartzog assumed the helm of the National Park Service, he knew that improving urban life and creating nearby outdoor recreation areas for city dwellers had become important issues.

Hartzog not only felt personally driven to expand the Park Service's involvement in urban recreation areas and programs but also recognized the strong outside incentives to do so. First, the report of Laurance Rockefeller's 1962 Outdoor Recreation Resources Review Commission set the stage by exposing serious problems in the country's accessible outdoor recreation resources and recommending ways to correct them. Second, secretary of the interior Stewart Udall was astute enough to act on many of the commission's recommendations and establish his own environmental vision for the country. Third, President Johnson and his wife created a receptive environment by promoting Great Society initiatives. Fourth, even President Richard Nixon's politically motivated support for national recreation areas aided Hartzog's quest for an expanded dimension to the park system. Finally, American citizens wanted an urban recreation emphasis, and their congressional representatives willingly funded it until budgetary restraints from a costly war forced them to slow domestic spending. In short, Hartzog paddled with the current, not against it.

※

The landmark study by the Outdoor Recreation Resources Review Commission set off a chain reaction of effort that would help direct federal and state activities for years to come. To the embarrassment of the Park Service, the commission found that the "lack of anything resembling a national recreation policy is . . . at the seat of most of the recreation problems of the federal government."[16] The Park, Parkway, and Recreational Area Study Act of 1936 had given the Park Service authority to coordinate the planning and development of adequate recreational parks, parkways, and recreation facilities at the local, state, and federal levels.[17] For many years, the Park Service led all other federal agencies in recreation planning and provision. By 1960, however, the Park Service would lose its supremacy and drop to third place behind the Corps of Engineers and the U.S. Forest Service in number of visitors.[18] While Mission 66 brought some badly needed support, the excitement generated by the program's projects sidetracked the Park Service from its duties of nationwide recreation assessment, planning, and development.

Given the lack of national leadership, the commission recommended that a special bureau be created to coordinate the activities of all federal recreation providing agencies. In 1962, Stewart Udall created such an agency, the Bureau of Outdoor Recreation. Although the new bureau highlighted the value the federal government placed on outdoor recreation, it was also a slap in the face to the Park Service, which had its authority stripped away. While Conrad Wirth had strenuously objected to its creation, Hartzog attempted to work with the sister agency, but competition and a series of difficult administrators made cooperative efforts difficult.

In addition to leadership problems, the commission pointed out that the populous East lacked easy access to the big parks like Yellowstone that were all located in the West. The commission reported that "three quarters of the people will live in these [urban] areas by the turn of the century. They will have the greatest need for outdoor recreation, and their need will be most difficult to satisfy as urban centers have the fewest facilities (per capita) and the sharpest competition for land use."[19] To purchase recreational lands, the commission recommended that a sizable amount of funding be made available and that particular emphasis be given to areas accessible to large populations. Their recommendations led to the creation of the 1965 Land and Water Conservation Fund, which would supply Hartzog with significant funding for park additions.

※

Although President Kennedy lacked a strong environmental record, he allowed his secretary of the interior, Stewart Udall, to take a national approach to dealing with the country's environmental problems and press for his "New Conservation" agenda. Like Kennedy, Lyndon Johnson had a weak environmental record, but he, too, interfered little with the Department of the Interior. If an idea was "good for the land and good for the people," Udall said, Johnson "bought it."[20]

Udall sought to make the environment a major government responsibility and a mainstream concern. His greatest strength, according to Bill Everhart, was his "ability to articulate a vision and environmental ethic."[21] Udall faced many problems but felt drawn to the urban environment, commenting that "more and more of my time is involved not in the problems of the West but in the problems of urban areas and urban environments."

In his book, *The Quiet Crisis*, Udall wrote that cities had grown too fast to grow well and that proper long-range planning had taken a backseat to the short-term profits of development. He encouraged people to move away from the idea that "all growth is good, all development is good."[22] He knew that polluted and congested cities with limited green spaces could not be healthy. He made it clear that cities needed the money and expertise to address such issues. "There is an unmistakable note of urgency in the quiet crisis of American cities," he wrote. "We must act decisively—and soon—if we are to assert the people's right to clean air and water, to open space, to well-designed urban areas, to mental and physical health. In every part of the nation, we need men and women who will fight for man-made masterpieces and against senseless squalor and urban decay."[23]

George Hartzog proved an ideal combatant to address Udall's "quiet crisis."[24] He knew he needed to provide aggressive new leadership in tune with Udall's agenda. His phenomenal success with the complicated Gateway Arch project in St. Louis gave him the confidence to think he could perform similar miracles in other cities. With Hartzog on board, Udall felt his greatest obstacle was convincing congressional leaders like Wayne Aspinall, the powerful, cantankerous chairman of the House Interior Committee, to accept urban parks and programs.[25]

※

President Johnson believed the federal government was obligated to help solve the country's problems. He envisioned his Great Society programs addressing them. One area of concern had to do with the quality of where Americans lived and worked. "Our country will never be great until our cities are great," he said. "It is harder and harder to live the good life in American cities today. The catalog of ills is long: there is a decay of the centers and the despoiling of the suburbs. . . . Open land is vanishing and old landmarks are violated. Worst of all, expansion is eroding the precious and time-honored values of community with neighbors and communion with nature. The loss of these values breeds loneliness and boredom and indifference."[26]

Given the way government works, these ringing sentiments almost certainly drew their inspiration if not the words themselves from lower echelons of the bureaucracy. According to Hartzog, presidential speechwriters frequently asked for statements from the Park Service. Often these appeared in the speeches of the president and First Lady.[27]

Some believed that the urban decay Johnson spoke of contributed to unrest and violence in cities. Despite his promise to mount a "national effort to make the American city a better and more stimulating place to live," U.S. cities erupted in racial strife.[28] Just five days after the Voting Rights Act of 1965 became law, a violent riot broke out in the Watts section of Los Angeles, leaving thirty-four dead and 20 square miles devastated. Few could deny that serious problems existed in black ghettos. For the next three "long hot summers," racial unrest erupted in 168 cities, killed 225 people, wounded 4,000, and damaged or destroyed property worth $112 billion.[29]

In response, Johnson established a commission to study what happened and why and to propose how future incidents could be prevented. The commission concluded that "our Nation is moving toward two societies, one black, one white—separate and unequal." The commission urged "national action—compassionate, massive, and sustained, backed by the resources of the most powerful and richest nation on this earth." Otherwise they warned that an explosive mixture of poor blacks might well blow the country apart and "threaten the future of every American."

According to the report, blacks cited the "poor recreation facilities and programs" as one of their twelve most serious grievances.[30] City parks were dying due to general neglect and the decreasing tax base that funded them. The city's poor, who lacked private backyards and money for exclusive golf and swim clubs, had the most critical needs but received the worst services and facilities.[31] Johnson told the nation that "the only genuine, long-range solution for what has happened lies in an attack—mounted at every level—upon the conditions that breed despair and violence."[32] The Park Service became part of this attack, and urban recreation areas and programs were a part of Hartzog's solution.

Despite such grandiose ideas, even Johnson knew there were limits to what the federal government and his Great Society programs could accomplish. He lacked the resources to "rebuild the entire urban United States," which is what he felt had to happen over the next forty years. Instead, in 1966, he developed an ambitious model cities program, which provided grants and technical assistance to rebuild blighted urban areas.[33] Ideally the efforts would stimulate businesses and overhaul schools, health care, transportation, and recreation facilities. Priced at more than $2 billion, only its planning component initially won funding from an increasingly cost-conscious Congress.

President Johnson struggled to get this and other domestic programs fully funded. By 1968, however, the Democratic Congress, facing rising inflation, had turned away from a president bogged down in Vietnam. While Johnson had wanted to believe he could support both his "guns and butter" agendas, a recalcitrant Congress gutted many of his efforts by refusing to fund them.

Although Johnson had only a mild interest in the environment, his wife, Lady Bird Johnson, became a strong proponent of conservation, parks, and natural beauty. The name of the committee she formed to carry out her beautification efforts—Committee for a More Beautiful National Capital— was criticized for having a "gimmicky tone," but these efforts greatly benefited the growing park and environmental movement as she continually pushed these issues before her husband and the nation.

For patriotic reasons and as a showcase for other cities, Mrs. Johnson began by beautifying national capital areas, which included Park Service holdings. Stewart Udall had told her that "Washington is a shabby city compared with most European capitals."[34] Washington suffered many of the ills common throughout the country—deteriorating inner cities, impoverished and segregated communities, and inadequate public housing and transportation. A critical *Harper's* article in 1963 described Washington as having, "dilapidated sidewalks, ugly and confusing clutter of traffic signs, decrepit benches, forbidding trash baskets, hideous parking lots, poorly lit, deserted, and crime ridden city parks, and a desperate dearth of amenities."[35]

As a result of the efforts of the First Lady's committee, flowers were placed in traffic triangles and squares, awards given for community beautification projects, and revitalization efforts begun on Pennsylvania Avenue and in Lafayette Park. As the *Washington Star* reported in October 1966, "with green-thumbed gloves and gilt shovel, the First Lady has traveled all over town planting pansies, azaleas, chrysanthemums, dogwoods and cherry blossom trees."

By 1967, with Park Service leadership, eighty park sites had been landscaped in addition to nine schools and eight playgrounds. Half a million flower bulbs, 83,000 flowering plants, 50,000 shrubs, 25,000 trees, and 137,000 annuals had been used. Cherry trees donated by the Japanese government had been planted, and new flowering trees and shrubs lined Pennsylvania Avenue.[36]

As director, Hartzog knew of and aided Mrs. Johnson's efforts in urban parks and her ambitious future plans for Washington, D.C. Secretary Udall also kept fully abreast of her activities. He served as a constant source of encouragement and ideas and accompanied her on ten to twelve official trips. He and her assistant would often talk months before a trip so the First Lady could incorporate some Interior business into her travels and he could promote his department's programs.

"Everyone knew that Mrs. Johnson had a great deal of influence on how we stood with the President," Udall said, "how we stood with the Administration, that our programs were important. . . . The liaison done was extremely good because we knew the President was following what she was doing. She talked with him all the time. If she thought something was good he would most likely think this was a good thing."[37]

Hartzog also appreciated Mrs. Johnson's importance. "With a little tea at the White House," he said, "Mrs. Johnson did wonders to convince doubting congressmen of the merits of our park proposals. Gracious, enthusiastic, articulate, always charming even when exhausted, she was our premier traveling saleslady. The head of steam she helped us build for new parks continued the momentum of the program for years after she left the White House."[38]

During her husband's presidency, Mrs. Johnson traveled with Hartzog to a number of Washington area parks in addition to distant ones such as Redwood, Point Reyes, Rocky Mountain, Grand Teton, Yellowstone, Big Bend, Blue Ridge, Shenandoah, Virgin Islands, and Padre Island.[39] Her visible interest and support helped Hartzog get park legislation passed through Congress.

❧

Hartzog lost valuable allies when the Johnsons left the White House in 1969. According to Hartzog, Richard Nixon never showed any real interest in the environment, but Nixon did ultimately support the establishment of urban parks and programs, if only for political reasons.[40] Nixon became president just as the environmental movement began taking off. Books such as Paul Ehrlich's *Population Bomb*, which sold more than three million copies, heightened people's concern about the impact of human beings on the environment. The January 1969 oil spill off Santa Barbara polluted 200 miles of California shoreline, and pictures of pitiful, oil-soaked birds filled the news media. Later in 1969, the Cuyahoga River in Ohio literally caught fire. Nixon could ill afford to ignore the political power of the environmental movement, especially after three million people across the country celebrated the first Earth Day on April 22, 1970.[41] So he cautiously supported environmental legislation, but he usually delegated responsibility for environmental initiatives to John Ehrlichman, his domestic affairs advisor; to John Whittaker, environmental advisor; or to Russell Train, who headed the President's Council on Environmental Quality and later served as undersecretary of the interior.[42]

John Whittaker, whom Hartzog described as "brilliant" and "one of the truly nice people that Nixon had in his administration," believed that the only environmental issue Nixon took interest in was national parks.[43] Whittaker attributed Nixon's interest to his childhood vacations to Yellowstone and Yosemite national parks. On more than one occasion, Nixon reportedly said, "We have to bring parks to people." Whittaker also recalled that when questions arose over how to divest of controversial surplus lands, Nixon would say, "When in doubt, make it a park."[44]

Nixon's new federalism publicly promoted local empowerment and fiscal responsibility, but privately, the president worked to concentrate more executive power under his control and usurp it from agency heads like Hartzog. Nixon opposed urban national recreation areas even though he publicly declared that "the creation of national parks and outdoor recreation areas near the large cities is as vital . . . as the reservation of the great forests and rivers of the West."[45] Developing federally run recreation areas in San Francisco and New York City ran counter to his new federalism approach and promised to be costly. Nonetheless, as the 1972 presidential election approached, assistant secretary of the interior Nathaniel Reed said the "oppose, oppose, oppose" stance changed to a "yes" with limits.[46] Nixon understood the importance of pleasing two states that together claimed 32 percent of electoral votes. Additionally, he had to pacify Representative Shirley Chisholm, a New York City Democrat and the first black woman elected to Congress, and Representative Phillip Burton, a Democrat from California and another power in the House.

Nixon hoped to sell the two urban parks on opposite coasts as a complete package rather than the first of many. Since both were located on harbors, he painted the two areas as complementary water "gateways," even going so far as to call them Gateway East and Gateway West. If he were lucky, he could support the two politically attractive parks, show voters his concern for urban conditions, and avoid having to fund similar parks in other cities.

≵

Hartzog and the Park Service felt that the country was encouraging if not demanding the government to place a greater emphasis on urban parks and programs. Similar pressures prompted Congress to add caves during the 1920s, parkways during the 1930s, and seashores during the 1950s to the National Park System. In the 1960s, people wanted urban parks. Wisely, Hartzog described his urban initiatives as demonstration projects for "innovation, validation and exportation." In other words, he would develop urban parks and programs, and if they were successful, he would help others do the same. He privately hoped for a whole string of urban recreation areas, but he knew that such grandiose plans would antagonize competing federal agencies and frighten Congress, so he openly promoted only two areas, hoping that success might heighten interest and fuel further expansion.[47]

Hartzog knew that urban recreation areas would not only expand the Park Service's management responsibilities but also add significantly to its base of power. Eastern congressmen increasingly complained that too much money was spent on western parks, where their constituents could not easily go.[48] As one Park Service administrator put it, "Hartzog was desperate to expand the political base of the system. He knew that a major urban park would bring the active support of a couple of dozen representatives while a new crown jewel would only affect one, and probably make him an enemy of the system at that."[49]

Although Hartzog objected to being described as "desperate," he agreed with the merits of pleasing the greatest possible number of congressional members—especially those on key House and Senate committees. Urban constituents and their congressional representatives, he believed, would play a critical role in the Park Service's future success. He felt that

unless the urban people of America have a stake in the National Park Service, it's not going to survive. And so if you want to reduce it to just a pure political equation—that's it! You know, the top 1 percent of the financial world . . . will never save the National Park System. It's the bottom 50% that are going to save it if it's to be saved. And they are not to be found among the membership of those elitist environmental groups, but they are to be found in the voting booths sending their representatives to the Congress . . . and he or she is going to vote their message. Now that in my judgment is the bedrock of the salvation of the National Park System.[50]

Hartzog also recognized that while most committee leaders who were key to the Park Service's agenda had come from western states, the balance of power was shifting east. Until urban constituencies and their congressional representatives understood the relevance of national parks to their lives, the National Park System would suffer.

To this end, Hartzog courted members of Congress. One of his key committee supporters was Julia Butler Hansen of Washington, who chaired

Interior's appropriations subcommittee in the House. Since Hansen exercised the power to add or take away authorized funding, Hartzog paid close attention to her interests. He also tried to engage her in his program initiatives. For example, after taking her to lunch one day, he drove her past some of Lady Bird Johnson's beautification projects, hoping that would impress her enough to authorize additional funding. When he got only a lukewarm response, he directed the driver to go past Lincoln Park in a very depressed section of Washington, D.C. As he described it, "You had these little children playing in the street, not a blade of grass in the park—pure desolation."[51]

Clearly moved, Hansen promised that if Hartzog came up with a suitable proposal to deal with that situation, she would fund it. Since she, like Hartzog, had grown up poor, she was sympathetic to underprivileged groups and simply used the power of her position to allocate $575,000 for what came to be known as "Summer in the Parks."[52] Without her influence, Hartzog believed this demonstration project would never have been funded by the Bureau of Budget (which in 1970 became the Office of Management and Budget). "Those damn bureaucrats didn't believe in that," he declared.[53]

Under Hartzog's watchful eye, the Park Service designed Summer in the Parks to meet the needs of many but concentrated on disadvantaged youth. Enhancing environmental awareness, developing outdoor recreation skills, and stimulating cultural awareness became cornerstones of the various youth programs. Ideally, such goodwill programs would also help quell the mounting tensions that had led to racial conflict in cities across the country.

Planning for Summer in the Parks did not begin until the end of March 1968. Funding levels were still in doubt by June for a July start date. Pulling such a program together with only several months lead time pushed Hartzog's staff hard. He recalled one meeting in which he questioned their lack of progress. Hartzog's regional chief of interpretation who was in charge of the initiative finally admitted that he believed the program could not possibly meet its deadline. "I thought that was the problem," an angry Hartzog erupted and told the man to wait outside while the meeting proceeded without him. Before the meeting's end, Hartzog installed William Whalen as head of Summer in the Parks, and the program's activities were back on track.[54]

Although the Park Service managed urban parks in and around Washington, the Summer in the Parks program took the agency into uncharted waters. As one key official said, "The needs were so different, the people, the suppliers, the hours—everything was a new ballgame." However, with a lot of creativity and the collaborative efforts of many different groups, the

Park Service managed to pull together a highly visible summer program in the capital city that involved an estimated three hundred thousand people. "In the spring of 1968, nobody in Washington had heard of Summer in the Parks. By the fall, practically everyone had."[55]

Many of the participants were disadvantaged city children who experienced the outdoors in a way they never had. They caught fish stocked by the Fish and Wildlife Service in the C&O Canal. They rode horses in Rock Creek Park. They visited a farm and petted the animals, went on a hayride, and later integrated their experiences into an arts and crafts program. They played in a tree house designed by an architecture student. Some took their very first boat ride. Park Service rangers developed a number of environmental education programs. One creative planner even heaped a pile of rocks near the water and allowed kids to do what came naturally—hurl them into the water. Part of the program's excitement lay in the "surprise trip" format. Each day participants would gather at schools or recreation centers to be picked up and spirited off to some unknown adventure for the day.

While Representative Hansen's first-year funding covered transportation for trips, she told Hartzog he would need specific authorizing legislation the following year. Desegregation and bussing had become political hot buttons. Representative Joe Skubitz of Kansas, ranking Republican on the legislative subcommittee overseeing the Park Service, opposed bussing and had the power to kill it. Hartzog reacted by contacting the superintendent at Fort Scott National Historic Site, a park in Skubitz's district. Without Skubitz's knowledge, Hartzog instructed the Fort Scott superintendent to pick the area's largest school district and transport the school's children to the fort for special living history programs. When the school superintendent wanted to thank Hartzog personally, he was told to call Skubitz and thank him.

Later, Skubitz called Hartzog into his office to discuss a recent phone call from a Kansas school superintendent who raved about the wonderful living history program Skubitz had initiated at Fort Scott. At first, Skubitz had been baffled until the official mentioned transporting the children to the fort. Immediately he realized that Hartzog had outflanked him. "If you want the damn legislation [for transportation costs]," he said, "tell Wayne [Aspinall, chair of the full committee] to go ahead."[56] According to Hartzog, Skubitz "got a bang out of it because it wasn't often that he got his deck trumped." Hartzog got his funding and continued transporting inner city youths to area parks.[57]

In addition to serving disadvantaged youths, Summer in the Parks put on midday concerts, which attracted office workers to the parks for their lunch breaks, and special evening programs that extended park usage. Due to Mrs. Johnson's beautification efforts, many of the city parks used had received face-lifts, such as brighter lighting, playground equipment, volleyball and badminton courts, multipurpose stages, and additional seating. Many credited these programs with helping decrease crime in volatile neighborhoods. Washington's officials even publicly acknowledged the program's importance in saving the city from more severe rioting.[58]

Increasingly, Hartzog sought innovative programs that would not only excite long-time users but also pull in those who had been little drawn to the national parks. To that end, he expanded Summer in the Parks to other areas outside the national capital. In milder climates, he broadened the summertime effort into Parks for All Seasons. He pressed to include new recreational facilities in park management plans such as at Fort Vancouver National Historical Site, which lay in Julia Butler Hansen's district. With prompting, Hartzog pushed for a children's playground. Originally opposed, Superintendent Eliot Davis relented, admitting that "you don't buck George and Julia, so the park went all out to do a good job." Within a short time, a western-themed playground with a frontier outpost, prairie schooner, and corral stockade appeared. Although parents were pleased to have a play area that was "away from town and freeway where there was no hippies, sailors or bums," others objected to its location and the intrusion into a historical area.[59]

To reach urban audiences, Hartzog also initiated new environmental education programs, telling a congressional subcommittee that "by allied efforts with schools, conservation organizations, and others we will help make available to school children . . . a fully integrated program to foster environmental perception." He went on to say that "the initial force of these efforts will be directed at the Nation's congested urban areas."[60] In 1968, the Park Service joined forces with Mario Menesini, director of Educational Consulting Services, to create the National Environmental Education Development program. This program aimed at developing environmental awareness and values in school-age groups and other park visitors. Parks were encouraged to set up environmental study areas where the program's materials could be used. In 1970, some sixty-three parks, including such urban areas as Jefferson National Expansion Memorial and Kennesaw Mountain National Battlefield Park, reported having study areas.[61]

Hartzog believed that living history programs provided another means of connecting with urban populations. He pressed for "a program of living interpretation at each of our historic areas."[62] As an incentive, he promised to add new funds to the park's budget since, according to Hartzog, "you can't change a superintendent's mind about a program without new money."[63] As Hartzog's wishes became known, parks responded, especially when he asked superintendents to report their progress. The resulting efforts varied. At Colonial National Historical Park, costumed interpreters demonstrated spinning and weaving, while personnel at Kennesaw Mountain National Battlefield near Atlanta attracted audiences to Civil War camp scenes, and cannon and musket firings. By 1973, Bill Everhart reported that, "almost every historical park has introduced living history programs."[64] Despite the legitimate concerns that such programs detracted from a park's primary purpose, they proved popular with visitors. Hartzog felt these types of well-liked and highly visible programs lent support to the growing movement to establish urban recreation areas.[65]

☙

In late December 1972, momentum building since the Johnson administration resulted in the creation of the country's first two urban recreation areas—Gateway and Golden Gate. The two parks added a new dimension to the National Park System, but their authorization would pose significant challenges for Hartzog. Gateway National Recreation Area, extending through three boroughs and into northern New Jersey, encompassed 26,000 acres of land, beaches, marshes, military installations, and wildlife habitat in the shadow of New York City. The composition of the 74,000-acre Golden Gate National Recreation Area near San Francisco was similar but also included a redwood forest and Alcatraz Island, a former prison facility. Since both were close to a large urban population and had over 10,000 acres of land and water, they fit the very general Park Service criteria for urban recreation areas.[66]

Located on opposite ends of the country, the two gateway parks shared similarities but also differed in many respects. Golden Gate's milder climate allowed year-round recreation activities, whereas Gateway's use was more seasonal. Golden Gate had better quality resources and lacked Gateway's pollution problems. Both consisted largely of lands already in government ownership, which reduced costly land purchases and made them particularly appealing. Gateway, for example, included such properties as Sandy Hook, a New Jersey state park unit under lease from the military; Floyd Bennett Field, a surplus Navy property; Forts Tilden and Wadsworth, military properties that guarded the harbors; Jacob Riis Park, a city park; and Breezy Point, a private cooperative with many summer homes.

Both parks benefited from having been owned by the military, which had kept them from being overdeveloped. Their boundaries included military lands and buildings still in use, but the lands would revert to the Park Service if ever declared surplus. Gateway's Fort Hancock, for example, had an elegant mansion that a commanding general on the East Coast wanted to live in, so until he moved, the property was withheld. At Golden Gate, Hartzog pushed to include the Presidio, a seaside military base. Although his staff deemed the Presidio nationally significant, he lacked the necessary local support. San Francisco's mayor Joseph L. Alioto objected since he feared losing his special golf privileges if the military's picturesque seaside course was opened to the public.[67] At the time, no one thought the bustling Presidio would ever close, and many thought Hartzog crazy to include a provision in Golden Gate's legislation annexing the base if that were ever to occur. (In 1989, the Presidio closed. On October 1, 1994, it was transferred to the National Park Service.[68])

Both the Gateway and the Golden Gate parks came with a number of existing structures. Hartzog knew that some at Gateway were in such bad shape that they needed tearing down. At Riis Park, however, he wanted to convert a partially completed apartment complex into lodging for children participating in environmental education programs. After he left, the Park Service instead destroyed it. As he observed, the agency often resolved the problem of what to do with questionable structures by just knocking them down.[69]

Another complication Hartzog faced was that the parklands were scattered in disjointed parcels. To be available to their target audiences, he knew that both areas needed accessible public transportation systems. Mass transit already served many of the Golden Gate units, but Gateway suffered a serious access problem. As Hartzog pointed out to the House Subcommittee on National Parks, Recreation, and Public Lands, "I think it is a very serious void in our entire recreation program . . . that we have got tens of hundreds of thousands of people in this country who don't have money to get to park areas in which they are in desperate need of having access to, and therefore if we are going to get them there somebody has got to provide some kind of transportation program."[70] Since Gateway parklands fell outside established public transportation routes, access for potential users without cars, which some estimated at 34 percent, would be severely limited.

Even car owners, however, found the roads leading to Gateway units often jammed with traffic. The Park Service discovered it could no longer plan a park or facility and expect road access to follow. When local communities foresaw additional traffic, they balked at upgrading existing access roads. Hartzog proposed using existing bus and subway systems to connect with a new ferry system linking the Breezy Point and Sandy Hook beaches. Without this interconnected public transportation system, he felt Gateway's intended audience could never get there. Congress greeted such proposals unfavorably.

Another challenge Hartzog faced was finding the right type of urban park employee. He believed that the typical outdoor-oriented professional with a strong resource management background would not be effective in an urban environment. He realized that the new professional needed to understand ethnically diverse populations and deal with urban issues and problems. His addition of sociologists, psychologists, and urban recreation and design specialists brought in persons with entirely new skills and orientation. The Park Service did not understand or warmly welcome such new recruits into its ranks.

Beginning in 1969, Hartzog directed that all entering park rangers go through an urban training program. The recruits first received specialized training at an eight-week orientation at Albright Training Center. Then they got on-the-job training with National Capital Parks, which included biweekly discussions that concentrated on special problems of cities, sensitivity workshops, ride-alongs with urban park police, college courses related to social and behavioral problems in urban areas, and an internship-type experience in an urban park environment. The Park Service wanted to "turn out a flexible person who can comfortably and effectively work with people of all ethnic and socio-economic backgrounds in an urban setting."[71] Hartzog wanted the Park Service to understand that "wilderness was not found only out in the woods." Cities had their own brand of wilderness.[72] Years after his directorate, park employees told him that they came to appreciate their forced urban experience even though they hated it at the time.[73]

❧

Many raised serious questions about Hartzog's drive to establish urban recreation areas and programs. Why should a federal agency like the Park Service move into urban recreation for a largely local population? Did the Park Service have the expertise to handle urban parks? How would an urban initiative fit into the Park Service mission of visitor use and resource preservation, and would urban parks measure up to agency standards? What would the urban park initiative cost? Would urban parks and programs become an accepted and important new component of the National Park

System? Hartzog tried to answer these questions and justify his agency's involvement.

No one in principle was against providing recreation for urban populations, but it was an open question whether managing urban recreation parks should be a Park Service responsibility. City parks are widely understood to be more or less a local government responsibility. Even Hartzog admitted as much in a 1965 speech when he said that "the need for parks, playgrounds, and gardens in our cities and metropolitan areas" has been "recognized traditionally as a local and state responsibility." But he went on to say that there exists a "dramatic interplay among federal, state, local and private programs in meeting . . . these needs."[74]

During the Hartzog directorate, the federal government stepped up its involvement by going beyond its traditional role to help cities in need. In speaking to the 1966 Congress for Parks and Recreation, Laurance Rockefeller said, "As the recent Senate hearings have brought out so vividly, the cities are in serious financial trouble. With their limited tax base, cities will not be able to meet park and recreation needs by themselves. They will need help."

Rockefeller urged states and the federal government to take "larger direct responsibility . . . in cities" by establishing national recreation areas or state parks in the very heart of cities.[75] To Rockefeller, agencies such as the Park Service could use federal funding and its in-house expertise to purchase, plan, and develop parks. Once initial development efforts were completed, the city could take over management responsibilities and expenses. While financially strapped cities would not have willingly accepted fiscal responsibility, this approach might have been a viable option for the National Park Service. However, it was not one Hartzog chose to follow. He saw the political potential in adding urban parks, and he was not about to take on the headaches of acquiring and developing them without reaping the long-term rewards for his agency. If Hartzog were an empire builder, as some suggest, he would never have let part of it slip away.

Hartzog and others within the Park Service had convinced themselves that the American people didn't care whose responsibility it was but just wanted the agency to move into urban parks. As Hartzog's chief historian Robert Utley said:

> The political process and its dynamics made it very clear that over-whelmingly the American people preferred to have the National Park Service run these [parks]. Not the Federal Government but

the National Park Service, because it had great credibility. . . . In my judgment the message was loud and clear and not very arguable at that time that this was something the people wanted the Park Service to do. I think when the situation is so persuasive the Park Service needs to respond positively and not drag its feet.[76]

Not one to drag his feet, Hartzog understood that if the government did not act promptly, areas with recreation potential would either be lost to development or become prohibitively expensive.

Part of Hartzog's sense of urgency also stemmed from the potential competition from other federal agencies. Some estimated that as many as twenty different agencies were vying to administer urban recreation areas. Federal recreation managing agencies, such as the Corps of Engineers, the Forest Service, the Fish and Wildlife Service, and Housing and Urban Development had likewise stepped up their interest in urban parks.[77] Hartzog wanted as much of the urban pie as possible, but he felt that the Bureau of Outdoor Recreation and its director, Ed Crafts, "were not kindly disposed to me having the whole pie."[78] As an administrative agency coordinating federal outdoor recreation policy, the Bureau of Outdoor Recreation had no authority to manage any parks unless it could metamorphose into one that did. Such a coup would have helped ensure the agency's survival and added yet another competitor for the Park Service.

According to Hartzog, each competing federal agency had philosophies and cultures that did not predispose them to managing urban areas. He objected to what he called the Bureau of Land Management's "mission to get rid of the public lands and those they don't get rid of, mine them or drill them or do whatever else that is necessary to get the goodies out of it." The Forest Service, on the other hand, was "in the business of raising trees for timber. Recreation didn't come into their focus until they recognized the phenomenal success which the Park Service was having."[79] In his opinion, only the Park Service among federal agencies had the expertise and appropriate management philosophy to deal with urban environments. He aggressively pursued urban parks because he felt his agency had the personnel, the opportunity, and the philosophy to "get it done now." While San Francisco and New York City were unable or unwilling to pull together a large urban park, Hartzog was both willing and able.

From a revenue-strapped city's perspective, a federal infusion of funds seemed like an ideal solution to the problem of providing inexpensive and accessible recreation for citizens. As historian Ronald Foresta writes, "One suspects that what the city governments really wanted the National Park Service to do was to take over the day-to-day management of the city parks, remove junked cars, put nets on the tennis courts and in essence make things look right by restoring the status quo ante."[80] The Park Service would give its respected name, expertise, and financial resources; the city would then be free to channel its scarce funds elsewhere.

Both San Francisco and New York City encouraged the Park Service to assume management of as many city-run parks as possible. New York City's Mayor John V. Lindsay suggested including the aging seaside Coney Island amusement park in Gateway.[81] While the Park Service successfully eluded the addition of Coney Island, it could not fight off Golden Gate's Sutro Baths, the ruins of an elegant former spa. Assistant secretary Nathaniel Reed, who did much of the negotiating, accused San Francisco's Mayor Alioto of "dumping off the Sutro Baths, which he didn't have the money to tear down, and the renovation of the area on the federal taxpayer. He won when the California delegation persuaded the Congress. The money spigot was on and they got what they wanted."[82]

While both cities gladly accepted federal financial aid and assistance, they balked at giving up complete control. Mayor Alioto fought to keep local control by declaring that it was a "condition of the city's necessary participation." The city backed down when Interior secretary Rogers Morton curtly called its bluff. New York City proposed that the federal government subsidize the city's mass transit system, which would be necessary to get people to Gateway, but that attempt to save the city money likewise failed.[83]

Some claimed the Park Service lacked the orientation and expertise to manage urban recreation areas that were so far removed from the agency's Yellowstone roots. Although Hartzog's close friend and confidante Bill Everhart admitted that moving into urban parks was a "big jump," Hartzog believed in his agency's capabilities.[84] He knew that the Park Service employed a wide range of expertise, from park planners and landscape architects to interpreters and park police. Few federal agencies or local park and recreation departments could boast such a varied and skilled workforce. Additionally, Hartzog actively pursued outside talents in diverse fields to bring fresh ideas and new expertise into the Park Service and to deal with the large number of historical, cultural, and recreation areas he was adding to the system.

Hartzog also justified the Park Service's involvement by pointing out that it had been managing parks in urban settings for years, that in fact it "had more urban parkland than most cities did."[85] In reality, aside from national capital parks, most of the urban parks he referred to were historical areas

with very different management goals. Resource protection and interpretation, not recreation, were the top priorities. More often than not, historical
areas guarded against inappropriate recreational uses. It was not thought
respectful to engage in activities such as picnicking, throwing Frisbees, and
playing baseball in places like battlefields where thousands died.[86] As one
historian put it, people "shouldn't be flying kites along [Antietam National
Battlefield's] Bloody Lane any more than there should be tennis courts at
Yosemite. The history should be enough, recreation profanes it."[87]

Urban historical areas aside, Hartzog did have to his credit the National
Capital Parks, which the Park Service had managed since 1933. He had been
applauded for his visible and creative Summer in the Parks program and had
stepped up the agency's living history and environmental education programs. Involvement in Job Corps also gave the Park Service familiarity with
inner-city youths and a staff comfortable dealing with urban issues. Of all
the federal agencies, the Park Service probably had the strongest claim of
expertise for developing and managing urban recreation areas.

⁂

While Hartzog tried to infuse the Park Service with his enthusiasm for
urban recreation areas, many in the agency had strong reservations about
how assumption of control of them would change the park system's mission. According to Robert Utley, the "National Park Service rank and file for
the most part opposed the idea of urban parks, and still do. They were a big
departure from the traditional. The gray and the green preferred to serve in
traditional parks; they shunned urban assignments. They thought Hartzog
should put his energies into caring for traditional parks and getting more."[88]
Urban recreation areas were the newest additions, and acceptance would be
slow in coming. Gateway and Golden Gate just felt different, and indeed in
some ways they were.

Theoretically, the Park Service protected the country's best natural,
historical, or cultural resources. Recreational use, if appropriate, would be
determined by the nationally significant resources that attracted a broad
audience from across the country. As a general rule, state agencies managed resources of lesser quality and significance, while local governments
concentrated on local needs with whatever remaining resources were easily
accessible and available.

Despite Hartzog's arguments that urban parks fulfilled a nationally
significant need, many inside and outside the Park Service struggled with
the agency's redefinition of significance. Part of the Service's foundational

creed had cautioned against additions that failed to uphold the "standards, dignity, and prestige" of the National Park Service.[89] To many, the new urban parks simply did not measure up. They lowered the overall standards and reputation of the Park Service. At Gateway, truckloads of trash with everything from rusty appliances to junked cars had to be hauled away before some areas could be opened to the public.[90] Pollution fouled the waters off some areas making them unsafe for bathing and unhealthy for indigenous plants and animals. Since Gateway and Golden Gate were the first two national urban recreation areas, the Park Service lacked clear criteria to judge them against. When compared with the resources of existing national recreation areas, such as the rugged and picturesque Lake Mead, they fared poorly.

Without the emphasis on protecting significant national resources, many feared the Park Service would experience a dilution of quality. The danger would arise not from one park with less than nationally significant resources but with more than one. As Everhart suggested, "If the park system began to include those areas, which are pleasant and moderately attractive, the distinction between truly national significance on the one hand and local pride on the other would be increasingly blurred and the original idea of national parks would steadily erode toward mediocrity."[91] To many, urban parks moved the Park System closer to mediocrity and further from the ideal.

Hartzog and others with the Park Service had convinced themselves that responding to a national "need" for accessible recreation outweighed the agency's desire to acquire only nationally significant resources. Although it could be claimed that both Gateway and Golden Gate had important resources in their former military installations or their beachfront properties, the case for national significance was weak. As Bill Everhart admitted:

> I think the most telling criticism . . . was that you took, in the case of New York, several old army posts and a few buildings and some beaches, none of which individually would be ranked very high for national significance, but by putting them together you somehow come up with a nationally significant area. And I think that was generally agreed to be a reversal of the customary, and in this case the resources weren't of national significance but the need was of national significance. . . . It is kind of turning it on its end, so therefore it made sense nationally to preserve this resource, which would be used only for the most part by local citizens.[92]

In essence, Hartzog argued that creating urban national recreation areas was in keeping with another part of the Park Service's 1918 creed, which said that all Park Service decisions should be based on the country's national interest.[93] During the 1960s and 1970s, national interest unquestionably centered on urban populations.

At the time, most local park and recreation departments lacked the money, the vision, and the boldness to develop large regional parks and instead concentrated on establishing and maintaining smaller parks throughout the city. Hartzog and the Park Service, on the other hand, were comfortable and experienced in proposing large, complex parks that contained thousands of acres. They also seemed willing to compromise standards of quality to provide desperately needed recreation. In a 1969 memo to Hartzog about a potential urban area, Lemuel A. Garrison, northeast regional director, wrote, "I believe the needs in northern Illinois are so pressing that we can accept considerably less than first quality standards of land form if this is all that is available, just so that we can make an approach to this problem."[94]

From Hartzog's perspective, significance was relative. The proximity of promising recreation areas to population centers made them significant. He could have found many parcels of Alaskan land with extraordinary wildness and beauty, but in Alaska such lands were commonplace. Near San Francisco or New York City, undeveloped land had become such a rarity that one could argue for national significance based solely on location. That visitors could seine for flounder at Gateway, or observe more than seventy different wading, shore, and marsh birds against the skyline of New York City made the area significant. For many inner-city children, Gateway had the only "natural" environment they had ever experienced.

Hartzog also argued that urban lands, even if they currently lacked pristine qualities, had a future potential that needed to be considered. The cutover areas included in Shenandoah National Park would not have impressed many with their wildness in the 1930s, but local support and proximity to eastern population centers smoothed its addition into the park system. Today, Shenandoah bears little evidence of past abuses and, to many, seems a wilderness park. Although Gateway might not have had ideal resources in the 1970s, Hartzog maintained that given time and proper management, it could recover.

Due to the country's shrinking resource base, Hartzog believed that the Park Service needed to consider marginal properties that could be held in a special reserve category for future inclusion. After he left the Park Service, he tried to convince Representative Joe McDade of Pennsylvania, the ranking minority member of the House Appropriations Subcommittee, to "take all those old abandoned coal mines that are pourin' acid water into the underground water system and make a great national park reserve. Those companies would have probably given us the damn land. . . . We would have had the greatest eastern hardwood national park in the world."[95] After the necessary cleanup and recovery time, the former coalfields could have provided recreational opportunities for many people in the surrounding area. The park could also have interpreted the cultural aspects of coal mining along with the environmental effects.

Critics failed to see this potential, and in addition to questioning national significance they were conflicted over the new parks' emphasis on recreational use. According to the Park Service's legislative mandate, resource preservation must be balanced with use by visitors. In urban recreation areas, however, the pendulum clearly tilted toward the use side. Since Gateway and Golden Gate were intended to provide high-density recreation, resource protection would become a clear second. To many, this presented a dangerous precedent. In many parks, overcrowding threatened resources, and management struggled to control recreational uses viewed as inappropriate. Purposely shifting the pendulum toward use was heresy for many.

While some argued that the urban parks would become windows to other national parks, others feared the urban park users would associate the park system with recreational use and enjoyment rather than with the preservation of a rich natural, historical, and cultural heritage for future generations. Although Hartzog wanted to been seen as erring in favor of resource preservation, those aspirations were offset by his interest in urban recreation parks.

⁂

Secretly George Hartzog aspired to a whole system of urban parks, and he was prepared to establish one if the opportunity presented itself and no one applied the brakes. As assistant secretary of the interior Nathaniel Reed said, "Once the genie is out of the bottle, look out Chicago and New Orleans."[96] If that happened, the potential cost could become exorbitant as city after city pressured their congressional delegations for their own urban parks. In fact, plans were being made for just that contingency.

In a June 1969 document, the Bureau of Outdoor Recreation initially proposed twenty-one urban areas of high priority and an additional fifteen areas of secondary importance for a total of more than a million acres at a cost to taxpayers of almost $2 billion. All areas were reportedly within 40 miles or one-hour's driving time of a major city.[97] A year later, in a memo addressed to secretary of the interior Walter Hickel, the bureau had narrowed the list to fourteen areas proposed for federal administration. At a cost of almost $500 million, they fell into three categories of readiness based on when studies would be sufficiently detailed to support legislation.[98] While only a small portion of them actually became urban parks, clearly there were high hopes for a series of federally run areas.

To Hartzog, speed was critical. The need would continue to rise and the price of the few remaining undeveloped lands would escalate, so delays could only worsen the situation. Even so, costs seemed prohibitive, especially as the economy worsened. In a report to Congress, the Park Service admitted that the development costs of its urban parks were "rather large by comparison to other areas in recent years." To justify the expense, Hartzog argued in congressional hearings that Gateway "on a visitation basis . . . will be the lowest capital cost to a visitor of any . . . in the whole national park system." Given Gateway's initial estimate of twenty million visitors per year and the estimated costs of $98 million over twenty years, he thought the price per person compared favorably to other parks. However, as one congressman responded, even if the unit cost at Gateway was low, the overall price tag for the 26,000-acre urban recreation area was still sizeable.[99]

Congress also worried about the estimated costs of Golden Gate, which was authorized at more than $61 million for land acquisition and $58 million for development.[100] In comparison, North Cascades National Park, a natural area in Washington, included 504,000 acres with an initial capped expenditure of $3.5 million.[101]

Even when compared to recreation-oriented lakeshores and seashores accessible to urban populations, Gateway and Golden Gate looked costly. In 1970, Congress authorized Michigan's 58,473-acre Sleeping Bear Dunes National Lakeshore for almost $39 million for the land and development costs.[102] The 1971 Gulf Islands National Seashore, with approximately 135,000 acres, was originally authorized at $3.1 million for land and $14.8 million for development. Indiana Dunes National Lakeshore, 50 miles from Chicago, was authorized in 1966 with a ceiling of $27.9 million (amended later to allow for inflation).[103]

Undoubtedly, urban recreation areas would be expensive to purchase and develop. Given the expected crowds, they would also be expensive to operate. Many worried that the new areas would pull essential funding from other parks that had desperate needs. Congress allocated only so big a pot of money to the park system. More parks dipping into the pot meant less for each one. Hartzog's view was that urban parks "brought along enough support that you just enlarge the pot." He maintained that "if an honest analysis were made," it would become clear that "these urban parks didn't cost the other parks a dime."[104] What people saw, though, was a gap between appropriations and the dollars necessary to protect resources, fix aging infrastructures, and hire adequate summer and full-time staff. Rightly or wrongly, urban recreation areas were seen as contributing to this shortfall.[105]

⁂

In *Searching for Yellowstone*, Paul Schullery argues that each generation rediscovers what Yellowstone means to them. The same could be said for each generation redefining what the National Park System should be.[106] During the 1960s and 1970s, the country was focused on social and civil rights, the Vietnam War, the health of the environment, and the urban landscape, where a majority of people lived. Udall wanted Hartzog to be receptive to the times, to develop progressive programs, and to add relevant parks. As Hartzog said, "In 1964, we had to change attitudes and motivate people to respond to the emerging needs of an urban America. That was a secretarial objective; it therefore became my imperative."[107] Personally, Hartzog justified his efforts as socially responsible, politically correct, and in the best interests of the Park System.

Hartzog may have shifted the Park Service more heavily into urban areas, but the agency's first urban park responsibilities came with the addition of National Capital Parks in 1933. Parkways and recreation demonstration areas of the 1930s and seashores of the 1960s added yet another dimension. Lake Mead and other reservoir parks expanded the agency's recreation management responsibilities. Hartzog simply added another dimension by pushing into the heart of cities on whatever lands were available, making that drive because he perceived the need as so profound.

Due to his strength as a leader, Hartzog was able to force the Park Service to accept an urban "shoe" many felt uncomfortable wearing. In true Great Society fashion, he tried to instill his agency with a social conscience by providing recreation opportunities for the underprivileged. Although urban recreation had not been a federal responsibility, under President Johnson, the federal government expanded into many areas where it had not previously ventured. Clearly the federal government was willing to improve urban environments, and if the Park Service did not step to the plate, a number of rival agencies would. The Park Service had let its supremacy in federal recreation slip away, and Hartzog resolved not to let that happen with the new urban frontier.

So Hartzog pressed change on his agency and pushed beyond its comfort zone. In doing so, he achieved much. He moved the Park Service away from the bricks-and-mortar mentality of Mission 66 to focus more on the park user. He was ahead of the times in his attention to urban recreational programming, living history, and environmental education. He encouraged his staff to work collaboratively with a variety of government and private groups—something the Park Service had historically shunned. For example, Summer in the Parks staff joined with the Fish and Wildlife Service and Boy Scout groups to take inner city children on fishing expeditions to the C&O canal. Kennesaw Mountain National Battlefield near Atlanta invited children selected by the local park and recreation departments to a museum tour, nature hike, and evening campfire program. Food was provided by the U.S. Department of Agriculture, and adult leadership included area high school students, members of Neighborhood Youth Corps, and Urban Corps college students.[108] For an agency that Hartzog said had "a reputation of thinking they knew more about how to do it than anybody in the world," such partnerships offered fresh approaches that would become increasingly important in the ensuing years of tight budgets.[109]

Fittingly, Gateway and Golden Gate were the last two park bills passed during Hartzog's directorate. These additions combined his passion for helping the less fortunate with his zeal for expanding the system in new directions. Had he held office longer, he might have succeeded in significantly expanding urban recreation areas and programs. If Congress had remained receptive to his programs, perhaps urban parks and programs would have materialized in many large cities and resulted in a major Park Service thrust. But he could not have foreseen the dampening effect of the Vietnam War on domestic policy, the brakes applied by an unfriendly Nixon administration, or his untimely departure as director.

Hartzog's successor, a Nixon political appointee, would inherit an urban program he had little understanding of or enthusiasm for. Hartzog could only watch from the sidelines as the Park Service backed away from his urban initiatives and over time dismantled much of what he had so painstakingly built. With Hartzog no longer at the helm, the vision for urban parks quickly faded.

Despite Hartzog's lofty ideals, development plans for Gateway and Golden Gate would change substantially. What he had envisioned as large, well-developed recreation complexes embracing the needs of many was transformed into areas serving far fewer and emphasizing low-density use. At Gateway, the biggest obstacle involved access. Without subsidized access from the inner city, those with the greatest recreation need could not get there. Although sites like Fort Sumter in South Carolina and New York's Statue of Liberty had ferry access, some in Congress were uncomfortable with subsidizing the transportation costs. Representative Joe Skubitz of Kansas worried that government funding would be "embarking on a very dangerous phase. . . . I don't know where this sort of program can end because if it's good for New York, it is good for Washington . . . Detroit . . . Chicago . . . and any place else in the country."[110]

Despite the reservations of Skubitz and others, congressional members such as Julia Butler Hansen of Washington and Shirley Chisholm of New York supported Hartzog. The greater difficulty according to Hartzog lay with Office of Management and Budget, successor to the Bureau of the Budget, which refused to subsidize bus, subway, or ferry access for Gateway. Hartzog had argued that the Park Service could build approach roads into parks, a practice that benefited only those who had their own transportation and could afford to go to national parks. He thought it hypocritical when budget office refused to help the poorest, who had the greatest need but not the means to access national parks.

Gateway plans would also shift away from the idea of supplying mass recreation for the city's neediest residents. New participatory planning practices that government agencies had to embrace in the early 1970s moved the park's plan in a totally different direction. Emboldened by the social movements of the 1960s, citizens now demanded a voice in how new parks were developed and how established ones were managed. After Gateway circulated its proposed management plans, most of the public comments came, not surprisingly, from those who lived closest to the park units and had the most to gain or lose. Park neighbors wanted the lands near their homes protected, but on their own terms. Gateway neighbors at Breezy Point knew of plans to turn Floyd Bennett airfield into a low-income housing development. They strenuously objected. The local government also resisted because of the costly infrastructure of a new housing development. Park neighbors worried that recreation access would clog their streets and might bring undesirable elements into what they viewed as their park. Only a few groups, such as the Gateway Citizen Commission, composed of upper-class philanthropic persons and poor underprivileged ones, supported developing the park to benefit inner city inhabitants. Public meetings often turned into hostile encounters between local neighborhoods fighting against a Park Service trying halfheartedly to protect an ideal.

The Park Service greased the squeaky wheel by appeasing the vocal park neighbors. Park superintendents knew their performance appraisals took into consideration their abilities to forge good relationships with a park's neighboring communities. Park planners understood the new emphasis on public input and the importance of not arousing vocal opposition that might reach congressional levels. As a result, Gateway's final plans dramatically deemphasized high-density recreation use and ease of public access. Instead, the plans emphasized the quality of the park experience, environmental education programs, and resource protection. Visitation increased only slightly over what it had been prior to national park designation.[111] While Gateway was justified by use estimates that ranged from twenty to fifty million per year, in 1999, for example, visitation figures were only about seven million.[112] Gateway failed to live up to Hartzog's original intent and metamorphosed into a local park benefiting its immediate neighbors.

While Hartzog had hoped to add a new dimension to the National Park System, a large urban component never materialized. Subsequent directors could "neither control their authorization nor gain the initiative in planning for their use." Instead of finding large appreciative constituencies to support the Park Service mission, they found agency discord, political constraints, and difficult urban problems to deal with.[113] Members of Congress eager to bring federal funding to inner cities forwarded many proposals, but only a limited number already in the pipeline were authorized. These included Cuyahoga Valley (1974) between Cleveland and Akron, Chattahoochee River (1978) in Atlanta, Santa Monica (1978) near Los Angeles, and Jean LaFitte National Historical Park and Preserve (1978) in New Orleans.[114]

While some of Hartzog's urban-oriented programs persevered, many would wither after he left. Funding for Summer in the Parks and other recreation-oriented programming would dry up. Recreational facilities such as Fort Vancouver's playground would face increasing scrutiny. Park managers found some of the coil-spring toys dangerous, much of the western-themed apparatus proved unpopular with children, and "every cat in Vancouver used the sandbox as a litter box" until it was removed. Park officials would attempt to phase out the playground, but community pressures on elected officials would not permit that, although a more appropriate location was found.[115]

Many environmental education programs, particularly those imposed on historical areas, would be phased out over time. While actively engaging the visitors was good, straying too far from a park's message and meaning was not. As chief of interpretation Bill Dunmire would say, "Our job is to interpret the resources and themes of our parks, not function as subject matter educators, or as spokespeople for special causes."[116]

Hartzog's living history emphasis would suffer the same fate. As chief historian Robert Utley noted in 1974, "I fear that we have let the public's enthusiasm for living history push us from interpretation of the park's features and values into productions that, however entertaining, do not directly support the central park themes." Another historian added that "living history is but one of several bandwagons upon which the Service has leaped with gay abandon." He went on to say that rather than costumed interpreters, perhaps visitors to historical areas would "prefer to walk with ghosts in silence." Later guidelines would reflect these concerns and encourage parks to make sure living history programs were both historically accurate and relevant to the park's theme.

Even Hartzog sadly admitted that while his urban initiatives "accomplish[ed] a lot," subsequent administrations "negated all of it."[117] He felt that "urban parks have not served an effective role in restoring a sense of community to our center cities as I had hoped they would."[118] He recalled from his childhood that despite the poverty, there still existed a strong sense of community. Years later, he believed this sense of community had eroded, especially for the poor inner-city youths who held special interest for him. Factors such as poverty, single-parent households, drug use, increasing ethnic populations, and lack of opportunity had separated and segregated society.

Hartzog's view was that the National Park System should help restore a sense of community, hope, and identity as a society. As he reflected in 1996:

> Where else can they [the young people] learn of the sacrifice and the courage and the innovation and the empathy and the love and the adventure that built this country? They're all right there in the National Park System. All you got to do is introduce 'em. . . . You're not going to experience that in an unruly classroom. They got to experience it. You want to inspire people you take them to George Washington Carver or Booker T. Washington. You take them to Abraham Lincoln's birthplace, his boyhood home. They can see these people were in the same condition I'm in, but they became somebody and so can I. But they can't without that exposure and that support. That's where I think the National Park Service's great role in our society is. Of course, it's scientific and of course it's preserving biodiversity, but it's also to preserve and interpret and

communicate our diversity as individuals and our commonality as one people, and that's what I think its great message is.[119]

He believed that national parks helped people answer the question "Who am I?" and "How do I fit in this continuum of civilization?" Some people might find the answer to those questions in the urban parks, and some would discover them only in a solitary hike in Yellowstone. But as Hartzog went on to say, "Unless you understand that question, 'who am I?' you cannot very well relate to the social and natural world in which you live, and to the other human beings with whom you associate."[120]

Overall, Hartzog' urban initiatives had the potential to grow and flourish, but they failed to withstand the test of time. Of his self-proclaimed accomplishments, this one seemed the most puzzling, even to those who knew him well. As close friend Bill Everhart exclaimed when asked why Hartzog chose to highlight it, "I'm not quite sure why George thought that that was such a big thing. . . . I mean why not say his contribution to Alaska, which . . . was huge . . . huge."

Despite the reservations of others, George Hartzog held steadfast in his assessment. "I tried to relate parks to an urban environment and they [the Nixon administration] came along and said the hell with it and the poor bastards that live in the cities."[121]

Expanding the National Park System

The timing for George Hartzog's rise to the directorate could not have been better. An environmental consciousness was sweeping the country along with a newfound respect for historical treasures. As people saw more resources being developed and polluted, citizen and conservation groups began prompting the government to act. Bowing to political pressures and finding its own environmental conscience, a Democratic majority in Congress passed significant environmental legislation and became increasingly mindful of the political benefits of park additions. The explosion of interest in outdoor recreation and the recommendations of the influential Outdoor Recreation Resources Review Commission seemingly begged those in government to acquire more effective and accessible parks. The new Bureau of Outdoor Recreation attempted to lead federal agencies in a nationwide effort to meet future demands for outdoor recreation and administered the all-important Land and Water Conservation Fund, which provided vital funding for land purchases. Spurred by the optimism of President Lyndon Johnson's Great Society and the First Lady's emphasis on beautification, park expansion fever became difficult for even the fiscally conservative Nixon administration to control.

George Hartzog understood the prevailing conditions and how best to use them to his advantage. "I think the times were right," he said. "I think we were organized for it. We had a good system! Good relations with Congress. And we had good relations with the administration, even when it changed."[1]

To move the Park Service in new directions, Hartzog had to rethink his predecessor's emphasis on construction and upgrading park infrastructures. To Hartzog, Mission 66's promise to bring all parks up to standard by the Park Service's fiftieth birthday was "an old emphasis on development, and I think that it had a very serious adverse impact in many places."[2] Taking a page from Mission 66, however, he vowed to "complete for our generation a National Park System by 1972," the hundredth anniversary of Yellowstone, the nation's first national park.[3]

Some worried that the National Park System might be growing too fast. In a letter to Hartzog, former director Horace Albright wrote that it was "already too big for one man and his few associates to plan for, direct and administer, do the job well and keep morale high throughout the huge organization without killing themselves."[4] He chose to ignore this advice and worked tirelessly to expand the system like no director before or after him.[5] Hartzog believed that acquiring parklands was a race against time. His strategy was to "acquire them now and if we made a mistake, then that's a challenge for my successor to straighten out. But if you leave it sit there, somebody else is going to develop it in a way you are not going to have it again."[6] To Hartzog, park additions also represented power, since each new park ideally brought with it appreciative members of Congress and their constituents, favorable publicity, additional staff, and increased funding.

Of his self-professed career accomplishments, Hartzog's skill in expanding the park system garnered the most accolades. In reality, he was an expansionist who interpreted "rounding out" the park system as "rounding up" as many worthwhile parks as possible. In doing so, he stretched the perception of what constituted a national park unit and experimented with new management options. He also laid critical groundwork for the later Alaska additions, which would more than double the size of national park holdings.

⁂

In his book, *Battling for the National Parks*, Hartzog acknowledged that many factors aided his park expansion efforts. When pressed in person for the three most important ones, he responded that "political leadership was a dominant factor because without it none of that growth would have been possible." A supportive president, secretary of the interior, and Congress all converged in nearly perfect alignment. Second, he felt the media "became an active partner in promoting preservation" and continually put environmental and preservation issues before the public. Third, the American people pushed to protect parklands and were willing to pay for them.[7]

While Hartzog reported strong support among the public, he experienced difficulties with fast-growing environmental organizations. Historically, they had supported the National Park System, as in the Sierra Club's classic early 1900s fight to save California's Hetch Hetchy Valley and the Audubon Society's efforts to protect Florida Everglades rookeries from plume hunters. By Hartzog's time, however, conservation groups offered selective support and at times open hostility. Although he listed cooperation with environmental groups as one of his 1964 priorities, he struggled to find a common ground with them.[8]

Prior to Hartzog's directorate, the tenor of environmental groups had been changing. The 1950s fight over Echo Park dam in Colorado had galvanized and mobilized them; some called it their "coming of age." The conflict had arisen over the development plans of the aggressive and powerful Bureau of Reclamation for a billion-dollar Colorado River storage project that included a dam on the Green River within Dinosaur National Monument in Colorado. In a show of solidarity, major environmental groups joined forces to fight the proposal and eventually defeat it.[9]

They did not, however, oppose the Glen Canyon dam, which was farther downstream and outside the national park. Too late they realized that Glen Canyon possessed qualities worthy of a national park. Reflecting upon their bittersweet success, environmentalists, including the hard-hitting executive director of the Sierra Club, David Brower, vowed not to ignore such areas in the future. Brower came to believe that since "what we save in the next few years is all that will ever be saved . . . much boldness [is] called for."[10]

As an outgrowth of the Echo Park fight, membership in about all environmental groups grew steadily, equipping them with even more money, power, and confidence.[11] The Sierra Club's membership, for example, doubled while the Wilderness Society's seventy-six hundred members of 1956 had increased to twenty-seven thousand by 1964.[12] At the same time, the well-mannered and gentlemanly veterans who had headed up these organizations were replaced by a younger, more aggressive and militant type that the old guard regarded as unfriendly and ill mannered. Hartzog would struggle to form supportive alliances with the new leadership despite their common goal of protecting more parklands.

With new leadership came a shift in thinking about such issues as the appropriate balance between visitation and resource protection. The new environmentalists pushed federal agencies like the Park Service to limit access to the swarms of people who wanted more services and amenities. They believed an ideal park experience should be more wild and less harmful to the environment. Pack mules and shelters made from freshly cut saplings were replaced by lightweight backpacks and tents.

Worried about how easily public lands could be altered, environmentalists rallied around legislation that would protect large tracts of wilderness in perpetuity. Special wilderness designation would halt any future plans by federal agencies to build intrusive roads, campgrounds, lodges, and parking lots in protected areas. After much conflict and many drafts, the Wilderness Act finally passed on September 3, 1964. It legally defined wilderness as an area "where the earth and its community of life are untrammeled by man, where man himself is a visitor who does not remain."[13]

Although Hartzog once called himself "a wilderness guy" because of his earlier experiences at Rocky Mountain and Great Smoky Mountains national parks, many would argue that he resisted wilderness designation for national parklands.[14] In his mind, however, he "was never opposed to wilderness." Hartzog claimed it was Conrad Wirth, his predecessor, who "had a great big damn falling out [with Udall] over the Wilderness Act." Wirth wanted national parklands exempt, arguing that the Park Service already preserved its roadless areas at a higher standard than that prescribed by the Wilderness Act. These arguments would lead to the act's eventual inclusion of the phrase "the designation of any area of any park, monument, or other unit of the national park system as a wilderness area . . . shall in no manner lower the standards evolved for the use and preservation of such park, monument, or other unit of the national park system."[15]

When Wirth retired in 1963, secretary of the interior Stewart Udall found a more complaisant supporter of wilderness. Hartzog inherited the push for wilderness legislation and recalled being put on a special administrative support group to promote the Wilderness Act. He recalled spending a tremendous amount of time politicking, lobbying, and testifying on the bill's behalf. He explained that "it was after I became director that Stewart Udall and I were able to get that wilderness bill through. . . . A great deal of that . . . was my relationship with Wayne Aspinall."[16] According to Udall, Aspinall was the "brakeman" who held the legislation up for four years. Udall and Hartzog both felt Aspinall finally withdrew his opposition in exchange for support of the Public Land Law Review Act (1964), which established a commission to review federal public land–use policies. Aspinall also made major changes in the legislation, which supporters reluctantly accepted in order to get the wilderness system started.[17]

The Wilderness Act required the secretary of the interior to study roadless areas exceeding 5,000 acres for possible wilderness designation. These recommendations would be forwarded to the president, who could then present them to Congress. According to assistant secretary Nathaniel Reed, "George just did not understand the relevance of the Wilderness Act to the National Park Service because he thought he was already providing wilderness and that any restrictions on future options should be avoided." Reed thought that Hartzog sought to keep his options open so that if, for example, he wanted to give the park visitor a view from a remote mountain he could install a cable car to get there.[18]

To Hartzog, wilderness designations favored young, robust individuals with the time and inclination to explore undeveloped areas. He remained cognizant of the greater number of park visitors who drove their cars around park roads, stayed in a developed campgrounds or nearby hotels, and only strayed short distances from parking lots.

Hartzog objected to what he regarded as the law's hypocrisy. As an example, he cited the romantic but damaging policy of allowing horses into wilderness areas. Given what a dozen horses who had bedded down for the night could do to an area, he said, letting them in ran counter to the notion that man's activities should have no impact on wilderness areas. He also disagreed with the sharp wilderness boundaries that could leave "a sawmill and wilderness cheek to jaw." He felt wilderness should not end suddenly at civilization's doorstep and proposed what he called an area of "man's influence on the wilderness." This transitional zone around all wilderness areas would allow modest development aimed at protecting and interpreting the wilderness itself. He envisioned, for example, firefighting towers and trails with modest interpretive exhibits but nothing as intrusive as a visitor center. He also saw a need for holes in the wilderness so mechanized equipment could be allowed into certain areas, to clean up, for example, after a large horse camp.[19] Wilderness advocates strongly objected to Hartzog's buffer zones because of the amount of land that would be required to establish them and their distrust of what future administrators might do in such areas.

Reed suggested that Hartzog lost interest in wilderness when his ideas were rejected. When it finally came to delineating proposed wilderness areas in the parks, Reed declared, his assistant had to "put the wilderness areas on the map because George simply refused to do it."[20] Hartzog strongly objected to Reed's allegations, saying that any reluctance on the part of the Park Service had more to do with higher priorities and limited budgets. The Park Service was aggressively pursuing new areas for inclusion in the National Park System. Preparing the necessary supporting materials for wilderness designation was time consuming and expensive and would draw resources away from more urgent priorities, such as the study of Alaskan lands. Hartzog also felt powerful members of Congress like Wayne Aspinall would not support wilderness designations.[21] By 1970, the Park Service had created wilderness areas only within Craters of the Moon in Idaho and Petrified Forest in Arizona—less than 94,000 acres.[22]

Environmental groups continued to press Hartzog for more additions to the wilderness system. As their coffers grew, they added professional staff such as economists, biologists, and lawyers. Organizations that had once relied on lobbying, educational materials, and letter-writing campaigns discovered the power of environmental lawsuits. "Sue the bastards!" became the new battle cry as the Environmental Defense Fund came into existence in 1967, followed by a host of other groups using the courts against government actions they opposed.[23]

Emboldened, environmental groups demanded more say in decisions affecting public lands. Many of the new leaders harbored a general distrust of all public bureaucracies and big businesses. Also, experience had shown leaders that a steady diet of conflicts and environmental causes kept up organizational interest and boosted the membership necessary for growth.

Rather than finding strong allies, Hartzog often found environmental groups to be nuisances. Even with park additions they favored such as Redwood, environmentalists criticized the proposed park boundaries, development and management plans, and compromises made in getting legislation through Congress. Hartzog felt that he protected the interests of the average visitor. In his view, environmental groups were either idealists who saw complex issues in black and white or elitists who wanted to close the parks to everyone but themselves.

> I tried to work with them. I tried to hear their concerns. And I tried to take them into account. I figured when I was catchin' hell from both of them [environmentalists and business interests], I was somewhere in the right spectrum. I had bitter, bitter critics in both camps. . . . I'm not sure that the Lord himself reincarnated could have satisfied them. And furthermore, there's no reciprocity on their part. In other words, you just do what I want done PERIOD. And I'm not going to do anything for you in return. I used to say to 'em, "You know, many of the problems that you complain about are money problems. I don't find any of you on the Hill testifying in support of my budget." Not a single damn one of them ever went up there to testify in support of the budget. All they do is complain about it.[24]

According to long-time Park Service employee William Brown, how-ever, much of the rift between the agency and environmental groups was staged for publicity's sake. Behind closed doors, the working relationship between the Park Service and environmental groups was closer than one would have suspected given the fiery rhetoric.[25] Both groups felt strongly about protecting lands from undesirable development; they simply differed on how it should be done.

Hartzog understood and used to his advantage the political and logistical processes involved in acquiring new parks. Working the crowd to generate interest for park additions seemed a task he was born to do. A comfortable, backslapping Southern charm combined with a quick mind, the ability to sidestep difficult questions, and the special attention he showered on key leaders added to his success in convincing Congress to add to the National Park System.

Hartzog explained that new parks are added in one of two ways. Most commonly, Congress passes legislation authorizing their creation. Second, and less commonly, a president can set aside a national monument under the Antiquities Act of 1906. Starting with Theodore Roosevelt, a number of presidents exercised this authority. Although once a powerful tool for protecting endangered lands before legislators could act, the Antiquities Act lost much of its appeal as Congress grew agitated over the president's ability to bypass its oversight. When President Eisenhower proclaimed the long-stalled C&O Canal Park a national monument in 1961, Congress reacted by withholding funds for many years. Congress wanted to send the president a clear message that while he could proclaim national monu-ments, they could never become functional parks without congressional appropriations. As a result, presidents grew reluctant to proclaim national monuments unless Congress supported them.[26] During Hartzog's tenure, for example, President Johnson was urged to set aside 7.5 million acres of parklands, but fearing congressional opposition, he refused to sign all the proclamations.

Hartzog understood this delicate balance between the executive and legislative branches. He knew that Congress creates national park units, determines their funding levels, and can decommission existing parks. As a balance, the president can proclaim national monuments and hold Congress in check by power of the veto. Both branches thus seek a level of commit-ment from the other before advancing any park bill.

Hartzog also understood that proposed additions were usually in the pipeline long before either the president or Congress considered them. Park proposals originated in a variety of ways, although some channels were more common than others. Frequently, a Park Service study team generated a list of possible areas that had been brought to its attention. Once listed, park staff scrutinized the park's feasibility, or the chance it would get through Congress, and its suitability, or level of national significance.[27] If Hartzog approved the park, staff would draw up a professional study report and gauge local support. Local public hearings could occur at this stage or later when Congress was considering legislation.

In Hartzog's experience, gaining strong local support was critical because "seldom if ever do you succeed in any legislation in which the local congressman opposes."[28] Not only could that congressman kill the park bill, but his friends could help as well. The attitude prevailed that "if you don't mess in my backyard, I won't mess in yours."[29]

Hartzog learned this lesson early in his directorate with a proposed prairie park in Kansas. Before he flew in for the public hearings, his people assured him of strong support. But, as he learned the hard way, "Your damn support didn't do any good if they're not there. . . . We didn't have a single solitary witness up there in support of Prairie National Park. Not one! I mean, those cattlemen, they fed us to those cows like forage. And that was the last hearing we ever had on Prairie National Park."[30]

After that experience, Hartzog revised his whole legislative program and adopted the "key man" approach. For each proposed park, he designated two key men. One stayed in Washington and assembled all the materials necessary to support the legislation, such as maps, data, and reports. The other, generally a superintendent from a nearby park, was expected to "get out and press the flesh and find out who's for me and who's against me and who's indifferent so that we know in advance when we go in there what we're moving into."[31] After his prairie park experience, he insisted that key men line up people willing to testify at public hearings on the park's behalf. To Hartzog, Congress needed to see visible support because "if there's nobody supporting the thing, they're not heroes, you know, trying to go to the Arctic by themselves. They want to make sure there's a crowd with 'em."[32]

If local support appeared sufficient, a park proposal was sent for recommendations to the secretary of the interior's Advisory Board on National Parks, Historic Sites, Buildings, and Monuments. If the advisory board approved, the proposal passed to the secretary. During Hartzog's tenure, the advisory board's opinions were taken seriously. In fact, Wayne Aspinall, chair of the House Interior and Insular Affairs Committee, always asked for its recommendations and made sure those recommendations were part of the public record before he considered any legislation.[33]

The advisory board consisted of at most eleven people. According to Hartzog, they were usually people of "great distinction in academia, business, and public service areas," people who were of "towering stature in their fields," and collectively possessed a knowledge of everything from history to science to archaeology. Although the board generally favored park additions, they never served as a rubber stamp and did reject some proposals. As an independent and unpaid group, the board remained largely immune to political pressures and that enabled it to render objective opinions. At times, the board could also head off bad proposals and allow the Park Service or a congressman to save face by saying that the area simply did not meet the test of national significance.[34] Hartzog worked as closely with this group as he did with members of Congress. According to Hartzog, "I never let 'em meet anywhere that I wasn't with 'em."[35]

Under the Nixon administration, Hartzog lamented that advisory board appointments grew increasingly political. He recalled a party for advisory board members in which he overheard a new member ask a very distinguished archaeologist, "How much did your seat cost you?" The new appointee proceeded to tell the flabbergasted board member the size of his contribution to the Nixon campaign. Once board positions started going to persons without professional competency, qualified people refused to take part, and the group lost much of its credibility and importance.[36]

During Hartzog's time, however, the advisory board studied and visited many proposed areas before passing its recommendations to the secretary of the interior. If the secretary supported the park, his office prepared a report that incorporated the input of the Bureau of Budget. His staff would examine testimony to be given in Congress, the cost of the proposal, and how the legislation would fit into the president's programs. During the later part of his tenure, Hartzog experienced "monumental problems with the Budget Bureau on 'Where does it all end?' or 'When are you going to stop expanding the National Park System?'"[37]

While the Park Service initiated many park proposals, some came from other sources. Regardless of its origin, worthy park legislation would advance to the appropriate House and Senate subcommittee for consideration. Generally, bills moved in the House before the Senate, but not always. If, for example, a park proposal had a pocket of local opposition, it might be introduced in the Senate first. The logic was that senators represented the entire state, so they could weather strong local opposition better than a House member. If a park bill began in the Senate, Hartzog knew any local opposition needed to be resolved before the measure would move in the House.[38] Regardless of where legislation began, each branch of Congress kept abreast of what the other was doing.

Hartzog knew well the finesse needed to deal with the legislators' many different temperaments. For the Park Service, the two most important congressional committees were the Interior and Insular Affairs for legislation and Appropriations for funding. Initial legislative work, however, began in the subcommittees, such as the House Subcommittee on National Parks, Recreation, and Public Lands. After disagreements had been ironed out, bills then went to the full committee for consideration. Traditionally, leadership in these crucial committees and subcommittees came from western states closely associated with cattle, lumber, mining, and other consumptive interests. During Hartzog's tenure, eastern congressmen gained more of a voice, and that altered the dynamics, priorities, and types of parks the committees favored.

When a park bill came up for consideration at the subcommittee level, someone from the Department of the Interior, usually Hartzog, testified. Here he learned some basic lessons of politics. A witness humbly testified before committees because "they were the supreme commanders of all they surveyed." Bill Everhart had witnessed Hartzog's predecessor, Conrad Wirth, openly criticize an appropriations committee for lack of park funding only to be put soundly in his place by an icy chairman. Drawing on his law background and his staff, Hartzog took pains to be well prepared for a hearing. He also kept extensive files on the parks in each committee member's district. "There was nothing," he remembered, "they got so much pleasure out of as tellin' you something you don't know anything about."[39]

Based on testimony from government agencies, concerned citizens, and various organizations, the subcommittee might revise the legislation before submitting it to the entire committee. Should a bill fail to gain subcommittee support, it died, since the full committee would never schedule it for a vote. Bills could also die if committee chairs chose to bury them. The objections of one key individual could be enough to stall or kill any bill. Hartzog had that lesson driven home by Charlotte Reid, a House representative from Illinois. He thought he had lined up adequate votes for Sleeping Bear Dunes National Lakeshore in Michigan, but when it came to a vote, they failed to show. Reid had apparently asked them to skip the meeting, which politically cost them nothing. Fortunately, one of Hartzog's supporters strategically voted against the legislation, which would allow it to come up for reconsideration, hopefully this time with a full complement of supporters. As Hartzog said, "She taught me how to count."[40]

Subcommittee members and particularly chairs wielded tremendous power over park legislation, and they knew it. According to Secretary Udall, powerful chairmen like Wayne Aspinall of Colorado presented one of the biggest obstacles to the passage of park legislation. Crotchety and difficult, Aspinall was a "strong-minded, one-man committee, and very dominant and domineering, so you have to kowtow to him, work with him, get as much as you could, take your half a loaf and settle for that."[41]

Fortunately for Hartzog, he had known Aspinall for years. They first met in the mid-1950s, when Hartzog was assistant superintendent of Rocky Mountain National Park in Colorado. Each year, the local chamber of commerce held a show-me day for the state's congressmen, during which they would tour a national park, have lunch, and evaluate the park's performance. Hartzog had been assigned to Aspinall, then the state's junior representative. Aspinall typically brought along his sons, and Hartzog arranged for sightseeing trips and other outdoor adventures. By the time he became director, he had known Aspinall for more than ten years and had established his credibility in Aspinall's eyes. Despite their friendship, Aspinall did not bow to Hartzog's whim. When asked how he dealt with Aspinall, Hartzog replied, "Like two porcupines making love. Very carefully!"[42]

Legislation approved at the subcommittee and committee level then moved to the floor, where the committee chair usually managed it. The committee chair, however, could hand the bill over to the subcommittee chair or a congressional representative from that district, especially if the district representative was prominent. Although Hartzog lost a number of bills at the subcommittee level, he never, as far as he could recall, lost a bill once it had made it to the full floor.[43] Usually House and Senate versions of a bill were similar, but on controversial parks such as Redwood, they could be significantly different and then it fell to a conference committee to reconcile the two versions.

If a bill passed, Hartzog then had to seek funds for land acquisition, development, and staffing from appropriations committees. For the National Park System, these acts originated in the House Appropriations Subcommittee of the Committee on Interior Department and Related Agencies. During Hartzog's tenure, that committee was chaired first by Ohioan Mike Kirwan until 1965, by Wendall Denton of Indiana until 1966, and then by Julia Butler Hansen from Washington. Hartzog described Hansen as ruling her appropriations subcommittee with an "iron fist in a velvet glove." Once when Hansen objected to a speech by a fellow congressman, she taught him a lesson by withholding funds for a park in his district.

Hansen wielded her power beyond the Hill by pointing out to Hartzog the management and service problems she observed in parks she had visited with her family. Hartzog dealt with her concerns promptly, since he knew she could cut his funding as easily as one could shut off a water spigot.[44] For example, one Monday morning she called Hartzog to ask him to come to her office *immediately*, which meant there was some problem. Hansen and her family had tried to visit the Jamestown-Yorktown area late one afternoon only to have a ranger close the gate in her face. Four hours of daylight remained on the summer day, but visitation ended at 5:00 pm. Thereafter, the Jamestown area extended its summer hours until dark.

While appropriation bills arose in the House, both the House and Senate considered the president's budget separately. Both held separate hearings and passed separate bills. As Hartzog explained:

> An item in the president's budget that is reduced or eliminated, for example, in the House subcommittee may be increased or added back in the Senate appropriations bills. Moreover, as frequently happens, each subcommittee may include items not in the president's budget but which are of particular importance to a member of either the House or Senate.[45]

Hartzog got his funding for the Summer in the Parks program by Hansen simply writing $575,000 into the budget without going through any other approvals.

To highlight their influence, Hartzog liked to say there were really three Congresses—the House, Senate, and Appropriations. The appropriation committees wrote "their own rules" and functioned as "individual empires."[46] While the House prohibited someone on the appropriations committee from serving on a substantive authorizing committee, the Senate allowed it. As a result, Alan Bible of Nevada chaired both the Senate appropriations subcommittee and the authorizing subcommittee on national parks. According to Hartzog, Bible had "total control," and no park would be created if he objected. Hartzog kept in almost daily contact with Bible, filling him in on the progress of all park legislation. Like Hansen, Bible routinely traveled to national parks and was quick to point out his concerns, which Hartzog dealt with immediately.[47]

Hartzog respected the power of key members of Congress and made their interests a top priority. He knew that for years Mike Kirwan, chair of the House Appropriations Committee, had refused to appropriate funds for the authorized Piscataway Park because he disliked one of the park's congressional supporters. Even after he stepped down, his replacement, Julia Butler Hansen, abstained from funding the park out of deference to him. When Alan Bible tried to allocate funds for the park in the Senate, the money was repeatedly lost in the conference committees that resolved differences in the House and Senate versions. Not until Kirwan agreed publicly to refrain from opposing funding did Piscataway Park finally get money for land purchases and scenic easements. When Kirwan wanted a statue of a prominent Irish poet and patriot placed along a District of Columbia avenue, Hartzog discreetly found a location without consulting the city's planning commission, which would likely to have objected to the proposed location.[48]

Although park legislation generally moved through typical channels, there were always notable exceptions, such as that for Steamtown National Historic Site.[49] According to Hartzog, Joseph McDade of Pennsylvania simply sat in his office, wrote an amendment authorizing the park, and attached it to a bill. The amendment never passed through any authorizing committee. As Hartzog said, McDade "was a ranking member of the Appropriations Committee in the House. There wasn't anybody gonna cross him. And that's the power that those old stags had."[50]

Getting park legislation passed was much like running a gauntlet where one well-placed blow could halt a bill's progress. Every year Congress considered far more park proposals than it passed. For example, during the ninety-first Congress (1969–1970), the House considered 108 new park proposals while the Senate looked at 51, but only 13 were authorized, although some would reappear and be approved in later years.[51]

For the parks that passed, the final legislation typically included compromises and concessions. To many, the compromises seemed too great, and they criticized Hartzog for being too willing to make deals. Even Newton Drury, former Park Service director and a man deeply committed to protecting redwoods, strongly objected to the final Redwood National Park legislation. Drury felt the park should have been larger and that some of the best stands of redwoods were excluded. Hartzog believed that "compromise is the essence of legislative art. Thus legislation is seldom perfect [but] happily it is never permanent." He reasoned that once a park was established, future directors could work out problems such as boundary delineations and do the necessary fine-tuning, which was done later in Redwood.[52] Protecting the area before it was lost remained his primary goal.

☙

Members of congress remain receptive to their constituents. As environmental concerns grew during the Hartzog directorate, legislators realized that adding large water projects was losing its political appeal. As they searched for alternatives, they increasingly looked to parks. Critics even suggested that Congress's "pork barrel" had become a "park barrel." Hartzog perceived that Congress was more receptive to historical parks because they were smaller and less costly. They also lacked the controversy of a Redwood, North Cascades, or Gateway. Furthermore, the comparatively small number of visitors rarely upset neighbors and rarely resulted in property condemnation that displaced locals. Federal funds also helped the local economy and won the support of local historical groups.[53]

As their interest grew, some in Congress cared less and less about a proposed park's suitability or its national significance. Hartzog found himself in the difficult situation of having to fend off unworthy park proposals without offending important legislators. Charles E. Bennett of Florida, for example, repeatedly proposed a "Southmost Battlefield of the American Revolution National Historic Site." Other than being the southern-most battlefield, its only other claim to fame was "that two equally incompetent commanders blundered into each other in the Florida swamps."[54] Rather than openly admit the proposal was unworthy, Hartzog stalled the proposal's progress until his chief historian was able to combine the battlefield with five other significant historic sites and suggest a Florida frontier rivers national park. Bennett embraced the new idea, but it failed to gain the necessary support in Congress.[55]

Stalling tactics were used with Representative Joe Skubitz, the ranking minority member of the House legislative subcommittee. According to Utley, Skubitz "urged one unacceptable project after another to put substandard properties from his Kansas district into the National Park System."[56] He usually succeeded.

If stalling failed, the negative recommendations of the secretary's advisory board sometimes proved sufficient to discourage impassioned supporters. Other times, Hartzog tried to deflect the heat by sending someone like his chief historian to deliver unpalatable messages to congressional members and their constituents. Later, Hartzog could blame the lack of Park Service support on "those goddamned professionals." If his staff could not justify the proposal, Hartzog regrettably said he could not fight for it.

Utley recalled a memorable Hartzog trick for dealing with one difficult park proposal. Joseph McDade, then ranking minority member of the House Appropriations Subcommittee, had wanted several abandoned coal mines in his home state of Pennsylvania proclaimed the National Coal Historic Site. To explain their proposal, several of McDade's constituents darkened his office and presented a slide show for Hartzog; Spud Bill, his second in command; and Utley. "When the lights went on, lo and behold, neither Hartzog nor Spud Bill were in that room," Utley recalled. "They had fled and left me to handle McDade and his constituents."[57]

Another Hartzog tactic involved burying insignificant properties in nationally significant ones. Fort Massachusetts, off the coast of Mississippi, saw little action since it was not completed until after the Civil War. A 1935 study reported that the barrier island fort lacked national significance. Despite this, Representative William Colmer of Mississippi strong-armed Hartzog into visiting the area. Very quickly it became clear to Hartzog that, given Colmer's influence, the Park Service would get Fort Massachusetts whether it wanted it or not. With this realization, he suggested that Colmer expand his horizons to include a whole string of barrier islands off the Mississippi, Alabama, and Florida coasts. The result was Gulf Islands National Seashore, authorized on January 8, 1971.[58]

Despite his best efforts, Hartzog took some parks and landmarks he could not seem to avoid, but he never pressured his professional staff "to provide him with information or justifications that ran counter to their professional principles."[59] However, his high-level administrators sensed the pressures to appease important congressmen. When the birthplace of William McGuffey of *McGuffey's Reader* fame in Ohio came up for national historic landmark consideration, the study group found "a hunk of real estate with nothing left on it that would even suggest a connection to anything historic. It was just a farm on the outskirts of Youngstown, with no structures surviving from McGuffey's time." The Park Service had already designated the place where McGuffey lived and wrote most of the books, so the case for a birthplace landmark designation was weak at best.[60]

Kirwan did not take the historians' pronouncement well and declared that if he did not get a national landmark in his district of Youngstown, he would cut off the money for all landmark designations. Since he knew any historian's report would be negative, Hartzog sent naturalist Howard Stagner, an assistant director, to investigate personally the site and present his findings to the Department of the Interior's advisory board. The advisory board knew at once what had transpired. They understood the site's only defense was that "Hartzog's got to do it for Mike. We owe Mike a lot, and I believe that we should suppress our professional dictates in this one instance and give Mike his landmark." Kirwan had done the Park Service many favors, including keeping the money flowing for Mission 66 initiatives. John Brew, an advisory board member and archaeologist, was also aware of how many millions Kirwan had directed into salvage operations. When it came to a vote, strong encouragement swayed a supposedly independent advisory board to support Mike Kirwan's landmark.[61]

As a few undesirables crept into the system, the Park Service had to accommodate them. As Utley said, "There is nothing the Service can do to ensure that you get only nationally significant sites for the simple reason that Congress is the ultimate authority on what goes into the National Park System. There will always be members of Congress sufficiently dedicated to hatching substandard sites who are also very powerful and make it likely that now and then it will happen."[62] According to Bill Everhart, however, the Park Service has accepted surprisingly few: "I think that on the whole when you think about how Congress moves and with the opportunity for slipping things in, there are a few parks in the system that shouldn't be there, but there are amazingly few, and I think the lesson is that you treat them all the same and even those you might say, 'This is marginal' because if you start doing that then the whole system buckles down."[63]

After Hartzog's departure, the Park Service experienced increasing difficulty warding off congressional pork. During the late 1970s, Representative Phillip Burton of California carried it to new extremes with "park omnibus bills" that included as many as a dozen new park proposals and twice as many expansions into one large bill. To gain widespread support in Congress, Burton packaged inferior sites along with the truly meritorious, leaving the Park Service to deal with the consequences for the integrity of the whole system.[64] While Hartzog admitted that some of Burton's additions lacked national significance, he admired Burton's ingenuity in what he called a "log-rolling operation." After his directorate, he ran into Burton and reportedly said to him that "I wish to heavens you and I had been together when I was director. We'd have made a park out of the whole United States."[65]

꙳

Land acquisition became critical to expansion of the National Park System. While early parks such as Yellowstone and Yosemite had been carved from western public lands, almost no public lands existed in the East or near urban population centers where parks were desperately needed. There were even fewer such lands for popular resources such as seashores, lakeshores, and waterways. In 1958, the Outdoor Recreation Resources Review Commission had strongly urged Congress to establish a fund to purchase recreation lands. Not until 1961, however, did Congress first appropriate money for land acquisition, when it purchased lands for Cape Lookout National Seashore in North Carolina. Pressures mounted to create special funding for park acquisition. Secretary Udall argued that "if we're going to enlarge the national parks system, we're going to have to spend thirty, forty, fifty million dollars a year in buying these lands. We're going to need a financing vehicle to do it."[66]

When Congress finally passed the Land and Water Conservation Fund Act in 1964, it created earmarked funds for land purchases and gave Hartzog's expansion efforts a huge boost. Initially, funding came from the proceeds of surplus federal lands, boat fuel taxes, and recreation fees at federal parks and forestlands. Udall said the program "got off to a bad start because we didn't have the funding."[67] That changed when they were able to add receipts from mineral leasing of the outer continental shelf, which effectively doubled the pool of authorized dollars to $200 million in 1969. By 1970, growing park demands moved Congress to authorize $300 million and to place special emphasis on urban parks and recreation areas.

As written, the legislation consisted of a federal and state component. The federal program supported land acquisition for the Park Service, Forest Service, Fish and Wildlife Service, and Bureau of Land Management. During Hartzog's tenure, the Bureau of Outdoor Recreation allocated most of the federal share to either the Forest Service or the Park Service. In reality, authorized funding far exceeded funds allocated for land purchases. Since 1965, the Park Service has reported spending on average closer to $100 million a year, reaching a peak of $369 million in 1979.[68]

The Land and Water Conservation Fund boosted Hartzog's legislative successes and helped him achieve a record of land acquisition superior to that of all previous administrations. Funds for land acquisition, according to Hartzog, were "the hardest money that we have ever tried to get from Congress."[69] Appropriations committees often delayed spending authorized money because they felt park funding could always "wait until tomorrow."[70] As Hartzog said, "with the Land and Water Conservation Fund there is a regular systemized funding for the purchase of land, and the Congress at its will can appropriate from it."[71] Not surprisingly, Congress was more willing to pass park legislation when it knew necessary funding existed. As Hartzog liked to say, "Nothing focuses attention like money."[72]

While Hartzog publicly complained that his agency "never got a fair shake because Ed Crafts, director of Bureau of Outdoor Recreation, was former deputy chief of the Forest Service," he knew the Park Service got significant amounts of funding. In his book, *Battling for the National Parks*, he wrote that historically the Park Service "had received the lion's share of the federal portion—approximately 67 percent."[73]

During Hartzog's tenure, accessible recreation areas, particularly those including seashores, lakeshores, and scenic rivers, became a top funding priority. All or much of the money for sixteen of the parks established or authorized during Hartzog's directorate came from the Land and Wildlife Conservation Fund. These included:

Appalachian National Scenic Trail (Maine to Georgia)
Apostle Islands National Lakeshore (Wisconsin)
Assateague Island National Seashore (Maryland and Virginia)
Biscayne National Monument (Florida)
Buffalo National River (Arkansas)
Cape Lookout National Seashore (North Carolina)
Cumberland Island National Seashore (Georgia)
Gulf Islands National Seashore (Mississippi, Alabama, and Florida)
Indiana Dunes National Lakeshore (Indiana)
North Cascades National Park (Washington)
Ozark National Scenic Riverways (Missouri)
Rocks National Lakeshore (Michigan)
Redwood National Park (California)
Sleeping Bear Dunes National Lakeshore (Michigan)
St. Croix and Lower St. Croix National Scenic Riverways (Wisconsin and
    Minnesota)
Voyageurs National Park (Minnesota)[74]

While the Land and Water Conservation Fund greatly enhanced park expansion, many grew frustrated with the yearly uncertainty of funding levels. Assistant secretary Nat Reed claimed that "one of the reasons I came to Washington in 1971 was to devise a strategy so that the Land and Water Conservation Fund didn't go up and down like a yo-yo. You know, I said, 'Mr. President, give me $300 million, $500 million, $700 million but I want it fixed so that it doesn't go up and down.'"[75] Even with Reed's and others' efforts, fund allocations failed to stabilize, making planning difficult.

≥

Aided by favorable conditions, the National Park System expanded as never before. Seventy-two new areas were added—over 70 percent more than in the preceding thirty years. Some of these additions included parks previously lost but successfully revived. Executive support for park expansion reached its zenith during the Johnson administration and waned during the Nixon years. Hartzog contended that during the Johnson years he had built up enough momentum that Nixon's crew could not stop him. As he explained, "the Nixon administration wasn't all that sympathetic. The whole thing is they were coping with a snowball that was already rolling downhill at a tremendous speed. And you know, you can slow it down, but you'd better not get in the way of it, otherwise you're liable to get wrapped up in it."[76] During the Johnson administration (1964–1968), a total of forty-six parks were added for an average of just over nine parks a year. During Nixon's time (1969–1972), only twenty-six parks gained entry for an average of six and a half parks a year.

As Hartzog expanded its numbers, he also broadened the concept of what constituted a national park unit. National rivers, national trails, a performing arts facility, and urban recreation areas entered the system. And he explored new types of management arrangements with other agencies and organizations.

As the National Park System had grown to include a diverse collection of parks, Hartzog recognized inherent differences between units. He recognized that one size did not fit all. To better deal with the differences, he drafted a memorandum to Secretary Udall in which he laid out his ideas about how to manage the system. On July 10, 1964, Udall officially sent the memo to Hartzog as a secretarial directive for management of the National Park System. For the first time, the Park Service officially recognized three different categories of park units—natural, historical, and recreational. Each category would require a separate management approach and a separate set of management policies but all would be coordinated to form one organic management plan for the entire system.[77] Natural areas would be guided by the 1918 directives and would be managed in such a way as to restore and perpetuate their natural values according to goals laid out in the 1963 Leopold report. This report urged the Park Service to restore each park to conditions as they were when the white man first visited the area so as to offer "a vignette of primitive America." Ecological principles received more attention, as did the important role of predators and fire.[78]

In largely historical parks, the emphasis shifted to protecting the historical resources for which the parks were established. In recreation areas, managers concentrated on providing visitors with a pleasing environment for outdoor recreation activities. If parks contained significant natural, historical, and recreation resources, they were divided into the appropriate management zones.[79]

Hartzog also felt the Park Service needed greater management flexibility. So with great flourish and fanfare, he abolished the fifty-six volumes of administrative manuals, even though he had personally penned several of them. To Hartzog, they stifled creativity and "imprisoned every manager in the same straitjacket."[80] They could not think freely or make timely and responsible decisions if they were continually forced to consult the manuals, many of which were out of date. As Hartzog described it, "when I got to St. Louis, and I ran into all those cotton pickin' manuals, I was totally convinced that they were an abomination to good management. I got into all kinds of arguments over those things, and then when I got to be director . . . their fate was sealed, even though I let them study it for a while. I knew the answer before the study started. They were gone."[81]

Hartzog replaced the cumbersome series with three slim administrative volumes—the blue book, the red book, and the green book—that he had written during the evenings at his home office. Manuals for natural, historical, and recreational areas outlined general policy purposes, presented prescriptions for common management problems, and discussed pertinent congressional administrative policies. He allowed his top staff to comment on his work, but he usually overruled objections, often in inelegant language.[82]

Hartzog's decision stunned the rank and file, who for years relied on the administrative manuals for guidance. As one bystander put it, "It left them in a boat without charts or even paddles. They drifted in different directions. Accountability weakened. Crises erupted that he had to quell."[83] According to Hartzog, his park managers eventually adapted and flourished. He said, "It was like turning seventy-five hundred cripples loose without a crutch. But you know in six months they started to walk on their own. And they were thrilled to death. They could throw their crutches away. They were human beings again."[84]

The difficulty many faced with their supposed freedom was the apprehension that their decisions would run counter to their director, whom many feared. Park managers with a combination of significant natural, historical, or recreational resources struggled to mesh policies from the different manuals. With subsequent directors, the administrative manuals reappeared and proliferated. In retirement, Hartzog scorned this development:

> The purpose of those manuals was to make sure that every guy in the field did everything exactly the way the guy in Washington wanted it done. Now you call that elucidation, education, efficiency? I call it a simple word "control." So when you have an organization that has six-foot shelves of books, you can bet your bottom dollar that the guy that's running that outfit has one purpose in mind. He is a decision maker and he is going to control every peon that moves in or out of that office. Do you want to know who has a good organization going? Go and look and see how many books he has on the shelf called administrative manuals, and if he's got zero, you know he's got talented, educated, wonderful people out there 'cause he's in business. The government approaches it exactly the opposite. The politicians come in and the first thing they want to do is review the administrative manuals and make changes so it reflects "our philosophy." For crying out loud! Give me a break! Give me a break! They now have seventy-eight volumes in the Park Service.

Later he added that "the problem is that the people in government that run the government don't trust the people in government that work for the government to have any common sense at all. So therefore, they write 'em handbooks."[85]

☙

Under Hartzog's direction, the Park Service experienced its largest expansion in historical areas. Although he lacked a strong interest in history, he oversaw the addition of thirty-four new historical areas, which was just shy of his combined total for natural and recreational areas. The new areas were located in twenty-seven different states and the District of Columbia, which furthered his goal of making parks relevant to members of Congress and their constituents. In fact, the many new historical areas vexed the Office of Management and Budget, successor to the Bureau of Budget. "Where would it all end?" the keepers of the purse wanted to know. How many new historical areas burden the president's budget and for how long? The answer was plain—forever, because history went on forever, and in whatever number history produced nationally significant places. That of course satisfied no budget writer, nor was it a reality Hartzog could concede. What was wanted was a "National Park System plan" that would define what was needed to "round out the system" and thus slow the flow of new historical parks.

In the studies conducted under the Historic Sites Act of 1935, Hartzog discovered an answer. A system of historical themes, such as European exploration and settlement and westward expansion, provided a framework for identifying the nation's worthy historic places and determining those of significance to the entire nation rather than a state or locality. The secretary of the interior, based on recommendations of his advisory board, declared these places national historic landmarks and attested their distinction with a certificate and bronze plaque. As national significance was the first requirement for a proposed historical addition to the park system, landmark status took on additional importance in both the executive and legislative branches.

The thematic approach to conducting the nationwide survey ordained by the Historic Sites Act seemed to Hartzog a simple (if simplistic) way to organize a bureaucratic answer to the repeated questions of what would round out the park system. "For Hartzog's purposes with OMB," said Utley, "we constructed some elaborate charts that purported to show an unbalanced National Park System and the themes in which we needed to acquire new parks in order to have a balanced representation of American history."[86]

A number of existing parks fit neatly into the framework, but creativity was called for to make others, such as Piscataway Park and Mount Rushmore National Memorial, do the same. Also, the approach had no way of accounting for the relative quality of the parks. A site like Independence National Historical Park would fit into the thematic framework the same as a Roger Williams National Memorial, which one park planner described as "a purely political park on a site of dubious connection to Roger Williams." Also, if a truly worthy and available historical area already had adequate thematic representation, the Park Service could have difficulty justifying its addition.[87] This proved embarrassingly true when the long-sought Lincoln Home in Springfield, Illinois, became available. The park system already included the Lincoln Memorial, Ford's Theatre, the house where Lincoln died, Lincoln's birthplace, and Lincoln's boyhood home.

Hartzog was aware of his plan's flaws but nevertheless hoped to use it as an instrument of communication to OMB. He reflected that "it was the only way to control what came in because otherwise it would become a political football and whoever had the most votes was going to get their way."[88]

He would justify certain parks by saying they were needed to round out the system. On the flip side, he could discourage areas he did not want by saying they failed the thematic test. In reality, his strategy probably had little substantive effect beyond addressing a bureaucratic problem.[89]

During the Hartzog directorate, ten parks were added under the political and military affairs theme. Seven of these commemorated past presidents. Although the Historic Sites Survey had established the useful rule that significance could only be truly assessed after the passage of fifty years, clearly some sites, such as those associated with nuclear energy and recent presidents, did not need fifty years to merit a finding of national significance.

A crisis intruded, however, when President Johnson insisted that his boyhood home in Texas be declared a national landmark, a first step toward addition to the park system. The advisory board balked because living persons had never been honored with a landmark. LBJ's demand placed Hartzog in an untenable position. In a lounge car in Alaska in 1965, he persuaded the board to adopt a policy that the very election of a president established national significance and that the Park Service should proceed at once to identify an associated landmark.

That relieved Hartzog's dilemma with President Johnson. But Utley pointed out that Harry Truman and Dwight Eisenhower were still living and that choosing landmarks for them was impossibly presumptuous. Utley therefore drafted a letter for Secretary Udall to send to each inviting them to make the selection themselves. Eisenhower promptly identified his Gettysburg Farm, which ultimately joined the park system. Truman responded that he did not believe in memorializing living people and declined to name a property. After his death, his home in Independence, Missouri, near his presidential library, joined the park system.

For Nixon, the new policy fell casualty to Watergate but was revived for Ford, whose Michigan home was designated a landmark but never considered for park status. Thereafter, the policy was overtaken by a congressional mandate to establish a theme study to identify a landmark for every U.S. president. Some, including the Lyndon B. Johnson National Historical Park and, more recently, the Jimmy Carter National Historic Site, entered the park system.[90]

A better test of the fifty-year waiting period occurred after the death in July 1967 of Carl Sandburg—popular poet, biographer, journalist, champion of the working poor, and winner of two Pulitzer Prizes. At a ceremony honoring him at Lincoln Memorial, Stewart Udall sat next to Sandburg's widow, who suggested that the National Park Service make his North Carolina farm a national historic site. Bill Everhart recalled inspecting the area and feeling ecstatic about its quaint and bucolic character. Less than a year after his death, the park bill sailed through Congress with little discussion or opposition. With Sandburg's great friend Roy Taylor of North Carolina chairing the House legislative subcommittee, Hartzog pointed out that enactment was certain. Less than fifty years after Sandburg's death, however, Everhart concedes that his true significance has so far eroded as to cast doubts on his claim to national significance and the likelihood that Congress would have considered a park bill now.[91]

The remaining twenty-four historical additions were distributed fairly evenly over the other eight themes. For the first time, three areas—Saint-Gaudens, Carl Sandburg, and Longfellow—were categorized under the contemplative society theme. With these areas, Hartzog helped move the Park Service beyond designating areas solely by reference to the traditional concept of historical commemoration. Before his directorate, he said "if it was a birthplace or battlefield it was automatically eligible 'cause that was the way we remembered history." Hartzog and his staff wanted to go beyond that and were exploring potential parks that would recall the panorama of creative efforts that helped define a nation.[92]

Hartzog also led the Park Service in efforts to preserve distinct cultures. The nation was reevaluating its melting pot philosophy and emphasizing its rich cultural diversity. Some believed the Park Service an ideal agency to help preserve representations of the country's culture. In 1972, the *National Parks for the Future* report prepared by the Conservation Foundation for the Yellowstone Centennial reaffirmed this direction. "It certainly serves the national interest to involve the Park Service in cultural diversity, just as the national interest is served by sustaining ecological diversity."[93] Hartzog was very receptive to the idea and even sought to develop a new category of "national cultural park." Since the Park Service could not purchase lands representing, for example, the Amish culture in Pennsylvania, other techniques would be necessary. Too much interference, such as land acquisitions, would destroy the very thing targeted for protection. Despite the interest and research, no such areas were set aside.

Where land acquisition presented problems, Hartzog looked for creative alternatives, such as the program with the Zuni Indians to jointly manage the historic pueblo in New Mexico until they gained enough expertise to take over completely. Although that effort died, the Park Service entered into a similar cooperative management arrangement at Nez Perce National Historical Park. Authorized in 1965, Nez Perce included twenty-three different sites spread across northern Idaho. It combined the efforts of the Park Service, other federal agencies, the state of Idaho, various local governments, the Nez Perce tribe, private organizations, and generous donors.[94]

Another new type of cooperative management agreement involved Fort Scott, Kansas. The fort lay in the district of Joe Skubitz, ranking Republican on the House parks subcommittee. He had long promoted the addition of the fort to the system but had been opposed by Park Service historians who questioned its suitability on the grounds that its surviving buildings had been incorporated into the city of Fort Scott as well its significance. The fort finally won landmark status based on its role in organizing some of the first black fighting units in the Civil War. Although still denying entry into the park system, in 1965, Congress allowed it to become an "affiliated area" by appropriating funds for the city to develop a park under guidance of the National Park Service. This formula proved unworkable, and in 1978, Congress authorized the Fort Scott National Historic Site as a unit of the system.[95]

Even so, the concept of "affiliated area" proved useful. The tool could be used to preserve significant places that were not federally owned or administered by the National Park Service. Some were recognized by congressional legislation, while others were designated national historic sites in nonfederal ownership by the secretary of the interior under powers granted by the Historic Sites Act of 1935.

⸶

During Hartzog's directorate, ten new natural areas were added. Of these, five were designated national parks, bringing the Park System total to thirty-eight.[96] North Cascades and Redwood involved long, bitter, emotionally charged battles that captured national attention. In both cases, the compromises made left no one completely satisfied. At North Cascades in Washington, Hartzog managed to pull the parklands away from its rival, the Forest Service. Although angrily fought by the Forest Service and its supporters, the strength of Henry "Scoop" Jackson, Washington's powerful senator, and public sentiment tipped the scales in Hartzog's favor, giving the Park Service what some called the "American Alps."[97]

The hard-fought struggle to add Redwood National Park featured many of the same protagonists as North Cascades. The Forest Service managed part of the potential parklands and objected to losing yet more land to the Park Service. Several timber companies owned other parcels, which they depended on to stay in business. Even park supporters strongly disagreed over which areas should be included, since buying all desirable redwood groves and enough upstream watershed for flood protection would prove prohibitively expensive. According to Hartzog, California governor Ronald Reagan further complicated matters by promising to add the redwood state parks to the proposed national park in exchange for surplus military seashore properties that were slated to be disposed of. But "the guy welched on the deal. . . . [Now] the state of California's got four state park superintendents, we got a national park superintendent, all there within yellin' distance of each other."[98]

The battles over North Cascades and Redwood showed how hard it was getting to be to establish new national parks and to secure sufficient funds to purchase private lands. The cost of Redwood's establishment and eventual enlargement at $1.5 billion for land acquisition alone made it unquestionably the most expensive national park to date.[99] The dwindling opportunity for new natural parks would encourage Hartzog and others within the Park Service to cast a wistful eye toward the vast Alaskan domain.

Three other national parks—Canyonlands, Guadalupe Mountains, and Voyageurs—entered the system with less controversy. Additionally, three national monuments having significant geological features were added—Agate Fossil Beds in Nebraska, Fossil Butte in Wyoming, and Florissant Fossil Beds in Colorado.

As he experimented with different management options, Hartzog helped create a new type of park called a scientific reserve. Authorized in 1964, Ice Age National Scientific Reserve was the result of a cooperative agreement between the Park Service and the state of Wisconsin. Prior to its authorization, Wisconsin had approached the Park Service to take over the area largely because the state lacked funds to complete land purchases. Hartzog sent a study team and visited the area personally but decided the state could adequately manage it. Under a new agreement, therefore, the Park Service would help develop a management plan, set standards of operation, and provide financial assistance, but the state would retain ownership and management. This kind of arrangement in Hartzog's view would protect the resource and save the federal government a lot of money and manpower, but after his departure no significant movement toward establishing other such joint ventures ever materialized.[100]

Joint management arrangements were encouraged, but they often fell short of the ideal. While public ownership presented the least problematic way to manage parklands, escalating costs forced Hartzog to explore other possibilities. Some ideas included "less-than-fee" options, which placed restrictions on development activities but did not give the federal government complete ownership, and scenic easement agreements, which protected scenic views along rivers, parkways, and seashores. As one example, Grant-Kohrs Ranch National Historic Site in Montana originally included 216 acres owned outright by the federal government with five times that much in less-than-fee agreement.[101]

Although alternative arrangements stretched limited dollars, both agency personnel and landowners often resisted. The Park Service frequently paid close to full fee for land but lacked full management powers. Park staff found policing these quasi parklands difficult and time consuming. Until a conflict arose, frustrated landowners often did not understand the full implications of the agreements they signed. As a result, park planners and budget officers tended to favor the new arrangements, while administrators and managers did not.[102]

Another means Hartzog employed to expand Park Service influence beyond park boundaries was the natural landmarks program. He inherited this program when he came into office. Established in 1962 under authority of the Historic Sites Act of 1935, it was modeled after the successful national historic landmark program, administratively created in 1960 to recognize places of national significance identified under the mandate of the Historic Sites Act of 1935. That act contained no hint of authority for a natural landmarks program, but Congress did not challenge it and, on the contrary, provided funding. Still, when it was finally described in detail in the Code of Federal Regulations, the authority named was the Historic Sites Act of 1935.

Despite its questionable legislative foundation, the natural landmarks program proved successful. By 1999, natural landmarks totaled 587 in forty-eight states, three territories, and Puerto Rico. A prospective natural landmark qualified as nationally significant if it was "one of the best examples of a type of biotic community or geologic feature in its physiographic province." Like historic landmarks, the secretary of the interior declared natural landmarks on public and private land with the hope that the designation would benefit from the protective measures conferred on historic landmarks by the National Historic Preservation Act of 1966 but relied on the owner to keep its resources inviolate. Although historic and natural landmarks are not units of the National Park System, and in fact are designated as a means of securing protection that does not entail federal acquisition, both historic and natural landmarks extended the reach of the Park Service. They also enhanced the agency's role as preserver of significant and representative areas.[103]

At the beginning of Hartzog's directorate, the National Park System had only sixteen areas with a heavy emphasis on recreation. Of these, five were parkways, five reservoirs, four seashores, and two recreation demonstration areas. Many in the Park Service felt uncomfortable with recreation areas, particularly those associated with man-made reservoirs. However, post–World War II prosperity combined with individuals' willingness to assume personal debt and reconnect with nature fueled an explosion in outdoor recreation. A greater number of three-day weekends, courtesy of new national holidays, provided opportunities for more intensive outdoor experiences, while the rapidly improving highway system shortened travel time. The growth of the airline industry also made it easier for people to connect to distant parks. Sales of boats, campers, motor homes, second homes, and recreational vehicles like motorcycles and all-terrain-vehicles likewise grew. By the time Hartzog came to office, the need for more outdoor recreation lands and facilities had approached "crisis proportions."[104]

Hartzog responded by adding twenty-five recreation areas—more than a 150 percent increase. To meet the country's obsession with water-based activities, the Park Service made special efforts to add seashores, lakeshores, and reservoir-based recreation areas. Additionally, the Wild and Scenic Rivers Act of 1968 led to a new system of protected riverways, while the National Trails System Act of 1968 designated new linear corridors that further diversified the park system.

During the 1960s, seashore development had continued unabated, leaving Hartzog fewer and fewer options for water-based parks. Prior to 1964, only Cape Hatteras in North Carolina (1937), Cape Cod in Massachusetts (1961), Point Reyes in California (1962), and Padre Island in Texas (1962) had been established. Using funds donated by the philanthropic Mellon family, the Park Service had previously identified and studied potential additions. Working from the list, Hartzog managed to gain five national seashores. Some even talked about a system of national seashores as a special category of the system.

Although a 1963 Recreation Advisory Board (consisting of cabinet-level officials from Interior, Agriculture, Defense, Commerce, Health, Education, and Welfare) stated that recreation areas "should be designed and located to achieve a comparatively high recreation carrying capacity," most within the Park Service emphasized natural resource protection over visitor use.[105] Pressures from environmental groups and park neighbors thwarted most efforts to enhance greater access. Since Park Service planners were more comfortable with resource management and protection roles than with mass recreation, they readily adjusted their park plans to satisfy vocal groups.

A classic example is Fire Island, Hartzog's first national seashore, authorized in September 1964. Fire Island legislation specified that the park provide accessible recreational opportunities that would benefit citizens from the heavily populated New York City area, which lay only 20 miles from the park's northern border. The legislation also instructed the Park Service to administer the area with the "primary aim of conserving the natural resources located there."[106] Any thoughts of providing easily accessible recreation for inhabitants of New York City quickly gave way to moves to protect the environment. The island's eventual development was good for the local inhabitants, who wanted the benefits of controlled tourism but not the headaches of too many visitors. Park designation protected large stretches of beach from future development while still allowing the towns to build and operate hotels, bars, and other businesses for tourists and local residents. In the first decade after Fire Island's designation, private development on the island increased 31 percent, most of which the Park Service had little control over.[107]

Assateague Island, a 35-mile barrier island along the Maryland and Virginia coasts, became Hartzog's next national seashore in 1965. Assateague had been targeted as a potential national seashore, but the development activities of a real estate promoter had made land prices exorbitantly high. Fortunately for the Park Service, a tropical storm destroyed homes and roads, changed the shoreline, and flooded parts of the island. This made sewage disposal risky and revived chances for national protection but not without compromises. The Maryland congressional delegation insisted that a controversial highway be rebuilt along the length of the island linking two access bridges. After heated debate and strong environmental pressures, these plans would be scrapped in 1976.[108] In order to help compensate for tax revenues lost from private holdings, a 600-acre site was set aside for commercial development.

Other concessions resulted in a three-way management agreement whereby the Fish and Wildlife Service would manage Chincoteague National Wildlife Refuge, the state of Maryland would oversee Assateague State Park, and the Park Service would be responsible for Assateague Island National Seashore. The famous Assateague Island ponies, on the Maryland side, were managed by the Park Service, while the Chincoteague Fire Company managed the Virginia herd and organized the well-known yearly pony penning event.[109] Although the arrangement almost guaranteed problems, Hartzog said saving the resource was the most important thing and that "time would straighten out the administration."[110] He recalled one property owner complaining bitterly that the Park Service would not compensate him for his property. Hartzog responded to the man, whose beach-front home lay largely submerged, by saying that "as soon as I can occupy the premises I'd be happy to pay, but until I do I'm putting one dollar in court and filing a declaration of taking, and that's how we got the front beach."[111]

Authorized in 1966, Cape Lookout consisted of three barrier islands with 56 miles of beaches that lay to the southwest of Cape Hatteras National Seashore. Since no bridges connected Cape Lookout to the mainland, access remained limited, the only means of getting to it being the public ferry or private boats. In 1971, Hartzog masterminded the addition of Gulf Islands, which included a chain of barrier islands off the coast of Florida, Alabama, and Mississippi, in addition to mainland areas in Perdido Key and the Naval Live Oaks Reservation.[112]

Cumberland Island became the last national seashore added during Hartzog's tenure. It was also one of the Park System's most pristine. Steel magnate Andrew Carnegie had kept the island largely free of development, but some of his heirs had sold their inheritance to a developer. Hartzog had been exploring options to save the island but could not seem to get anything going. Unbeknownst to him, Paul Mellon's personal lawyer, Stoddard Stevens, had become enthralled with Cumberland Island after visiting friends on an adjacent island. He convinced his boss to buy most of the island and give it to the Park Service. They unveiled their plans to Hartzog during a private luncheon at the Mellons' on March 17, 1970, which happened to be Hartzog's fiftieth birthday. According to their agreement, Hartzog would have a land acquisition officer negotiate for various properties, and Mellon would give final approval. Lands would be held by the congressionally chartered National Park Foundation, a nonprofit partner of the Park Service that could accept such gifts until such time that Congress enacted legislation. Mellon bought most parcels recommended to him, but he rejected one that was overpriced. At a New York meeting, he quipped, "George, you can always spend money."[113]

Protected in such a way as to preserve its primitive characteristics, Cumberland Island maintains few facilities, limits the number of daily visitors, and is reachable only by boat. Additions such as Cumberland Island protected invaluable islands and beaches from uncontrolled growth, but provided limited relief for the large numbers of people seeking seashore access.

To protect disappearing lakeshores and provide additional areas for water-based recreation, Hartzog added a new lakeshore category to the

National Park System. Between 1966 and 1970, four national lakeshores in the Great Lakes area entered the system. Pictured Rocks, the system's first lakeshore, hugged Michigan's Lake Superior shoreline for more than 40 miles but only extended 5 miles inland. Authorized in 1966, the park protected unique sandstone cliffs, beaches, sand dunes, and northern forestland.

Apostle Islands, along Lake Superior's Wisconsin shoreline, was finally established in 1970 after ten years of legislative wrangling. Located within 250 miles of Minneapolis and St. Paul, it protected twenty of the twenty-four Apostle Islands. The park had become a pet project of Senator Gaylord Nelson, former governor of Wisconsin and one of the chief founders of the country's first Earth Day. Nelson and other environmentalists had pushed to set the areas aside before its timber could be harvested and more summer homes built. Although original plans included Indian lands, the Chippewa tribe successfully fought efforts to make lands within Red Cliff Reservation part of the national lakeshore. Hartzog later explained that his "argument was not so much with the Indians but with the white brothers who are advising them and exploiting them. . . . The speculators and promoters were what hurt the Apostle Islands project and caused all the trouble over Indians lands. . . . The Park Service had little to do with the proposal itself." Hartzog looked at the mainland reservation lands as an important component of the park, but in the end he was willing to "take what you get."[114]

Indiana Dunes on the southern shore of Lake Michigan and Sleeping Bear Dunes along Lake Michigan's upper portion also entered the system during Hartzog's tenure. Ironically, Indiana Dunes was one of the first parks Stephen Mather proposed when he became the Park Service's first director, but the measure failed. Some fifty years later Hartzog would testify on the park's behalf, this time with success but not without some strategic maneuvering.[115]

In the 1960s, steel companies on the shores of Lake Michigan wanted to enlarge the harbor to accommodate their ships. Senator Paul Douglas of Illinois opposed this plan on account of the environmental damage it would cause. Hartzog recalled how he and the dignified senator, fresh from a meeting, had taken off their socks and shoes and proceeded to roll up their business suits so they could hike to the top of the dunes. There, Hartzog recalled his companion making an impassioned statement:

> When I was thirty-eight years old, I volunteered for the Marine Corps to save the world, and . . . I came back to Chicago from the war and I did not save the world, so I ran for alderman Southside

Chicago. I decided if I couldn't save the world I would save Chicago. And you know this was during the Daley administration with a crook going to jail every morning, . . . and I did not save Chicago. I ran for the Senate and I'm in my last term and I want to tell you I'll be damned if I'm not going to save Indiana Dunes.[116]

As a member of the Public Works Committee, Douglas could stop the Corps of Engineers from enlarging the harbor to the detriment of the proposed park.

Hartzog's other great challenge was how to stop Inland Steel from building a new plant that was slated to lie adjacent to the proposed lakeshore park. According to Hartzog, he and Phil Stewart, his Washington office chief of land acquisition, hatched an idea to buy the land that would be necessary for constructing the railroad that would provide access to the new plant. As Hartzog told it:

> The night that the bill was signed I said to Phil Stewart "I want you to put the best people you've got in Indiana tomorrow morning, and I want that connection cut from the highway to the lake." And away we went and the railroad is there, Inland Steel is there, and the Park Service is there buying land like crazy. Phil Stewart called me after midnight and he said, "We got it!" And I said "Tell me about it." He said, "We all wound up at this country store. This old man had the last piece that either let the railroad through or cut them off. And we are there with our contracts and blank numbers. And he said, 'I think you're all a bunch of sons of bitches, and I don't want to do business with any of you, but if I gotta do business, I'm gonna do business with the Park Service.'" And he signed our option.[117]

Soon after, Hartzog got a call from thwarted Inland Steel about the sale of their lakeshore property for the Indiana Dunes National Lakeshore. The Park Service's "quick footwork" had turned the tide.[118]

Before the Hartzog directorate, the Park Service had managed five reservoir areas: Lake Mead (1936) in Nevada, Coulee Dam (1946) in Washington, Shadow Mountain (1952) in Colorado, Glen Canyon (1958) in Arizona, and Whiskeytown-Shasta-Trinity (1962) in California.[119] By the end of his directorate, eight more reservoir-based recreation areas were added. Managing reservoir lands was seldom warmly embraced by those within the Park Service, who objected to flooding natural environments. But even Hartzog had trouble resisting some additions. "If we were going to get them, sometimes we were for them."[120]

Authorized in 1965, Delaware Water Gap National Recreation Area in Pennsylvania included the proposed Tocks Island Reservoir. Strong objections based on a dam's adverse environmental impacts to the Delaware River basin forced Congress to transfer management of the area to the Park Service and designate its waterway as a wild and scenic river, which precluded any future impoundments.[121] In 1968, Ross Lake and Lake Chelan national recreation areas in Washington were established to provide water-based recreation and to help safeguard North Cascades National Park by concentrating intensive use outside the national park boundaries.

Four other reservoir areas were run by cooperative management agreements with other agencies. Initially, several were called "recreation areas" to distinguish them from Park Service properties, but later they all became national recreation areas. Amistad National Recreation Area in Texas provided recreation opportunities on the U.S. side of the Amistad Lake, an international reservoir along the Rio Grande. The Park Service entered into cooperative agreements with Bureau of Reclamation for three other areas: Arbuckle in Oklahoma, Sanford (later renamed Lake Meredith) in Texas, and Bighorn Canyon in Montana and Wyoming.

※

With poetic justice, Ozark National Scenic Riverways became the country's first national scenic river and the first park bill passed under the Hartzog directorate. (It was there that Hartzog first met Stewart Udall, making a lasting impression on him.) When he was superintendent at Jefferson National Expansion Memorial in St. Louis, he had traveled many miles back and forth across Missouri serving as the contact or key man for the proposed Ozark area. The Park Service sought to protect portions of three rivers—Jack's Fork, Current, and Eleven Point—in a national monument but local opposition had stalled the project. Hartzog's mission was to move the project forward. Aided by his love of fishing, his people skills, and rural roots, he could deal with what he described as the "creative, insular, and suspicious" Ozark locals who feared hunting bans typical of national park units. Residents also feared national park status would harm the local economy instead of bolster it.

After a year, Hartzog realized the original proposal would never fly, so he explored alternatives with a group of interested locals. They determined that it needed a local organization to "disseminate information, monitor opposition meetings, challenge their misinformation, and arrange for speaking opportunities."[122] Over time, the resulting Ozarks Natural History Association helped gain support for the park proposal and helped Hartzog overcome a lot of local opposition by negotiating compromises on the hunting issue. Secretary Udall's 1962 visit also boosted local and political support. According to Udall, Hartzog "knew all the arguments, all the facts" and had already conceived of how to turn the river into a new type of park. His understanding of the area's people also gave Udall insights into how to "play my cards to disarm the anti-biases of the 'hillbillies' who lived along these rivers."[123]

Finally authorized in August 1964, the Ozarks included 140 miles of free-flowing waters along the Current and Jack's Fork but excluded the Eleven Point River, which the Forest Service fought hard to retain. Hartzog had been instrumental in crafting a new type of park that foreshadowed the forthcoming wild and scenic rivers legislation.

In 1965, Stewart Udall convinced President Johnson of the need for a new wild rivers bill as a companion piece to the 1964 Wilderness Act. The Wild Rivers Bill, as it was initially known, would slow the rapid rate at which the country's rivers were being dammed, diked, diverted, and degraded with pollutants. According to Udall, Wayne Aspinall, chair of the House Interior and Insular Affairs Committee, balked at considering such a ridiculous notion as legislating protection for free flowing rivers and for three years refused to consider any bills even though they had the president's endorsement. Finally Aspinall's objections faded under a strong Senate bill, the support of House minority leader John Saylor, the president's continued high placement of the bill, and vocal public support.[124] On October 2, 1968, President Johnson signed the Wild and Scenic Rivers Act, protecting a new system of free-flowing rivers to be managed by the Park Service, Forest Service, Bureau of Land Management, Fish and Wildlife Service, and other state and Native American concerns.

Wild and scenic rivers could be designated by Congress or the secretary of the interior with approval from the governor of any state involved. Unlike wilderness designation, the wild and scenic rivers bill protected rivers from being dammed or impounded and improved their water quality, but it did not give the federal government complete control over development along their banks. In particular, the federal government was limited in its ability to interfere if the development was not deemed damaging to the resource's values.[125]

The original act included eight river segments in nine states and called for the study of twenty-seven others. Only one of the original eight, St. Croix in

Wisconsin, fell under National Park Service management.[126] In March 1972, Buffalo National River followed despite the protests of private landowners, who disliked government interference, and the Corps of Engineers, which wanted to construct flood-control dams along the river. Several months later, the Lower St. Croix National Scenic Riverway in Minnesota was added.

On the same October day in 1968 that President Johnson signed the Wild and Scenic Rivers Act, he signed the National Trails System Act. This encouraged the addition of scenic trails, especially in areas accessible to urban populations. Only Congress could designate national scenic or historic trails, while the secretaries of interior and agriculture could establish national recreation trails or connecting trails with the consent of the state and any administering agencies involved. Of the four kinds of trails, recreational trails became the most numerous.

The trails act immediately added Appalachian National Scenic Trail, administered by the Park Service, and Pacific Crest Trail, managed by the Forest Service. Appalachian National Scenic Trail originated in 1921 as the vision of forester and philosopher Benton MacKaye and opened in 1937 after being built largely by volunteers. It ran from Springer Mountain, Georgia, to Mount Katahdin, Maine, passing through a total of fourteen states. Serious studies of other trails, such as the Continental Divide, North Country, and Oregon Trail, began during Hartzog's tenure but were not added until later.[127]

☙

In August 1972, Congress authorized the John D. Rockefeller Jr. Memorial Parkway, the last national parkway and the only one in the West. Intended to commemorate Rockefeller's generous philanthropy, the 82-mile parkway connected the south boundary of Yellowstone with the northern boundary of Grand Teton, traversing the intervening national forest. Over the years, John D. Rockefeller and his foundations had purchased considerable lands in Great Smoky Mountains, Acadia, Shenandoah, and Grand Teton national parks and had financed museums in a number of other parks. His son Laurance carried on the tradition by chairing the Outdoor Recreation Resources Review Commission of 1958 and donating land for the Virgin Islands National Park. During Hartzog's directorate, Rockefeller financed Hartzog's show-me tours, gave a $1 million grant for environmental education curriculum development and programs, supplied "seed money" for the newly created National Park Foundation, which accepts gifts for the benefit of the park system, and provided financial support for National Recreation and Park Association, founded in 1965.[128] After Hartzog left the Park Service, he kept his connection with Laurance Rockefeller by doing both paid and volunteer legal work for various Rockefeller endeavors.

With the authorization of Wolf Trap Farm for the Performing Arts on October 15, 1966, the Park Service moved into a completely new type of park. Wolf Trap was the brainchild of Catherine Filene Shouse, a department store heiress and patron of the arts, who donated the land and provided funding for a performing arts facility on the outskirts of Washington, D.C. Despite construction problems and Shouse's heavy-handed involvement, the center hosted its inaugural summer series in 1971. Hartzog and others hoped the new park would become a prototype of a new system of cultural parks, but that never happened even though the Park Service assumed temporary custody of the John F. Kennedy Center for the Performing Arts in 1972.[129] Congress later turned the Kennedy Center over to a board of trustees, and Wolf Trap remains the only site set aside exclusively for the performing arts. Other areas, such as Chamizal National Memorial in El Paso and the restored Ford's Theatre in Washington, D.C., accommodate performing groups, but both have historically significant resources, which Wolf Trap does not. Wolf Trap, a stretch for the Park Service, did not fit neatly into its natural, historical, and recreational classification scheme. Hartzog supported the park's inclusion because it was available and had the potential to begin expansion in a new direction.

Hartzog repeatedly stretched the Park Service in different directions to test the waters. Designating an area with such labels as "demonstration area," "prototype," "scientific reserve," or "affiliated area," or some other nebulous title, he could watch how the area played with Congress and the public and determine how best to proceed, if at all. His final two additions of Gateway and Golden Gate national recreation areas were just such experiments intended to entrench the Park Service in the urban recreation business.

❧

While George Hartzog packaged his park expansion efforts as a rounding out of the national park system, he knew the system would continue to grow long after he was director. The thematic framework for natural and historical areas and other tactics were merely tools he cleverly used to help expand the park system and set aside areas that might otherwise be lost to development. As an expansionist, Hartzog took all the parklands that he could somehow justify or that an influential congressman made it difficult to refuse.

Part of the credit for park expansion needs to rest with the optimal conditions present during the Hartzog administration. The nation increasingly valued preserving its natural, cultural, and historical heritage and sought more parks for its outdoor enjoyment. A strongly Democratic Congress willingly passed park legislation while the Johnson administration encouraged federal agencies to seek solutions to national problems. Secretary of the Interior Stewart Udall allowed the director a great deal of latitude in running the Park Service and actively encouraged park additions. The Land and Water Conservation Fund provided a source of funding that proved especially important for recreation areas near population centers.

Under such conditions even a commonplace director might have presided over moderate park growth simply because the people wanted it and a responsive Congress would have given it to them. Since no one would call George Hartzog commonplace, much credit for extent of park expansion rests with him and his staff. Even his strongest detractors had to admire his talents and the fact that he managed to get things done.

Cajoling park proposals through the appropriate channels was a job at which George Hartzog excelled. As a farmer's son, he acquired a reverence and respect for the land. He also suffered the pain of having that land taken away during the Depression. He grew up with the barter system, so he was comfortable with the horse trading and the compromises inherent in the legislative process. His background in the ministry, law, politics, and business served him well. With each proposed park addition, Hartzog seemingly ascended to the pulpit to preach about the park's many merits, trying like a minister to sway the congregation to his view. His law background gave him an appreciation for good research and made him comfortable with the legal lingo of park legislation. His law training also allowed him not to be intimated by the threat of lawsuits. They "never bothered me," he said, "because a lot of people were suing me all the time." Hartzog said he had a "whole sixth floor of guys in the Interior Department that don't have a damn thing to do except go to court and represent me," so he refused to cower as some might have.[130]

Unlike many of his predecessors, Hartzog loved the political aspects of the directorate and could comfortably and effectively hobnob with key Washington politicians. As director, he focused on legislation and appropriations. He made it his business to befriend influential congressmen, particularly those with power over park legislation and funding, such as Alan Bible, Wayne Aspinall, Julia Butler Hansen, Henry "Scoop" Jackson, and Warren Magnuson. Hartzog knew where his support lay and what the grounds were of any given objection to a proposed park. Additionally, he possessed an uncommon flair for testifying before congressional committees, which helped move park legislation along.

While Hartzog's record for park additions is impressive by any standards, one of his greatest contributions to park expansion materialized after his directorate with the additions in Alaska. Much of the credit here has to go to his early groundbreaking efforts.

In addition to expanding park numbers, Hartzog broadened the idea of what should be included in the National Park System. Urban recreation areas, national lakeshores, national trails, wild and scenic rivers, scientific reserves, and cultural areas like Wolf Trap Farm for the Performing Arts put a vivid new stamp on the system. While the park system had naturally evolved over the years before Hartzog became director, he aggressively moved it in new directions that expanded the Park Service's role in protecting the country's resources and added to the agency's political support.

Hartzog developed a bold vision for the Park Service and Park System, but many of his ideas never fully materialized. Proposed additions in Alaska dragged on for years and proved to be a bittersweet victory for Hartzog, who had wanted more Park Service land. Joint management of some Native tribal lands in the continental United States would come years later, but suspicious tribes never relinquished much control. Hartzog never acquired desirable military properties, many of which were little used but nicely situated to protect coastlines, river passages, and cities. Wresting them away from the military proved difficult even for Hartzog. He had wanted more seashores, lakeshores, cultural parks, and urban recreation areas.

Hartzog also wanted to add parks "to memorialize the creative achievements of the people who came here" and began the effort with Saugus Iron Works and Wolf Trap Farm. He wanted a park to commemorate the nation's medical achievements and had searched the Boston area for one. He supported an Agricultural Hall of Fame National Cultural Park, a park that celebrated the labor movement, and areas that highlighted the accomplishments of ethnic groups and the women's movement.[131] Had he remained director, there is little doubt his empire would have continued to grow and expand.

While we can only speculate about the parks George Hartzog might have added, his legacy is astonishing:

1964 (ten areas)
Ozark National Scenic Riverways (Missouri)
Fort Bowie National Historic Site (Arizona)

Saint-Gaudens National Historic Site (New Hampshire)
Johnstown Flood National Memorial (Pennsylvania)
Allegheny Portage Railroad National Historic Site (Pennsylvania)
John Muir National Historic Site (California)
Fort Larned National Historic Site (Kansas)
Fire Island National Seashore (New York)
Canyonlands National Park (Utah)
Bighorn Canyon National Recreation Area (Wyoming, Montana)

1965 (fourteen areas)
Arbuckle Recreation Area (Oklahoma)
Curecanti National Recreation Area (Colorado)
Sanford National Recreation Area (later Lake Meredith) (Texas)
Nez Perce National Historical Park (Washington, Idaho, Montana,
    and Oregon)
Agate Fossil Beds National Monument (Nebraska)
Pecos National Monument (New Mexico)
Golden Spike National Historic Site (Utah)
Herbert Hoover National Historic Site (Iowa)
Hubbell Trading Post National Historic Site (Arizona)
Alibates Flint Quarries National Monument (Texas)
Delaware Water Gap National Recreation Area (Pennsylvania,
    New Jersey)
Assateague Island National Seashore (Maryland, Virginia)
Roger Williams National Memorial (Rhode Island)
Amistad National Recreation Area (Texas)

1966 (ten areas)
Cape Lookout National Seashore (North Carolina)
Fort Union Trading Post National Historic Site (North Dakota)
Chamizal National Memorial (Texas)
George Rogers Clark National Historical Park (Indiana)
San Juan Island National Historical Park (Washington)
Guadalupe Mountains National Park (Texas)
Pictured Rock National Lakeshore (Michigan)
Wolf Trap Farm for the Performing Arts (Virginia)
Ansley Wilcox House National Historic Site (later Theodore Roosevelt
    Inaugural National Historic Site) (New York)
Indiana Dunes National Lakeshore (Indiana)

1967 (two areas)
John Fitzgerald Kennedy National Historic Site (Massachusetts)
Eisenhower National Historic Site (Pennsylvania)

1968 (ten areas)
National Visitor Center (D.C.)
Saugus Iron Works National Historic Site (Massachusetts)
Appalachian National Scenic Trail (Georgia to Maine)
Lake Chelan National Recreation Area (Washington)
Ross Lake National Recreation Area (Washington)
North Cascades National Park (Washington)
Redwood National Park (California)
St. Croix National Scenic Riverway (Minnesota / Wisconsin)
Carl Sandburg Home National Historic Site (North Carolina)
Biscayne National Monument (Florida)

1969 (four areas)
Marble Canyon National Monument (Arizona)
Florissant Fossil Beds National Monument (Colorado)
Lyndon B. Johnson National Historical Park (Texas)
William Howard Taft National Historic Site (Ohio)

1970 (four areas)
Apostle Islands National Lakeshore (Wisconsin)
Andersonville National Historic Site (Georgia)
Fort Point National Historic Site (California)
Sleeping Bear Dunes National Lakeshore (Michigan)

1971 (five areas)
Chesapeake and Ohio Canal National Historic Site (Maryland)
Voyageurs National Park (Minnesota)
Gulf Islands National Seashore (Florida, Louisiana, Mississippi, Alabama)
Buffalo National River (Arkansas)
Lincoln Home National Historic Site (Illinois)

1972 (thirteen areas)
John F. Kennedy Center for the Performing Arts (D.C.)
Pu'ukohola Heiau National Historic Site (Hawaii)
Grant-Kohrs Ranch National Historic Site (Montana)

John D. Rockefeller Jr. Memorial Parkway (Wyoming)
Longfellow National Historic Site (Massachusetts)
Thaddeus Kosciuszko National Monument (Pennsylvania)
Mar-A-Lago National Historic Site (Florida)
Hohokam Pima National Monument (Arizona)
Fossil Butte National Monument (Wyoming)
Cumberland Island National Seashore (Georgia)
Lower St. Croix National Scenic Riverway (Minnesota, Wyoming)
Golden Gate National Recreation Area (California)
Gateway National Recreation Area (New York and New Jersey)

During a period of unparalleled park growth, Hartzog oversaw the addition of seventy-two parks in just under nine years for an average of eight a year.[132] Today that remains his most lasting legacy.

CHAPTER EIGHT

Alaska, the Last Park Frontier

"I hope that the Alaska bug bites you—and I don't mean mosquitoes," wrote Doris Leonard to George Hartzog in June 1965 prior to his first visit. "There is something about that place that haunts one," the enthusiastic conservationist and wife of a former Sierra Club president professed. "You have a great responsibility and tremendous opportunity to capture and protect whatever that haunting quality is."[1] In August 1965, Hartzog traveled to Alaska and experienced for himself a landscape that evoked such passion. "Once I was introduced to Alaska," he said, "I was obsessed with saving the best of that."[2]

As Hartzog ascended to the directorate, long ignored Alaskan land issues were being forced to the forefront. Land selections that were permitted to the new state by the Alaska Statehood Act of 1958 increasingly conflicted with Native land claims.[3] Land managing agencies like the National Park Service, environmental organizations, and some in Congress turned evermore wistful gazes toward Alaska. They began arguing that Alaska possessed resources of national significance and therefore needed federal protection. The discovery of valuable oil reserves on the Arctic coastal plain provided the catalyst that would speed the growing controversy over land ownership toward eventual resolution in Congress but not without a lengthy and impassioned battle.

What would unfold in Alaska was without precedent. While George Hartzog was but one of a number of key players in this process, his role was critical. As the director of a preservation agency, he was on the leading edge of a national movement to federally protect the state's unspoiled resources. Early in his directorate, he had recognized that Alaska held immense promise and was "ripe for the taking."[4] He grasped the potential, but he was savvy enough to realize he needed to move cautiously lest he anger Alaskans and the leadership in other federal agencies.

Initial Park Service studies of Alaskan lands, which had begun in the 1920s and 1930s, laid important groundwork but lacked sufficient support to yield park additions. President Lyndon Johnson stopped just short of leaving the country an Alaskan legacy before he left office. The crucial turning point would come when Hartzog persuaded a key member of Congress to sponsor a critical amendment to the 1971 Alaska Native Claims Settlement Act. This amendment opened the door to what would become an unrivaled but hotly contested conservation legacy. For Hartzog, the quest for Alaska parks alternated between elation and frustration.

Hartzog and those associated with Alaska labored hard to save significant resources before they were lost. They had vowed not to repeat mistakes made with previous parks in the lower forty-eight states. Past additions, once buffered by large expanses of unsettled lands, had become wilderness islands, as development pressed in from all sides. Resulting problems, such as those encountered in Florida's Everglades National Park, where the park's lifeblood of water lay outside its boundaries, left park managers facing resource management and protection nightmares. With Alaska, an immense area well over twice the size of Texas, they believed they had an unparalleled opportunity to protect entire ecosystems and do things right the first time.

※

Many called Alaska the last unsettled frontier, but hardy souls had occupied its harsh lands as early as 6000 BC. Eskimos lived mostly along the northern and western coasts and in pockets of the interior. Aleuts occupied the Aleutian Islands. Hugging the more moderate shorelines of southeast Alaska were coastal Indians, largely Tlingits and Haidas, while Athabascans occupied the interior. Over the years, Native peoples had established their own territories and subsistence patterns that later served as the basis for their land claims.

Around 1741, Russians sailed to Alaska and quickly began exploiting the natural resources and spreading devastating diseases. After more than a century, troubles at home and a dwindling fur supply led Russia in 1867 to sell her claims in Alaska to the United States for $7 million.[5] After purchasing "Seward's Folly," the United States did little to assimilate Alaska and its inhabitants into the rest of the country. Communication difficulties, inhospitable climate, and distance proved significant obstacles. Nevertheless, enterprising Americans found ways to use Alaska's rich natural resources. They picked up whaling where the Russians left off and opened up salmon-processing canneries at seaports.[6] Discoveries of gold from the 1860s to early 1900s brought prospectors seeking instant wealth and opened American eyes to the land's potential.

Shortly after the turn of the century, concerns about Alaska's exploited resources grew. The federal government responded by withdrawing millions of acres for conservation purposes but paid scant attention to Native communities. In 1902, the first elements of what became the 16-million-acre Tongass National Forest in southeastern Alaska was set aside, followed in 1907 by the 4.9-million-acre Chugach National Forest. Between 1909 and 1912, five wildlife refuges were protected. In 1910, Sitka National Monument, which protected sacred totems and the Russian-Tlingit battlegrounds, was established by proclamation and became Alaska's first national park unit.

On February 26, 1917, those who advocated for a national park for the wilderness expanse in Mount McKinley finally overcame stiff resistance to the idea in Congress. The 1.4-million-acre park, Alaska's first "national" park, protected an abundance of wildlife and included Mount McKinley, the highest mountain on the North American continent.[7] After their experience with McKinley, the Park Service hesitated to advance legislation for Katmai, which showed the effects of a violent 1912 volcanic eruption, but in 1918, President Woodrow Wilson was persuaded to bypass congressional approval by proclaiming Katmai a national monument.[8]

As the federal government withdrew more lands from the public domain, opposition from independent-minded Alaskans grew. In a terse 1918 letter to Stephen Mather, Alaska's territorial governor Thomas Riggs wrote, "I cannot help but feel that the withdrawal of land embraced in this monument [Katmai] was ill advised, owing to the intense feeling which is aroused in Alaska through additional withdrawals."[9] Alaskans resented the distant federal government imposing laws and making decisions regarding "their" lands, and these feelings would only intensify in the time leading up to the Hartzog directorate. Many Alaskans had trouble understanding why such large desolate stretches needed protection in the first place, or how the government could justify restricting millions of acres when they might be needed for Alaska's future growth and development.

Despite opposition, the federal government withdrew more public domain lands in 1923, when it created the 23-million-acre Naval Petroleum

Reserve in the Arctic. Two years later, President Calvin Coolidge proclaimed Glacier Bay a national monument.[10] Although the Alaska park units now comprised more than 40 percent of the Park Service's total acreage, they received limited manpower and money. As the infant Park Service struggled to staff and fund all its parks, Alaska sites consistently received less than others. Fortunately, Alaska's remoteness and few inhabitants spared the parks serious damage, but the lack of oversight would make future enforcement of Park Service policies more difficult and controversial.

World War II pushed Alaska into the American consciousness. The Japanese attack on Pearl Harbor in 1941 dramatized the strategic location of Alaska and the need for better connections with the "lower forty-eight."[11] Congress authorized the construction of the 1,523-mile Alaskan Highway from Dawson Creek, British Columbia, through the Yukon Territory to Fairbanks, Alaska. In just over eight grueling months of work, the Army Corps of Engineers, working in cooperation with Canadian engineers, completed the rugged overland supply road to link the lower forty-eight with the Alaska Territory. The construction of military bases, airfields, ports, roads, and other infrastructure laid the essential foundation for postwar development.

After the war, the U.S. military pumped significant funds into the economy, and the territory's importance as an international air crossroads grew. Timber companies, the oil industry, fisheries, and mining companies continued to grow and draw additional workers. Many whites prospered, while Natives—who lived in isolated rural areas—struggled economically. Potential industries looked toward Alaska's natural resources with great interest. As white populations increased, conflicts with Native groups mounted over land ownership.[12] During this period, Alaska Natives repeatedly asked the government for protection from encroachment but were generally ignored. Meanwhile, convinced that benefits outweighed drawbacks, a broad array of Alaskans pushed for statehood.

On January 3, 1959, President Dwight D. Eisenhower signed the proclamation making Alaska the forty-ninth state, thereby increasing the nation's acreage by 20 percent. To lay a firm economic base, Congress granted the new state 104 million unappropriated acres of land, which amounted to roughly the size of California. Congress also gave Alaska a huge share of revenues from mineral leases on the public domain—a whopping 90 percent compared to 37.5 percent for most western states. At the time of statehood, federal land reserves totaled 92.4 million acres. Of that, 23 million acres were in the Naval Petroleum Reserve, another 27 million in power reserves, over

20 million in national forests, 7.8 million in national wildlife refuges, 6.9 million in national parks and monuments, and 4 million in Indian reservations. Federal reserves aside, roughly 271.8 million acres remained from which the state could select its share.[13]

While Native claims were discussed, few seemed willing to tackle the complex issue of state and Native land selections. With the statehood act, Congress reaffirmed its authority to settle it, but until that time, no lands were supposed to be disposed of where "the right or title" was held by Natives or held in trust for them.[14] What that meant remained unclear.

The statehood act gave Alaska twenty-five years to make its land selections, but the state proceeded slowly and cautiously because little was known about the vast lands and their economic potential. By late 1960s, during the Hartzog directorate, the state had chosen only 28 million acres, leaving almost 73 percent of its allotment unselected. In the early 1960s, Alaska Natives made up less than 20 percent of the state's population but formed a clear majority in many of the two hundred small, isolated communities. As the state began to explore rural land selections, inevitable conflicts arose.[15]

Realizing that their lands and lifestyle were in jeopardy, the unorganized and diverse Alaska Natives began to speak up for their rights. They established a newspaper, the *Tundra Times*, which first rolled off the presses in 1962, in an effort to organize and strengthen the Native populations. In 1966, the Alaska Federation of Natives emerged as a collective and politically powerful voice for Native positions. A showdown between Native, state, and national interests was inevitable.

Although slow to recognize Alaska's potential, the Park Service eventually joined the fray over Alaska lands. Since the addition of Glacier Bay in 1925, no new Alaska parks had been set aside. The Park Service had studied potential parklands, but none had gained enough support to move forward. Admiralty Island with its brown bears and Lake George, a self-dumping glacial lake northeast of Anchorage, were among those studied. Director Conrad Wirth reportedly said that Admiralty Island had been declined more times "than there are Alaskan brown bears."[16] Another area with park potential was the glacier-clad mountains of the Wrangell-St. Elias bordering Canada. Some envisioned a great international park, but negotiations over the years proved unsuccessful.

In 1950, George Collins, Pacific Northwest regional chief of recreation resource planning, oversaw an Alaska recreation survey team that spent several summers investigating and inventorying Alaska resources. The team quickly realized that, given how little was known about Alaska, they could contribute significantly to an understanding of the state's resources.

Using Mission 66 funding in 1960, Collins put Roger Allin, a long-time Fish and Wildlife employee who had transferred to the Park Service, in charge of developing a recreation plan for Alaska that would also look at resources worthy of federal, state, or local protection. Working with Allin was Theodor Swem, a park planner who would later play a critical role in the Alaska effort. Over the next several years, they looked at a number of areas, but in the resulting *Parks for America* publication (1964), Allin would conservatively suggest only two additions—the Wrangell-St. Elias Mountains (800,000 acres) and Lake Clark Pass (330,000 acres).[17] It would take the boldness of George Hartzog to broaden that vision.

※

Author John McPhee wrote that the federal government "used to watch over Alaska with one eye, and with so little interest that the lid was generally closed."[18] That lid fluttered opened during the Hartzog administration as the federal government was pushed to resolve the complex land claims. Under Hartzog, the National Park Service stepped up efforts begun in the Wirth administration. Alaska was a land of opportunity, and Hartzog was convinced his agency had done a poor job of embracing it.

Park planner and writer John Kauffmann, born into an influential newspaper publishing family, helped focus Hartzog's attention on Alaska. After a 1964 trip to assist in preparations for a Park Service film about Alaska parks called *Magnificence in Trust*, Kauffmann soundly criticized the Park Service for opportunities lost, lack of a coherent plan of action, and limited attention from Washington. He wrote that "after more than forty years as an organization, the Service is the Cheechako [Alaskan derogatory term for newcomer] of all federal agencies at work in Alaska."[19] In a letter to Hartzog, Kauffmann said that the National Park Service had a good team at Glacier Bay National Monument, but they "feel like stepchildren and are frankly wistful in their hope of getting more attention from Washington."

After assessing existing Alaska parks and making recommendations, such as providing enhanced facilities for visitors, Kauffmann went on to eloquently describe prospective park areas. Flying over the Wood-Tikchik and Merrill Pass-Lake Clark Pass areas in southwestern Alaska, he said "left us numb, speechless and emotionally drained." He urged swift action since summer cabins were creeping onto the edges of lakes along the area's southern edge. The Mount St. Elias and Mount Logan areas were "among the most awesome sites in Alaska (and neighboring Canada)." Its rugged remoteness, glacial features, and long common border made it a perfect candidate for an international scientific reserve. He urged Hartzog to see the areas for himself, adding that the staff at various park units would be "transported with joy if you were to visit them."[20]

Hartzog responded by appointing a task force in 1964 to evaluate existing studies, review park possibilities, and suggest future directions. The task force included Sigurd F. Olson, a member of the secretary of the interior's advisory board and chairman of the Wilderness Society; George Collins, the now retired National Park Service employee who had conducted the recreation survey in 1950s and had been coaxed back into service; Doris Leonard, environmental activist; Bob Luntey, landscape architect; and John Kauffmann, whom Hartzog described as a writer/editor.[21] In their Operation Great Land report, the task force described Alaska as a "complex land mass of amazing variety and beauty, . . . a land of permafrost, rain forests, arctic tundras, glaciers, mountains, and continental ice fields with violent extremes of temperature" that still retained its wilderness and frontier character. Despite this magnificence, few visited, and "unless immediate steps were taken neither Alaskans nor the rest of the country would support the Alaska program."

The report identified thirty-nine zones and sites across Alaska that contained significant natural, historical, or recreational resources but did not make specific recommendations regarding potential national park units.[22] The group did, however, recommend the development of a history program, the opening of an Alaska field office, and the exploration of cooperative land preservation efforts with Canada, the state of Alaska, and other federal agencies. Emphasizing its importance by underlining, the task force wrote: "There must be no question . . . that Alaska's scenery and the story . . . is worth a massive investment."[23]

Although Hartzog would later call Operation Great Land the cornerstone of all subsequent studies in Alaska, he decided not to circulate the report. In fact, Ted Swem, his assistant director in charge of new park areas, recalled Hartzog asking him to hide the few remaining copies under lock and key in Swem's desk. According to Swem, Hartzog did not want to ruffle the feathers of the Bureau of Sport Fisheries and Wildlife (later folded into the Fish and Wildlife Service), Forest Service, or Bureau of Land Management, under whose jurisdiction the thirty-nine identified areas intruded.[24] In a June 1965 memo to task force member Bob Luntey, Hartzog commended the group for their superb work but added that

I believe that if the Park Service proceeds on its own to take leadership, that action may be misconstrued and resented even though no usurpation of the prerogatives and the programs of other agencies would be intended. It is for this reason that I do not believe we should circulate this report, since it may be construed as a Service attempt to take over Alaska resource planning. What I think is called for in Alaska is a type of cooperative and coordinated planning that was represented on a smaller scale in our North Cascade study.

During his upcoming trip to Alaska, Hartzog believed that he would learn how best to proceed.[25]

While Hartzog did not circulate the 1965 report, he did follow up on many of the recommendations. In August 1965, he traveled to Alaska as suggested. Accompanying him was the secretary's advisory board on its annual field trip. Additionally, three members of the House Subcommittee on National Parks—Alaskan Ralph Rivers, the subcommittee chair; Roy Taylor of North Carolina, the ranking majority member; and Joe Skubitz of Kansas—joined the group. Traveling with Ralph Rivers allowed the group a more intimate look at the possible park areas. Through meetings he arranged with local government officials, the group could better gauge the feelings of Alaskans. Secretary of the Interior Stewart Udall joined the group for part of the trip, which helped heighten his interest.

Hartzog's first visit to Alaska left him awestruck. By rail, air, and automobile, the group traversed vast areas of the state, including zones identified by the Alaska task force. They watched as great blocks of ice at Glacier Bay "calved," sending up large plumes of water. They toured a gold mine, watched Native dancers, saw a play about the gold rush, and narrowly missed a confrontation with a Kodiak bear as they were fishing for salmon. To Hartzog, Alaska was indescribable. "It's different than anything that we had left in the lower forty-eight. You go there and you want it all because it is all so magnificent—the wildlife, the landscape."[26] He wrote, "This trip gave great encouragement and impetus to the work of the staff then being assembled in Alaska by Assistant Director Theodor Swem for our great push forward."[27]

Following up on other task force recommendations, Hartzog opened a field office in Anchorage in 1965. By May 1967, the Alaska Field Office included three permanent Park Service employees: a landscape architect, a biologist, and a secretary. Administratively, the unit fell under the direction of Mount McKinley's superintendent, who served as Alaska state coordinator and liaison with the state government and other federal agencies. A

Park Service reorganization two years later (1969) created the Seattle-based Pacific Northwest Regional Office, which assumed some responsibilities in the Alaska effort. A new San Francisco service center also assisted by developing master plans for existing Alaska parks. As the effort became more involved, and as more disparate groups gained responsibilities in the Alaska effort, territorial strife and disagreements arose.

In keeping with Hartzog's strategy to work cooperatively so as not to be seen as preempting other state and federal agencies, he met in 1967 with Alaskan governor Walter Hickel, a man who later became President Richard Nixon's first secretary of the interior. Hartzog briefed the governor about his current national park program in Alaska and tried to initiate some joint-planning ventures at Wood-Tikchik, Alatna-Kobuk, and Skagway. While cordial, Hickel showed an interest only in Skagway, an Alaskan frontier mining town that had served as a gateway to the Yukon Gold Rush of 1898. Several months later, Hartzog heard from Hickel's assistant, Carl MacMurray, who had traveled to Skagway and found locals interested in having the Park Service study the area. Hartzog followed up with a letter to Hickel about other areas of interest but received no response.[28]

Undeterred, the Park Service continued its Alaskan park studies. The agency started investigating potential additions to its National Natural Landmarks program, patterned after the successful National Historic Landmarks program. Natural landmark studies identified areas possessing the best examples of biological and geological features regardless of whether they were publicly or privately owned. These studies added to the growing body of knowledge about Alaskan lands that would later prove invaluable. By 1968, fifteen natural landmarks had been designated. Although natural landmarks identified significant resources that Hartzog hoped might one day be considered for a national park, landmark designation alone offered no legal protection.[29]

Meanwhile, Native land claims had continued to heat up in Alaska. As various groups studied state land-selection recommendations, the claims of Alaska Natives refused to go away. Finally, in 1966, Secretary Udall, who oversaw the Bureau of Indian Affairs, froze all lease sales, homesteading, and disposition of federal lands pending settlement of Native claims. Championing the Alaskan Native, according to Udall, resulted in a "head-on conflict with Governor Hickel of Alaska" and a "very bitter controversy."[30] Hickel branded Udall's actions as illegal and filed suit to allow state land transfers to continue. Later, the federal court upheld the rights of Alaska Natives to make land claims, and in January 1969, just before leaving office, Udall formalized the land freeze with Public Land Order 4582. The 1969 freeze prevented the immediate construction of an Alaska pipeline and preserved Native land rights until Congress could resolve the long-standing issues.

≹

Despite a number of attempts, efforts to protect new Alaska park units after Glacier Bay's addition in 1925 had failed. One notable near miss during Hartzog's tenure occurred in January 1969 just before President Lyndon B. Johnson left office. Secretary Udall tried to convince Johnson to set aside a package of national monuments, mostly in Alaska, as a parting Christmas gift to the American people. Udall had called Hartzog during the summer of 1968 and asked him to begin developing park proposals to present to the president. He had also sent Johnson a memorandum outlining how departing presidents had used their Antiquities Act powers to create monuments, thereby enlarging the National Park System.[31]

Udall knew that some in Congress, especially Wayne Aspinall, chair of the House Interior and Insular Affairs Committee, took exception to such executive powers. Aspinall had even written to Udall on May 20, 1961, that "some of us feel that it would be better that these new park units be established by Congress because the Congress is being committed to the appropriations of funds for their operation and maintenance." He requested that Congress be notified thirty days in advance of when the president planned to establish a unit.[32]

To minimize the vocal objections he expected, Udall opted to proceed with quiet caution. He tried to convince Johnson that in this instance, since he was leaving the White House, he should not care what Congress thought and should instead focus on what would benefit the country. Sometime in the fall of 1968, Johnson gave Udall the go-ahead to review and present the proposals to him. Comfortable with thinking big, Hartzog and his park planners recommended large additions in some fifteen areas. Udall "didn't want to rile up Congress too much," so he thought it would be best to scale the requests back.[33]

Udall knew that when President Eisenhower proclaimed the C&O Canal area near Washington, D.C., Aspinall retaliated by stalling the park's legislation and funding. But after eight years in office, Udall wanted something big and significant as his parting action. His narrowed recommendations came to 7.5 million acres in seven parks that included a 4-million-acre Gates of the Arctic, a 2-million-acre addition to Mount McKinley, extensions to Katmai, and several smaller parks in the continental United States. Playing to President Johnson's ego, Udall had pointed out that if President Herbert Hoover could proclaim 4 million acres, he thought 7 million would be just about right for him.[34]

In mid-November, Udall and Hartzog joined with other representatives from the National Park Service and the Bureau of Sport Fisheries and Wildlife to make a presentation to the president, the First Lady, and many staff members. Johnson staffers asked a lot of questions after the presentation, and Udall sensed trouble, but he came away hopeful. Johnson wanted reassurance from Udall that he had cleared it with Alaska's congressional delegation and the appropriate congressional committee members. "I told them [Johnson's staff] from the very beginning that Aspinall hated the Antiquities Act. He thought it was the biggest mistake that Congress ever made." Udall thought that "there's no point in getting him to approve it."[35]

Hartzog begged Udall to reconsider, predicting that Aspinall would be receptive if a section were added promising that no appropriations would be sought until Congress approved the areas. Udall held firm, however, and refused to brief Aspinall.[36] Udall and Hartzog did talk to and get support from such members of Congress as Senator Henry "Scoop" Jackson of Washington, chair of the Senate Interior and Insular Affairs Committee, and Representative John Saylor of Pennsylvania, ranking Republican on the House Interior and Insular Affairs Committee. Even the Alaska senators had agreed not to oppose the measure publicly.

Hearing that Alaska governor Walter Hickel had been selected as secretary of the interior by the incoming Nixon administration, Udall became even more determined to push the monuments through, since Hickel would undoubtedly oppose them. In mid-December, Udall got a tentative green light to prepare the paperwork and press releases but was pointedly warned to get clearances from key members of Congress. Udall reported enthusiastic support from the Hill but acknowledged that Aspinall was out of town.

Udall had hoped Johnson would sign the papers before Christmas, but an untimely illness sent him home to Texas, and the papers remained unsigned.[37] Udall remained hopeful and felt that the president had implied his intentions in his last State of the Union address on January 14, 1969, when he said that while much land had already been protected, "there's more going to be set aside before this administration ends."[38]

Wayne Aspinall found out about the proclamations. Furious, he voiced strong opposition since the additions did not appear to be emergency situations. The Park Service had already added many new areas that would require funding, and budgets were getting increasingly tight. Aspinall warned that if the proclamations were signed, there would be no appropriations for the areas.

Despite Aspinall's objections, Johnson appeared ready to proceed when he scheduled a signing ceremony for January 17. But he delayed the signing, forcing Udall and Hartzog to wait by their phones for word from the White House. By January 18, Udall knew that time was running out. Still hoping that the president would create the national monuments, however, Udall released information. Hearing the media announcements, an infuriated Johnson called Udall and ordered him to retract the news releases since he had not yet made a decision.[39]

On the morning of his last day in office, Johnson signed proclamations boundary adjustments for Arches, Capitol Reef, and Katmai; he also established Marble Canyon National Monument, which was later assimilated into Grand Canyon National Park.[40] Of the larger Alaskan proposals he said that "the taking of this land without opportunity for Congressional study would strain the Antiquities Act far beyond its intent. Such action, I am informed, would be opposed by leading members of Congress having authority in this field."[41] Johnson directed the secretary of the interior to submit the remaining proposals to Congress for consideration by the Interior and Insular Affairs committees.

The reasons for Johnson's refusal to sign all the proclamations remained a topic of speculation, and only he knew for sure. Udall accepted Lady Bird Johnson's insights; she had written in her diary that Johnson had confided to her that he did not want to offend important members of Congress. "If that's what he told Lady Bird, then . . . I have to accept it 'cause he wouldn't talk to me," Udall remarked.[42] Udall and Hartzog were understandably upset over Johnson's decision, but one wonders whether success might have adversely affected later and much larger land reservations. Alaskans could then have argued that an adequate amount of land had already been protected.

⁑

Hartzog knew his park program would likely change significantly under the new Nixon administration. In contrast to the environmentally sensitive Udall, incoming Secretary Hickel brought a prodevelopment reputation that dogged him throughout his less than two years in office. Hartzog was already aware that political leanings in Alaska had shifted. As George Hall, his Alaska state coordinator, had warned in December 1968, "The political tide in Alaska has changed in dramatic fashion during the month with the death of Senator Bartlett and the appointment of Ted Stevens to his position and the appointment of Governor Hickel to the Secretary of the Interior." He went on to predict that the "general climate for single purpose agencies will be poor for some time." Multiple-use agencies allowing more consumptive activities, he felt, would fare much better.[43]

In 1969, Congress would begin in earnest to sort out the complex land issues in Alaska. A year earlier, the Atlantic Richfield Oil Company had reported the discovery of huge oil reserves on state lands at Prudhoe Bay on Alaska's North Slope. To move the valuable oil to the ice-free port at Valdez, a pipeline crossing hundreds of miles of contested Alaska land would have to be built. The Udall land freeze meant Congress had to settle the land claims before the project could get underway. Oil, rather than justice for the Alaska Natives, appeared the stronger force compelling Congress to act.

As Congress and the courts struggled to settle competing state and Native land claims, a third competitor emerged. Increasingly, conservationists and others like Hartzog argued that Alaska's large public domain was held in trust for all Americans—not just Natives and other state residents. If something was not done before the land freeze was lifted, they envisioned a frantic land grab of millions of acres of public domain.

The idea of establishing new national parks and refuges while settling the Native claims gained support and resulted in a provision added to a July 1970 Senate bill that directed the secretary of the interior to

> review all public lands in Alaska and within three years recommend to Congress areas appropriate for inclusion in the National Park System and National Wildlife Refuge System.[44]

On July 15, 1970, the Senate passed S. 1830 by a wide margin with a modified version of the provision. Despite the Senate support, the House Interior and Insular Affairs Committee failed to act and the bill died with the ninety-first Congress.[45]

Hartzog was quick to understand the potential implications were such a measure to pass, and as a result, the Park Service "greatly expanded its vision" of what was possible in Alaska. When asked why this expanded vision did not appear in Park Service maps and park proposals until late in 1971, he said that "I tried to explain to my staff that why pick a damn fight before you have to? If we had written all that stuff down and come out with those maps those special interests would probably have killed it."[46]

At the start of the 1971 congressional year, lobbyists for commercial interests, the state of Alaska, the Alaska Natives, and national interest lands organized for the upcoming battle. Rogers C. B. Morton, a Maryland congressman, had replaced Walter Hickel as secretary of the interior. Conservation groups had joined forces to form the Alaska Coalition, which pressured Congress to include a national lands interest provision. Alaska's new governor, William Egan, let it be known he would be "flexible" in the coming settlement claims without going into any specifics about this flexibility.[47] Even the often divisive Alaska Native groups tried to present a united front.

In Congress, the Senate waited for the House to act. The House debated a number of Native claims bills, including one by John Saylor and Morris Udall that included a strong national interest lands provision. Hartzog recalled being asked not to get involved in lobbying because it might cast a shadow on the effort, making it look like "just another one of Hartzog's parks bills."[48] Many opposed the Udall-Saylor amendment, including Nixon lobbyists, the state of Alaska, organized labor, consumptive users like the mining and logging industries, the Alaska Federation of Natives backed by civil rights groups, and House Interior and Insular Affairs Committee chair Wayne Aspinall. Ardent supporters fought hard but lost by a vote of 177 to 217.

Despite the loss, the vote showed strong support for such a measure. A similar provision in the Senate would be critical, and differences could be worked out in a House-Senate conference.[49] Saylor, among others, called Hartzog about approaching key Senate members to gain such a measure. He knew well Hartzog's influence with certain members of the Senate.

Hartzog immediately approached Senator Henry "Scoop" Jackson, chair of the Senate Interior and Insular Affairs Committee. Although Jackson supported the measure, he told Hartzog that he would have to consult with Alan Bible, chair of the Subcommittee on National Parks, Recreation, and Public Lands, who had primary responsibility for that legislation.[50] Hartzog would have preferred lobbying Jackson because he was the more conservation-minded of the two. He had great respect for Bible and was a close personal friend of his, but he recognized that a Nevada senator was kept in office by water and mining, not parks.

True to form, Bible told Hartzog that without firsthand knowledge of the Alaska situation he would rely heavily on the opinions of the two Alaska senators, Mike Gravel and Ted Stevens. To that Hartzog jokingly bemoaned, "Oh, my broken back. They don't want what I want."[51] Determinedly, Hartzog suggested that Bible accompany him to Alaska, promising the "damnedest vacation you ever had." Jackson joined Hartzog in pressuring Bible to see

Alaska for himself. A "quiet behind the scenes workhorse" who seldom took time off, Bible confessed that he and his wife had already made vacation plans with Bob McDonald, his former law partner, Dr. Fred Anderson, a long-time family friend, and their wives. It was to be a second honeymoon for the couples, but they promised to consider Alaska as an alternative. In the interim, Hartzog described himself as a "deflated bird . . . just like somebody had pulled out the long feathers in the wings." He felt on "pins and needles" until Bible called to say they would all go.[52]

Hartzog understood that Senator Bible held the key to success in Alaska. He and his staff worked hard to deliver a memorable trip for the Bibles and their traveling companions. In discussions with the media, Bible portrayed his trip as simply a vacation with friends over the August congressional recess. Reports exist of their travel to existing parks, but nothing appeared about travel to proposed areas. Hartzog realized they "didn't want to incense Ted Stevens and Mike Gravel any more than they already were. They would have been furious had they realized." Although Hartzog was on friendly terms with Stevens, he knew that many Alaskans disliked the Park Service.[53]

For two weeks, using a variety of plane, train, bus, and boat connections, the group explored the vast Alaska landscape. Influential people joined the group along the route, which included stops at existing park units and areas under study. The party first converged in Fairbanks, where Vide Bartlett, the gracious widow of former Alaska senator Edward Lewis "Bob" Bartlett, threw a party in Bible's honor. She managed to turn out the academic and political establishment in Alaska and start the trip on a positive note. Since she was so politically connected, Hartzog would periodically call for her assessments of the changing Alaska political scene.[54]

Edgar Wayburn, president of the Sierra Club, and his wife, Peggy, a writer and an equally strong advocate, joined the group for part of the trip. Aboard a twin-engine Otter, the group headed for the proposed Gates of the Arctic National Park amid cloudy skies. After two hours, the clouds finally parted and exposed a surreal landscape. Wayburn saw Bible "glued to the window. His stunned silence conveying more than words. . . . Coming from Nevada's desert country, I don't think he could have imagined that such country existed."[55]

By train the group traveled to Mount McKinley National Park. Along the route, the train slowed or stopped to allow better viewing of the abundant wildlife, reportedly some of the best of the trip. At the park, the group flew to the park boundaries and proposed extensions. Bible saw how the continent's highest mountain was only protected within park boundaries on its northern side. Hartzog recalled the pilot flying the group so close to the glaciers that it seemed he was attempting to climb them. It about "scared the liver out of Alan Bible and me."[56]

During this flight, Wayburn's exuberance for Alaska pushed Bible to his limits. As the Wayburns buzzed around the plane leaning over Bible to show him landmarks out the window, Hartzog could see that Bible was becoming increasingly annoyed. When the plane landed, Bible pulled Hartzog aside and said that if the Wayburns were on the next flight, he would be heading home to Reno. They were not on the next flight, and Bible remained in Alaska.[57]

The group continued to Katmai and Glacier Bay with planned overflights of Lake Clark and the Wrangell Mountains, weather permitting. They caught salmon, boated at Glacier Bay, and watched Chilkat dancers with their carved masks and traditional costumes. At opportune times, Hartzog spread out maps and supporting materials so he could talk about current Park Service needs and potential park proposals. He recalled introducing Bible to a number of people enthusiastic about the possibilities in Alaska.[58] In addition to a landscape that spoke for itself, he thought supportive Alaskans and Bible's traveling companions, the Andersons and the McDonalds, were critical persuaders.[59]

Strategically, Hartzog wanted to appear collegial with other federal agencies. Prior to the trip, he had sent a cryptic letter to Spencer Smith and Burt Silcock, directors of the Bureau of Sport Fisheries and Wildlife and the Bureau of Land Management, respectively, saying he would be traveling with Bible and asking "if there is any special thing that I can do for you on this trip."[60] He received no response. While traveling, Hartzog had asked Bible if he wanted to talk to representatives of the Forest Service and Bureau of Sport Fisheries and Wildlife. Bible thought that was a good idea, so Hartzog arranged an informal meeting with coffee and light snacks. He did not attend the meeting, but later Bible gave him the impression that "their plea was for some limited additional acreage to round out some of their units." Hartzog later pointed to this meeting as evidence that the Bureau of Sport Fisheries and Wildlife and Forest Service did not become interested in Alaska until after he had done all the work to elicit Bible's support for a national interest lands amendment to the Alaska Native Claims Settlement Act.[61]

The Bible party disbanded after spending sixteen days in Alaska. Hartzog felt the experience simply "blew their minds because nobody's ever seen anything like Alaska until you go see Alaska."[62] The McDonalds and the Andersons appeared simply awestruck and as enthusiastic as children about the experience. They urged Bible to protect everything they saw. Although Hartzog felt that Alaska's magnificence registered with Bible, he proved to be much harder to read. Coming from the great gambling state of Nevada, he often played his cards close to his chest. Hartzog felt under enormous pressure to sell Bible on Alaska, so as each day slipped away during the trip, he grew more exasperated and came no closer to guessing the senator's intentions.[63]

"Bible didn't indicate one damn thing about what he was going to do about Alaska until we got back to the States," Hartzog recalled. The Bibles had already extended an invitation to the Hartzogs to spend several days with them at their Lake Tahoe summerhouse. Finally, on the second day of the visit, as they sat outside the cabin, Bible brought up Alaska. Hartzog recalls him very simply saying to "go ahead and give me language to get done what you want to get done." Hartzog immediately called his legislative staff to have them begin drafting language.[64]

With characteristic bravado, Hartzog would claim that "Senator Bible was so thoroughly impressed with those areas that if I had insisted at that moment in time, we could have actually created these parks in '71 instead of just preserving them for study."[65] While this view may have been overly optimistic, even taking in account Hartzog's power in Congress, there remains no doubt that the trip to Alaska transformed the senator. He would sponsor legislation based on his own personal experiences rather than relying on the perspectives of the Alaska senators.

Hartzog returned to Washington and forwarded the draft language of the national interest lands amendment to Bible. Confusion still exists about whose language provided the basis for section 17(d)(2) of the Alaska Native Claims Settlement Act, commonly called "the Bible Amendment." Park Service historian G. Frank Williss claimed that the materials he examined and the people he contacted, including George Hartzog, Thomas Flynn (Hartzog's deputy director for legislation and cooperative programs), Ted Swem, Senator Bible, and three congressional staff members, failed to provide a definitive answer. Hartzog did ask Tom Flynn and his staff to prepare a draft for Bible, but no copies of that draft have been found in Hartzog's extensive collection of personal papers.[66]

By the time Bible introduced his amendment to Senator Jackson's S. 35 on November 1, 1971, few senators remained on the floor to contest what Bible called a "reasonable and non-controversial amendment."[67] With only minor objections from Senator Stevens of Alaska, the Senate overwhelmingly passed its version of the Alaska Native Claims Settlement bill with Bible's section 17(d)(2) amendment securely attached. The amendment instructed the secretary of the interior to "conduct detailed studies and investigations of all unreserved public lands in Alaska . . . for inclusion in the National Park and National Wildlife Refuge Systems."[68]

It now fell to the conference committee to work out, among other things, the difference between the House amendment and Bible's Senate version.[69] With minimal debate, the conference committee added the Forest Service and Wild and Scenic Rivers System as possible beneficiaries. The addition of the Forest Service arose from pressures to include a "multiple-use" agency to appease Alaskans who were concerned that single-use conservation systems would forever lock up the state's valuable resources. The committee would also add the amount of national interest lands that were to be reserved for study—80 million acres.

Hartzog remembers purposely leaving blank the number of acres in the Park Service version of the section 17(d)(2) amendment. However, he said he relayed to Bible the Park Service's interest in some 76 million acres. Given the interest of the Forest Service and Bureau of Sport Fisheries and Wildlife in small "boundary adjustments" during their meeting with Bible in Alaska, Hartzog reasoned that Bible added 4 million acres to his request to arrive at the 80-million withdrawal specified in the amendment.[70]

Hartzog also believed that Bible meant for the bulk of the lands to enter the National Park System, but Bible's section 17(d)(2) amendment made no such assertions. According to Williss, some evidence supports Hartzog's belief. Bible had a strong interest in parks and recreation. He was good friends with Hartzog and listened closely to advice regarding parks.[71] Senator Bible reportedly mentioned to Senator Stevens three park areas—the proposed Gates of the Arctic and extensions to Mount McKinley National Park and Katmai National Monument—just prior to his introduction of the amendment. Furthermore, Senator Jackson, cosponsor of the amendment, described it as a "park study" amendment.[72] While that may have been his intent, the actual bill instructed the secretary of the interior to study the withdrawn areas for possible inclusion in four systems: national parks, wildlife refuges, national forests, and wild and scenic rivers.

The additions Hartzog and his staff envisioned for the National Park System were monumental. Williss credits Hartzog with thinking "in much larger terms than nearly anyone inside or outside the Service at that time." On a map of Alaska, Hartzog's staff had colored proposed additions, including a huge Gates of the Arctic park that stretched north from the Arctic Circle across the naval petroleum reserves to the Arctic Ocean. A great Wrangell-St. Elias park spread over into protected areas in Canada. Sizable additions would extend the boundaries of Katmai and Mount McKinley. Several historic sites and four cultural centers representing the major Native groups were proposed. He wanted to convert the Arctic National Wildlife Refuge into an international park that would adjoin its counterpart in northwestern Canada. In Hartzog's view, later controversies over drilling for oil in the Arctic National Wildlife Refuge probably would have been circumvented had the Park Service gained the areas he wanted.[73]

Hartzog's vision seemed as vast as the landscape he hoped to protect. Using state-of-the-art scientific thinking, the Park Service lobbied for the inclusion of entire ecosystems and watersheds. In the past, most park boundaries had been drawn without knowledge of the requirements of ecosystems, watersheds, or wildlife habitats. The entire migratory ranges of caribou, for example, could lie within a single park and thus circumvent problems like those at Yellowstone, where elk and bison traveled out of the park's protective boundaries. In Alaska, the Park Service and other conservation agencies realized they could establish park boundaries using scientific knowledge.

⁂

Signed December 18, 1971, the Alaska Native Claims Settlement Act became the most generous settlement for Native Americans ever and set the stage for the later additions to the country's conservation systems. Briefly, the act settled Native claims by giving them some 44 million acres of land and close to $1 billion in compensation for lands taken, thereby extinguishing all future claims. The act set up a system of twelve regional corporations and over two hundred village corporations. To help preserve their cultural heritage, Natives could continue subsistence use on public lands that were being studied under the act's section 17(d)(2) provision. The act's section 17(d)(2) amendment required initial land withdrawals to occur within nine months, and final recommendations for the up to 80 million acres of national interest lands intended for inclusion in one of four conservation systems were to be submitted by December 18, 1973. Section 17(d)(1) allowed the secretary of the interior to withdraw other lands in the public's interest. Congress gave itself until December 18, 1978, to debate the land recommendations and pass any new park legislation. According to the Alaska Native Claims Settlement Act, a new joint federal-state land-use planning commission would provide advice for a fair and equitable division of lands among Native, state, and federal interests. Despite its advisory nature, the commission would come to play an important role in final land decisions.[74]

With just two years to make final recommendations, assistant secretary Nat Reed directed the Park Service and Bureau of Sport Fisheries and Wildlife to study and prioritize their choices. Hartzog had lost no time in appointing the well-qualified and knowledgeable Ted Swem to coordinate from Washington what would prove to be a massive Park Service task in an impossibly short time. Swem tried to convince Hartzog not to appoint him since he was deeply involved in other efforts, but "George wasn't a person you talked out of things."[75] Even though park funding had become scarce, Hartzog would channel the necessary money to the Alaska effort and give Swem considerable latitude to operate.

Three days after the signing of the act on December 18, 1971, undersecretary of the interior William T. Pecora called a meeting of all the top people within the department. Hartzog was not invited to this or any subsequent meetings on Alaska. "They closed the door on me," he recalled.[76] Swem went in his place and remembered clearly that "it was very obvious with one or two exceptions no one knew anything about the [legislation]," which made planning difficult.

To meet deadlines outlined in the legislation, the Park Service had to make many important decisions about parks and boundaries based on only cursory information. Swem moved quickly to bring in Richard Stenmark of the Alaska office in Anchorage to help delineate areas of initial interest. By January 4, Stenmark had identified twelve natural areas and ten areas with significant historical or archaeological resources. These initial areas were submitted to Reed on January 7, 1972, but many revisions and refinements were made in these recommendations until mid-March, when they were forwarded to Secretary Rogers Morton.

As Interior officials struggled to implement the section 17(d)(2) provision, interpretation of it evolved. Early in 1972, they began viewing the claims settlement legislation as an 80-million-acre withdrawal under section 17(d)(2) and an additional withdrawal under the sister section 17(d)(1) section. House leaders John Saylor and Morris Udall concurred with Interior's interpretation. By March 2, Reed had reviewed the information from his department's agencies and had also received input from Native leaders, Alaska officials, conservation groups, and others with an interest in Alaska lands. Reed made a recommendation of 148 million acres to Morton.

As time went on, Hartzog felt that special interest groups were exerting more and more influence on the recommendations. "The commercial hunters, the diggers and the cutters [i.e., mining and timber interests] zeroed in on section 17(d)(2) and began to apply the heat to put much of the land into the forest system and the Fish and Wildlife Refuge System. It would be easier for them to get at it there in the future."[77]

Commercial interests knew that national parks generally forbade oil exploration, mining, logging, hunting, and dam building. Wildlife refuges, on the other hand, might allow any or all of these development activities if found to be compatible with the refuge's significant resources. National forests allowed the greatest range of uses, including logging, grazing, hunting, and oil and mineral development. To developers, therefore, if lands had to be set aside, setting them aside for national forests and wildlife refuges were far preferable to setting them aside for national parks.

In frustration, Hartzog wrote Morton a heartfelt letter on March 6, 1972, that challenged the secretary to rethink the direction he was leaning. It read in part:

> The pressures are enormous . . . but the opportunities are awe-inspiring. For the most part, we have preserved our heritage—both natural and cultural—as residual values. In Alaska, we have the opportunity to re-order this priority. Shall we interpret the law to reserve the option to the people—through their Congress—to choose a "Legacy" or an economic gain?[78]

On March 15, Morton slimmed down Reed's proposed 148 million acres to 125 million—80 million under section 17(d)(2) and 45 million under section 17(d)(1) authority. At the same time, the secretary opened millions of acres for possible state and Native selection. He and Reed also shifted much of what Hartzog wanted for the parks to the national forest and wildlife refuge systems.[79] According to Morton's initial withdrawals in March, the Park Service had something over 33 million acres in fourteen areas to study, while the Bureau of Sport Fisheries and Wildlife would study 49 million acres. Although these withdrawals were not final, Morton's split deeply disappointed Hartzog, who called them a "complete disaster."[80]

Morton's decision not only disheartened the Park Service. Alaskans also raged against "a massive land grab" by the federal government. In April 1972, the state sued over the March 1972 preliminary withdrawals that overlapped with state selection preferences. In a September closed-door session, Secretary Morton and Alaska governor William Egan resolved the lawsuit in an out-of-court memorandum of understanding.[81] In the agreement, the state gave up a large part of the disputed acreage in exchange for some national interest lands Morton had withdrawn in March. The lands Morton surrendered included magnificent gateway areas to the proposed Gates of the Arctic and parts of the proposed extensions to Mount McKinley that the state wanted for summer-home development. In a sharply worded telegram to Morton, seven major environmental organizations found the memorandum

> . . . disturbing . . . since it appears that your future options for retention or disposal of federal lands have been severely limited. More specifically, the designation of entire viable ecosystems as (d)(2) withdrawals could be seriously hampered by this action. . . . Equally disturbing is that negotiations on this matter were conducted with no opportunity for public knowledge or involvement.[82]

According to angry environmental groups, Morton gave away tracts of land that were of national-park caliber before those in either federal agencies or Congress could assess their value.

As the battles over land selection raged in Washington, the Park Service was busy developing a management framework and assembling field teams. Hartzog and Swem both realized that management freedom and flexibility would be critical. Therefore, they developed a radically new system whereby Swem reported directly to Hartzog, bypassing established management hierarchy. Swem controlled hiring, program development, staffing, and budgeting and represented the Park Service in intradepartmental dealings. Logistical support would come from the Alaska Field Office, the Pacific Northwest Regional Office, and the Denver Service Center. On paper the roles of each appeared clear, but in reality overlapping responsibilities would create severe tension within the various offices.[83] While this unprecedented approach made some unhappy, Bob Belous, chief liaison for the Alaska task force, believed it "extremely important" to later successes in Alaska.[84]

Hartzog had made Alaska his top priority and told Swem he could recruit the best people. Barring special family considerations, no one was protected from being drawn into the effort. To head the field study operations, Swem selected Albert G. Henson, a park planner with experience in park management and new area planning. Next, he picked a core group permanently assigned to Anchorage. Swem recalled Hartzog inviting them to breakfast at his house, where he impressed on them the importance of the task that lay ahead and the need for their complete commitment. This core group would receive additional support from a number of people temporarily detailed to Alaska for four to six months.[85]

As Alaska's brief field season approached, the Park Service sent study teams into the field to assess parklands suggested in the March 1972 withdrawals. Each study team consisted of a team captain, ecologist, landscape architect, and interpretive planner who would look at three to four areas that could include both section 17(d)(2) and section 17(d)(1) lands. Since assistant secretaries wanted recommendations by July 20, prior to an August 10 presentation to Morton, the field teams had just weeks to analyze the areas, justify any changes, and make recommendation for the final September withdrawals. They worked seven days a week from sunup to sundown. Reed called them "the brightest team you ever laid eyes on."[86] Given the sheer size of the Alaska withdrawals, however, the teams recognized their study efforts as superficial at best.

By July, after an almost round-the-clock effort, the Park Service recommended eleven areas consisting of almost 49 million acres to Reed for his review and passage to Morton. The Park Service urged Morton to recommend protecting not just the integrity of wildlife habitats but also entire watersheds and areas of geologic importance. Since the activities of one federal, state, or Native group could affect the resource values marked for protection by another group, the Park Service strongly urged that land-use planning embrace a regional approach. The Park Service also suggested large areas be studied for archaeological, historical, and paleontological resources worthy of protection by the appropriate federal, state, or Native organization.[87]

According to the 1971 legislation, the secretary had to finalize his study area withdrawals by September, nine months after the bill was signed. Areas not specifically selected could then be chosen by the state of Alaska. Morton's final section 17(d)(2) withdrawals included twenty-two areas over 79.3 million acres, falling just shy of the 80-million-acre limit. Of that acreage, the Park Service could now focus on some 41,685,060 acres in eleven areas as follows:

Noatak	7,874,700 acres
Gates of the Arctic	9,388,100 acres
Great Kobuk Sand Dunes	1,454,400 acres
Imuruk	2,150,900 acres
Yukon River	1,233,660 acres
Mount McKinley National Park additions	2,996,640 acres
Katmai National Monument additions	1,411,900 acres
Lake Clark Pass	3,725,620 acres
Kenai Fjords	95,400 acres

| Wrangell-St. Elias | 10,613,540 acres |
| Aniakchak Crater | 740,200 acres |

Although he publicly expressed disappointment with some of the areas not included in the September decisions, Hartzog got much of what he wanted.[88]

As one Herculean effort wound down, another began. With the September withdrawals behind, the Park Service now shifted to the deadline of December 18, 1973, by which time the secretary had to make final legislative recommendations. These recommendations had to include each proposed park's master plan with an environmental impact statement, detailed support information, and final park boundaries. Boundaries that had been rough angular rectangles on a map had to reflect more realistic borders. The Park Service also needed to be ready with individual park legislation and have a person well acquainted with each area to testify on its behalf in Congress. Conflicts between government, Alaska, and Natives over withdrawals needed resolution. In addition, the Park Service knew that it had to improve its relationship with Alaska Natives, because it believed that park preservation could be compatible with Native interests and subsistence lifestyles.

On December 31, 1972, Hartzog stepped down as director of the National Park Service with many of his efforts unrealized. In the years following his dismissal, Hartzog kept close watch on Park Service happenings through his many loyal contacts. He seemed particularly interested in the Alaska drama. In reflecting on his record, he said that "one of the most important parts was saving that land in Alaska, so I was certainly interested in how it all came out. That's why I was so upset when Morton sent his recommendations."[89]

The recommendations Hartzog referred to came on December 17, 1973, and involved Morton's recommendations for the national interest lands that would be considered for Congressional action. In the months leading up to the December decision, Morton seemed to fall increasingly under the spell of a multiple-use philosophy. In what some called a power struggle between secretary of the interior Rogers Morton and secretary of agriculture Earl Butz, the multiple-use forces seemed to carry the day. In a series of offers, counteroffers, and compromises between the two secretaries, Morton finally agreed to include some 18.8 million acres of new forest reserves in his recommendations of 83,470,000 acres. He recommended that the wildlife refuge system gain nine areas totaling 31,590,000 acres and that the Wild and Scenic Rivers System add 820,000 acres. The total recommended acreage for the Park Service fell to 32,600,000 acres from September 1972's figure of 41,685,060 acres:[90]

Potential NPS Parklands	September 1972 Acreage	December 1973 Acreage
Noatak	7,874,700	0
Gates of the Arctic	9,388,100	8,360,000
Great Kobuk Sand Dunes (later Kobuk Valley)	1,454,400	1,850,000
Imuruk	2,150,900	2,690,000
Yukon River (later Yukon-Charley)	1,233,660	1,970,000
Mount McKinley National Park additions	2,996,640	3,180,000
Katmai National Monument additions	1,411,900	1,187,000
Lake Clark Pass	3,725,620	2,610,000
Kenai Fjords	95,400	300,000
Wrangell-St. Elias	10,613,540	8,640,000
Aniakchak Crater (later Caldera)	740,200	440,000
Cape Krusenstern	0	350,000
Total	**41,685,060**	**32,600,000**

Morton's total exclusion of the Noatak distressed Park Service officials, who valued it as one of the agency's best selections. The Park Service also felt the sting of losing valuable low-lying acreage in Wrangell-St. Elias, which made the proposed park what some called a "rock and ice" park. The Park Service's recommendation for regional planning to help guide Alaska's future land-use decisions received no mention, and Gates of the Arctic lost its wilderness designation. Furthermore, Morton suggested that sport hunting continue to be allowed contrary to a long-standing tradition that prohibited such activities in national park units.[91]

Fortunately, the suggestions that Morton made would change over the years leading up to the final resolution in 1980. In the intervening years, emotions ran high in Alaska over how the state should be developed. Alaska faced what John McPhee called a "tension of preservation versus development, of stasis versus economic productivity, of wilderness versus the drill and the bulldozer, and it had caused the portentous reassignment of land that now . . . was altering, or threatening to alter, the lives of everyone in the state."[92]

As the December 1978 deadline neared, Hartzog and everyone else knew that lands not legislated by Congress into one of the conservation systems would become eligible for state selection. Shortly after his election in 1976,

President Carter directed his secretary of the interior, Cecil Andrus, to make Alaska one of the administration's top issues. Congress responded by introducing a number of legislative proposals. Representative Morris Udall of Arizona introduced H.R. 39, which reserved some 115,300,000 acres in Alaska with 64,100,000 acres earmarked for the Park Service. In the opening debate, the tall and well-respected Udall told the House that "we shall vote on no more vital, far reaching or more memorable conservation measure. As others have said, this will indeed be the land and wildlife vote of the century."

In May 1978, following heated arguments, impassioned testimonies, conferences between House members, and a flurry of letters and telegrams, the House resoundingly supported the bill, voting to protect more than 100 million acres by a 279–13 vote. Senator Henry "Scoop" Jackson had forwarded a similar bill in the Senate. Opposition from the Alaska senators Ted Stevens (R) and Mike Gravel (D) delayed and weakened the Senate version, which finally moved out of committee in October 1978. In a feverish effort to reach a compromise before adjournment, Senate and House members met but were thwarted by Gravel's unreasonable demands and delaying tactics. Hours later, Congress adjourned—leaving the national interest lands issue unresolved by the December 1978 deadline.[93] Hartzog recalled "panicking along with a lot of other people," wondering what would happen.[94]

Prepared for such a contingency, Secretary Andrus withdrew from state selection in mid-November some 110,750,000 acres using a 1976 Bureau of Land Management law. On December 1, 1978, President Carter followed up by using his Antiquities Act powers to establish seventeen national monuments amounting to 56 million acres.[95] Carter's proclamations gave Congress time to reach a legislative agreement. For the next two years, the battle raged inside and outside Congress. Meanwhile, the Park Service struggled with its own management difficulties and angry Alaska residents, who opposed government restrictions on what they viewed as their lands. In some Alaska areas, park employees were refused service at restaurants, received death threats, and were generally shunned.[96]

Finally, in the waning days of the 1980 congressional session, a compromise bill was reached. Supportive congressmen, conservationists, and others favoring national parks and wilderness designations recognized the importance of reaching a settlement before President Ronald Reagan and his development-oriented administration came into office. Reagan had chosen James Watt as his secretary of the interior, and most expected a hostile political climate to follow. On December 2, 1980, President Carter signed the Alaska National Interest Lands Conservation Act. The Bureau of Sport

Fisheries and Wildlife gained the most with 53,720,000 acres, which represented over 22 million acres more than Morton had recommended in 1973. The National Park Service ended up with 11 million acres over what Morton had recommended with 43.6 million acres. The Forest Service took the biggest hit, ending up with only 3.25 million acres, a decrease of 15.5 million acres. The Wild and Scenic Rivers System ended up with 1.2 million acres. A total of 56.4 million acres received wilderness designation.

National Park System additions included the following acreage:

Aniakchak National Monument and Preserve	514,000
Bering Land Bridge National Preserve	2,457,000
Cape Krusenstern National Monument	560,000
Gates of the Arctic National Park and Monument	7,952,000
Kenai Fjords National Park	570,000
Kobuk Valley National Park	1,710,000
Lake Clark National Park and Preserve	3,653,000
Noatak National Preserve	6,460,000
Wrangell-Saint Elias National Park and Preserve	12,318,000
Yukon-Charley Rivers National Preserve	1,713,000
Glacier Bay National Park additions and National Preserve	580,000
Katmai National Park additions and National Preserve	1,345,000
Denali (formerly Mount McKinley) National Park additions and National Preserve	3,756,000
Total	**43,600,000**[97]

In assessing the long struggle to protect national interest lands in Alaska, the 1971 Alaska Native Claims Settlement Act remains the critical turning point. Williss writes, "There is no question that George Hartzog played a crucial role in securing a national interest lands provision in the Alaska Native Claims Settlement Act of 1971." The August 1971 Alaska trip that Hartzog arranged for Senator Alan Bible profoundly changed the Nevada senator. As a result, he was impelled to sponsor the all-important section 17(d)(2) amendment, which recognized the need to study and protect resources important to the country and not just to Alaska and its residents.[98] Bible retired in 1974, leaving others to press forward using all their political prowess and influence to secure as much worthy parklands as possible.

To Hartzog, the ups and downs of the Alaska parks movement were reminiscent of a roller coaster ride. "One day you're up and you're going to get it all and then next day, you're zilch and you're going to lose it all."[99] The final legislation left him pleased that lands had been protected but disappointed that more had not been saved and that the National Park Service had not gained a larger share. The final may not have included all that Hartzog sought, but it doubled the size of the National Park System and remained what some called "the greatest single conservation act of the century."[100]

CHAPTER NINE

More New Directions

I n reflecting on his administration's accomplishments during a 1996 interview, George Hartzog initially mentioned three things—diversifying the work-force, making parks more relevant to urban populations, and expanding the National Park System. In the ensuing years, he would expand this list.[1] One addition, for example, was using scientific research to help guide resource management decisions. Another was developing programs to better educate the public about the environmental issues.[2] Most dealt with getting important legislation passed, something at which he excelled.

Of all the Park Service directors, Hartzog was the most politically savvy. Rather than view politics with disdain, he had been intrigued by it since his early study of law and work with political campaigns in South Carolina. He believed the United States had "the most glorious system of government on the earth," though he did acknowledge its flaws.[3] He recognized Congress as key to his programs since it constitutionally had the final say in public land policy. To be an effective director, he knew he had to work the system. A master at reading people and situations, he knew how to adjust his tactics as necessary. The gracious southern gentleman with the proper level of deference could transition to a bartering horse trader, a sharp and witty story-teller, a hard-drinking smoking companion, or a hardball player you crossed at your own peril.

Hartzog admitted to being "obsessed with legislation."[4] He made it his business to get involved with or at least stay abreast of any legislation that impacted the National Park System. Sometimes he worked in concert with others, such as when he served with the director of the Bureau of Outdoor Recreation and chief of the U.S. Forest Service on an administrative support team. Together, they lobbied for the Wilderness Act (1964), the Land and Water Conservation Fund Act (1965), the Wild and Scenic Rivers Act (1968), and the National Trails System Act (1968). Other times, he lobbied for legislation specific to the National Park System.

What follows touches on three legislative initiatives related to historic preservation, park volunteers, and private donations that he worked on. With each he was a major player, but not the only player. The last section discusses the promotion of scientific research in the parks and its use to help steer management decisions. All brought change to the National Park System, but the change driven by legislation would provide a firmer foundation and yield more lasting results.

⁂

One of George Hartzog's most significant legislative coups involved historic preservation. While many rightly link former director Horace Albright with historical parks and preservation, few recognize Hartzog's importance. Albright changed the national park system forever when he convinced Franklin Roosevelt to put large numbers of historic areas under Park Service control. With this 1933 reorganization, historical areas almost quadrupled in number and eclipsed natural areas. Rather suddenly, the Park Service entered the historic protection and preservation field. Thirty-three years later, Hartzog helped engineer the next big step forward.

Hartzog benefited from good timing. Americans had grown increasingly alarmed over the loss of their historic resources. Communities witnessed historic neighborhoods and buildings demolished to make way for an expanding interstate highway system, new commercial development, and suburban housing. A country that had often viewed old buildings as impediments to progress began realizing that their destruction meant an important historical memory for communities and an irreplaceable part of the country's heritage was being lost. The government had taken steps to protect its historical areas but was being pushed to do more.

Throughout its history, the United States moved slowly to protect its historic and cultural resources. Some of the earliest protective efforts included the city of Philadelphia saving Independence Hall, the Mount Vernon Ladies' Association acquisition of George Washington's home in Virginia, and the military's protection of Revolutionary and Civil War battles sites. It would take the vandalism of prehistoric Native American sites in Colorado to prompt Congress to enact the 1906 Antiquities Act. This act allowed the president to set aside public areas with significant resources being threatened with destruction. Less than a month after its passage, President Theodore Roosevelt exercised his new authority by protecting the ancient Pueblo remains that would become Mesa Verde National Park.

When the National Park Service was created in 1916, it assumed responsibility for Mesa Verde as well as other historical areas. The agency's founding legislation mandated that it "conserve the scenery and the natural and historical objects and the wildlife therein." In reality, historical areas were hardly a priority. Historical areas would, however, gain more attention with the 1933 reorganization that transferred them to the Park Service. Many well-known parks like Gettysburg in Pennsylvania, Appomattox Court House in Virginia, and Ford's Theatre in Washington, D.C., passed to Park Service management.

Depression-era work programs also moved the Park Service into the preservation of state and federal historical areas. For example, the agency initiated the Historic American Buildings Survey, which put unemployed architects, photographers, and draftsmen to work drawing and photographing the country's significant architectural structures. Such activities extended the Park Service's preservation role far beyond its national park boundaries and would help position the agency as a leader in historic preservation.[5]

With an increased emphasis on historic preservation came the realization that little was known about the nature and extent of the country's historic resources and whether they were being adequately preserved. In response, Congress enacted the 1935 Historic Sites Act, which entrusted the Park Service with establishing a national policy for preserving historic places and a plan for identifying those of national significance. Under the able leadership of historian Ronald F. Lee, numerous inventories were conducted of important areas and determinations made of their significance. (These later came to be known as National Historic Landmarks.) When the United States entered World War II in 1941, survey and other historic preservation efforts all but ceased.[6]

After the war, interest in historic preservation slowly revived. Park Service staff tried to resurrect the national historic survey, but lack of funding kept efforts to a minimum. It would take Mission 66, a ten-year development program begun in 1956, to modestly fund such efforts as the Historic Sites Survey and Historic American Buildings Survey.[7] In the late 1950s, regional historians began limited studies to ascertain which historic sites might be suitable for inclusion in the National Park System and which might not. In 1960, these historians established the Registry of National Historic Landmarks, which listed nationally significant historical areas officially designated by the secretary of the interior. Legally, landmarks could be privately or publicly owned and managed. While the registry's intent was to promote preservation, no legal action could be taken against property owners who altered or destroyed the landmarks. Preservationists wanted stronger measures and protection to extend to places of less than national significance.

As President Lyndon B. Johnson expanded the role of federal government in the mid-1960s, it assumed more responsibilities in the realm of historic preservation. Johnson established committees on natural beauty that also examined historic preservation and set the stage for new legislation. Meanwhile, concerned taxpayers complained about their tax dollars supporting federal interstate construction projects and urban renewal programs that destroyed historically significant and aesthetically pleasing buildings and neighborhoods. They argued that such areas enhanced a community's unique character, imparting a sense of continuity that helped link the past to the present.[8]

When Hartzog came into office, he redirected the agency away from the building frenzy of Mission 66 that at times needlessly intruded on natural and historical areas. Instead he sought new, innovative programs and looked for ways to expand his agency and extend its influence beyond park boundaries. Historic preservation presented such an opportunity. In January 1964, he asked his solicitor, Bernard Meyer, to explore ways the National Park Service could provide financial support to localities for historic preservation. Meyer said the agency could not provide grants to states for protecting areas that had only state or local interest but only for protecting areas of national significance. New legislation would be needed.[9]

Hartzog claimed a long-standing interest that heightened during his tenure (although not everyone was sure this enthusiasm was genuine). As a child, he recalled "holding onto artifacts, the ones that were left that we could afford to keep and didn't get burned up in a fire or sold for groceries." His wife's business in buying and selling antiques, in addition to his living in a home filled with them, also influenced him.[10]

He got involved in historic preservation soon after becoming director, when President Johnson established the Committee for the Preservation of the White House, whose task it was to advise the president on the acquisition, use, and display of historic and artistic objects in the White House. Since the White House was a unit of the Park System, Hartzog became ex officio director and remained a member at large until 1998.

Members of Hartzog's staff also helped keep him focused on historic preservation. Ronald Lee, who had played a key role in historic preservation since the Historic Sites Act of 1935, undoubtedly exerted the greatest influence.[11] To Hartzog, Lee was "the single most able guy in this field of preservation I ever met, because he had a sweep of understanding and a philosophy as well as a flexibility that made his ideas achievable." According to historian Robert Utley, "Lee's word was gospel, and if it was not embraced and put into place, it was for political reasons."[12] Using his influence, Lee urged Hartzog to reassert the Park Service's claim as the primary federal historic preservation agency.

Another factor that enhanced Hartzog's growing interest in historic preservation was his trip to Europe. In 1965, the U.S. Conference of Mayors sponsored a blue ribbon committee to look at the nation's historic resources. Albert M. Rains, a former chair of the House Subcommittee on Housing, led a special group studying historic preservation. To gain perspective, the group visited European cities with strong preservation records and prepared a report on its findings. The committee also invited members of the heads of federal agencies involved in preservation or in financing construction projects. Representatives from the General Services Administration, Interior, Housing and Urban Development, and Commerce agreed to go. Hartzog represented the Department of the Interior. Joining the group were Gordon Gray, chair of the National Trust; several congressmen; and Hartzog's good friend Raymond R. Tucker, mayor of St. Louis.

Hartzog toured England and France with the group before being called back to testify on legislation. During the trip, he recalled visiting parts of Paris that had been reconstructed after heavy World War II damage. In England, he saw Stratford-upon-Avon, William Shakespeare's childhood home. In each area, the group met with the cultural ministries and local politicians. Hartzog was impressed with France's restoration projects and with England's concept of parks, which included significant private lands.[13] He credited the trip with heightening his "sensitivity to the part that historic preservation can play in making the culture more relevant to the current generation."[14] Hartzog and others found evidence that, with proper planning, progress and historic protection could coexist. They also saw that European governments assumed a primary role in the preservation of their historic buildings and sites, and they came to the conclusion that the United States needed to do the same.

In January 1966, the Rains committee report, titled *With Heritage So Rich*, outlined recommendations for a national preservation program. The committee's ideas included establishing a National Register of Historic Places that would list the country's significant resources, a register that would be compiled by drawing on each state's comprehensive inventory of its historical areas. Hartzog lobbied hard for the committee to recommend that the National Park Service maintain this register and oversee a grants program for states and localities. The committee also suggested that a special advisory council be set up to help resolve conflicts between agencies and to persuade them to consider impacts to historic resources before beginning any development activities.[15]

Encouraged by the Johnson administration, the Rains committee, and the Park Service, Congress introduced preservation bills in early 1966. Since Hartzog anticipated a possible role for the Park Service, he appointed a three-person committee in May to examine the Park Service's existing historic preservation policies and to brainstorm possible future directions. The committee consisted of historian Ronald Lee and two people from outside the Park Service. John O. Brew was a Harvard-trained archaeologist and director of Harvard's Peabody Museum, while Ernest A. Connally possessed expertise in historic architecture and was on the faculty of the University of Illinois. Connally had previously helped the Park Service with several building surveys and some historic preservation projects. Among other things, the committee recommended that staff and funds related to historic preservation be consolidated into a single unit reporting to the director.[16]

Meanwhile, Hartzog competed behind the scenes with other federal agency heads to become the favored agency in the developing legislation. He faced his first battle with the Department of Housing and Urban Development. Preservation legislation first appeared in the housing committee, and the Department of Housing and Urban Development seemed the likely agency to administer the desirable grants-in-aid program. Undaunted, he worked his close ties on the Hill to get the grants program shifted to the Interior and Insular Affairs Committee for consideration.

Hartzog argued that the new legislation simply "expanded and maintained" what the Park Service had already been authorized to do by the 1935 Historic Sites Act. He maintained that his agency had in essence been keeping a National Register of Historic Places and that the new legislation would simply broaden the scope to include places of state and local concern. To Utley, "it was this tactical move, more than anything, I think, that captured the new program for the Park Service and away from the housing people." Hartzog relished such intellectual tactics and proved exceptionally good at them.[17]

Hartzog recognized that capturing the register piece would ensure that the Park Service was given authority over most of the whole historic preservation program.[18] He fought to keep it an intact unit by saying that most European countries placed preservation responsibilities in a similar cultural resource management agency. In the United States, the Park Service managed nationally significant historic sites and had traditionally been recognized as the lead federal agency for historic preservation. That made the Park Service, he said, the heir apparent. Additionally, keeping the nation's preservation program all together would be more administratively effective and less costly. While Hartzog proved aggressive in his efforts, he was always careful to prevent adversarial conflicts with members of Congress.

Hartzog worked hard to cultivate friendships on the Hill and credited his congressional connections with keeping him informed of any new developments. One day he got a call. "Ripley is trying to take your foreign responsibility under the Historic Preservation Act and he's already got the money in the House bill." The caller failed to identify himself, but Hartzog had worked the Hill long enough to recognize his informant's voice. S. Dillon Ripley, head of the Smithsonian Institution, wanted the international recognition attached with such responsibilities. "I went to the Hill on the Senate side and I got my Senate friends organized and nobody ever saw that damn language again. It didn't even show up in the conference [committee]. It was gone!" Hartzog boasted.[19]

Historic preservation legislation was considered in the Senate before the House because the chair of the House Interior and Insular Affairs Committee, Wayne Aspinall of Colorado, failed to place a high priority on the measure and therefore consider it. On July 11, 1966, S. 3035 passed. Despite success in the Senate, the bill initially failed in the House due to opposition by conservative congressmen. The measure then moved to the House Rules Committee, which controls the flow of legislation, where it stalled. All seemed lost until Gordon Gray, chair of the board of the National Trust for Historic Preservation, interceded. Gray had been a secretary of the army, president of the University of North Carolina, and member of the National Security Council. As a result, "he enjoyed a formidable reputation and when he spoke all listened."[20] Gray approached his good friend "Judge" Howard W. Smith, the House Rules Committee chair, and asked him to reconsider the bill.[21] Once the bill was released, the House expanded on the Senate version, strengthening its protective components.

On October 15, 1966, President Lyndon B. Johnson signed the National Historic Preservation Act (Public Law 89–655) into law. Title 1 authorized the secretary of the interior to maintain a National Register of Historic Places. To assist with this, the secretary could grant matching funds to states to conduct statewide surveys and develop preservation plans. These plans would serve as the basis for making grants that would help acquire, preserve, and develop historic properties. Additional funding could channel through the National Trust to benefit private organizations trying to preserve worthy sites. Section 106 of Title 1 added protective teeth to the bill, requiring federal agencies to consider the effects of any activities on areas included in the register before government funding or licenses could be issued.

Title 2 created the Advisory Council on Historic Preservation, which would among other things resolve conflicts arising from section 106 of Title 1. The council consisted of representatives from six federal agencies, the chair of the National Trust, and ten nonfederal presidential appointees. Additionally, the council would advise the president and Congress on historic preservation, encourage government and private preservation, guide states and localities in developing legislation, and promote professional training in the field. The National Park Service director would serve as the executive director. Hartzog's intense lobbying had paid off and ensured a dominant role for the Park Service.[22]

Once the National Historic Preservation Act was enacted, the Park Service faced the challenge of implementing what it coined as its "new preservation" program. The much-expanded effort would swell the ranks and necessitate a partnership between federal, state, and local governments as well as the private sector. In November 1966, Hartzog turned to Ronald Lee to assemble four senior administrators to conceive a plan for implementing Title 1 of the preservation act. The group suggested that a special task force develop criteria, standards, and a procedure for disseminating grants-in-aid funding. The group also made recommendations of nominees for the advisory council and suggested that a letter be drafted for the secretary to send to each state requesting they name a special liaison that would oversee each state's program.[23]

The new task force, under chief historian Robert Utley, lost little time in developing criteria that would determine which properties warranted inclusion in the new register. The task force believed eligible properties should be associated with important events or persons in history or with inspirational American ideals. Sites important for illuminating certain periods, showing distinctive styles of construction or workmanship, or that might be significant for research would be strong candidates. Generally, cemeteries, birthplaces, and religious buildings were excluded. Based on their statewide surveys, states would nominate worthy properties. Each state would prepare a preservation plan in order to be eligible for matching funds.

To head the new preservation effort, Hartzog hired Ernest Connally, hoping with this hire to further enhance the agency's academic respectability and standing. Connally accepted on the condition that a new organizational unit to administer the National Historic Preservation Act be created. To a meeting of the Society of Architectural Historians in 1967, Hartzog said, "the Office of Archeology and Historic Preservation will be viewed . . . as the equivalent of the European monuments offices. . . . I intend it to be as effective and as prestigious as its European counterparts. I intend it to be a scholarly institution drawing strength from such groups as the Society of Architectural Historians and the College Art Association."[24] Due to his university obligations, Connally had to delay taking up a new position until June 1967 when the school year ended, leaving Utley as the acting head.

The new Office of Archeology and Historic Preservation brought archaeology, historic architecture, and history together in one unit. Ideally, all projects would be overseen from their inception and research stages through the final construction and supervision stages. To staff the new positions, Hartzog agreed with Connally that they needed to hire people with respected academic qualifications, knowledge, and links to the preservation movement, which generally meant PhDs. While the new recruits gave the office credibility, they found it difficult to mesh with existing Park Service culture.[25]

Although Hartzog promised a European monument–style office, it did not last long. In one of his many reorganizations, he would weaken the all-inclusive Office of Archeology and Historic Preservation concept by moving the historical researchers and those involved in construction out to the service centers. Hartzog and his senior staff argued that this allowed better collaboration with park planners and that the move gave the impression that the Park Service had reduced its Washington overhead as it was being pressured to do. But it has been suggested that they wanted to diminish the growing power of Connally and squash his perceived attempts to break away into a separate monuments office.[26]

The new office faced other problems, such as lack of congressional funding. While Congress authorized $2 million for the 1967 fiscal year and an additional $10 million for each of the next three fiscal years, appropriations fell far short. Congress released no funding for the first year. In 1968 fiscal year, only $447,000 of the $10 million was appropriated. Of that, $300,000 went to the grant-in-aid program and the rest to establishing the advisory council. Since the state liaison systems were still being established and the funding was minimal, it was decided that the National Trust, which was firmly established, would get the initial grant funding. Funding shortfalls also kept the Park Service from hiring the new positions needed to help administer the National Historic Preservation Act.

Hartzog did his best to increase funding by emphasizing to key appropriations committee members the large sums requested by their home states. State liaison officers (later retitled state historic preservation officers) were urged to contact their congressional representatives and request their assistance. Despite such efforts, the escalating expense of the Vietnam War eclipsed domestic programs. For the 1969 fiscal year, funding dropped to $100,000 for the grants-in-aid program, one one-hundredth of the $10 million authorized. The Park Service got $82,500 to be divided among fifty states. Only twenty-five states bothered to submit funding requests. Awards, based on a percent of the state's total request, ranged from $11,745 to $788.51. With the need so great, no one was pleased.[27]

With so little money appropriated, attempts to develop federal and state partnerships withered and almost died. Fortunately, the next year funding increased to a more respectable $969,000 with nearly a third going to the National Trust. States responded to the financial incentives and began working on statewide surveys and preservation plans. In 1970, Congress would agree to extend funding for three more years.[28]

Although Hartzog had argued successfully to Congress that the National Register of Historic Places was simply an expansion of the National Historic Landmarks program, it operated much differently in practice. The landmark program identified and listed buildings and areas of national significance. Conversely, the National Register of Historic Places became a planning tool for all levels of government. Initially, only areas designated as national landmarks were added. As the Park Service developed criteria and received funding, state historic preservation officers made recommendations for additions. Based on a state's inventories and preservation plans, they decided which sites warranted grant-funding requests for acquisition, restoration, or protective measures. Whereas the landmarks program included nationally significant places, the states added areas of state and local significance to the register, thereby changing the character of the list and greatly expanding it. Additionally, all listings were now subject to section 106.

Hartzog agreed to publish an attractive copy of the register for reference and to help publicize the program. He also promoted the volume to Congress as a means of encouraging local tourism. The first preliminary version appeared in July 1968; the completion of final copy coincided with the arrival of Walter Hickel, the new secretary of the interior, in January

1969. Hartzog ceremoniously presented the book at a candlelight reception at the National Trust's Decatur House.[29]

Implementing Title 2 of the National Historic Preservation Act was delayed until July 1967, when funding became available. As legislated, the Park Service director would serve as executive director of the advisory council, but Hartzog chose to delegate that responsibility to Ernest Connally. Hartzog asked for and received suggestions for council appointees. He added a few names of his own and forwarded the list to Secretary Udall, who made his own adjustments and then sent the list to President Johnson. Those Johnson appointed were strong supporters of historic preservation, but they also enjoyed the support of prominent members of Congress.

Ideally, the advisory council would recommend historic preservation policies and ensure compliance with section 106. Soon, however, ensuring compliance took precedence.[30] Hartzog selected Robert R. Garvey Jr., an outspoken critic of the "federal bulldozer" from the National Trust, as the liaison between the Park Service and the advisory council but could not hire him until 1968 fiscal year funds became available. In the meantime, Utley oversaw issues related to section 106, such as a new highway that threatened the historical character of the Spanish American village of Las Trampas in New Mexico. In this first test case, Hartzog intervened and helped force the state highway commission to reach a solution with local preservationists. When Garvey became executive secretary, Hartzog instructed him to help fulfill the council's legislative mission, to prevent adversarial relationships between the Park Service and Congress, and to stay in control of the council's direction.

The council spent its first few years establishing procedures for how section 106 of Title 2 would be administered and how conflicts would be resolved. A number of cases would test the council's authority. Their outcomes clearly showed the council's power to force special considerations for historic preservation.[31] Undoubtedly a favorable climate arising from Johnson's Great Society, Udall's environmentalism, and the country's growing concern about protecting its natural and cultural resources helped.

While the council proved successful at resolving conflicts, the Park Service's unique involvement with it presented special challenges. The Park Service exerted great influence over the council leadership, making Hartzog happy, and also provided administrative support. However, Garvey's job as Park Service liaison and executive secretary resided in the Office of Archeology and Historic Preservation. Tensions grew between Connally, serving as acting director of the council, and Garvey, as both tried to steer the advisory council. Garvey maintained that the council looked biased to other federal agencies as long as the Office of Archeology and Historic Preservation was involved. Eventually, Hartzog under Garvey's urgings removed Connally as executive director and promoted Garvey to a special assistant position under his direct supervision. Garvey essentially became de facto executive director, and Connally lost a bit more power.

Hartzog refused to acknowledge any potential conflicts of interest, even though the Park Service oversaw the council and supplied it with professional investigative recommendations on which it based its decisions. To some, the Park Service gave the impression that since it was the premier preservation agency, it could do no wrong. In extreme cases, Park Service staff was called on to make assessments from opposing perspectives. For example, during the intense controversy over the Gettysburg Tower, agency employees prepared justification for why the Park Service should grant an easement for the tower and also assessed the impact such a tower would have on the historical qualities of the battlefield. Since a Park Service employee presided over the advisory council's deliberations, some wondered how an unbiased resolution was possible.

Perhaps Hartzog felt that since the Park Service was the premier historic preservation agency, it should be immune from any oversight. Some Park Service superintendents fought compliance with section 106 and wanted no outside interference in their parks. For example, Yellowstone superintendent Jack Anderson angrily complained to Hartzog when state historic preservation officials identified Yellowstone properties that warranted registry protection and therefore subjected him to section 106 restrictions.[32] Hartzog sided with Anderson, saying the Park Service would conduct its own inventory and there was no need for the state to duplicate the effort.[33] In May 1971, President Nixon would direct all federal agencies through Executive Order 11595 to locate, inventory, and nominate areas for inclusion in the national registry.

Hartzog kept control of the advisory council despite efforts to make it an independent federal entity. In 1976, after he had left office, legislation was proposed to make the council independent. He volunteered to travel to the Hill to help kill it, but then-director Gary Everhardt refused. Hartzog would later say that letting the advisory council go was the biggest mistake Everhardt ever made and that following the separation the council's edicts were not as well implemented.[34]

Without question, Hartzog played a significant role in the passage of the National Historic Preservation Act of 1966, which some call the most far-reaching historic preservation legislation ever enacted in the United States. It created a fundamental shift in how the country viewed its historic resources and also reasserted the Park Service's role as lead federal agency for historic preservation. National Park Service influence with the state and local governments grew owing to partnerships necessitated by the national registry program. Currently, the National Register of Historic Places has over eighty thousand listings. This number includes all historical areas of the National Park System, the over twenty-four hundred National Historic Landmarks designated by the secretary of the interior, and additional properties with state and local significance nominated by governments, organizations, or individuals.

Where there had once been a disjointed preservation effort, cooperation now extended across all government levels and beyond to the grassroots level. As funding levels increased, states responded to the financial incentives by actively working on statewide surveys and preservation plans. Such efforts would shift the emphasis in historic preservation. Instead of states just seeking to protect individual landmarks, they might start looking more holistically at neighborhoods with worthy historic resources. Old buildings were renovated for modern uses and adaptive uses were found for historic districts.

Membership in professional organizations, such as the National Trust for Historic Preservation, grew.[35] The field became much more professionalized as college and universities began offering degree programs. People increasingly recognized the economic benefits from related jobs, tourism, enhanced quality of life, and heightened property values. Additional protective amendments and supportive measures (i.e., tax credits, rehabilitation grants, etc.) have since been passed.[36] While much has been accomplished since 1966, the fight to protect the country's historic resources continues.

❧

Another of Hartzog's legislative achievements with long-lasting benefits was the formalization of the park volunteer program. He recalled that the idea for a volunteer program originated during a visit to the Arlington House, also called the Custis-Lee Mansion. Overlooking Washington, D.C., the house was built by George Washington's adopted son, George Washington Parke Custis, and eventually passed to his daughter, who married Robert E. Lee. Lee and his wife had lived there prior to the outbreak of the Civil War, and it was to that period that the house had been restored. Hartzog favored the elegant mansion for entertaining important congressmen and philanthropists like Paul Mellon.

Unpaid docents staffed the house and interpreted its rich history for visitors. On one of his visits, Hartzog struck up a conversation asking them what they did and why. It occurred to him that a system-wide program of volunteers might benefit both the volunteer and the Park System.[37] He appointed a task force to study the feasibility. The task force reported favorably, but the report came in the final year of the Johnson administration. Hartzog knew that bills introduced toward the end of a president's tenure had a significantly reduced chance of passing. Secretary Udall concurred, so Hartzog slipped the proposed legislation in his desk drawer to await a new administration. When Nixon appointed Walter J. Hickel as secretary of the interior, Hartzog lost little time in presenting the volunteer bill as a new initiative. Hickel gave him enthusiastic support.[38]

The timing was excellent for promoting volunteerism. John F. Kennedy had earlier challenged the country to "ask not what your country can do for you but what you can do for your country."[39] Lyndon Johnson had followed suit when he initiated his War on Poverty with such programs as Volunteers-in-Service-to-America, or VISTA as it was commonly called. Even Richard Nixon felt pushed toward national service and formed a cabinet-level committee on voluntary action.

Hartzog faced few objections to the proposed Volunteers-in-Parks bill. He did remember discussing certain points with a concerned George Meany, president of the AFL-CIO. Meany needed reassurance that the volunteers would not replace unionized park maintenance positions. Hartzog also faced the usual reluctance of Senator Alan Bible. Chair of the parks and recreation subcommittee in addition to appropriations subcommittee, Bible was often hesitant to approve new programs that would need funding. On friendly terms with Bible, Hartzog enjoyed their lively bantering but knew when to back off deferentially.

During an Interior and Insular Affairs Committee meeting, Bible queried Hartzog about the $54,000 requested for the program's overhead and staffing needs. Bible grilled Hartzog about the need for a GS-13 "bureaucrat" to run the program, fearing the anticipated costs would escalate.

"Next year will the GS-13 need a secretary?" Bible asked.

"I suspect he will," Hartzog replied.

"The year after that he will need an assistant?" To which Hartzog, who knew Bible's concerns, answered, "I don't think so."

Bible fired back that "with all due deference and with my regard for you, you sure try to get a little more in on it."

The bantering continued with Bible at first threatening to remove funding for the GS-13 employee but then ending the lengthy inquisition by saying that maybe both the overhead costs and the personnel funding could be saved.[40] Hartzog said Bible's position on both subcommittees made him unique because he "caught you on legislation and then he could reexamine the whole picture when it got to appropriations."[41]

With few difficulties, Public Law 91–357 was enacted on July 29, 1970. Mrs. Nixon attended the legislation's inauguration ceremony held at the Custis-Lee Mansion, where she helped recognize the first two male and forty-two female volunteers.[42] Hartzog had estimated a hundred volunteers would eventually enroll in the first year and that there would be a steady increase in numbers thereafter as funding became available.

In April 1972, which was less than two years later, an impatient Hartzog fired off a critical letter to his regional directors about the volunteer program's lack of progress. He charged the directors with failing to fully use that fiscal year's funding. For each region, he included the amount of funds allotted and the amount spent to date, which made the gap evident. "The record would seem to indicate you have not done very well at this late date in the fiscal year to implement this program, . . . one of the high priority programs of the First Lady."[43] Regional directors knew such a letter warranted their immediate attention. Frank Kowski, regional director for the Southwest Region, quickly sent a pointed letter to his superintendents saying that since he had gotten his "butt chewed off," he would apply similar pressure to help Hartzog "put this program over the top."[44]

By December 1, 1972, the Park Service had released a press statement bragging that in the preceding year 144 parks had established Volunteers-in-Parks programs with some six thousand volunteers contributing 196,000 hours. Volunteers had participated in battlefield reenactments, given interpretive walks and talks, provided medical assistance during performances at Wolf Trap Farm for the Performing Arts, assisted in archaeological digs, and demonstrated various arts and crafts like candle making and weaving. To would-be volunteers, Hartzog was quoted as saying "You must have a skill and the park must have a need."[45]

Over the years, the Volunteers-in-Parks program has flourished. In 2005, the program touted 137,000 volunteers, who contributed 5.2 million hours of work for an estimated value of $91.2 million.[46] Despite the program's success and benefit to the Park System, some, including Hartzog, worried that a budget-strapped Park Service had come to rely too heavily on volunteers at the expense of permanent and seasonal staff. To Hartzog, that was never the intent of the legislation.[47]

※

A third legislative success story involved outside donations to the National Park System. As funding became increasing difficult to secure from Congress, Hartzog looked to other sources. He knew that philanthropy had enriched the National Park System in ways the federal government could not. Many parks owed their existence in whole or part to generous donors. Those passionate about parks gave millions, such as philanthropic giants like the Mellons and Rockefellers, while others, like the schoolchildren who contributed to Shenandoah National Park in Virginia, gave pennies. Supporters also donated period furnishings and artifacts, built buildings, funded special educational programs, and gave in innumerable other ways. When Hartzog became director, he inherited what he found to be an outdated trust fund governing private donations.

The National Park Trust Fund bill had been passed on July 10, 1935. Gifts or bequests made to the trust fund were overseen by a board consisting of the secretary of the interior, director of the National Park Service, and two people appointed by the president. Financial management of the funds fell to the secretary of the treasury.

According to Hartzog, this board proved unsatisfactory for two reasons. First, the secretary of the treasury quickly established a rule whereby all donations, whether stocks, bonds, or land, were converted to cash and then invested into treasury bonds. But bonds yielded low rates of returns when compared with stocks and other investments, and wealthy donors benefiting from the economic resurgence after the Depression hated to see their contributions diminished. The second problem, according to Hartzog, was that taxpayers seemed reluctant to send the federal government more money, especially after hefty tax payouts.[48]

Hartzog credits his predecessor, Conrad Wirth, with discussing the trust fund's limitations with secretary of the interior Stewart Udall. Udall responded by hiring Donald Thurber, a financial consultant from Detroit, to investigate and make recommendations. Thurber assembled a small committee of experts in law, regulations, and legal research to assist him.[49] He finished his report as Hartzog assumed the directorate. Thurber recommended that the ineffective trust fund be abolished and that a new foundation replace it. Private trustees would manage the fund instead of the secretary of the treasury, thereby giving it the financial freedom needed to make more prudent investments. Udall enthusiastically supported the recommendations, and Hartzog set out to gain congressional support.

Timing seemed favorable since the bill coincided with a growing interest in purchasing proposed parklands while prices were low. Increasingly Hartzog saw that once congressional approval was granted, parkland prices often skyrocketed and areas taken by condemnation were awarded "outrageous prices."[50] He found committee members generally supportive of the bill, but he encountered some issues that needed his diplomatic skills. Senator Harry F. Byrd of Virginia briefly held up the legislation because he worried that a foundation flush with donations might provide incentive to condemn lands in advance of congressional authorization.[51] Once Hartzog convinced him that would not happen, he withdrew his opposition and the legislation moved forward.

Hartzog's next challenge arose when an assistant secretary of the treasury balked at giving up control of the trust fund. The assistant convinced his superiors in Treasury to withhold a favorable report to the Bureau of Budget. He knew that without it, congressional committees would halt the bill's progress. After months of haggling without success, Hartzog switched tactics and visited the aging Senator Byrd, who served as chair of the Senate Finance Committee. After hearing a brief explanation of the problem, Byrd suggested that Hartzog wait in an adjoining room since Harry H. Fowler, the secretary of the treasury, was scheduled to arrive for a meeting at any moment.

Shortly after the secretary arrived, Byrd invited Hartzog to join him in explaining the problem to Fowler. Byrd pointedly told Fowler he would like to see a favorable report sent to the Bureau of Budget. That afternoon, Hartzog got a call from Bureau of Budget saying Treasury had cleared the report. An amused Hartzog remembered hearing that Treasury officials were livid about his going over their heads and having them overruled.

Hartzog recalled another problem involving Rogers Morton, who then served on the House Interior and Insular Affairs Committee. Morton insisted on adding a sentence that said the board "shall not engage in any business."[52] Hartzog had objected, but the insertion remained. When Morton later became secretary of the interior and chairman of foundation, Hartzog said he was "bound by his own stupid legislation." Morton would learn that his insertion hampered foundation activities and kept it, for example, from accepting small businesses that people without an heir apparent might want to donate.[53]

On December 18, 1967, Congress established the tax-exempt, charitable National Park Foundation (Public Law 90–208). As the official nonprofit partner of the National Park Service, the foundation could solicit, accept, and administer gifts of real and personal property for the benefit of the national parks. The secretary of the interior served as chairman of the foundation, while the director of the National Park Service fulfilled the role of secretary. A minimum of six private citizens appointed by the secretary served initially staggered terms until a full six-year term could be put in place. Board members included such heavyweights as philanthropist Laurance S. Rockefeller; Paul H. Douglas, former Illinois senator; retired Supreme Court justice Thomas C. Clark; Rudolph Peterson from Bank of America; and Margaret Wentworth Owings, conservationist and wife of well-known architect and engineer Nathaniel Owings. Hartzog tried to interest Mrs. Lyndon B. Johnson, but she declined.[54]

The National Park Foundation started with a beginning balance of $784,386.72, the amount transferred over from the old trust fund account.[55] At the first board meeting, Laurance Rockefeller pledged to donate property adjacent to Grand Teton National Park, valued at over $1 million. Much of the money would be directed toward developing environmental education materials for schoolchildren. Initially, the board put the most emphasis on education, land acquisition, support of conservation programs, and the donation of funds by others.

Additionally, the board supported a variety of smaller projects. These included such things as buying and refurbishing a beloved community carousel from a Washington, D.C., amusement park so it remained in the city; providing grant money for the Christian ministries program in the national parks; giving $2,000 to National Geographic to help protect archaeological remains at Stanton Cave; and granting $7,500 to the fledgling Student Conservation Society, a nonprofit volunteer organization that placed volunteers in parks.[56] By June 30, 1971, the National Park Foundation's coffers had grown to $9.2 million, due largely to Andrew W. Mellon Foundation's infusion of funds that would allow the purchase of lands on Cumberland Island in Georgia.[57] When Congress authorized the new seashore park, the foundation turned over the lands that had been purchased with Mellon funding to the Park Service to manage.

Hartzog had worried about covering management costs, and he had successfully inserted a provision that allowed him to use government employees to operate the foundation and pay for its overhead. After Hartzog left, he recalled that Representative Sidney R. Yates of Illinois, chairman of the Park Service's appropriations subcommittee, abolished federal support, forcing the foundation to fund its own office space and pay administrative employees.[58] That hurt the foundation financially, but eventually it rebounded. Today, the foundation grants over $31 million each year in cash, services, or in-kind donations to the Park Service.[59]

⁑

While George Hartzog excelled at cajoling legislative support in Congress, he discovered implementing legislation, new policies, and innovative ideas within his agency more challenging. From the beginning, he found changing the traditional agency mindset easier said than done. He had faced difficulties with broadening the type of employee hired. Women, ethnic minorities, PhDs, and those with degrees outside resource management fields simply did not fit the mold and were not readily accepted. Urban programming and parks stood in stark contrast to the crown jewels and faced resistance.

On a smaller scale, Hartzog tried to create an agency emblem more reflective of the Park System. He thought the arrowhead-shaped one with a large sequoia tree, bison, distant lake, and mountains outdated. A new triangular emblem would better represent the Park System's natural, historical, and recreational areas, while cannon balls in the center would reflect the new historic preservation dimension. Stiff resistance from the field and the unfavorable comments of Horace Albright to secretary of the interior Walter Hickel rapidly shot down the new symbol, and the familiar one remained.[60] So while Hartzog wanted to embrace change, he faced an agency often reluctant to give up its traditional ways.

Initially, Hartzog thought that by using his power as director he could force change on the agency. In some instances, he succeeded through intimidation, coaxing, personnel changes, transfers, and positive or negative incentives. The hardest lesson he had to learn, however, was that real change only occurred "with the permission of the organization."[61] He learned that one could lead only if the troops agreed to follow.

When outside forces pushed the Park Service to increase its science effort, Hartzog faced considerable resistance. He wanted the Park Service to be seen as innovative and progressive, but, as he said, "they liked it the way it was."[62] He was embarrassed by the stinging public criticism over the Park Service's lack of scientific data to support its management decisions, particularly with regard to its elk and bison reduction programs. He knew that public redemption lay in ratcheting up the science program.

Hartzog credited George Wright, not himself, with beginning a research program in the national parks. Wright, who came from a wealthy family, studied forestry before accepting an assistant park naturalist position in

Yosemite National Park in 1927. Concerned that the Park Service understood little about its wildlife populations, he personally financed a wildlife survey program. In 1930, he became the first chief of the wildlife division and proceeded to initiate studies to assess wildlife populations, identify problem areas, and make management recommendations.[63]

In a departure from customary management practices, the new cadre of biologists suggested that parks be kept in or returned to a natural condition, that nonnative species needed to be controlled, that predators merited protection, and that scientific research was essential. Tragically, Wright was killed in an automobile accident before the importance of the idea of scientific research became firmly entrenched in Park Service culture.[64]

"After that, science just kind of plugged along," according to Hartzog.[65] Instead of establishing a research unit in the Park Service, wildlife biologists were transferred to the Bureau of Biological Survey. Although the biologists often kept their duty stations within the national parks, their influence within the parks diminished. Soon the Biological Survey was combined with Bureau of Sport Fisheries and Wildlife to become the Fish and Wildlife Service. The former Park Service biologists found themselves at odds in the new agency that seemed more focused on the commercial and recreational uses of wildlife than with preservation.

The forties and fifties was "one of the bleakest periods of science in the NPS."[66] Severe budget cuts during World War II forced the Park Service to operate with a skeletal staff. After the war, the need for making informed management decisions based on scientific knowledge grew, but funds were limited and few research positions were created. Instead, the Park Service allowed independent researchers and foundations to conduct scientific studies in the parks.[67] Little improved with the Conrad Wirth administration. A landscape architect by profession, Wirth concentrated on implementing his heavily funded Mission 66 program of building park infrastructure to meet the demands of soaring postwar visitation. In 1958, the budget for research studies (excluding salaries) stood at just $28,000, a minute amount compared to that directed toward development and construction.[68]

"Everybody knew that you needed it but it didn't press itself as a priority until the sixties," Hartzog recalled.[69] Several internal reports criticized the agency's failure to embrace the need for scientific knowledge in the management of parks. One report released in October 1961 called *Get the Facts and Put Them to Work* chastised the agency for its poorly funded research program and its lack of "continuity, coordination, and depth."[70] The secretary of the interior's advisory board mirrored such concerns. Environmental groups also increasingly challenged the basis on which the government made management decisions on public lands.

What helped bring these concerns to the forefront was the public affairs nightmare created by sport-hunting controversies in the national parks. While sport hunting was traditionally banned in national parks as required by law, the Park Service had been conducting reduction programs for ungulates, such as elk, in select parks. For example, it allowed "deputized park rangers" to participate in hunts at the Grand Teton National Park. Increasingly, hunters pushed for more access to hunting opportunities in new and existing parks.

The controversy erupted at Yellowstone, when resource managers concerned about range degradation planned to reduce by half the northern elk herd of around ten thousand animals. Hunters clambered to participate while environmentalists questioned the scientific basis for such a reduction program. Wirth originally seemed agreeable to allowing public participation, only to back off under heavy pressure, further incensing hunting groups. Critics feared that if national parks opened their doors to public hunting, they could never close them.[71]

Secretary of the interior Stewart Udall responded to the uproar by calling for thorough studies of science and resource management. To gain credibility and outside perspectives, he asked the National Academy of Sciences to study the "natural history research needs and opportunities" in the national parks.[72] The academy chose William J. Robbins, a prominent biologist from the National Science Foundation, to head the blue-ribbon committee. To assess wildlife management practices, Udall persuaded A. Starker Leopold, son of the prominent ecologist Aldo Leopold, to head a second committee. For the first time, the Park Service would have an independent and in-depth assessment of its research and wildlife management policies.

In March 1963, less than a month after George Hartzog became associate director, the widely publicized *Wildlife Management in the National Parks*, or Leopold report as it became known, appeared. Rather than deal with specific management problems like the elk reduction programs, Leopold's committee developed a philosophy of wildlife management based on emerging ecological thinking. The group wrote that each park should "be maintained, or where necessary recreated, as nearly as possible in the condition that prevailed when the area was first visited by the white man. A national park should represent a vignette of primitive America."[73]

The committee acknowledged that given changes over the preceding 350 years this would not be easy and would require a radical shift in thinking for the Park Service. Park Service managers were urged to "recognize the enormous complexity of ecologic communities and the diversity of management procedures required to preserve them." The report went on to say that the Park Service was best suited to direct its own research activities, although it could continue to benefit from the outside researchers.

Five months later, in August 1963, the National Academy of Science delivered its sharply critical analysis, often referred to as the Robbins report. Research in the parks, it charged, "lacked direction, has been piecemeal, has suffered because of failure to recognize the distinction between research and administrative decision making, and has failed to insure the implementation of the results of research in operational management." The committee found it "inconceivable" that an agency charged with protecting national treasures lacked competent research scientists. The committee made twenty recommendations, including a number that targeted Park Service organizational structure, personnel, and budgeting. Although Wirth gave the impression that he supported the report, secretly he resented the public chastisement and made little effort to implement changes before he retired.[74]

The best chance for change lay with George Hartzog, who wanted to be seen as a progressive leader. Hartzog disliked the negative image portrayed by the reports and so wanted to address the deficiencies. He hired George Sprugel, a respected National Science Foundation biologist, as chief scientist. Sprugel would run a new Division of Natural Sciences Studies, thus establishing an "identifiable" research unit as recommended in the Robbins report. Hartzog declined to establish a direct link to the director as recommended, opting instead to have the unit answer to Howard Stagner, one of six assistant directors but also a strong advocate for the science program.

In setting up the new research unit, Sprugel and his team of largely PhD scientists wanted to develop long-range studies to gain better ecological understandings of the park resources rather than settle immediately into studying specific resource management problems. Ideally, each park would develop its own research program. Early plans were developed for Isle Royale in Michigan, Everglades in Florida, Great Smoky Mountains in North Carolina and Tennessee, and Haleakalā in Hawaii. By the late 1960s, these plans would be included in park resource management plans.[75]

Off to a slow but promising start, the fledgling science program would suffer from two problems—lack of funding and lack of power. The Robbins report pointed out that the Park Service from 1960 to 1962 had spent less than 1 percent of its appropriations on research, which compared most unfavorably to the approximately 10 percent spent by comparable federal agencies.[76]

By 1965, Hartzog had managed to raise science funding to $105,000, which was $80,000 more than 1963 levels, but still woefully inadequate. Even Hartzog admitted the science program had not progressed as he hoped and that results were mixed.[77]

Hartzog maintained that he could not convince members of Congress to fund research. He recalled approaching Michael J. Kirwan, chair of the House Interior Appropriations Subcommittee, about research funding. Hartzog remembered Kirwan gathering his thoughts and looking down at his stomach. Hartzog knew from past experience that when Kirwan "contemplated his navel," the outlook was not promising. "Research . . . research . . . research," Kirwan said. "NIH does research." Hartzog responded that he wanted to study the park resources, to which Kirwan replied that "I think NIH is doing enough."[78] Realizing the futility of asking for "research" dollars, Hartzog looked at previous organizational charts and found the title "resource studies." He resubmitted his request under the new name, and all the requested funding was appropriated. While funding did grow under Hartzog, park scientists felt it paled compared to what other divisions within the Park Service received, and it remained far below the science funding in comparable federal agencies.[79]

Hartzog faced funding issues with most, if not all, of his initiatives, especially as the escalating costs of the Vietnam War resulted in significant drops in domestic appropriations. Deciding whether the Alaska effort or minority hiring or urban programs or a myriad of other programs should get priority could not have been easy. While Hartzog supported the science program, it was not one of his top priorities. Had it been, he would have found a way to better fund it. Hartzog favored programs that would give him the most bang for his buck and impress congressional committees. Given limited funding, long-term research studies compared poorly with more flashy initiatives.

Additionally, Hartzog lacked a science background and was on occasion guilty of not understanding the value of research in assisting with management decisions. He came through the ranger ranks, where decisions likely were made by reference to "gut" feelings based on years of field experience. In response to a request to study wild boars in the Great Smoky Mountains, where Hartzog had served as assistant superintendent, he bellowed, "Do with them? . . . I can tell you what to do with them! Shoot the goddamn beasts."[80]

In addition to funding problems, the new science unit suffered from lack of power. While the Robbins report had recommended that the science unit operate independently so it could conduct studies that might yield results critical of current management practices, Hartzog would never have allowed that level of freedom and power in his organization. The Robbins report had also recommended that research "must form the basis of all management problems" and that every phase of management be "under the jurisdiction of biologically trained personnel."[81] But this would have meant a shift in power that those in the traditional hierarchy would have fought hard.

While Sprugel supposedly controlled his park scientists, he found that park superintendents and regional directors had line authority and ultimate control over his program. Sprugel found Hartzog "friendly" toward his efforts but saw his top lieutenants as obstructionists.[82] In frustration over funding and lack of support, Sprugel left in September 1966. He said he felt like an outsider that Hartzog had "thrust down the throats" of managers unwilling to accept the new science focus.[83] A sharply worded *Bioscience* article following Sprugel's departure noted that the Park Service "had turned its back on scientific advice" of the Leopold and Robbins reports. Given that three years had passed since the reports were published, the Park Service's efforts were described as "sorry at best."[84]

Shortly following Sprugel's departure, Hartzog raised the science program's sagging reputation by hiring the well-respected A. Starker Leopold. As lead author of the 1963 *Wildlife Management in the National Parks*, Leopold understood the challenges faced by the Park Service. He had refused the first offer, but Hartzog had persisted, saying he was key to changing the Park Service management practices his report had criticized. Finally Leopold accepted after working out an arrangement whereby he kept his position at the University of California and ran the National Park Service's science program from there. Hartzog held immense respect for Leopold, saying that "whatever he said I took as gospel."[85] Hartzog elevated the science division to a new Office of Natural Science Studies with a direct link to the directorate, which gave it a coveted spot in the director's inner circle.

With Leopold stationed in California, Robert Linn, his deputy, handled much of the day-to-day operations in Washington. To establish credibility, advanced degrees including doctorates were needed to run the science initiative, but the Park Service lacked such credentialed employees. The agency not only hired scientists but also agreed to send promising employees back to school.

The science program's elevated stature proved short lived. After only a year, Leopold resigned in June 1968, after he realized that he could not do justice to the two positions. He suggested Robert Linn replace him, which Hartzog supported. In August 1969, Hartzog again reorganized his administration, this time burying the science program far from the director's ear.

Less than a year later, in early 1970, he reorganized again, and this time grouped the science program with the new Harpers Ferry Center and the newly combined service center now located in Denver. Two more reorganizations would follow; the final December 1972 one moved science back to a more prominent spot just before Hartzog left office.[86]

Throughout Hartzog's many reorganizations, tensions over who controlled scientific research intensified. Superintendents, who believed themselves captains of their own ships, disliked the independence of scientific researchers in their parks. As Robert Barbee, whom the Park Service had elevated to a superintendent after paying for him to earn an advanced science degree, said "managers felt scientists should be influential but should be working for managers." They continually put pressure on Hartzog to give them more control. Perhaps succumbing to such pressures, Hartzog transferred Washington staff scientists to the regional offices. Scattered throughout the country, the scientists' ability to communicate with each other and to plan interdisciplinary research programs diminished. As was typical of his management style, Hartzog had failed to give Linn warning of the move. After the announcement, he asked Linn whether he had real "heavy objections." Caught by surprise, Linn came to deeply regret not more forcefully fighting the decision. In reality, even had he objected strongly, Hartzog would not have changed his decision.[87]

Linn believed most people in the Park Service failed to understand the importance of research, which they viewed as research "hobbies." Some of the new science hires were PhDs who hadn't come up through the ranks and therefore were not seen as true "green bloods." The new scientists struggled to find common ground with other employees, who regarded them as impinging on the traditional rangers' resource management responsibilities. Not surprisingly, when superintendents were faced with difficult decisions, they commonly sided with rangers' seasoned opinions over those of the more cautious scientists, who felt uncomfortable making snap decisions based on incomplete research.

Regional managers and superintendents wanted scientists at their disposal for help with specific management problems and not sidetracked by long-term research studies. Hartzog claimed his reorganizations did not result in a loss of the scientists' "professional independence" but reigned in "an uncontrolled and oftentimes irregular administrative process." The research program, he said, was determined by the chief scientist.[88] Chief scientist Robert Linn saw it differently, claiming to have witnessed what he called the "end of a centrally directed science program."[89]

Exercising their new control, superintendents and regional directors cut budgets for research projects and redirected funds to more pressing and immediate problems such as dangerous tree removal, fire suppression, and visitor services. Ken Baker, a scientist at Hawaii Volcanoes, watched helplessly as his $5,200 research budget simply disappeared, leaving him nothing. With scientific studies no longer centralized, determining the level of spending became difficult to measure and therefore hard to criticize.[90]

Additionally, scientists trained to seek peer review and publish their work faced an agency that carefully guarded its image. Hartzog and other administrators would not have allowed critical and embarrassing reports to circulate. As a result, park scientists published little in professional journals compared to other scientists and infrequently attended professional meetings.

Park scientists' stature improved with new legislation that helped provide legitimacy for their work. Passed in 1969, the National Environmental Policy Act required federal agencies to complete environmental impact statements before taking any major action on their lands. The science program stood to benefit by lending its expertise to assess the proposed action, such as building a new campground, for its impacts and then help develop alternatives. But the Park Service resented the intrusion, feeling that as a preservation agency its practices remained above reproach. Compared to other federal agencies, it responded slowly and reluctantly.[91]

To help comply with the requirements of the National Environmental Policy Act, the Denver Service Center added just three full-time scientists supplemented with three part-timers. In comparison to the hundreds of people involved in planning and development activities, scientists, who would help determine the impacts of proposed activities, represented a very small minority. In a memorandum to Hartzog, Johannes E. Jensen, an assistant director, wrote that he would need many more scientists than six to prepare 120 environmental impact statements for the coming year and provide input for at least another 75. He went on to say that given their available combined workdays, it would be impossible to complete them, even if he borrowed other personnel.[92] As a result, the overloaded scientists often merely rubber stamped Park Service activities instead of carefully assessing impacts and helping develop ecologically sound projects and alternatives. With time, however, the National Environmental Policy Act and other environmental legislation such as the Clean Water Act, Clean Air Act, and Endangered Species Act would create the need for specially trained scientists within the Park Service.[93]

Another positive step for the Park Service's science efforts involved the development of cooperative park study units. During the contentious hearings for the proposed North Cascades in Washington, Senator Henry "Scoop" Jackson pushed the Park Service to establish a cooperative research agreement with the University of Washington in the hope that such an arrangement would provide a better understanding of the ecological and sociological aspects of the park. In April 1970, the first study unit was established at the University of Washington to the mutual benefit of both groups. The university benefited from the arrangement by being able to add Park Service scientists as adjunct faculty and by being awarded research contracts. The Park Service benefited from the access to technological and educational amenities, the comparatively low overhead, and the boost to its tarnished science reputation.

To Hartzog, the arrangement brought an additional political benefit. Most people, he said, failed to realize the tremendous political clout of the Association of University Presidents. "So my thought was . . . to put those units in the university and you not only have the university speaking on your behalf to raise money for them, you just got yourself a first class lobbying organization. They got more power than you got."[94]

The University of Washington cooperative park study unit became the prototype for an expanding system. By 1973, the Park Service had entered into agreements with eighteen universities. While the program allowed the Park Service to better study and understand its resources, the agency carefully controlled what research it funded and permitted to be conducted in the national parks. Studies of controversial issues such as grizzly bear declines or elk overpopulation that might create embarrassing political situations were avoided.[95]

Overall, Hartzog advanced the science program slowly. He did increase funding and created an office dedicated to research, but at the same time the program was hampered by considerations having to do with his political agenda. Secretary Udall had directed the Park Service to incorporate the recommendations of the Leopold report into its administrative policies.

Hartzog would include the report in its entirety in his slim administrative policy manual for natural areas.[96] But in practice, Hartzog chose to selectively follow the recommendations in his policy manual. For example, bowing to the public outcry over the reduction of the Yellowstone elk herds, Hartzog crafted a political solution rather than one having a sound ecological basis. In the national spotlight, hunters had lined up against those opposed to the killings, putting Senator Gale W. McGee on the defensive and precipitating a congressional hearing. In a secret meeting prior to the hearings, Hartzog had met with McGee and agreed to halt the shooting.

During the hearings, Hartzog strategically sat close to the testimonial table. After Wyoming's governor Stanley K. Hathaway had launched a scathing attack on the Park Service and asked that the elk be shipped to other areas, Hartzog stepped into his path. Exuding his considerable charm, he thanked the governor for his comments. After each testimonial, Hartzog repeated his actions. By the time Hartzog stood to testify, the crowd gave him a standing ovation. When he revealed his plan to halt the shooting, those opposed to the hunts were mollified. Hunters were also pacified since the reduction program had been halted.

On the governor's suggestion, elk were live trapped and relocated to other areas in Wyoming until ranchers objected that the elk were eating grassland intended for their livestock and the governor was forced to ask that the program be stopped.[97] The political firestorm died, but the problem of elk overpopulation and range depletion remained. The Park Service's new elk policy became letting nature take its course to determine a natural population level despite no scientific evidence to support such an approach and despite the Leopold report's recommendation that the elk population be reduced.[98]

Another example of a political solution was the way Hartzog handled the problem of the explosion in the population of feral goats in Hawaii Volcanoes National Park, which had wreaked havoc with native plant species. To save the plants, park staff tried, where possible, to keep them out with fences, but if necessary they simply shot them.[99] The vocal concerns of local hunters who enjoyed hunting the goats prompted Hartzog to fly to the island with Representative Patsy T. Mink. According to Hartzog, "We decided we're going to deputize 'em [the local hunters], and she and I go over there and we had a great big shootin' festival. We kill goats until hell won't have 'em."[100] To placate the hunters, Hartzog stated that the Park Service had "no intention of exterminating goats from Hawaii Volcanoes National Park."[101]

This directive came despite the clear recommendations in the Leopold report to concentrate management efforts on native species. The report even stated that "a visitor who climbs a volcano in Hawaii ought to see mamane trees and silver-swords, not goats."[102] Pressure from environmental groups prompted Hartzog to justify the new policy by saying that some exotic plants "may be held in a state of equilibrium by the pressure of the exotic goat."[103] Ken Baker, the park biologist, called the reasoning "poor thinking." Superintendent Gene J. Balaz also disagreed and continued work to reduce goat populations in order to restore the natural ecosystem. Hartzog promptly removed Balaz from the Hawaiian Volcanoes superintendency in August 1971.[104]

The Park Service continued to face controversies over its lack of supporting scientific evidence for its actions. In 1968, Yellowstone National Park decided it wanted to force garbage-fed bears to forage naturally and so began closing its open garbage dumps, with the final closure slated for 1971. John and Frank Craighead, well-respected bear experts who had studied the bears since 1959, cautioned the Park Service to close the dumps more gradually, thereby allowing the bears to adjust. Based on no scientific evidence to the contrary, the Park Service refused to back down and the closures proceeded. Human-bear conflicts spiked, as did the number of "problem bears" killed. Some eighty-eight grizzlies were euthanized in the Yellowstone area in the two years following the closures, leaving many to wonder whether the animal would survive in the park. In 1975, it was listed as a threatened species. Through various interagency efforts, grizzly numbers would eventually stabilize and gradually increase.[105]

Despite its problems in some areas, the Park Service's research program progressed well in its fire research, even though it was strongly resisted by park managers. The Leopold report helped open the door by calling fire "an essential management tool" and suggesting that its suppression had led to unnatural plant communities and a buildup of dangerous fuel.[106] Those used to total fire suppression and used to seeing all fire as the enemy, on the other hand, objected to any shifts in policy. Hartzog recalled a meeting attended by former director Horace Albright, who berated the Grand Teton National Park superintendent for allowing a fire to burn in the park. Calling it heresy, Albright pushed for a resolution to suppress all fires in national parks. When he asked Hartzog what he planned to do, Hartzog replied, "Horace, we love you but we're going to let it burn."[107]

The Park Service had successfully experimented with prescribed fire in the 1950s in the Everglades and began similar efforts in other parks such as Sequoia and Kings Canyon in the mid-1960s. The 1968 administrative handbook for natural areas that Hartzog penned noted that "the presence or absence of natural fire within a given habitat is recognized as one of the ecological factors contributing to the perpetuation of plants and animals native to that habitat." Fires within park-established boundaries would be allowed to "run their course."[108] The Park Service led the way for other agencies in experimenting with fire and shifting its official fire policy.[109]

While the Hartzog directorate record's with respect to advancing scientific research in the parks was inconsistent, future administrations likewise struggled, as evidenced by subsequent critical reports. In 1977, Durwood Allen and Starker Leopold reviewed the Park Service's science program and found that it still lacked adequate funding, staffing, and influence within the agency. Pressured by Congress to study the condition of its parks, the Park Service responded with *State of the Parks—1980: A Report to Congress*, in which it found widespread and serious threats to the national parks. It called for the Park Service to "significantly expand its research and resource management capabilities," which were "clearly inadequate to respond to the needs of the Service." Outside reports, such as the National Park and Conservation Association's 1988 and 1989 reports and a 1992 report from the National Academy of Sciences, urged better scientific research to understand threats and protect resources. Finally, some twenty-six years after Hartzog left office, Congress passed the National Parks Omnibus Management Act of 1998 (Public Law 105–39), which mandated that the Park Service use scientific research and information to manage its parks. The Park Service still struggles with implementing that mandate as evidenced by a National Park Science Committee 2004 report entitled *National Park Service Science in the 21st Century: Recommendations Concerning Science and Future Directions for Science and Scientific Resource Management*.[110]

⁂

As Hartzog continued to reassess his career, he added to his list of accomplishments with the help of former senior staff, such as William Brown, Bill Everhart, and Robert Utley. Examination of these achievements provided further insights into his leadership of the National Park Service. Clearly Hartzog excelled in the legislative arena. Capture of the National Historic Preservation Act showcased his political maneuvering at its finest. A convincing argument as to why the Park Service should manage the country's historic preservation effort combined with his influence and the support of political friends stole the legislation from competing organizations. Once enacted, he used the new preservation responsibilities to extend Park Service influence beyond its traditional boundaries to state and local entities.

Hartzog grew to enjoy the power of his position and was always looking for ways to gain more control over the agency and influences affecting the Park System. With the National Historic Preservation Act, he won total control of the historic preservation program and got a lead role for the Park Service on the Advisory Council on Historic Preservation. Previously park volunteers had received little oversight, so formalizing the program gave the agency greater control over their activities. With the National Park Foundation, Hartzog supplied administrative support, which kept him informed and helped him influence the board members. His role as executive secretary also allowed him to exert considerable influence when it came to what projects were funded.

Within the Park Service, Hartzog left no doubt that he was in charge. When Ernest Connally appeared to be amassing too much power, Hartzog reorganized, stripping some of it away. When his advisors worried that scientists had too much freedom, one of his many reorganizations placed them more firmly under regional and superintendent control. Those who crossed him stood to be severely reprimanded and possibly moved to less desirable positions.

Hartzog set high standards and expected everyone to meet them. He wanted the Park Service viewed as a professional outfit and not "a maintenance crew."[111] To that end, he moved away from hiring the "jack-of-all-trades" and added specialists in a variety of disciplines. With historic preservation and the science program, he wanted credibility and so brought in well-respected academicians like Ernest Connally and Starker Leopold. Having expert opinion, however, did not guarantee that he would follow the advice offered. Such advice had to be considered in light of his political agenda and what he saw as the best interests of the Park System.

Assistant secretary Nathaniel Reed recalled the goat situation in Hawaiian national parks as a case in point of Hartzog ignoring expert advice because heeding it would have interfered with his plans. Reed had paid for the study showing the vegetative effects of fencing out goats but was told the final version of it had been delayed. An anonymous tip, however, suggested that he look "inside George Hartzog's third desk drawer" for the completed report. Conning Hartzog's secretary into retrieving it for him, Reed read the report, which explained how native vegetation returned in areas without goats. In a heated confrontation with Hartzog, Reed asked why he hadn't released the report. Hartzog replied that "if we kill the goats . . . , we will lose the native Hawaii support for additional national parks and I've got ideas for at least two more." Reed fired back that "you mean to tell me we sacrificed [one park] so you can have two more?" To Hartzog, it seemed a reasonable trade, but Reed found it unacceptable and ordered the fencing and killing of goats to proceed.[112]

When asked about his reputation for wanting to control and micromanage the agency, he laughed, preferring to call it a "hands-on" management style. He said he was interested in everything going on in the Park System, especially since he knew Congress or the president's staff could quiz him about any aspect of park operations at any time.[113] His law background ingrained in him the need to be well briefed.

Hartzog carefully monitored the daily goings on in the Park System and was sensitive to negative publicity. Such publicity not only reflected poorly on his agency, it might also impede his ability to effectively work the Hill. When riots broke out in California's Yosemite National Park in July 1970, he flew out and traveled around incognito to assess the situation. During the elk-hunting controversy, he participated in the hearings and worked to defuse the uproar. Sometimes, negative publicity led to change, as with the science program. But when the furor receded, often so did the attention and support. Given limited resources, Hartzog favored high-profile, innovative programs and activities that would catch the public eye and reflect well in Congress.

Hartzog knew that Congress held the key to his success, and he learned to thrive in that realm. Legislation was seldom perfect, but by using his skills, he often managed to tweak it in desirable directions. "If you know what you're going to do, and you know how to do it, it can be done. It may not be done the way you thought it was going to be done, but it can be done."[114]

Figure 9: Hartzog shaking hands with President Lyndon B. Johnson, while Lady Bird Johnson looks on, 1965. Hartzog's park programs meshed well with Johnson's Great Society initiatives and his wife's interests in beautification and parks. Courtesy of Clemson University, Clemson, SC. Hartzog Papers, photographs and negatives, folder 40.

Figure 10:
Hartzog with former directors (l-r) Newton B. Drury, Horace M. Albright, and Conrad L. Wirth at the dedication of the Stephen Tyng Mather Home, a registered National Historic Landmark, July 17, 1964. Each man put their own unique stamp on the National Park Service during their tenures. Courtesy of the Department of the Interior. National Park Service Historic Photograph Collection, HPC-000358, Harpers Ferry Center, WV. Jack E. Boucher, photographer.

Figure 11: Each year, Hartzog promoted his programs and initiatives to a show-me tour group. By giving these tours, he hoped to enhance his support from key members of Congress and their staff by exposing them to nearby natural, historical, and recreational parks that represented a microcosm of the National Park System. Courtesy of the Hartzog family.

Figure 12:
Director Hartzog faced a number of challenges, including the "3 Cs"—cars, crowds, and crime. He encouraged alternative forms of transportation, such as the new shuttle system being tested here in Washington, D.C., in September 1966. He felt that the Park Service could not accommodate the increasing

number of cars and at the same time maintain the environment a quality park experience called for. Courtesy of the Hartzog family.

Figure 13: Hartzog ascends the steps of the Jefferson Memorial for the annual wreath laying ceremony on April 13, 1964, to honor the birthday of Thomas Jefferson. Courtesy of the Hartzog family.

Figure 14: Hartzog often held meetings in the sitting area adjoining his office. Each day he oversaw an organization of some thirteen thousand employees that managed close to 30 million acres of parklands. Courtesy of the Hartzog family.

Figure 16: Hartzog and others at the 1970 unveiling ceremony for the new women's
uniforms held at Independence National Historical Park. The stylish uniforms
proved to be a disaster in the field. Courtesy of the Department of the Interior. National
Park Service Historic Photograph Collection, HPC-001115, Harpers Ferry Center, WV.
Cecil W. Stoughton, photographer.

Figure 17:
On April 22, 1970, Hartzog addressed a crowd at the Washington Monument for the first celebration of Earth Day. Under Hartzog, the Park Service became an early leader in the environmental education movement. Courtesy of the Hartzog family.

Figure 18:
Hartzog looks on, ca. 1970, as secretary of the interior Walter J. Hickel shakes hands with Julia Butler Hansen, chair of the subcommittee on appropriations. Hartzog excelled in the political arena of Washington politics and paid close attention to administrators and congressional delegates like Hansen who wielded power over his programs. Courtesy of Clemson University, Clemson, SC. Hartzog Papers, photographs and negatives, folder 30.

Figure 19: First Lady Pat Nixon accompanies Hartzog to help kick off a Summer in the Parks event, June 1970. Hartzog found Nixon's administration to be significantly less supportive of his park programs and initiatives than Johnson's, but he nevertheless believed that the momentum he had built up during the Johnson administration would prove hard for Nixon to slow. Courtesy of the Hartzog family.

Figure 20: George and Helen Hartzog riding to Sperry Chalet in Glacier National Park during one of their many trips into the field. Courtesy of the Hartzog family.

Figure 21: Members of the secretary of the interior's Advisory Board on National Parks, Historic Sites, Buildings, and Monuments visiting Canyonlands National Park and Glen Canyon National Recreation Area, 1967. During Hartzog's tenure, the board consisted of well-respected individuals from business, academia, and public service areas. Their assessments of existing and proposed park units mattered to members of Congress. Courtesy of Department of the Interior. National Park Service Historic Photograph Collection, HPC-001121, Harpers Ferry Center, WV.

Figure 22:
Hartzog and Teton's Superintendent Fagergren present Lady Bird Johnson with a certificate appointing her as First Lady honorary park ranger, while Stewart Udall looks on, in August 1964. Recognizing her influence with the president, Hartzog called her the National Park System's "greatest saleswoman" due to her strong interest in

beautification and park-related efforts. Courtesy of the Hartzog family.

Figure 23:
Hartzog in the
the director's
chair of a
jonboat as it
motors down the
Current River in
Missouri. While
superintendent at
Jefferson National
Expansion
Memorial, he
spent many
weekends here
trying to garner
local support for a
new type of river
park. It was here

in the fall of 1961 that he first met and impressed Stewart Udall, who immediately
sensed in Hartzog "a good leader, driving type, full of enthusiasm and interest."
Fittingly, Ozark National Scenic Riverways became the country's first national
scenic river and the first bill passed during the Hartzog directorate. Courtesy of the
Hartzog family. Hadley K. Irwin, Missouri State Park System, photographer.

Figure 24:
Hartzog at
the newly
authorized Nez
Perce National
Historical Park
with Josiah
Red Wolf, last
survivor of the
Nez Perce War,
and Richard
Halfmoon.
Hartzog
envisioned
adding to the
National Park

System a whole series of Native American parks. Courtesy of the National Park
Service. Nez Perce National Historical Park, NEPE-HI-2532.

Figure 25: Hartzog holds the "ribbon" as Laurance S. Rockefeller and his wife, Mary (center), prepare to dedicate the 82-mile Rockefeller Memorial Parkway linking Yellowstone and Grand Teton national parks in 1972. The parkway commemorated the significant contributions of Laurance's philanthropic father, John D. Rockefeller Jr., to the National Park System. Laurance proved to be a valuable friend to Hartzog by financing his show me tours, providing critical funding for his environmental education efforts, and offering him legal work when he left office. Courtesy of the Hartzog family.

For George - To remember the big day we won our case with the President! Stewart L. Udall Dec. 1968

Figure 26: Before President Johnson left office, Steward Udall and Hartzog tried to persuade him to use his Antiquities Act powers to set aside parklands in the continental United States and in Alaska. They nearly succeeded with the Alaska additions, but then Johnson balked at the last moment because of powerful opposition from Wayne Aspinall, chair of the House Interior and Insular Affairs Committee. In anticipation of their victory, Udall sent Hartzog this photograph inscribed with "For George—To remember the big day we won our case with the President! Stewart L. Udall, Dec. 1968." Courtesy of Clemson University, Clemson, SC. Hartzog Papers, photographs and negatives, folder 72.

Figure 27: Hartzog and Pat Nixon attend the inauguration ceremony for the newly implemented Volunteers-in-Parks program held at the Custis-Lee Mansion in 1970 (Arlington House). Since its inception the program has grown significantly; millions of hours of volunteer help are now provided each year to the National Park System. Courtesy of the Department of the Interior. National Park Service Historic Photograph Collection, HPC-001557, Harpers Ferry Center, WV. Cecil W. Stoughton, photographer.

Figure 28: Hartzog at Cumberland Island during a National Park Foundation meeting. Hartzog reworked the old Park Service system governing private donations into the National Park Foundation, which more easily allowed the Andrew Mellon Foundation to donate substantial funds for the purchase of parkland on Cumberland Island. Courtesy of the Department of the Interior. National Park Service Historic Photograph Collection, HPC-001128, 1972, Harpers Ferry Center, WV. Cecil W. Stoughton, photographer.

Figure 29: Hartzog surprises his successor, Ronald H. Walker, by throwing him a party to welcome him to the Park Service in 1972. Walker had served Nixon as advance man setting up domestic and international travel, but he lacked any park management experience. Courtesy of the Hartzog family.

CHAPTER TEN

Going Fishing

Life After the National Park Service

George Hartzog knew in 1969 that the political winds would shift with the incoming Republican administration. While Johnson's Great Society initiatives had encouraged the federal government's expansion, Nixon had campaigned on a new federalism that promised to cut taxes and reduce government spending. Hartzog also knew he would lose his great ally Stewart Udall when Nixon appointed a new secretary of the interior. How this would influence management of the National Park System remained to be seen.

Hartzog first met Richard M. Nixon in 1960 in Chicago when Hartzog was superintendent of Jefferson National Expansion Memorial. Nixon, then vice president for Dwight D. Eisenhower, was seeking the nomination for president. Nixon had contacted Hartzog to use St. Louis's Old Courthouse for a reception. Their next encounter came nine years later when Nixon finally won the presidency.[1]

Nixon selected Walter J. Hickel as his secretary of the interior. Hartzog understood that the incoming political appointee would develop his own agenda, but Hartzog, as a careerist much more familiar with the Park Service and its policies than Hickel, hoped to steer Hickel in the direction he wanted to go. To a certain extent, he did when he supplied Hickel with a memorandum on how the Park Service should be run. With few changes, Hickel accepted the document as his own.[2] Hartzog continued on much as he had before but under increasing scrutiny, with less support, and with more conflict.

Nixon inherited an austere federal budget from the previous administration that included deep cuts to the National Park Service operations budget. Faced with an expanding Park System, a spike in visitors, and proposed budget cuts, Hartzog reacted to the cuts by restricting the hours at some national parks, including at very visible ones like the Washington Monument, conveniently located near congressional offices. Tourists complained loudly, prompting Congress to add $17 million to Hartzog's park operations budget. While Hartzog's bold actions, dubbed the "Washington Monument Strategy," succeeded in restoring needed funds, it angered some in Congress. Senator Clifford P. Hansen of Wyoming objected to what he called blackmail and urged Nixon to fire Hartzog.[3]

Had he been able to, Nixon would have replaced Hartzog in 1969 when he named his political appointees. Nixon, however, had narrowly defeated Hubert Humphrey, so initially he lacked political muscle. Hartzog, on the other hand, had amassed an impressive level of support with both political parties. Also, historically, the Park Service directorate did not change with a new administration.

Hartzog felt that from the beginning Nixon never embraced his park expansionist program. In contrast, many in Congress loved its political benefits—new parks brought jobs and tourists to their home districts. Hartzog felt he had created a "tidal wave" of park legislation that the Nixon administration found itself powerless to stop.

After just two years in office, Nixon fired Walter Hickel for publicly criticizing White House policies. Rogers C. B. Morton, a former congressman from Maryland and chairman of the Republican National Committee, replaced him. In May 1971, Morton brought in Nat Reed as his assistant secretary. Reed and Hartzog, both with volatile personalities, clashed often. Hartzog believed Reed wanted to usurp his power as director. Morton believed Hartzog could "go through an assistant secretary easier than I can jump over a three-legged stool."[4] Reed had been told by Nixon to "keep an eye on that damn George Hartzog."[5]

Recurrent rumors of a possible Hartzog firing continued to circulate. "They hated my insides. And you know I'd have been fired on the spot, except my job was saved on the Hill by contacts on both sides of the aisle." Hartzog believed that the "art of politics is that you have no enemies."[6] His extensive social network of friends had blossomed, keeping him informed about behind-the-scenes political maneuvering and the identities of his powerful enemies.

In addition to the likes of Cliff Hansen, Hartzog knew some of the more militant environmental organizations were pushing for his removal to make way for a more preservationist-oriented director. Friends of the Earth publicly called for his dismissal in the summer of 1972, alleging that he supported piecemeal development in the parks, resisted wilderness, participated in parkland "giveaways," and too rapidly transferred personnel. Morton publicly defended Hartzog, addressing each of the charges against him and saying that "your unsupported allegation that Mr. Hartzog is intentionally destroying national parks is totally and absolutely rejected by this office."[7]

Rumors of powerful enemies persisted. Making careful inquiries, former director Horace Albright was able to add another name to Hartzog's enemy list—Charles "Bebe" Rebozo. At first the name meant little to Hartzog until he investigated further. Rebozo, a millionaire developer, banker, and business owner with alleged ties to the mafia, had become fast friends with the Nixons. Rebozo often dined with the Nixons in the White House or vacationed with them in Florida, where he owned a house close to their "Florida White House" in Key Biscayne.

Although Hartzog had never met Rebozo, he later connected him to an incident at Biscayne National Monument in Florida. When the National Park Service acquired the lands for the new park, it purchased a private island club called the Cocolobo Club. Owned by wealthy shareholders, including Rebozo, the club passed to the Park Service. As was custom when purchasing such properties, the Park Service retained the property's caretaker, who happened to be Rebozo's brother-in-law and who, along with his family and friends, had enjoyed exclusive use of the island's boat dock. Rebozo and Nixon used the dock as a favorite landing spot during their jaunts on Rebozo's luxury boat. Rebozo's mother liked fishing from the houseboat he often kept tied to the dock. Both Nixon and Rebozo were outraged when the Park Service ended that privilege.[8] Rebozo's increasing influence with Nixon would spell trouble for Hartzog.

In September 1972, just prior to the November presidential elections, Hartzog attended the second World Conference on National Parks held in Yellowstone National Park. The event brought together leaders from over a hundred nations to discuss park-related concerns and helped commemorate the hundredth anniversary of Yellowstone, the world's first national park. President Nixon had been invited but had sent Mrs. Nixon instead. Hartzog was pointedly told not to appear in any photo sessions with the First Lady or to accompany her on a sightseeing tour of the geysers. Such an intentional slight further fueled rumors of Hartzog's imminent firing.

Horace Albright attempted to intercede on Hartzog's behalf by meeting with Rogers Morton. Morton talked of Hartzog's powerful enemies, Rebozo's being the only name he chose to release.[9] Fighting for his job,

Hartzog continued to call on such influential supporters as Billy Graham, Lyndon Johnson, and friends in Congress to put in a good word for him. Information about continuing in his position remained mixed. One correspondent had written that "skids have been greased in the 'highest levels' for you to take a disability pension." Another assured him that there is "no possibility of you not being [re]appointed."[10]

With Nixon's landslide reelection in November 1972, things turned grim for Hartzog. Nixon's power had grown appreciably and the Watergate scandal had yet to break. As Nixon's chief of staff, H. R. Haldeman, wrote in his book, *The Ends of Power*, Nixon wanted to bring all government agencies under his control. Nixon felt his appointees ineffective because careerists, many left over from the Johnson administration, really ran the show. He wanted loyal men in key positions. "Clean the bastards out. . . . Take that Park Service, they've been screwing us for years."[11]

Soon after his election, Nixon began a systematic housecleaning of top officials, which the *New York Times* called "one of the most sweeping in any department in years."[12] Hartzog had heard through his sources that Morton's reappointment depended on his dismissing Hartzog. In *Battling for the National Parks*, Hartzog describes his last meeting with Morton. He went to Morton's office armed with his termination papers and noted that the usually friendly Morton was clearly conflicted over what needed to happen. When he handed him the papers, Morton initially refused to sign them and asked for time to approach the administration about shifting Hartzog over to the vacant assistant secretary for Indian affairs position. Since he possessed a special interest in Indian issues and thought he could benefit the agency, Hartzog agreed to discuss the possibility with his wife, Helen.

That night, the Hartzogs discussed their options but came to the conclusion that the Park Service directorate was the only job they'd be happy with. Hartzog believed that assistant secretaries had no authority and no money and therefore no real power.[13] The next day, Morton reluctantly confessed that Nixon would not support such an appointment and so was relieved when Hartzog informed him that he wasn't interested. Hartzog dated his termination for December 31, 1972. "Rogers and I never discussed the reason for my dismissal; he volunteered no reasons and I asked for none."[14]

While Hartzog had his admirers, he also had his detractors. "There were a helluva lot of happy people when I got fired," he recalled.[15] That elation turned to concern when his replacement was announced. Michael McCloskey of the Sierra Club reported being "disturbed that somebody has been named who has none of the credentials we expected."[16] Hartzog chuckled, "Better the devil you know than the devil you don't know."[17]

Morton announced on December 13 that Ronald H. Walker would replace Hartzog as director. The thirty-five-year-old former insurance and marketing executive had entered the Washington scene in 1969. He had served briefly in Interior as an assistant to Walter Hickel before becoming an advance man to Nixon, coordinating and planning all the president's domestic and international trips. Nothing in his background suggested that he possessed any knowledge of how to manage three hundred national park areas. Walker was totally unqualified for the helm of the National Park Service. Even Walker admitted to Hartzog that, "I know I have much to learn and your offer of help was much appreciated."[18] To Walker, Hartzog wrote that he was stepping into "the best job in the whole world." He counseled Walker to heed George Washington's advice and quoting from a plaque that hung on his office wall wrote:

> Do not suffer your good nature
> When application is made,
> To say "yes" when you should say "no"
> Remember it is a public
> Not a private cause that is to be
> Injured or benefited by your choice.[19]

Hartzog lamented leaving the Park Service family he had been a part of for twenty-six years. During his retirement party, fellow Park Service employees good-naturedly lampooned his many reorganizations by showing him walking down a hall with each door marked "reorganization." A shuffle board game allowed participants to pick their next park assignment based on where the puck landed. A wood carving of a bass signified one of his favorite fishing retreats at Fort Jefferson in Florida. During the evening, Helen Hartzog graciously announced her donation of money to the National Park Service women's organization, to which Hartzog quipped, "Here I am unemployed and she gives away $500."[20] When asked by a reporter what he planned to do next, he replied that he was "going fishing."[21]

While Hartzog did spend more time with family and friends, he also focused on shifting career directions. For a short time, he traveled to various paid speaking engagements but quickly tired of it. What would pay the bills would be a return to practicing law. Shortly after Hartzog's dismissal hit the press, Laurence Rockefeller called to offer him legal work.[22] As Hartzog sought additional clients, he interviewed with Washington law firms. He selected Ragan and Mason due to its strong client base, the nature of its work, and its small and more intimate size. In such an environment, he felt he could "make an imprint."[23] In July 1974, he was admitted to the Virginia State Bar. By July 1976, he made partner. His client base consisted largely of concessionaires and other recreation-related businesses, and he often represented them before federal agencies.[24]

At the same time that he was practicing law, Hartzog also started the planning firm of Hartzog, Lader, and Richards based in Washington, D.C., and Hilton Head, South Carolina. While they got a couple of contracts to do recreation planning in South Carolina, the business failed to prosper. "People just didn't believe we had the expertise to do park planning."[25]

After leaving the National Park Service, Hartzog faced some of the most difficult times of his adult life. Private practice "paled by comparison to the excitement and challenge of public service."[26] From the sidelines, he saw many of his pet initiatives weakened or dismantled. He watched as his environmental education and urban programs such as Summer in the Parks were scrapped. Funding for the Land and Water Conservation Fund was gutted, urban areas were ignored, and scientists were intimidated and displaced.[27] Through it all, he continued to keep in touch with his many friends in the Park Service and met with each successive director. He kept extensive files on the Park Service, including newspaper clippings and magazine articles. Such efforts allowed him to keep a connection with the Park Service he still cared deeply about and benefited his law practice.

Two years after leaving public office, Hartzog came under federal scrutiny for activities prior to and after leaving the Park Service. Some dealt with conflict-of-interest charges related to Title 18 USC 207a, which puts restrictions on former government employees' dealings with government agencies they previously worked for.[28] One of his first problems arose over his renegotiation (less than two years after leaving office) of a contract due to expire for Landmark Services, an operator of Washington tourmobiles. Hartzog had asked assistant solicitors and officials with the Park Service ahead of time whether they were concerned about his involvement and was told "No."[29] Later, Interior officials questioned the propriety of "going on the other side of the fence and representing a company he was closely and directly involved with as a government official." News of the investigation leaked to the media and Hartzog decided it best to withdraw from the negotiations.[30]

Other charges related to purported activities while Hartzog was director. Another conflict-of-interest investigation looked into the hiring procedures for an architect doing design work for the Washington, D.C., and St. Louis visitor centers.[31] Rumors also circulated that Hartzog had taken bribes and kickbacks from concessionaires while in office, which prompted additional involvement from the FBI and the IRS, which audited all his tax records.

Hartzog denied any wrongdoing. To Hartzog, "I had a very simple rule. I never spent a night in an accommodation that I did not pay for. If I could eat it and drink it in one sitting, that was okay. I would not take anything with me." He recalled often arriving at rooms "lined with whiskey bottles. Whatever I drank, I drank. I left the unfinished bottle. I never took a bottle out of a hotel room unless I bought and paid for it."[32]

Hartzog continued to get calls and letters from friends saying they had been questioned about his activities as director. Gary Everhardt, Park Service director from 1975 to 1977, sent a note saying he had been requested to provide memos, follow-ups, and notes from the Hartzog directorate but had refused unless ordered to do so.[33] His former chief of personnel, Ivan Parker, wrote saying he had responded to the questions in a rather "profane manner since I know you so well and know that you would rather shoot your best friend before you would take a kickback from him."[34]

Clearly, these legal battles angered him long afterward. Pounding the table for emphasis during an interview, he declared he followed the simple rule: "If it doesn't look right, doesn't feel right, and doesn't smell right, it probably ain't right." He attributed the attacks to a personal and political vendetta designed by Republican incumbents to discredit a former Democratic appointee.[35] After five years and tens of thousands of dollars in legal fees, Hartzog was cleared. He credited his successful defense with keeping a daily log, keeping meticulous records, and saving all his banking records since starting with the Park Service.[36] The experience left him bitter about the toll it took on him, his career, and his family. "I had played hardball all of my public life—I like the game—but this was dirty ball."[37]

At sixty-five, Hartzog retired from Ragan and Mason and became general counsel to Guest Services, Inc., a hospitality management company providing food, lodging, special event planning, and recreation services. The company operated a number of facilities in national parks. He also opened his own private law practice at his farmhouse in McLean, Virginia. For several years, he taught as an adjunct professor at University of Southern California's Public Affairs Center in Washington, D.C., where he enjoyed lecturing about policy and public administration. He remarked that had it paid as well as law, he would have enjoyed teaching full-time.

In 1988, he completed and published *Battling for the National Parks*, in which he wrote of his experiences and lessons learned while in office.[38] "When I finished my book," he recalled, "I was as proud as a peacock—imagine a country boy on the brink of a published book. It was false pride! Nobody wanted it." With his damaged ego in check, he employed a good editor. After much back and forth, the book was finally published. "When I held that first copy in my hand, scar tissue immediately sealed over my still open sores."[39]

Not one to sit idly, Hartzog also served on many boards and as a trustee in a number of organizations after leaving the Park Service. Some of these affiliations, such as his long relationship with the White House Historical Association, began while he was in office. As director, he automatically served as an ex officio member of the White House Historical Association. After leaving office, he was asked to become a member at large, and eventually he served a term as president. He continued to serve the organization until 1998 when health and mobility issues forced his resignation. During his tenure, he used his legal skill on a pro bono basis to charter and organize an endowment fund with the goal of raising $25 million to support the preservation of the White House public rooms and the collection of fine and decorative arts.[40] Hartzog led a legislative effort to mint a White House commemorative coin, which contributed $5 million to the fund. In 1998, the $25 million endowment goal was finally reached and the trust established.[41]

He served as the director or a trustee of a number of other organizations he had affiliations with, including Wolf Trap Foundation for the Performing Arts, Camden Military Academy, American Forestry Association, Yosemite National Institute, Archaeological Conservancy, U.S. Capitol Historical Society, National Recreation and Park Association, and Christian Ministry in the National Parks. He donated legal expertise to the Christian Ministry in the National Parks and served as general counsel for some twelve years for the National Park and Recreation Association as it struggled to get established and become financially solvent.[42] As his health failed, he increasingly limited such activities.

Throughout his life, Hartzog never forgot his roots and maintained a special fondness for his home state of South Carolina. Knowing of this attachment and his commitment to parks, his good friend Bill Everhart and his wife, Mary, established the Hartzog Fund at Clemson University, the state's land grant university, in 1978. The Everhart gift, along with donations from other friends and foundations, funds the annual Hartzog lecture series and the luncheon and awards ceremony and also provides financial aid for graduate students. Each year, the fund brings prominent figures in the parks and conservation field to campus to speak.[43]

To build on the success of the Hartzog Fund, Clemson officials approached Hartzog in 2005 about developing a research and training facility in his name. Clearly moved by the idea, he launched into helping make it a reality. In fact, his was the "biggest fingerprint" on what eventually developed.[44] Meanwhile, the recently formed Coalition of National Park Service Retirees likewise expressed a desire to develop a center to address what they saw as serious problems with the National Park System, especially in light of the Park Service's upcoming centennial in 2016.

In an April 2006 meeting at the Cosmos Club, Hartzog helped convince both groups to join forces, arguing that two groups with similar goals would divide and weaken necessary support. What resulted was the George B. Jr. and Helen C. Hartzog Institute for Parks that would be housed at Clemson University but would legally be a separate nonprofit entity. The institute would concentrate on four areas: training and leadership development, applied research, efforts to make parks relevant to people's lives, and the promotion of partnerships and collaborations. Until the end, Hartzog stayed mentally alert and energetically engaged in setting up the institute, selecting board members, and defining its mission.[45] Just days before his death, legal documents officially registering the institute were completed.

On June 22, 2008, George Hartzog passed away. His death occurred less than a week before his sixty-first wedding anniversary. On what would have been their anniversary, eleven red roses arrived from the florist for his wife, Helen, as they had for many, many years. Hartzog had first sent Helen eleven roses when wooing her. Pleased with her first gift of roses but baffled by eleven and not the usual dozen, he explained that she was the twelfth rose. He never missed sending roses on their anniversary.

Hartzog's memorial service was held at Green Pond Methodist Church in Smoaks, South Carolina. The intimate ceremony, attended by family, close friends, and a National Park Service color guard accompanied by director Mary A. Bomar, took place in the same church where he had delivered his first sermon. George and Nancy, his two oldest children, both of whom had gone on to become ministers, delivered a moving service during which they read some of their father's favorite passages from the Bible.[46] His grandson, Dietrich, played the violin while the boy's mother sang and played the piano. He was laid to rest in nearby Walterboro next to his parents and under a large, stately live oak tree draped in Spanish moss. The country boy had come full circle.

CHAPTER ELEVEN

The Hartzog Legacy

S tewart Udall hired forty-three-year-old George Hartzog to bring a fresh, innovative perspective to the National Park Service and mold it into a more contemporary agency responsive to the shifting needs of the American people. That edict plus the Park Service's mission to provide for the visitors' enjoyment while protecting resources formed the basis of Hartzog's tenure from January 1964 to December 1972.

Many remember Hartzog as a powerful and controversial director. Some can still picture him sporting his cream-colored Stetson, wearing his big, silver Indian bolo tie, and carrying a double-sized briefcase. Bob Utley, his chief historian, perhaps best describes him. He was

> bluff, gruff, hearty, amiable, articulate, not merely self-assured but overflowing with certitude, intensely ambitious, a human dynamo, hyperkinetic, workaholic, mind always in motion, driven, funny but sometimes with cutting wit, sarcastic, demanding, pragmatic, fulsome in praise, devastating in criticism, immoderate in food, drink, and tobacco (he often had a cigarette and cigar going at the same time; I've seen him down a tumbler of straight Scotch at lunch).[1]

Michael Frome, an environmentalist and critic of Hartzog's remembers him as breezy, tireless, overweight, a hard drinker and heavy smoker, puffing cigarettes in between big cigars, a super salesman for new parks . . . who spent considerable time cultivating politicians.[2]

Nat Reed, assistant secretary of the interior, recalls:

a magical man . . . who had the vision and imagination and bravery to make some tough decisions, and of course as a politician there was nobody better.[3]

His long-time friend and colleague Bill Everhart writes:

Boldness or perhaps audacity may have been his best quality. Incorrigibly optimistic and famously demanding of his staff, he had the saving grace of being even more demanding of himself, sweeping his colleagues along with the force of his personality. . . . He energized us and made us all eager to go out and bust our butt for him. He was confident, and so, after seeing him in action, were we.[4]

Such accounts paint a picture of a dynamic man who relentlessly drove himself and those around him to run a complex, multidimensional agency that managed a wide variety of parks. Hartzog was a politician at heart who loved the challenge, excitement, power, and human dimensions of how governments operated. Influenced by his business training, he said he looked on the Park Service as a business operation. As its manager, he paid particular attention to the services rendered, the people who ran the parks and those who visited, and the flow of money.[5]

Hartzog remained a difficult man to pin down on sensitive issues such as the agency's commitment to achieving a balance between use and preservation. He repeatedly said that "parks are for the people but not all people at all times for all things." According to Hartzog, his critics conveniently left off the last part, which allowed them to suggest that he supported any type of use, even though that was not his policy. Pounding the desk for emphasis, he said,

I still believe parks are for people. If people aren't in parks, then it's not a park. It may be something else. Maybe a national forest. Maybe a wildlife refuge. Maybe any number of other preserves, but it ain't a park without people 'cause by definition that's what a park is. But that doesn't mean it's for all people for all things at all times. There's got to be limitations on it. Otherwise it soon won't be anything except a playground, and interestingly that's the language that was used in establishing Yellowstone . . . a pleasuring ground, a play yard.[6]

Hartzog saw his policies as lying somewhere between what environmentalists wanted and what development interests desired. Hartzog believed he hugged the middle, erring toward resource protection over use, but most critics put him as erring on the side of use. "He talked a good preservation line, but in a pinch between preservation and some of his eye-catching initiatives, use won."[7]

Driven to develop new initiatives and direct a pioneering agency, Hartzog forced change on a tradition-loving agency happy with the status quo. Many questioned the agency's countless changes in direction. A common criticism from staff was that Hartzog made changes too quickly and "shot from the hip" without doing adequate research and seeking input. His many organizational and management changes led to a sense among some of disorientation and alienation within the Park Service.[8] But as Stewart Udall recalls, "everyone who saw him in action . . . remembers his sense of mission, and the zest and drive he transmitted to his co-workers."[9]

Mercurial and full of contrasts, Hartzog was at once an "inspirator" and "nemesis" to those who worked with him.[10] One moment he could be an abusive tyrant with a hair-trigger temper and the next a compassionate and caring friend. Deeply religious and anchored in southern rural values where "your word was your bond," he swore prodigiously, smoked incessantly, and could recover seemingly unfazed from a late-night meeting infused with alcohol. The Hartzog years were "exciting times" but "full of stress."[11] He was widely feared but at the same time respected for his ability to get things done and his "extraordinary accomplishments."[12] As John McPhee has said, had it not been for Hartzog there would be no St. Louis arch.[13] Although they failed to recognize it at the time, many now fondly remember him as the finest director they served under during their long careers and feel those were the golden years of the Park Service.[14] Many say Hartzog was the last powerful director before the position fell to political appointees and the real power moved into the secretary of the interior's office.[15]

So what should we remember Hartzog for besides his outsized personality? His most notable legacies involved expanding the National Park System, diversifying the workforce, putting more emphasis on urban environments, and actively lobbying for important legislation.

⁂

Hartzog's skill in expanding the park system garnered him the most praise and remains his most lasting legacy. While other directors may have added more parks in selected years, none have matched his sustained record of growth. Over his nine-year tenure, a record seventy-two new parks came into the National Park System for an average of eight new parks a year. His broad vision of what a national park unit should be went well beyond that which defined the traditional, large western parks like Yellowstone and Yosemite. Urban recreation areas were the most controversial of the additions, but his directorate also saw the addition of wild and scenic rivers, national trails, national lakeshores, and cultural parks such as Wolf Trap Farm for the Performing Arts. He also experimented with new management ideas like the joint operatation of scientific reserves and the comanagement of Native American lands.

In part, Hartzog owes his park expansion success to an ideal set of circumstances. An intense interest in outdoor recreation gripped the country, and parks overflowed with people. People grew increasingly concerned about the loss and deterioration of their natural and historical resources. A strongly Democratic Congress willingly passed protective legislation and supported setting aside more of the country's resources. George Hartzog possessed the political talents and know-how to exploit this momentum.

As a masterful bureaucrat, Hartzog knew the political system intimately and understood how best to work it. His down-home charm and storytelling flair belied a calculating mind and keen intellect. He recognized the importance of cultivating influential people and spent considerable time promoting his agency's programs. As Utley said, "He knew how to be responsive to his superiors and those on the Hill who held his fate in their hands."[16] A prime example of his political savvy is his convincing Senator Alan Bible to travel to Alaska to view potential parklands. As a result of that trip, Bible become a key supporter and laid the legislative basis for setting aside national interest lands in Alaska. Legislative battles raged for years, but eventually, after Hartzog left office, culminated in the 1980 Alaska National Interest Lands Conservation Act, which doubled the size of the National Park System.

Many criticized Hartzog as being too much of a "wheeler dealer" when adding parks and delineating their boundaries. Perhaps due to his country roots and comfort with horse trading, he believed that government works best when bipartisan compromises between opposing opinions can be forged. To Hartzog, a less than perfect park that could be fixed at a later time was better than no park at all.

⚜

When Hartzog became director in 1964, the Park Service was filled with rugged, white male rangers with similar educational backgrounds. Hartzog changed that by actively recruiting women and minorities, a shift that more accurately reflected the country's diversity.

In the 1960s and 1970s, workforce change became inevitable as ethnic groups and women asserted themselves and forced the federal government to examine its abysmal lack of diversity. Agencies like the Park Service had to respond, and, considering everything, Hartzog chose a fairly aggressive path. He appointed the agency's first woman, first black, and first Native American superintendents and hired the first black head of a major police force. He also moved beyond the traditional ranger hires, bringing in employees with more diverse educational backgrounds to infuse the agency with fresh ideas and perspectives.

Comfortable with its traditions, the Park Service struggled with its staffing transformation. As Hartzog said, increasing workforce diversity was "a cultural change and those are difficult."[17] Even he struggled with some of the personnel changes he effected. Despite the influence of a tough and talented mother, Hartzog had difficulty allowing women to be treated like men, particularly when it came to letting them carry out the physically demanding and potentially dangerous tasks that were part of the job for ranger and police forces. However, once the diversity issue gained his attention, he coaxed, bullied, and applied whatever means available to admit employees of different gender, race, and educational backgrounds. He searched within and outside his own agency for talent, established special recruiting programs, and expanded training opportunities for disadvantaged groups. Despite his efforts, the Park Service was slow to accept the new employees, especially if they did not put in their time and move up the ranks in the traditional manner. In order for Hartzog to show progress, some women and ethnic minorities were moved rapidly through the ranks, creating dissension.

A clear indication of how Hartzog changed the face of the Park Service can be seen by comparing a 1963 photograph of inductees at the Albright Training Center at Grand Canyon National Park to 1964, 1968, and 1972 photographs. The 1963 picture clearly shows the white, all-male face of the Park Service prior to Hartzog's tenure with a lone woman a part of the training center staff. The 1964 photograph shows a slight crack in the armor, while the 1968 and 1972 pictures show the growing mosaic of future Park Service leaders. Given Hartzog's autocratic management style, that transformation would not have occurred without his consent and direction.

⚜

George Hartzog recognized the importance of being responsive to the country's shifting demographics. As a result, he brought parks and programs to an increasingly urban society. When he was superintendent of Jefferson National Expansion Memorial (1959–1962), he had witnessed how the gateway arch and its surrounding parklands revitalized downtown St. Louis. Emboldened by his success, he needed little encouragement to view urban areas as being ripe for expansion, especially given President Johnson's Great Society push to improve the country's cities. Hartzog increasingly believed that the future of the National Park System depended on selling the importance of national parks to an urban constituency that might never visit a Yellowstone or one of the other large western crown jewels.

Therefore, Hartzog pushed to add urban recreation areas. Although he publicly packaged Gateway National Recreation Area in New York City and Golden Gate National Recreation Area in San Francisco as prototypes, he was too much of an expansionist to settle for only two areas. He envisioned many more. Not surprisingly, this proved unsettling for many who felt this new direction strayed too far from the tradition of protecting the country's nationally significant resources. Some criticized federal involvement in what appeared to be a local recreation concern and one best left to local or state governments. Congress feared that many cities would demand similar federally funded efforts and worried what the price tag would escalate to, especially given the costly Vietnam War. All were valid concerns, and so once Hartzog was dismissed, the urban parks emphasis would wane.

Despite the brakes applied to his urban parks push, Hartzog's programs succeeded in broadening the agency's western-leaning orientation. Accordingly, Robert G. Stanton, Park Service director from 1997 to 2001, said Hartzog made the agency "more responsive and sensitive to the change of demographics of our society" and emphasized that

> every member of our society should have an opportunity to become acquainted with the values of national parks and understand that these parks are theirs as part of their educational diversity, their recreational uses as well as inspirational values.

Stanton went on to say that Hartzog's programs "allowed the Park Service to reach out to the various communities that heretofore had not really connected with national parks or programs of the Park Service."[18] Hartzog accomplished this by actively promoting creative and innovative programs. New living history programs made the past more interesting and relevant to visitors, while cutting-edge environmental education programs informed members of the public about problems facing their world and inspired them to protect their environment. Hartzog's Summer in the Parks program followed by the Parks for All Seasons effort brought outdoor recreation opportunities to urban communities. His collaborative efforts that forged new partnerships between agencies also proved pioneering.

According to Stanton, these types of programs "laid the foundation for a new ethos in park management."[19] Mary Bomar, director from 2006 to 2009, likewise remarked that "his vision of what the national parks should be and should mean to the American people left an indelible mark on the agency he so loved and believed in. His goal of making the National Park Service relevant to people who previously had been overlooked, especially minorities and women, has strengthened our agency."[20]

꧁

According to James M. Ridenour, Park Service director from 1989 to 1993, Hartzog "probably had a closer relationship with members of Congress than any director, before or after him."[21] Consequently, he proved a master at shepherding legislation through Congress. He kept close tabs on the movement of all new park legislation while actively lobbying for and testifying on its behalf. With the National Historic Preservation Act of 1966, he successfully wrestled legislation away from rival agencies and kept all the act's provisions intact and under National Park Service control. The bill revolutionized the historic preservation field and remains its most far-reaching legislation, saving structures, sites, and historic districts in every state. His 1970 Volunteers-in-Parks bill created a mutually beneficial program that formalized the arrangement whereby talented volunteers helped with a variety of tasks at national park units. Since the bill's passage, the numbers of volunteers has steadily risen.[22]

Hartzog also pushed for National Park Foundation legislation that would provide a better means of accepting donations to help fund programs and purchase lands. He played important but less prominent roles in lobbying for other important environmental legislation, such as the Wilderness Act of 1964, the Land and Water Conservation Act of 1965, and the 1968 Wild and Scenic Rivers Act. To Hartzog, the key to politics was that "you have no enemies. . . . The guy that's fightin' you tooth and nail today maybe the very guy you depend on tomorrow to help you get something else."[23]

⁂

As the agency's seventh director, George Hartzog led the National Park Service for almost nine years, making him the fourth longest-serving director. Hartzog had lasting effects on the organization, leaving an indelible mark on the both the agency and the National Park System. "Institutional evolution went into high gear" as he flooded the organization with new ideas and programs, some of which thrived and others of which faded away.[24] Former secretary of the interior Stewart Udall considers him to be the "best director of this century," while his chief historian Robert Utley believes that after the agency's cofounders, he is "the greatest director in the entire history of the Service."[25] According to Udall, "Hartzog was able to leave behind a legacy that to this day is unsurpassed in the amount of land acquired and the amount of legislation passed."[26]

Figure 30: When asked what he would do after he left the Park Service, Hartzog replied that he was "going fishing." Courtesy of Pat Canfield. National Park Service Historic Photograph Collection, Harpers Ferry Center, WV.

Figure 31: Hartzog at an August 25, 1989, Founder's Day dinner celebrating the seventy-fifth anniversary of the signing of the Organic Act, which created the National Park Service in 1916. Even after leaving office, Hartzog kept abreast of Park Service matters through an extensive network of friends. Courtesy of the Department of the Interior. National Park Service Historic Photograph Collection, Harpers Ferry Center, HPC-001125, WV.

Figure 32: Hartzog in Yellowstone National Park, 1972. Hartzog became a bold, innovative, and ambitious director who relentlessly drove himself and his staff to carry out the Park Service's inherently difficult mission of providing for the enjoyment of its visitors while protecting park resources for future generations. Gifted with shrewd political instincts, he cultivated influential friends in Congress to advance his agency's parks and programs. Many consider him the last powerful director of the Park Service. Courtesy of the Department of the Interior. National Park Service Historic Photograph Collection, HPC-001129, Harpers Ferry Center, WV. Cecil W. Stoughton, photographer.

Figure 33: Secretary of the interior Stewart L. Udall autographed his photograph to Hartzog with "For George—one of the best of the parkmen!" In fact, Udall felt Hartzog was the best director of the twentieth century. Courtesy of Clemson University, Clemson, SC. Hartzog Collection, photos and negatives, folder 74.

Figure 34: Hartzog left an indelible mark on the National Park Service. Just days before his death on June 22, 2008, the legal documents establishing the George B. and Helen C. Hartzog Institution were finalized. Ideally, the institute located at Clemson University in his home state of South Carolina will extend that legacy by serving as a research, education, and training center for current and future park professionals. Courtesy of the Hartzog family.

Notes

Introduction

1. Everhart, *The National Park Service*, 27.
2. Frome, *Regreening the National Parks*, 69–79.
3. Mengak, "Hartzog and Udall Reminisce."
4. Weisner, "The Value of Historical Research."
5. Hartzog, interview with Mengak, March 23, 1996.
6. Utley, e-mail correspondence with Mengak, May 10, 2002.
7. Hartzog, interview with Mengak, June 9, 1999.
8. Hartzog, interview with Mengak, July 7, 1997.
9. Utley, interview with Mengak, March 31, 1999.
10. Everhart, interview with Mengak, July 30, 1998. Hartzog made no objection to Everhart's version.
11. Reed, interview with Mengak, September 11, 2000.
12. Hartzog, interview with Mengak, July 30, 1998.
13. McPhee, "Ranger," 74.
14. Sherwood, "George B. Hartzog, Jr."
15. Hartzog, interview with Mengak, March 23, 1996.

Chapter One

1. McPhee, "Ranger," 74; Hartzog, *Battling for the National Parks*, 14.
2. Hartzog, interviews with Mengak, March 23, 1996, and July 30, 1998.
3. Hartzog, interview with Mengak, May 11, 1996.
4. Ibid.; Hartzog, interview with Mengak, March 23, 1996.
5. Ibid.
6. Hartzog, interview with Mengak, May 11, 1996.
7. Ibid.
8. Hartzog, interview with Mengak, July 30, 1998.
9. Hartzog, interview with Mengak, May 11, 1996.
10. Ibid.
11. Ibid.
12. Hartzog, interview with Mengak, March 23, 1996; Hartzog, *Battling for the National Parks*, 16.
13. Hartzog, interview with Mengak, May 11, 1996.
14. Hartzog, interview with Mengak, May 11–12, 1996.

15. Hartzog, *Battling for the National Parks*, 13–14.
16. Hartzog, interview with Mengak, May 11, 1996.
17. Hartzog, interview with Mengak, July 30, 1998.
18. Hartzog, interview with Mengak, March 23, 1996.
19. Hartzog, *Battling for the National Parks*, 14.
20. McPhee, "Ranger," 74.
21. Hartzog, interview with Mengak, May 11, 1996; Hartzog, *Battling for the National Parks*, 14.
22. Hartzog, *Battling for the National Parks*, 15.
23. Ibid.
24. Hartzog, interview with Mengak, May 11, 1996.
25. Hartzog, interview with Mengak, March 23, 1996.
26. McElvaine, *The Great Depression*, 18.
27. Hartzog, interview with Mengak, May 11, 1996.
28. Bird, *Invisible Scar*.
29. Elder, *Children of the Great Depression*, xv.
30. Long after the age when he might have retired, Hartzog kept working. He continued to live in the comfortable but not showy farmhouse he purchased outside Washington, D.C., in McLean, Virginia. His beige Volvo car and battered Volkswagen bus were plain and well past the age when most people would have traded them in for newer models. Hartzog became a man who lived comfortably but well below his means.
31. Hartzog, interview with Mengak, March 23, 1996.
32. Hartzog, *Battling for the National Parks*, 16; Hartzog, interview with Mengak, March 23, 1996.
33. Hartzog, interview with Mengak, March 23, 1996.
34. Hartzog, interview with Mengak, May 11, 1996; Hartzog, *Battling for the National Parks*, 16.
35. Hartzog, interview with Mengak, March 23, 1996; Hartzog, *Battling for the National Parks*, 17.
36. Hartzog, interview with Fry, April 14, 1965.
37. Hartzog, *Battling for the National Parks*, 17–20.
38. Hartzog, *Battling for the National Parks*, 18; Hartzog, interview with Mengak, May 11, 1996.
39. Hartzog, *Battling for the National Parks*, 21; Hartzog interview with Mengak, March 23, 1996.
40. Hartzog, interview with Mengak, May 11, 1996.
41. Ibid.
42. Hartzog, *Battling for the National Parks*, v, 24.

Chapter Two

1. For the early years of the national parks, see Runte, *National Parks*, chaps. 1–4.
2. Ibid., 71–72.
3. Biographies of the two founding fathers include Shankland, *Steve Mather of the National Parks*, and Swain, *Wilderness Defender*.
4. Albright and Schenck, *Creating the National Park Service*, 39–40.

5. Ibid., 18, 70–71.

6. The following account of the creation of the parks bureau is drawn largely from Albright and Schenck but is also cited in other sources. A history of the National Park Service is Everhart, *The National Park Service*.

7. Albright and Schenck, *Creating the National Park Service*, 148.

8. Albright, Dickenson, and Mott, *The National Park Service*, 11.

9. This important part of the Park Service history is authoritatively detailed in Sellars, *Preserving Nature in the National Parks*, 50–56.

10. Albright and Schenck, *Creating the National Park Service*, 239.

11. Albright tells the story engagingly in his pamphlet *Origins of National Park Service Administration of Historic Sites*. For the executive order and its results, see Mackintosh, *The National Parks*. This is an updated version of Lee, *Family Tree of the National Park System*.

12. Old Kasaan, the only natural area addition in Alaska, was later transferred to the Forest Service on July 26, 1955, so this reorganization did not add to the Alaskan park system.

13. Mackintosh, e-mail correspondence with Mengak, February 17 and 24, December 29, 1999; Utley, e-mail correspondence with Mackintosh, March 31, 1999. Both men agreed that Albright ranked as most influential, followed by George Hartzog and Stephen Mather. Utley writes, "I share your sense that Albright was responsible for getting the NPS up and running. Mather just was not there to help. That was a tremendous achievement for one so young, with no precedent to guide him. And I do agree that the revelations in this book [*Creating the National Park Service*] diminish Mather's significance. Of the two Albright was the more significant. But without Mather, Albright could not have done it. Each made his own unique contribution, which the other could not have made. History has been badly distorted by the common assumption that Mather did it all, a distortion to which Horace himself contributed, probably decisively."

14. See Bearss, "Arno B. Cammerer," for a biographical sketch.

15. Paige, *The Civilian Conservation Corps and the National Park Service*.

16. Mackintosh, *The National Parks*, 44–56; Wirth, *Parks, Politics and the People*.

17. Paige, *The Civilian Conservation Corps and the National Park Service*; Mackintosh, "Revising the Mission."

18. Qtd. in Foresta, *America's National Parks and Their Keepers*, 48–49.

19. Qtd. in Sellars, *Preserving Nature in the National Parks*, 143.

20. Foresta, *America's National Parks and Their Keepers*, 47–51, provides a good evaluation of the Drury era.

Chapter Three

1. Hartzog, interview with Mengak, March 23, 1996.

2. Ibid.

3. Gilliam, "Parks Are for People to Have Fun In."

4. Hartzog, interview with Mengak, May 11, 1996.

5. Hartzog, *Battling for the National Parks*, 22.

6. Ibid., 25; Hartzog, interview with Mengak, May 11, 1996. Although Lake Texoma was managed by the Corps of Engineer, the Park Service was

involved in the project because it was charged with providing recreational opportunities around the lake.

7. Hartzog, interview with Mengak, May 12, 1996.
8. Hartzog, interviews with Mengak, August 10, 1996, and July 30, 1998.
9. Hartzog, *Battling for the National Parks*, 25–26; Hartzog, interviews with Mengak, May 11, 1996, July 19, 1999, and September 15, 2003. According to Hartzog, he did try to finish his master's degree when he returned to Washington as associate director in 1963. He was told by the dean that if he completed the one remaining class required for the degree, American University would grant him a diploma. In August, while serving as associate director, he took the required seminar class at night in a room lacking air conditioning. By the time the class finished, a new dean had come and the "son of a bitch said, 'No because it had been a delay of seven years. It's out of date. You've got to do it all over again.' I said, 'Thank you very much and let me tell you what you can do with it, which I didn't.'" Hartzog was furious and enlisted the former dean's help, to no avail. Ironically, American University bestowed an alumni recognition award on Hartzog in May 1966.
10. Hartzog, interview with Fry, April 14, 1965.
11. Hartzog, interview with Mengak, March 23, 1996.
12. Ibid.
13. Hartzog, *Battling for the National Parks*, 26–29.
14. Ibid.
15. Ibid., 31–32.
16. Ibid, 35–36; Hartzog, interview with Mengak, May 11, 1996.
17. Hartzog, interview with Mengak, May 11, 1996; Hartzog, interview with Moore, October 25, 1994.
18. Hartzog, interview with Mengak, March 26, 1996.
19. Capps, "Eero Saarinen"; Everhart, interview with Moore, October 25, 1994.
20. Hartzog, interview with Mengak, May 11, 1996; Hartzog, interview with Moore, October 25, 1994.
21. Hartzog, interview with Moore, October 25, 1994.
22. Hartzog, *Battling for the National Parks*, 44.
23. Everhart, interview with Moore, October 25, 1994.
24. Hartzog, *Battling for the National Parks*, 42–47.
25. Hartzog, interview with Moore, October 25, 1994.
26. On August 10, 1976, the Museum of Westward Expansion opened to the public, and in 1985, the George B. Hartzog Visitor Center was officially dedicated.
27. Hartzog Papers, series 2, box 16, folder 119A.
28. Hartzog, *Battling for the National Parks*, 76; Hartzog, interview with Fry, April 14, 1965; Hartzog, interviews with Mengak, March 23, 1996, August 10, 1996, and September 8, 2001.
29. Udall, introduction, *Battling for the National Parks*, xi.
30. McPhee, "Ranger," 78, 80.
31. Frome, *Regreening the National Parks*, 65–67.
32. McPhee, "Ranger," 80; Hartzog, *Battling for the National Parks*, 74.
33. Hartzog, *Battling for the National Parks*, 74–76.

34. Everhart, interview with Mengak, July 28, 1999.

35. Ibid. For the draft of the book, see Hartzog Papers, Clemson University, series 3, box 1, folder 1.

36. Hartzog, *Battling for the National Parks*, 78; Blair, "Park Service Due for Big Changes," *New York Times*, October 17, 1963.

Chapter Four

1. Utley, interview with Mengak, March 31, 1999.

2. Fred Overly to Hartzog, February 2, 1965, in Hartzog Papers, series 1, box 76, folder 916.

3. Utley, interview with Mengak, March 31, 1999.

4. Dave and Fay Thompson, remarks dated April 1985, in Hartzog Papers, series 4, box 8, folder 66; Edwin Winge, remarks dated May 4, 1985, in Hartzog Papers, series 4, box 8, folder 66; Ted Swem, remarks dated May 8, 1985, in Hartzog Papers, series 4, box 8, folder 66; McPhee, "Ranger," 60.

5. Benson to Hartzog, April 13, 1985, in Hartzog Papers, series 4, box 8, folder 66.

6. Hartzog, interview with Mengak, March 23, 1996.

7. Utley, interview with Mengak, March 31, 1999.

8. Reed, interview with Mengak, September 11, 2000.

9. Everhart, interview with Mengak, June 8, 1999.

10. Hartzog, interview with Mengak, March 23, 1996.

11. Utley, interview with Mengak, March 31, 1999.

12. William (Joe) Kennedy, remarks dated April 24, 1985, in Hartzog Papers, series 4, box 8, folder 66.

13. Mintzmyer, interview with Mengak, September 6, 2000.

14. Hartzog, interview with Mengak, May 11, 1996.

15. Hartzog, interview with Mengak, March 23, 1996.

16. Hartzog, interview with Mengak, May 12, 1996; Frome, *Regreening the National Parks*, 74, 117–21.

17. Hartzog, interview with Mengak, June 8, 1999.

18. Reed, interview with Mengak, September 11, 2000.

19. Stanton, interview with Mengak, October 1, 2000. Stanton listed this as one of Hartzog's greatest strengths as director.

20. Hartzog, interview with Mengak, May 12, 1996.

21. McPhee, "Ranger," 47.

22. Mintzmyer, interview with Mengak, September 6, 2000.

23. Hartzog, interview with Mengak, May 11, 1996.

24. Hartzog, interview with Mengak, July 7, 1997.

25. Hartzog, interview with Mengak, November 4, 2000.

26. Hartzog, *Battling for the National Parks*, 137.

27. Reed, interview with Mengak, September 11, 2000.

28. Hartzog, *Battling for the National Parks*, 118.

29. Hartzog, interview with Mengak, July 28, 1999.

30. Mackintosh, "For Public Outdoor Recreation Use and Enjoyment," in *Assateague Island National Seashore*, http://www.nps.gov/history/history/online_books/asis/adhi8.htm (accessed August 19, 2011).

31. Everhart, interview with Mengak, March 23, 1996.

32. Hansen, remarks dated May 7, 1985, in Hartzog Papers, series 4, box 8, folder 66.

33. Hartzog, interview with Mengak, November 4, 2000.

34. McPhee, "Ranger," 68.

35. Everhart, interview with Mengak, March 23, 1996.

36. Hartzog, interview with Mengak, May 12, 1996.

37. Hartzog, *Battling for the National Parks*, 122–24; Hartzog, interview with Mengak, March 23, 1996.

38. Utley, e-mail correspondence with Mengak, October 6, 2003.

39. Hartzog, interview with Mengak, February 4, 2004.

40. Hartzog, interview with Mengak, May 12, 1996.

41. Johnson, "The Great Society," May 22, 1964, American Rhetoric, http://www.americanrhetoric.com/speeches/lbjthegreatsociety.htm (accessed March 4, 2011).

42. Udall, interview with Frantz, April 18, 1969.

43. Utley, interview with Sellars and Webb, September 24–December 27, 1985, 147.

44. Everhart, interview with Mengak, August 10, 1996.

45. Hartzog, interview with Mengak, March 23, 1996.

46. Everhart, interview with Mengak, March 23, 1996.

47. Dallek, *Lone Star Rising*, 131.

48. Ibid., 132.

49. Utley, interview with Sellars and Webb, September 24–December 27, 1985, 41.

50. Hartzog, interview with Mengak, March 26, 1996.

51. Reed, interview with Mengak, September 11, 2000; Reed, e-mail correspondence with Mengak, August 28, 2000; Hartzog, *Battling for the National Parks*, 185.

52. Nixon did attend the dedication of the Lady Bird Johnson Grove in Redwood National Park on August 27, 1969.

53. Hartzog, interview with Mengak, March 26, 1996.

54. Reed, interview with Mengak, September 11, 2000.

55. Frome, *Regreening the National Parks*, 23.

56. Udall, interview with Frantz, April 18, 1969.

57. Ibid.

58. Frome, *Regreening the National Parks*, 26.

59. Udall, interview with Frantz, April 18, 1969.

60. Everhart, interview with Mengak, March 23, 1996.

61. Hartzog, interview with Mengak, March 23, 1996.

62. Hartzog, *Battling for the National Parks*, 183–90; Hartzog, interview with Mengak, May 11, 1996.

63. Hartzog, interview with Mengak, May 11, 1996; Hartzog, *Battling for the National Parks*, 183. According to Hartzog, Hickel's main change to his proposal was scratching the section that advocated Park Service campgrounds being run by concessioners.

64. Hartzog, *Battling for the National Parks*, 95–96.

65. Hartzog, interview with Hosmer, August 5, 1981, 18.

66. Frome, *Regreening the National Parks*, 31–33.

67. Utley, interview with Sellars and Webb, September 24–December 27, 1985, 61.

68. Frome, *Regreening the National Parks*, 33.

69. Hartzog, *Battling for the National Parks*, 188.

70. Reed, biographical information, in Nathaniel Reed Public Statements, 1971–1976, Gerald R. Ford Library, Ann Arbor, MI. In a July 28, 1999, interview Hartzog recalled first meeting Reed when he was working in the Florida governor's office. Reed had helped Hartzog "a great deal in getting that assured water supply to the Everglades." When Hartzog refused the job of assistant secretary, he recommended Nat Reed to Morton, and after meeting him in Florida, Morton offered Reed the job. In a September 11, 2000, interview with me, Reed acknowledged that "George has always claimed that he was responsible for my assistant secretary's position, but I've always seriously doubted it." Reed attributed his securing the position to his connections with Morton, Nixon, and Bebe Rebozo. Morton was a "very close friend of my eldest brother who farmed near him on the eastern shore and was a great supporter of him in Congress. I shot with him. I rode with him."

71. Reed, interview with Mengak, September 11, 2000.

72. Hartzog, interview with Mengak, July 28, 1999.

73. Everhart, interview with Mengak, July 28, 1999.

74. Hartzog, interview with Mengak, March 23, 1996.

75. Reed, interview with Mengak, September 11, 2000.

Chapter Five

1. Hartzog, interview with Mengak, June 8, 1999, and May 11, 1996. Hartzog must have kept up with Aunt Lula's son, since he knew his playmate had become a Baptist preacher in South Carolina.

2. Hartzog, interview with Mengak, June 8, 1999.

3. Hartzog, interview with Mengak, May 11, 1996, and June 8, 1999.

4. Hartzog, interview with Mengak, March 23, 1996.

5. See Banner, *Women in Modern Times*; Chafe, *The Paradox of Change*; and Kessler-Harris, *Out to Work*.

6. Hartzog, interview with Mengak, July 30, 1998.

7. Hartzog, interview with Mengak, July 28, 1999.

8. Hartzog, interview with Mengak, June 8, 1999.

9. Ibid.

10. Levy, *The Civil Rights Movement*, 29; Branch, *Parting the Waters*, 271–73.

11. O'Reilly, *Nixon's Piano*, 197.

12. Qtd. in Levy, *The Civil Rights Movement*, 173.

13. Qtd. in ibid., 177.

14. Hartzog, interview with Mengak, July 28, 1999.

15. Kennedy, Executive Order 10925, http://www.eeoc.gov/eeoc/history/35th/thelaw/eo-10925.html (accessed March 4, 2011).

16. See Levy, *The Civil Rights Movement*, 94.

17. Ibid.

18. Albright (as told to Cahn), *The Birth of the National Park Service*, 145.

19. Kaufman, *National Parks and the Woman's Voice*, 65–78, 121. See also the collection of materials related to the National Park Women's Organization in the National Park Service History Collection.

20. Kaufman, *National Parks and the Woman's Voice*, 78–79.

21. Qtd. in ibid., 80.

22. Ibid., 89.

23. Hartzog, interview with Mengak, July 28, 1999.

24. Hartzog, interview with Mengak, March 23, 1996.

25. Kaufman, *National Parks and the Woman's Voice*, 115–16.

26. Levy, *The Civil Rights Movement*, 103–19.

27. Friedan, *The Feminine Mystique*, 1–27.

28. Sealander, "John F. Kennedy's Presidential Commission on the Status of Women"; Hartman, *From Margin to Mainstream*, 50–53.

29. Harrison, *On Account of Sex*, 142–46, 225–27.

30. Reed, interview with Mengak, September 11, 2000; Hagood, interview with Mengak, August 31, 2000; Hutchinson, interview with Mengak, August 4, 2000; Stanton, interview with Mengak, October 1, 2000.

31. Hartzog, interview with Mengak, March 23, 1996; Kaufman, *National Parks and the Woman's Voice*, 152–53.

32. Kaufman, *National Parks and the Woman's Voice*, 121.

33. Committee on Women's Employment and Related Social Issues, *Women's Work, Men's Work*, 38–39.

34. Doll, "Women Don't Mind Park Service Limits."

35. Qtd. in Kaufman, *National Parks and the Woman's Voice*, 126.

36. Doll, "Women Don't Mind Park Service Limits."

37. Committee on Women's Employment and Related Social Issues, *Women's Work, Men's Work*, 53.

38. Hartzog, interview with Mengak, June 8, 1999.

39. Doll, "Women Don't Mind Park Service Limits."

40. Knight, interview with Mengak, October 10, 2000.

41. Mintzmyer, interview with Mengak, September 6, 2000; Mintzmyer, e-mail correspondence with Mengak, October 23, 2000.

42. Doll, "Women Don't Mind Park Service Limits."

43. Bowen, interview and e-mail correspondence with Mengak, July 26–27, 2000.

44. Keller and Turek, *American Indians and the National Parks*, 237.

45. Stanton, interview with Mengak, October 1, 2000.

46. Floyd, *Race, Ethnicity, and Use of the National Park System*, 1.

47. Gwaltney, interview with Mengak, August 31, 2000.

48. Stanton, interview with Mengak, October 1, 2000.

49. Keller and Turek, *American Indians and National Parks*, 237.

50. Everhart, *Take Down Flag and Feed Horses*, 86.

51. Hartzog, interview with Mengak, July 28, 1999.

52. Lerner, *Statistical Abstract of the United States*.

53. Grove, e-mail correspondence with Mengak, September 20, 2000.

54. Udall, interview with Mengak, October 3, 2000.

55. Stanton, interview with Mengak, October 1, 2000.

56. Hartzog, interview with Mengak, June 8, 1999.

57. Hartzog, interview with Mengak, September 2, 2000.

58. Hartzog, interview with Mengak, November 4, 2000.

59. Chapman, e-mail correspondence with Mengak, October 23, 2000.

60. Hartzog to superintendents, "Special Information Memorandum No. 48—EEO Affirmative Action," August 25, 1969, in Hartzog Papers, series 2, box 22, folder 156; Hartzog, interview with Mengak, June 8, 1999. This memo was sent in a blue envelope, which signified it contained important information, and it was supposed to route directly to the desks of the superintendents, who were expected to pay special attention to its contents.

61. John A. Rutter to Hartzog, "EEO Workshop, Pacific Northwest," April 29, 1971, in Hartzog Papers, series 2, box 24, folder 162D.

62. Hartzog, interview with Mengak, March 23 and August 10, 1996; Hartzog, *Battling for the National Parks*, 99.

63. Hartzog, *Battling for the Parks*, 78.

64. Hartzog, interview with Mengak, July 30, 1998.

65. Hartzog, interview with Mengak, August 10, 1996.

66. Everhart, interview with Mengak, June 8, 1999.

67. Utley, interview with Webb and Sellars, September 24–December 27, 1985, 80.

68. Stanton, interview with Mengak, October 1, 2000.

69. Hagood, interview with Mengak, August 31, 2000.

70. Stanton, interview with Mengak, October 1, 2000.

71. Davis, interview with Mengak, October 19, 2000; "Biography of Gentry Davis, Deputy Regional Director, National Capital Region, National Park Service, Washington, D.C.," http://www.nps.gov/ncro/biogent.html (accessed March 4, 2011); National Park Service press release, "Gentry Davis and Joseph M. Lawler Named Deputy Regional Directors of Park Service's National Capital Region," August 3, 2001, http://www.nps.gov/ncro/Public Affairs/PressReleases/xx_New_Deputy_Directors_Named_25FEB98.htm (accessed March 4, 2011).

72. Hagood, interview with Mengak, August 31, 2000.

73. Everhart, interview with Mengak, August 10, 1996; John D. Neal, phone conversation with Mengak, November 20, 2000.

74. Mintzmyer, interview with Mengak, September 6, 2000.

75. Civil Service Commission, "Background on Changes in National Park Service Uniform Classification Series," in Hartzog Papers, series 1, box 74, folder 909A; Kwandrans, "Is FOST Dead?"

76. Hartzog, interview with Mengak, July 28, 1999.

77. Ibid.

78. Bowen, interview with Mengak, July 26, 1999.

79. Hartzog, interview with Mengak, July 28, 1999.

80. Hartzog, interview with Mengak, August 30, 2004.

81. Hartzog, interview with Mengak, July 28, 1999.

82. Udall, speech, Western Governor's Conference, Las Vegas, NV, April 26, 1966, in Hartzog Papers, series 1, box 95, folder 1198.

83. Hickel to Hartzog, "Management of the National Park System," June 18, 1969, in Hartzog Papers, series 1, box 98, folder 1229. Hickel's directive was, as I have already noted, actually drafted by Hartzog.

84. Udall, excerpts from speech, National Convention of League of United Latin-American Citizens in Phoenix, AZ, June 24, 1967, in Hartzog Papers, series 1, box 95, folder 1200.

85. Lewis to Midwest Region, "Indian Liaison, Midwest Region, Points to Ponder," March 20, 1970, in Hartzog Papers, series 1, box 32, folder 398.

86. Hartzog to all regional directors, service centers, and training centers, "Secretary's June 18 Policy Directive—Training Task Force," October 9, 1969, in Hartzog Papers, series 1, box 98, folder 1229.

87. Hartzog, interview with Mengak, May 12, 1996.

88. Stanley Hulett to Nathaniel Reed, "Accomplishments Since January 1969," July 17, 1972, in Hartzog Papers, series 1, box 32, folder 398.

89. John Cook, e-mail to Robert Utley, September 22, 2004. "The American Indian/NPS formal relations program . . . was actually started by Stu Udall and Connie Wirth with the appointment of Meredith Guillett to [Canyon] de Chelly and as Indian Relations Officer back in 1962."

90. Hartzog, interview with Mengak, May 11 and August 10, 1996; Lewis to Midwest Region, "Indian Liaison, Midwest Region, Points to Ponder," March 20, 1970, in Hartzog Papers, series 1, box 32, folder 398; Hulett to Reed, "Accomplishments Since January 1969," July 17, 1972, Hartzog Papers, series 1, box 32, folder 398.

91. Kaufman, *National Parks and the Woman's Voice*, 130.

92. Chapman, e-mail correspondence with Mengak, October 15, 2000.

93. Kaufman, *National Parks and the Woman's Voice*, 131; Knight, e-mail correspondence with Mengak, October 19, 2000.

94. Kaufman, *National Parks and the Woman's Voice*, 131, 136, 144; Bowen, interview and e-mail correspondence with Mengak, July 26–27, 2000.

95. Chapman, e-mail correspondence with Mengak, October 15, 2000.

96. Sealander, "John F. Kennedy's Presidential Commission on the Status of Women," 256.

97. Kaufman, *National Parks and the Woman's Voice*, 126.

98. Foresta, *America's National Parks and Their Keepers*, 132–33.

99. Utley interview with Sellars and Webb, September 24–December 27, 1985, 84, 51, his emphasis.

100. The information about the kinds of trainees who participated in twenty-ninth session in 1969 was provided by participant Doris Osmundson Bowen.

101. Bowen, interview and e-mail correspondence with Mengak, July 26–27, 2000.

102. Kaufman, *National Parks and the Woman's Voice*, 131.

103. "CSC Limits 'One Sex Only Job Slots,'" *National Park Courier*, c. 1971, in Hartzog Papers, series 1, box 67; Kaufman, *National Parks and the Woman's Voice*, 132.

104. Hartzog, interview with Mengak, May 12, 1996.

105. Hartzog, interview with Mengak, July 28, 1999.

106. Hartzog, "Goals for 1971," December 22, 1970, in Hartzog Papers, series 1, box 32, folder 398. Before 1971, Hartzog's goals had danced around the issue of

enhanced diversity. See other yearly goals in Hartzog Papers, series 1, box 32, folder 398.

107. Kaufman, *National Parks and the Woman's Voice*, 132.

108. Levy, *Civil Rights Movement*, 99.

109. Reed, interview with Mengak, September 11, 2000; Everhart, *The National Park Service*, 239–40.

110. Rutter to Hartzog, "EEO Workshop, Pacific Northwest," April 29, 1971, in Hartzog Papers, series 2, box 24, folder 162D.

111. Everhart, interview with Mengak, August 10, 1996.

112. Stanton, interview with Mengak, October 1, 2000.

113. Hartzog, interview with Mengak, November 4, 2000.

114. Knight, interview with Mengak, October 10, 2000.

115. Stanton, e-mail correspondence with Mengak, October 20, 2004.

116. Davis, interview with Mengak, October 19, 2000.

117. Hagood, interview with Mengak, August 31, 2000.

118. Everhart, *Take Down Flag and Feed Horses*, 84.

119. Mintzmyer, interview with Mengak, September 6, 2000.

120. Suggs, interview with Mengak, November 2, 2000.

121. Mintzmyer, interview with Mengak, September 6, 2000.

122. Bowen, interview and e-mail correspondence with Mengak, July 26–27, 2000.

123. Mintzmyer, interview with Mengak, September 6, 2000.

124. Knight, interview with Mengak, October 10, 2000.

125. Mintzmyer, interview with Mengak, September 6, 2000.

126. Hagood, interview with Mengak, August 31, 2000.

127. Davis, interview with Mengak, October 19, 2000.

128. Mintzmyer, interview with Mengak, September 6, 2000.

129. Kaufman, *National Parks and the Woman's Voice*, 134–36, 143.

130. Ibid., 154.

131. Hartzog, interview with Mengak, August 10, 1996.

132. Rutter to Hartzog, "EEO Workshop, Pacific Northwest," April 29, 1971, in Hartzog Papers, series 2, box 24, folder 162D.

133. Hagood, interview with Mengak, August 31, 2000; Hutchinson, interview with Mengak, August 4, 2000.

134. Zone conference notes, Southwest Region, Grand Canyon, April 22–23, 1968, in Hartzog Papers, series 1, box 97, folder 1222.

135. Rutter to Hartzog, "EEO Workshop, Pacific Northwest," April 29, 1971, in Hartzog Papers, series 2, box 24, folder 162D.

136. Hartzog, interview with Mengak, June 8, 1999.

137. Hartzog, interview with Mengak, March 23, 1996.

Chapter Six

1. French, "The Decline and Deterioration of the American City Park."

2. House Committee on Interior and Insular Affairs, *To Provide for the Establishment of the Gateway National Seashore in the States of New York and New Jersey, and for Other Purposes*, 378.

3. Foresta, *America's National Parks and Their Keepers*, 173.

4. Hartzog, interview with Mengak, March 23, 1996.

5. Foresta, *American's National Parks and Their Keepers*, 169.

6. Hartzog, interviews with Mengak, March 23, 1996, and May 12, 1996.

7. Qtd. in Nash, *Wilderness and the American Mind*, 113–14.

8. Sellars, *Preserving Nature in the National Parks*, 183.

9. Foresta, *America's National Parks and Their Keepers*, 30–77.

10. Unrau and Williss, "Reorganization of Park Administration," pt. C, "Reorganization of 1933," in *Administrative History*, http://www.cr.nps.gov/history/online_books/unrau-williss/adhi2c.htm (accessed August 19, 2011).

11. Qtd. in ibid.

12. Qtd. in Foresta, *National Parks and Their Keepers*, 170.

13. Hartzog, interview with Mengak, March 23, 1996.

14. Hartzog, interview with Mengak, July 28, 1999.

15. Everhart, interview with Mengak, July 8, 1997.

16. Outdoor Recreation Resources Review Commission, *Outdoor Recreation for America*, 1.

17. Unrau and Williss, "New Initiatives in the Field of Recreation and Recreational Area Development," pt. D, "The Park, Parkway, and Recreational-Area Study Act of 1936," in *Administrative History*, http://www.cr.nps.gov/history/online_books/unrau-williss/adhi4d.htm (accessed August 19, 2011).

18. Outdoor Recreation Resources Review Commission, *Outdoor Recreation for America*, 1.

19. Ibid., 2.

20. Udall, interview with Frantz, April 18, 1969.

21. Everhart, interview with Mengak, March 23, 1996.

22. Udall, interview with Frantz, December 16, 1969.

23. Udall, *Quiet Crisis*, 172.

24. Ibid., viii.

25. Udall, interview with Frantz, December 16, 1969.

26. Johnson, "The Great Society," May 22, 1964, American Rhetoric, http://www.americanrhetoric.com/speeches/lbjthegreatsociety.htm (accessed March 4, 2011).

27. Hartzog, interview with Mengak, January 18, 2005.

28. Johnson, State of the Union address, January 4, 1965, http://www.lbjlib.utexas.edu/johnson/av.hom/streaming-index.shtm#1965 (accessed March 4, 2011).

29. Kearns, *Lyndon Johnson and the American Dream*, 305.

30. U.S. Riot Commission, *Report of the National Advisory Commission on Civil Disorder*, 1, 12.

31. French, "The Decline and Deterioration of the American City Park," 227–28.

32. Lyndon B. Johnson, "Address to the Nation, June 27, 1967," http://millercenter.org/scripps/archive/speeches/detail/4040 (accessed August 19, 2011).

33. Johnson, "The Great Society," May 22, 1964.

34. Gould, "Lady Bird Johnson and Beautification," 150, 155.

35. Von Eckardt, "Washington's Chance for Splendor," 55.

36. Gould, "Lady Bird Johnson and Beautification," 158–60.

37. Udall, interview with Frantz, May 16, 1969.

38. Hartzog, *Battling for the National Parks*, 177.

39. Ibid., 177–81.

40. Hartzog, interviews with Mengak, March 23, 1996, and July 7, 1997.

41. Small, *The Presidency of Richard Nixon*, 196–200.

42. Tom Wicker, *One of Us*, 507–16; Reed, interview with Mengak, September 11, 2000.

43. Wicker, *One of Us*, 507–16; Hartzog, interview with Mengak, March 23, 1996.

44. Wicker, *One of Us*, 513.

45. Nixon, "America's Natural Resources," October 18, 1968, in Hartzog Papers, series 2, box 22, folder 156A.

46. Reed, interview with Mengak, September 11, 2000.

47. Hartzog, interview with Mengak, July 7, 1997.

48. Everhart, interview with Mengak, July 8, 1998.

49. Qtd. in Foresta, *America's National Parks and Their Keepers*, 174.

50. Hartzog, interview with Mengak, July 30, 1998.

51. Hartzog, interview with Mengak, March 23, 1996.

52. While Hartzog's memory remained surprisingly sharp, sometimes he misquoted information. He repeatedly referred to the initial funding as amounting to $275,000. According to a brochure called *Summer in the Parks* put out by the Park Service in the summer of 1968, Congress appropriated $575,000. Congressional documents also put the amount at $575,000.

53. Hartzog, interview with Mengak, June 8, 1999.

54. Everhart and Hartzog, interview with Mengak, June 8, 1999; Hartzog, interviews with Mengak, January 20 and April 5, 2005.

55. National Park Service, *Summer in the Parks*, n.d., in Hartzog Papers, series 1, box 97, folder 1217.

56. Hartzog, *Battling for the National Parks*, 143–44.

57. Hartzog, interview with Mengak, July 8, 1997.

58. National Park Service, *Summer in the Parks*, n.d., in Hartzog Papers, series 1, box 97, folder 1217; Foresta, *National Parks and Their Keepers*, 178.

59. Merritt, "Site Planning and Development at Fort Vancouver," in *Administrative History*, http://www.nps.gov/history/history/online_books/fova/adhi/chap4.htm (accessed August 19, 2011).

60. "Statement of George B. Hartzog, Jr. Director, National Park Service, Department of the Interior, Before the Subcommittee on Parks and Recreation of the House Interior and Insular Affairs Committee, January 18, 1968," in Hartzog, interview with Fry, April 14, 1965, app. C, 74.

61. Mackintosh, "New Directions," pt. 4, "Environmental Interpretation," in *Interpretation in the National Park Service*, http://www.cr.nps.gov/history/online_books/mackintosh2/directions_environmental.htm (accessed August 19, 2011).

62. Ibid.

63. Hartzog, interview with Mengak, February 14, 2005.

64. Macintosh, "New Directions," pt. 3, "Living History," *Interpretation in the National Park Service*, http://www.cr.nps.gov/history/online_books/mackintosh2/directions_living_history.htm (accessed August 19, 2011).

65. Hartzog, interview with Mengak, March 23, 1996.

66. Neuman, "Golden Gate, Gateway: First Urban NRA's." According to Ed Peetz, chief of the NPS's division of Urban Park Planning, preference in establishing federal urban national recreation areas would be given to areas within a 40-mile radius of a city with a population of 250,000 or more and in which the population within a 250-mile radius was more than 10 million people. The gross land acreage should not be less than 10,000 acres. As Peetz put it, "We're not talking about vest-pocket parks or tot-lots, but something of a more regional nature."

67. Utley, e-mail correspondence with Mengak, December 2004. According to Utley, Hartzog "quizzed me about whether I could make a case for national significance of Presidio and Alcatraz Island. I said, 'Yes.'"

68. Hartzog, interview with Mengak, September 2, 2000; National Park Service, "Presidio: From Post to Park," http://www.nps.gov/prsf/historyculture/post-to-park.htm (accessed March 4, 2011).

69. Hartzog, interview with Mengak, November 11, 2000, and January 18, 2005.

70. House Committee on Interior and Insular Affairs, *To Provide for the Establishment of the Gateway National Seashore in the States of New York and New Jersey, and for Other Purposes*, 397.

71. James Hansen to Hartzog, "Washington Area Urban Training and Work Experience Program for New Uniformed Personnel," August 18, 1970, in Hartzog Papers, series 1, box 110, folder 1347.

72. Hartzog, interview with Mengak, September 2, 2000.

73. Hartzog, interview with Mengak, November 11, 2000.

74. Hartzog, "Open Spaces for All Americans," Outdoor Recreation Congress for the Pacific Northwest, Wenatchee, Washington, April 1, 1965, in Hartzog Papers, series 1, box 92, folder 1154.

75. Rockefeller, keynote address, Congress for Parks and Recreation, October 10, 1966, Washington, D.C., in Hartzog Papers, series 1, box 95, folder 1191.

76. Utley, interview with Sellars and Webb, September 24–December 27, 1985, 56.

77. Hartzog, interview with Fry, April 14, 1965, 38.

78. Hartzog, interview with Mengak, July 8, 1997.

79. Ibid.

80. Foresta, *America's National Parks and Their Keepers*, 194.

81. Ibid.

82. Reed, interview with Mengak, September 11, 2000.

83. Foresta, *America's National Parks and Their Keepers*, 195.

84. Everhart, interview with Mengak, July 7, 1997.

85. Hartzog, interview with Mengak, July 8, 1997.

86. Rettie, *Our National Park System*, 46–47.

87. Foresta, *America's National Parks and Their Keepers*, 162.

88. Utley, interview with Mengak, March 31, 1999.

89. Lane, "Secretary Lane's Letter on National Park Management, May 13, 1918," 51.

90. Chuck Pellicane, "Remembering Gateway," National Park Service, Gateway National Recreation Area, http://www.nps.gov/gate/homepage/pellicane.htm (accessed July 7, 1999).

91. Everhart, *The National Park Service*, 140.

92. Everhart, interview with Mengak, July 8, 1997.
93. Lane, "Secretary Lane's Letter on National Park Management, May 13, 1918," 48.
94. Garrison to Hartzog, "NERO Recreation Area Potentials," November 14, 1969, in Hartzog Papers, series 1, box 110, folder 1346.
95. Hartzog, interview with Mengak, July 7, 1997.
96. Reed, interview with Mengak, September 11, 2000.
97. Bureau of Outdoor Recreation, "Proposed Urban Recreation Areas," June 30, 1969, in Hartzog Papers, series 1, box 110, folder 1346.
98. G. Douglas Hofe Jr. to Hickel "Acquisition of Recreation Areas to Serve Urban Needs," June 26, 1970, in Hartzog Papers, series 1, box 79, folder 999. The following table shows June 1970 proposed outdoor recreation areas to meet urban needs.

Table of 1970 Proposed Bureau of Outdoor Recreation Areas

Parks	Population Served	Timing	Estimated Acquisition Costs
C&O National Historical Park	Washington, D.C.	Ready to go	$20.4 million
Gateway NRA	New York City	Ready to go	$2 million
Connecticut River NRA	Metropolitan New England	Ready to go	$58 million
Golden Gate NRA	San Francisco	Almost ready	$ 0 (all federal land)
Meramec NRA	St. Louis	Almost ready	$22 million
Buffalo Bayou NRA	Houston	Ready in early 1971	$5 million
Anacostia NRA	Washington, D.C.	Ready in early 1971	$3 million
Chattahoochee Recreation River	Atlanta	Ready in early 1971	$40 million
Four Seasons NRA	Denver	Ready in early 1971	$42 million
Upper Mississippi NRA	St. Louis, Minneapolis/ St. Paul	Ready in 1971–1972	$200 million
Lake Michigan Beach Lakeshore	Chicago-Milwaukee area	Ready in 1971–1972	$35 million
Lake Erie Lakeshore	Detroit, Toledo, Cleveland	Ready in 1971–1972	$20 million
Huck Finn NRA	Memphis, Arkansas, Mississippi	Ready in 1971–1972	$50 million
Total Estimated Acquisition Costs			**$ 497.4 million**

99. Senate Committee on Interior and Insular Affairs, *To Provide for the Establishment of the Gateway National Seashore in the States of New York and New Jersey, and for Other Purposes*, 87. An unedited version of this report can be found in Hartzog Papers, series 1, box 104, folder 1275.

100. Rothman and Holder, *The Park That Makes Its Own Weather*, 29.

101. Louter, "Contested Terrain: The Establishment of North Cascades National Park," in *Contested Terrain*.

102. Karamanski, *A Nationalized Lakeshore*, app. 4. Sleeping Bear Dunes National Lakeshore reported 777,000 visitors in 1975.

103. Colby-Ghiatis, e-mail correspondence with Mengak, March 16, 2001; Szarka, e-mail correspondence with Mengak, March 19, 2001.

104. Hartzog, interview with Mengak, July 8, 1997.

105. George Siehl, *Alternative Strategies for Providing Urban Parks*. The Department of the Interior would later concede that urban recreation areas were a drain on the system and needed reassessment. "Urban park operation," according to Siehl, "strained the manpower and financial resources of the Service, to the detriment of traditional park areas such as Yellowstone and Yosemite."

106. Schullery, *Searching for Yellowstone*.

107. Hartzog, *Battling for the National Parks*, 97.

108. Capps, "Interpretation," in *Kennesaw Mountain National Battlefield Park Administrative History*, http://www.nps.gov/history/history/online_books/kemo/adhi/adhi4.htm (accessed August 19, 2011).

109. Hartzog, interview with Mengak, January 20, 2005.

110. House Committee on Interior and Insular Affairs, *To Provide for the Establishment of the Gateway National Seashore in the States of New York and New Jersey, and for Other Purposes*, 377.

111. Foresta, *America's National Parks and Their Keepers*, 189–212.

112. Facts on File, "20 Most-Visited Sites in the National Park System, 1999," http://2facts.es.vrc.scoolaid.net/icah_story.aspx?PIN=wusf30855 (accessed June 24, 2011).

113. Foresta, *National Parks and Their Keepers*, 219.

114. Ibid., 180–81.

115. Merritt, "Site Planning and Development at Fort Vancouver," in *Administrative History*, http://www.nps.gov/history/history/online_books/fova/adhi/chap4.htm (accessed August 19, 2011).

116. Macintosh, "New Directions," pt. 4, "Environmental Interpretation," in *Interpretation in the National Park Service*, http://www.cr.nps.gov/history/online_books/mackintosh2/directions_environmental.htm (accessed August 19, 2011).

117. Ibid.; Hartzog interview with Mengak, January 20, 2005.

118. Hartzog interview with Mengak, March 23, 1996.

119. Hartzog, interview with Mengak, May 11, 1996. See also Hartzog, interviews with Mengak, March 23, 1996, July 8, 1997, and July 30, 1998.

120. Hartzog, interview with Mengak, July 7, 1997.

121. Hartzog, interview with Mengak, January 20, 2005.

Chapter Seven

1. Hartzog, interview with Hosmer, August 5, 1981, 17.
2. Hartzog, interview with Mengak, May 12, 1996.
3. Sellars, *Preserving Nature in the National Parks*, 206.
4. Qtd. in ibid., 341.
5. Rettie, *Our National Park System*, 15–16.
6. Hartzog, interview with Mengak, July 8, 1997.
7. Hartzog, interview with Mengak, April 25, 2005.
8. Hartzog, *Battling for the National Parks*, 95.
9. Reisner, *Cadillac Desert*, 17.
10. Qtd. in Foresta, *National Parks and Their Keepers*, 62.
11. Ibid., 314.
12. Fox, *The American Conservation Movement*, 286–89.
13. Public Law 88–577 (16 USC 1131–36), 88th Congress, 2nd session, September 3, 1964.
14. Frome, *Regreening the National Parks*, 72; McCloskey, "What the Wilderness Act Accomplished in Protection of Roadless Areas Within the National Park System," 461.
15. Hartzog, interview with Mengak, April 25, 2005; Hartzog, interview with Mengak, May 11, 1996. Hartzog, however, explained that "there's a lot of misperception about the Wilderness Act. The Wilderness Act had a provision in it that nothing in this act shall be construed as in effect . . . and I can't quote it precisely . . . as lowering the preservation standards for national parks. So, you know, when you come right down to it the Congress said when they passed the Wilderness Act that the preservation in the national parks was already at a standard higher than that prescribed in the Wilderness Act. And that none of those exceptions written into the Wilderness Act should be implemented in the national parks if they would lower the standards of preservation in the national parks. But all these guys choose to ignore that now because wilderness sells. Parks do not. So they're selling wilderness" (interview with Mengak, May 11, 1996).
16. Hartzog, interviews with Mengak, March 23, 1996, November 4, 2000, and April 25, 2005.
17. Hartzog, interview with Mengak, September 13, 2005; Udall, interview with Mengak, September 19, 2005.
18. Reed, interview with Mengak, September 11, 2000.
19. Hartzog, interviews with Mengak, November 4, 2000, and September 6, 2005.
20. Reed, interview with Mengak, September 11, 2000.
21. Hartzog, interview with Mengak, September 13, 2005.
22. Frome, *Regreening the National Parks*, 72.
23. Fox, *The American Conservation Movement*, 304.
24. Hartzog, interview with Mengak, March 23, 1996.
25. Brown, interview with Mengak, June 13, 2001.
26. Rothman, *America's National Monuments*, 233–39.
27. Everhart, interview with Mengak, July 7, 1997.
28. Hartzog, interview with Fry, April 14, 1965, app. C, 46.

29. Frome, *Regreening the National Parks*, 26.

30. Hartzog, interview with Mengak, July 7, 1997.

31. Hartzog, *Battling for the Parks*, 122; Hartzog, interviews with Mengak, March 23, 1996, and April 22, 2005. Although Hartzog had served as key man in the Ozarks during the time he was superintendent at Jefferson National Expansion Memorial, he said that approach was not at that time well established and was only implemented on an "ad hoc basis." After his experience at Prairie Park, he institutionalized the key-man approach for all proposed areas.

32. Hartzog, interview with Mengak, July 7, 1997.

33. Ibid.

34. Utley, interview with Sellars and Webb, September 24–December 27, 1985, 56.

35. Hartzog, interview with Mengak, April 25, 2005.

36. Hartzog, interview, July 7, 1997.

37. Utley, interview with Evison, May 17, 1973.

38. Hartzog, interview with Fry, April 14, 1965, 47.

39. Hartzog, interview with Mengak, July 7, 1997.

40. Ibid.

41. Udall, interview with Frantz, December 16, 1969.

42. Hartzog, interview with Mengak, May 11, 1996.

43. Hartzog, interview with Mengak, July 7, 1997.

44. Hartzog, *Battling for the National Parks*, 140–41.

45. Ibid., 150.

46. Hartzog, interview with Mengak, July 7, 1997.

47. Ibid.

48. Hartzog, *Battling for the National Parks*, 150–51.

49. Steamtown National Historic Site was authorized on October 30, 1986.

50. Hartzog, interview with Mengak, July 7, 1997.

51. Everhart, *The National Park Service*, 137.

52. Hartzog, *Battling for the National Parks*, 174.

53. Foresta, *National Parks and Their Keepers*, 149.

54. Utley, interview with Sellars and Webb, September 24–December 27, 1985, 31; Hartzog to Thomas Flynn and Joseph Holt, "Personnel Attention," February 25, 1971, in Hartzog Papers, series 2, box 48, folder 597. Hartzog wrote, "I am advised that Congressman Bennett is pushing on this [Florida Frontiers Rivers]."

55. Eventually the idea was reshaped into Timucuan Ecological Historic Preserve, which was designated February 16, 1988.

56. Utley, interview with Sellars and Webb, September 24–December 27, 1985, 31.

57. Ibid., 49–50; Hartzog, interview with Mengak, July 7, 1997.

58. Hartzog, *Battling for the National Parks*, 130–32.

59. Utley, interview with Sellars and Webb, September 24–December 27, 1985, 16.

60. Ibid., 32–33.

61. Ibid.

62. Ibid., 54.

63. Everhart, interview with Mengak, August 10, 1996.

64. Foresta, *National Parks and Their Keepers*, 80–81.

65. Hartzog, interview with Mengak, July 7, 1997.

66. Udall, interview with Frantz, May 19, 1969, 17.

67. Udall, interview with Mengak, September 19, 2005.

68. National Park Service, "The Land and Water Conservation Fund," http://www.nps.gov/lwcf/history.html (accessed August 5, 2011).

69. Hartzog, interview with Fry, April 14, 1965, 56.

70. Udall, interview with Frantz, May 19, 1969, 17.

71. Hartzog, interview with Fry, April 14, 1965, 56.

72. Hartzog, interview with Mengak, July 8, 1997.

73. Hartzog, *Battling for the National Parks*, 267; Bureau of Outdoor Recreation, "History of the Implementation of the Land and Water Conservation Fund Program," November 25, 1968, in Hartzog Papers, series 1, box 47, folder 578.

74. National Park Service, "The Land and Water Conservation Fund," http://www.ncrc.nps.gov/lwcf (accessed September 9, 2005).

75. Reed, interview with Mengak, September 11, 2000.

76. Hartzog, interview with Hosmer, August 5, 1981, 17.

77. Mackintosh, "Shaping the System," pt. 5, "Mission 66 and the Environmental Era, 1952–1972," in *The National Park System*, http://www.cr.nps.gov/history/online_books/mackintosh1/sts2d.htm (accessed August 19, 2011); Rettie, *Our National Park System*, 41.

78. Leopold, Cain, Cottam, Gabrielson, and Kimball, *Wildlife Management in the National Parks*; Udall to Hartzog, "Management of the National Park System," July 10, 1964, in Hartzog Papers, series 2, box 1, folder 2. The 1964 memo from Udall to Hartzog can be found in Dilsaver, *American's National Park System*, 272–76.

79. Mackintosh, "Shaping the System," pt. 5, "Mission 66 and the Environmental Era, 1952–1972," in *The National Park System*, http://www.cr.nps.gov/history/online_books/mackintosh1/sts2d.htm (accessed August 19, 2011); Rettie, *Our National Park System*, 41–44.

80. Utley, interview with Mengak, March 31, 1999.

81. Hartzog, interview with Mengak, May 11, 1996.

82. Utley, e-mail correspondence with Mengak, July 2005.

83. Utley, interview with Mengak, March 31, 1999.

84. Hartzog, interview with Mengak, May 11, 1996.

85. Ibid.; Hartzog, interview with Mengak, August 7, 1997.

86. Utley, interview with Sellars and Webb, September 24–December 27, 1985, 14.

87. Foresta, *National Parks and Their Keepers*, 152.

88. Hartzog, interview with Mengak, April 25, 2005.

89. Foresta, *National Parks and Their Keepers*, 139–48.

90. Utley, e-mail correspondence with Mengak, July 2005.

91. Everhart and Hartzog, interviews with Mengak, July 7, 1997, and April 25, 2005.

92. Hartzog, interviews with Mengak, July 8, 1997, and April 25, 2005.

93. Foresta, *National Parks and Their Keepers*, 231.

94. Lee, *Family Tree of the National Park System*, 73. Today Nez Perce National Historical Park includes thirty-eight sites in the states of Idaho, Oregon, Washington, and Montana.

95. Utley, interview with Sellars and Webb, September 24–December 27, 1985, 47. Utley said the whole Park Service opposed the park, much to Skubitz's dismay. And from this arose Skubitz's "contempt for Park Service historians, especially those specializing in the West, because on the face of it anyone who thought that Fort Scott wasn't significant couldn't be a very good historian."

96. Lee, *Family Tree of the National Park Service*, 66–71.

97. Louter, "The Making of a New Park (1968 to 1978)," in *Contested Terrain*, http://www.nps.gov/history/history/online_books/noca/adhi/part2.htm (accessed August 19, 2011).

98. Hartzog, *Battling for the National Parks*, 169–75; Hartzog, interview with Mengak, July 7, 1997.

99. Mackintosh, "Shaping the System," pt. 5, "Mission 66 and the Environmental Era, 1952–1972," in *The National Park System*, http://www.cr.nps.gov/history/online_books/mackintosh1/sts2d.htm (accessed August 19, 2011).

100. Lee, *Family Tree of the National Park Service*, 68–69.

101. Foresta, *National Parks and Their Keepers*, 238–42; McChristian, "Going Into the Cattle Business: NPS Acquisition," in *Ranchers to Rangers*, http://www.nps.gov/grko/parkmgmt/upload/adhi1.pdf (accessed August 19, 2011).

102. Ibid.

103. Foresta, *National Parks and Their Keepers*, 237–38; Gibbons, "National Natural Landmarks Program"; Shafer, "The National Landmark Program."

104. Lee, *Family Tree of the National Park System*, 60.

105. "Criteria for National Recreation Areas," *NPS Criteria for Park Lands*, in Hartzog Papers, series 1, box 61, folder 761.

106. Mackintosh, "Shaping the System," pt. 5, "Mission 66 and the Environmental Era, 1952–1972," in *The National Park System*, http://www.cr.nps.gov/history/online_books/mackintosh1/sts2d.htm (accessed August 19, 2011).

107. Foresta, *National Parks and Their Keepers*, 216, 281–82.

108. Mackintosh, "Shaping the System," pt. 5, "Mission 66 and the Environmental Era, 1952–1972," in *The National Park System*, http://www.cr.nps.gov/history/online_books/mackintosh1/sts2d.htm (accessed August 19, 2011). The National Environmental Policy Act of 1969 required the government to examine the environmental impacts of any development plans it had for an area.

109. First held in 1924 to raise money for the local fire department, pony penning starts in late July, when the "saltwater cowboys" herd the ponies to the mainland. Most of the year's foals are sold, and the remainder of the ponies are returned to the island. Ideally, the herds are kept to a combined total of 150 in both states to minimize environmental damage from their grazing and daily movements. Contrary to popular beliefs, the ponies are probably not direct descendants of a shipwrecked Spanish galleon. More than likely, the feral horses originated from settlers who instead of fencing their horses on the mainland used the barrier islands to corral them. Having them off the mainland also allowed the owners to escape taxation on them. See National Park Service, "Assateague's Wild Horses," http://www.nps.gov/asis/naturescience/horses.htm (accessed March 4, 2011).

110. Macintosh, "Becoming of the Seashore," in *Assateague Island National Seashore,* http://www.nps.gov/history/history/online_books/asis/adhi1d.htm (accessed August 19, 2011).

111. Hartzog, interview with Mengak, April 25, 2005.

112. National Park Service, "The Live Oak Story," http://www.nps.gov/guis/historyculture/the-live-oak-story.htm (accessed August 6, 2011). Owing to their tolerance to salt spray, their relative density compared to other oaks, and their resistance to disease and decay, live oaks were widely used for shipbuilding during the eighteenth and early nineteenth centuries. Thus, in 1828, the United States purchased land to protect the valuable trees, and the following year, President John Quincy Adams created a federal tree farm exclusively for the Navy. Among the ships constructed from live oaks were the revolutionary privateer the *Hancock,* the USS *Constellation,* and "Old Ironside" herself, the USS *Constitution.* By the 1860s, the development of the ironclad ship would eliminate the tree's importance as a construction material.

113. Hartzog, interview with Mengak, April 25, 2005; Hartzog, *Battling for the National Parks,* 198–200.

114. Keller and Turek, *American Indians and the National Parks,* 3–16.

115. Hartzog, *Battling for the National Parks,* 128.

116. Hartzog, interview with Mengak, July 8, 1997.

117. Ibid.

118. Cockrell, *A Signature of Time and Eternity,* 98–101; Engel, *Sacred,* 271–82; Douglas, "*In the Fullness of Time,* 536–45. According to Douglas, "I felt we were in the grip of an almost irreversible force, which would overrun those who loved the Dunes and sweep on to Michigan City and beyond. Then we would have a continuous jungle of asphalt and steel, with pollution of air and water, with no place for the millions of pent-up city folk to seek refuge, quiet, and renewal. It seemed impossible to stop this movement, but one moonlit evening I made a secret pledge that if I could help to do so I would" (76–77). Despite the long, drawn-out struggle, Douglas felt the that fight "quickened my interest in preserving all places of natural beauty" (543), and he became a strong supporter of park legislation.

119. Lee, *Family Tree of the National Park System,* 52. Shadow Mountain in Colorado was transferred to the U.S. Forest Service in 1979.

120. Hartzog, interview with Mengak, April 25, 2005.

121. Hartzog, interview with Mengak, November 4, 2000.

122. Hartzog, *Battling for the National Parks,* 59, 59–69.

123. McPhee, "Ranger," 78; Udall, introduction, xi–xii.

124. Udall, interview with Frantz, December 16, 1969, 9.

125. See the Wild and Scenic Rivers Act (16 USC 1271–87).

126. Other rivers designated by the 1968 act and managed by the Forest Service included Eleven Point in Missouri, which Hartzog had tried to include in the Ozark National Scenic Riverways; Middle Fork of the Clearwater in Idaho; Feather River in California; Rio Grande in New Mexico; Rogue River in Oregon; and Middle Fork of the Salmon River in Idaho. The last of the eight rivers, the Wolf River, was scheduled to be acquired by the Park Service from the Menominee Indians, but the tribe resisted transfer of management responsibility. See Lee, *Family Tree of the National Park Service,* 81–82, and

Mackintosh, "Shaping the System," pt. 5, "Mission 66 and the Environmental Era, 1952–1972," in *The National Park System,* http://www.cr.nps.gov/history/online_books/mackintosh1/sts2d.htm (accessed August 19, 2011).

127. Lee, *Family Tree of the National Park Service,* 81; National Park Service, "National Park Trails," http://www.nps.gov/nts (accessed March 4, 2011).

128. Daugherty, "John D. Rockefeller, Jr."; Hartzog, *Battling for the National Parks,* 197–202; Hartzog, interview with Mengak, July 28, 1999. According to Hartzog, "I didn't have any role in getting it [the National Recreation and Park Association] started, but I served them for over twenty years as a director and as an unpaid general counsel. See, that was Laurance and Connie Wirth that pulled all those organizations together. And I became Director of NRPA . . . I reckon Orville Freeman [secretary of agriculture] and I were on the board at the same time, and that would have been just a couple or three years before the end of the LBJ administration, when Orville's turn was up he left and I stayed 'cause I was elected for another term which took me through the Nixon administration on through my firing by the Nixon administration. When that term was up one of the people I was working for at that time was Laurance Rockefeller, who was the first client I got when I left the Park Service. And Laurance suggested his interest in NRPA was sufficient that I ought to help him with their legal work, so the board elected me as general counsel and I served in that capacity I reckon for twelve or thirteen years without any compensation." He went on to say that Rockefeller's interest in NRPA came out of the ORRRC study. "He saw all of these small organizations having no political impact because they didn't have money enough to, as splinted as they are. He came up with the idea to join all these and got a first class manager, . . . and he was a very accomplished professional who understood the political process and they got off to a very good start" (Hartzog, interview with Mengak, July 28, 1999).

129. Hartzog, interview with Mengak, April 22, 2005. Hartzog, a member of the Kennedy Center's board, said the building had serious roof leakage problems, and after a rain, patrons would have to navigate around embarrassing drip buckets. A fellow board member approached him and asked him to take over the building so the leak and other problems like difficult access to the facility could be fixed. The Park Service assumed management responsibilities on June 16, 1972, while the board retained control over programming. By the time of Hartzog's departure, the building leak had been fixed, but access problems remained.

130. Hartzog, interview with Mengak, June 8, 1999.

131. Hartzog, interview with Mengak, July 8, 1997; "Legislative Program, 93rd Congress, 1st Session," November 8, 1972, in Hartzog Papers, series 1, box 49, folder 599.

132. Hartzog, *Battling for the National Parks,* 152. According to Hartzog, from 1963 to 1972 "an average of nine new parks each year" were added to the system.

Chapter Eight

1. Leonard to Hartzog, July 1, 1965, in Hartzog Papers, series 2, box 2, folder 11.

2. Hartzog, interview with Mengak, March 23, 1996; Hartzog, *Battling for the National Parks,* 105.

3. Public Law 85–508, 72 Stat. 339, July 7, 1958.

4. Hartzog, interview with Mengak, December 9, 2005.

5. Black, *Russians in Alaska, 1731–1867.*

6. Mitchell, *Sold American*, 99–147.

7. Prior to 1980, Mount McKinley National Park (later renamed Denali National Park) was the only Alaska area given the "national park" title.

8. Williss, *"Do Things Right the First Time,"* 1. I rely extensively on this definitive work in this chapter.

9. Qtd. in ibid., 2.

10. Butcher, *Guide to National Parks*, 44.

11. Japan actually captured two of the Aleutian Islands early in the war effort, making a strong U.S. presence there all the more critical.

12. Potter, *Alaska Under Arms*, 161.

13. Williss, *"Do Things Right the First Time,"* 32.

14. Public Law 85–508.

15. Williss, *"Do Things Right the First Time,"* 33.

16. Qtd. in ibid., 8.

17. Qtd. in ibid., 10.

18. McPhee, *Coming into the Country*, 83.

19. Williss, *"Do Things Right the First Time,"* 10.

20. Kaufman to Hartzog, July 7, 1964, in Hartzog Papers, series 2, box 2, folder 11.

21. Hartzog, *Battling for the National Parks*, 205; Williss, *"Do Things Right the First Time,"* 13.

22. Hartzog, *Battling for the National Parks*, 211. Hartzog would write that the "OPERATION GREAT LAND task force had developed proposals totaling approximately seventy-six million acres." Close examination of the document reveals that the task force identified very broad zones of interest that totaled far more than that. For example, the Brooks Range and Arctic Slope zone, one of the thirty-nine identified zones, totaled 120,000 square miles, which converts to 76.8 million acres.

23. U.S. Department of the Interior, *Operation Great Land*, 7, in Hartzog Papers, series 2, box 5, folder 21; George Collins to Sigurd Olson, February 1, 1965, Hartzog Papers, box 2, folder 11. Collins asked what steps should be taken to get the advisory board to Alaska, adding "Shouldn't we all undertake a campaign to that end?"

24. Swem, interview with Mengak, September 16, 2005.

25. Hartzog to Luntey, June 21, 1965, in Hartzog Papers, series 2, box 2, folder 11; Swem, interview with Schneider, October 10, 1991. In this interview, Swem recalled that Hartzog "spent some time going over the report and decided because it identified so many areas involving lands administered by other agencies such as the Fish and Wildlife Service and the Forest Service and to a lesser degree the Bureau of Land Management that it really went further than he had contemplated it would and that although this could serve as a basis for identifying areas that the Park Service might want to study in the future, he decided this report should not be released and actually it never was. We kept a few copies of the report but we kept them very definitely under wraps."

26. Hartzog, *Battling for the National Parks*, 207–11; Hartzog, interview with Mengak, July 8, 1997. See also various thank-you letters in Hartzog Papers, series 2, box 2, folder 11.

27. Hartzog, *Battling for the National Parks*, 207.

28. Williss, *"Do Things Right the First Time,"* 14; Swem, interview with Schneider, October 10, 1991; Hartzog, *Battling For the National Parks*, 183. Studies of the area eventually led to its establishment as Klondike Gold Rush National Historical Park in 1976.

29. Williss, *"Do Things Right the First Time,"* 17.

30. Udall, interview with Frantz, July 29, 1969.

31. Udall, interview with Frantz, October 31, 1969.

32. Aspinall to Udall, May 20, 1961, in Hartzog Papers, series 1, box 40, folder 494.

33. Udall, interview with Frantz, October 31, 1969.

34. Ibid.

35. Udall, interview with Mengak, September 19, 2005.

36. Hartzog, interview with Mengak, March 13 and May 5, 2006.

37. Cahn, "How National Park Plan Slipped Away"; Udall, interview with Frantz, October 31, 1969.

38. Johnson, State of the Union address, January 14, 1969, http://www.presidency. ucsb.edu/ws/index.php?pid=29333#axzz1QPLEm5gt (accessed June 25, 2011). In his address, Johnson said, "Part of the American earth—not only in description on a map, but in the reality of our shores, our hills, our parks, our forests, and our mountains—has been permanently set aside for the American public and for their benefit. And there is more that will be set aside before this administration ends." Udall took his last sentence to mean that Johnson was publicly announcing the impending proclamations.

39. Cahn, "How National Park Plan Slipped Away."

40. In 1975, Marble Canyon National Monument was added to Grand Canyon National Park.

41. Larrabee, "How Udall's Park Plans Collapsed."

42. Udall, interview with Mengak, September 15, 2005; "Five Versions."

43. Hall to Hartzog, December 31, 1968, in Hartzog Papers, series 2, box 2, folder 11.

44. Williss, *"Do Things Right the First Time,"* 35; Cahn, *The Fight to Save Wild Alaska*, 11. Williss credits Joseph Fitzgerald, chair of the Federal Field Committee for Development Planning in Alaska, as being the originator of the idea that settlement of Native claims must also take the entire country's interests into consideration. The committee was created in 1964 to help prepare long-range economic and development plans for a state recovering from a devastating March 1964 earthquake. Fitzgerald believed that a "park complex" was important to that recovery. David Hickok, a staff member of Fitzgerald's is credited with suggesting the provision be added to the Senate bill.

45. Williss, *"Do Things Right the First Time,"* 35.

46. Hartzog, interview with Mengak, May 5, 2006.

47. Berry, *The Alaska Pipeline*, 139–41.

48. Hartzog, interview with Mengak, May 5, 2006.

49. Cahn, *The Fight to Save Wild Alaska*, 12; Berry, *The Alaska Pipeline*, 185–86.

50. Elliot, *Alan Bible and the Politics of the New*, 138. In 1965, when Jackson took on the chairmanship of the Interior and Insular Affairs Committee, Bible assumed leadership of the newly created Parks and Recreation Subcommittee, which helps explain why Jackson deferred to Bible about Alaskan park issues.

51. Hartzog, interview with Mengak, March 23, 1996.

52. Hartzog, interview with Mengak, March 26, 1996; Hartzog, *Battling for the National Parks*, 212; Elliot, *Senator Alan Bible and the Politics of the New West*, 206.

53. "Bible Says Gravel Effective despite Pentagon Papers Row"; Hartzog, interviews with Mengak, December 16, 2005, and September 8, 2001.

54. Hartzog, interviews with Mengak, September 6, 2005, and September 8, 2001.

55. Wayburn, *Your Land and Mine*, 228–31.

56. Hartzog, interview with Mengak, December 9, 2005.

57. Hartzog, interviews with Mengak, September 8, 2001, September 13, 2005, and December 9, 2005.

58. Among others, Hartzog credits Ginny Hill Wood and Celia Hunter, who started Camp Denali, a wilderness vacation ranch in the Kantishna mining district, adjacent to Denali National Park where the group stayed, with being an important influence on Bible. When asked why they were influential, Hartzog replied, "They were businesswomen in the community[,] . . . in the top social echelons of Alaska. So that a word out of them . . . just carried a lot of weight" (Hartzog, interview with Mengak, May 12, 2006).

59. Hartzog, interview with Mengak, September 8, 2001.

60. Hartzog to Smith and Silcock, July 26, 1971, in Hartzog Papers, series 2, box 2, folder 14.

61. Hartzog, *Battling for the National Parks*, 213; Hartzog, interviews with Mengak, December 6, 9, and 15, 2005. Hartzog felt that since he had gone to all the effort and expense of getting Bible to Alaska and convincing him to sponsor a national interest lands amendment, he was entitled to the largest share. Ted Swem could not concur with Hartzog on this point. He noted that the Fish and Wildlife Service had a long history in Alaska and had just published an important document, *To Have and to Hold, Alaska's Migratory Birds*. "It was a warning to us that they were very interested in playing the same game that we wanted to play. They wanted to follow up and identify the type of areas that they felt should be their responsibility." Swem felt that the Fish and Wildlife Service knew better at that time what it wanted than the Park Service (Swem, interview with Schneider, October 10, 1991; Swem interview with Mengak, September 6, 2005; U.S. Department of the Interior, *To Have and to Hold, Alaska's Migratory Birds*).

62. Hartzog, interview with Mengak, March 23, 1996.

63. Hartzog, interview with Mengak, December 9, 2005.

64. Ibid.; Hartzog, interviews with Mengak, March 23, 1996, and September 13, 2005.

65. Hartzog, interview with Mengak, July 8, 1997.

66. Williss, *"Do Things Right the First Time,"* 39, 46. Williss said two versions were apparently drafted but that he found copies of neither.

67. Ibid., 41.

68. *Congressional Record*, Senate, November 1, 1971, 38451.

69. Since the House version had failed, the conference senators (including Alan Bible) had to get the House members to allow the Bible amendment to remain in the overall bill (Hartzog, interview with Mengak, November 17, 2006).

70. Hartzog, interviews with Mengak, March 23, 1996, May 11, 1996, July 8, 1997, September 6, 2005, and May 5, 2006. In a September 2005 interview, Ted Swem was not able to corroborate Hartzog's reported interest in "76 million acres."

71. Elliot, *Senator Alan Bible and the Politics of the New West*, 138.

72. Williss, *"Do Things Right the First Time,"* 39.

73. Ibid., 39; Hartzog, interview with Mengak, September 6, 2005.

74. Public Law 92–203, December 18, 1971.

75. Swem, interview with Schneider, October 10, 1991.

76. Hartzog, interview with Mengak, May 12, 2006.

77. Hartzog, *Battling for the National Parks*, 214.

78. Ibid., 214; Hartzog Papers, series 4, box 3, folder 15.

79. Hartzog, interviews with Mengak, November 4, 2000, September 6, 2005, and September 13, 2005. Hartzog felt Reed was more predisposed toward wildlife refuges than national parks. As evidence he pointed to the donation of Reed family land in Florida to the Hobe Sound National Wildlife Refuge in 1969. The refuge came from family lands not put into family's real estate development of the area.

80. Qtd. in Williss, *"Do Things Right the First Time,"* 52.

81. "Memorandum of Understanding Between the State of Alaska and the United States," in Hartzog Papers, series 4, box 3, folder 16A.

82. "Secret Memo Clouds Alaska Land Decisions," *Wilderness Report*, November 1972, in Hartzog Papers, series 4, box 3, folder 16A.

83. Williss, *"Do Things Right the First Time,"* 53; Swem, interview with Mengak, September 16, 2005.

84. Belous, interview with Schneider, October 8, 1991.

85. Swem, interview with Mengak, October 10, 1991.

86. Reed, interview with Mengak, September 11, 2000.

87. Williss, *"Do Things Right the First Time,"* 56.

88. Ibid.

89. Hartzog, interview with Mengak, July 8, 1997.

90. Williss, *"Do Things Right the First Time,"* 67–71.

91. Ibid.

92. McPhee, *Coming Into the Country*, 83.

93. Williss, *"Do Things Right the First Time,"* 84–100.

94. Hartzog, interview with Mengak, November 17, 2006.

95. Duscha, "How the Alaska Act Was Won," 8.

96. Brown, interview with Mengak, June 13, 2001; Williss, *"Do Things Right the First Time,"* 140. During this transition period, Williss reports that "someone . . . fired five shots through Regional Director John Cook's office window one night, and another assaulted an individual known to be friendly to rangers assigned at Wrangell-St. Elias. On September 11, an arsonist destroyed a plane chartered for the use of the three rangers manning that area" (140).

97. Williss, *"Do Things Right the First Time,"* 112. These figures represented estimates presented at the time the legislation was passed. More precise acreages have since been calculated.

98. Ibid., 39.

99. Hartzog, interview with Mengak, May 12, 2006.

100. Connally, "d-2," 8.

Chapter Nine

1. Hartzog, "Summary of Achievements of George B. Hartzog, Jr. as Director of the National Park Service, 1964–1972."

2. I mentioned this accomplishment with regards to urban parks and programs in chapter 6.

3. Hartzog, interviews with Mengak, August 10 and March 23, 1996.

4. Hartzog, interview with Mengak, May 5, 2006.

5. Mackintosh, *The Historic Sites Survey and National Historic Landmarks Program*, 5.

6. Ibid., 21.

7. Ibid., 33.

8. See Jacobs, *Death and the Life of Great American Cities*, and Martin Anderson, *The Federal Bulldozer*. Hartzog recalled seeing one proposal for an interstate highway slated to go right through Washington, D.C., and felt pressure for other roads to be built into parklands (Hartzog, interview with Mengak, October 9, 2006).

9. Glass, *The Beginnings of a New National Historic Preservation Program*, 8.

10. Hartzog, interview with Mengak, September 1, 2006.

11. Hartzog, interview with Hosmer, August 5, 1981, 7. Ronald Lee had served as chief historian and regional director and as a special assistant to Hartzog.

12. Utley, interview with Sellars and Webb, September 24–December 27, 1985, 77.

13. Hartzog, interview with Mengak, March 23, 2007.

14. Hartzog, interview with Hosmer, August 5, 1981, 5.

15. Glass, *The Beginnings of a New National Historic Preservation Program*, 10–13.

16. Woodbury, "John Otis Brew, 1906–1988"; Park, "Dr. Ernest Allen Connally."

17. Utley, interview with Sellars and Webb, September 24–December 27, 1985, 40.

18. Glass, *The Beginnings of a New National Historic Preservation Program*, 57.

19. Hartzog, interview with Mengak, May 5, 2006.

20. Utley, "What Were They Thinking?" "Any lesser figure than Gordon Gray could not have gotten that bill back on the floor."

21. Hartzog, interview with Mengak, March 23, 2007.

22. Glass, *The Beginnings of a New National Historic Preservation Program*, 18–19.

23. Ibid., 23.

24. Hartzog, speech, Annual Meeting of the Society of Architectural Historians, Cleveland, OH, January 27, 1967, in Hartzog Papers, series 2, folder 1156.

25. Utley, interview with Sellars and Webb, September 24–December 27, 1985, 80. Archaeologists rebelled against the new Office of Archeology and Historic Preservation and thought Connally failed to support their efforts in favor of historic preservation. See Binkley, *Science, Politics, and the "Big Dig,"* 62–71.

26. Utley, interview with Sellars and Webb, September 24–December 27, 1985, 82; Mackintosh, *The National Historic Preservation Act and the National Park Service*, 7.

27. The National Trust argued that Congress had intended the entire amount to go to it. The previous year, it had started on expensive preservation efforts, and the limited funding would all but halt progress. States were unhappy with how funding was disbursed. Missouri, for example, a state not known for its wealth of historical sites, submitted the largest funding request and therefore got the largest share, despite the needs in such historically rich states as Virginia.

28. Glass, *The Beginnings of a New National Historic Preservation Program*, 35–39.

29. Mackintosh, *The National Historic Preservation Act and the National Park Service*, 35.

30. Section 106 (16 USC 470f) states that "the head of any Federal agency having direct or indirect jurisdiction over a proposed Federal or federally assisted undertaking in any State and the head of any Federal department or independent agency having authority to license any undertaking shall, prior to the approval of the expenditure of any Federal funds on the undertaking or prior to the issuance of any license, as the case may be, take into account the effect of the undertaking on any district, site, building, structure, or object that is included in or eligible for inclusion in the National Register. The head of any such Federal agency shall afford the Advisory Council on Historic Preservation established under Title II of this Act a reasonable opportunity to comment with regard to such undertaking."

31. Glass, *The Beginnings of a New National Historic Preservation Program*, 41–52.

32. Utley, interview with Sellars and Webb, September 24–December 27, 1985, 38.

33. Mackintosh, *The National Historic Preservation Act and the National Park Service*, 86–90.

34. Hartzog, interview with Mengak, March 23, 2007; Utley, interview with Sellars and Webb, September 24–December 27, 1985, 44.

35. National Trust for Historic Places website, http://www.preservationnation.org/about-us/.

36. Lusignan, e-mail correspondence with Mengak, September 4, 2008. Also see "Laws, Executive Orders, and Regulations," http://www.nps.gov/history/laws.htm (accessed March 4, 2011).

37. The Student Conservation Association claims that the National Park Service modeled the new Volunteers in Parks program after it ("History," http://www.thesca.org/about/history [accessed March 4, 2011]). Hartzog's response to their claim was that the "SCA is claiming credit in a rather unique way. It's the only voice of authority supporting that point of view" (interview with Mengak, March 23, 2007).

38. Hartzog, interviews with Mengak, August 18, 2006, and February 8, 2007.

39. Kennedy, inaugural address, January 20, 1961, http://www.jfklibrary.org/Asset-Viewer/BqXIEM9F4024ntF17SVAjA.aspx (accessed March 4, 2011).

40. Senate Committee on Interior and Insular Affairs meeting, July 2, 1970, in Hartzog Papers, series 1, box 103, folder 1270A.

41. Hartzog, interview with Mengak, March 23, 2007.

42. Hartzog recalled a man sent by the Nixon administration as a "must hire." They placed him in the legislative division where he spent considerable time

with his feet up on his desk allowing everyone to admire that day's selection of brightly colored socks. Hartzog doubted his closeness to the Nixons until the inauguration of the Volunteers-in-Parks program. As Hartzog and the Nixon "friend" waited, Mrs. Nixon's limo pulled up. "Out stepped Mrs. Nixon and the first damn thing she did was reach out and grab him around the neck and smack him right there on the lips. He resolved my doubts immediately that day" (Hartzog, interview with Mengak, March 23, 2007).

43. Hartzog to John Rutter, Russell Dickenson, and Frank Kowski, April 27, 1972, in Hartzog Papers, series 1, box 103, folder 1270A.

44. Kowski to superintendents, c. April 1972, in Hartzog Papers, series 1, box 103, folder 1270A.

45. "Volunteers in the Parks Helping Park Come Alive for Visitors," Department of the Interior press release, December 1, 1972, in Hartzog Papers, series 1, box 103, folder 1270A.

46. National Park Service Volunteer website, http://www.nps.gov/volunteer (accessed February 20, 2007).

47. Hartzog, interview with Mengak, March 23, 2007.

48. Hartzog, interview with McDonnell, September 7, 2006, 146–47.

49. Thurber to Robert Garvey Jr., September 6, 1968, in Hartzog Papers, series 1, box 60, folder 748.

50. Hartzog, interview with Mengak, September 1, 2006.

51. Hartzog, interview with Mengak, February 8, 2007.

52. See National Park Foundation Congressional Charter, Public Law 90–209, 90th Congress, 2nd session, S. 814, December 18, 1967, section 4.

53. Hartzog, interview with Mengak, February 2, 2007.

54. Hartzog to Thurber, July 26, 1968, in Hartzog Papers, series 1, box 60, folder 748. In 1970, Secretary Hickel would appoint Richard Mellon; William Paley from CBS; timber capitalist Frederick Weyerhaeuser; William M. White Jr., chair of Great Western United Corporation; and Courtney Burton, associated with mining and shipping.

55. Udall to Lyndon B. Johnson, August 1, 1968, in Hartzog Papers, series 1, box 60, folder 748.

56. National Park Foundation minutes, June 5, 1969, in Hartzog Papers, series 1, box 60, folder 748. Stanton Cave is located along the Colorado River in Grand Canyon National Park. A major archaeological expedition looking for prehistoric artifacts was conducted during the summers of 1969 and 1970. See Quinn and Petterson, "A Grand Effort in the Grand Canyon."

57. Report of National Park Foundation, July 1, 1970–September 30, 1971, in Hartzog Papers, series 1, box 61, folder 758.

58. Hartzog, interview with Mengak, February 2, 2007.

59. National Park Foundation, "NPF Grants and Programs," http://www.nationalparks.org/npf-at-work/our-programs/apply-grants-programs (accessed August 10, 2007).

60. Hartzog, interview with Mengak, September 1, 2006.

61. Hartzog, interview with Mengak, June 8, 1999.

62. Hartzog, interview with Mengak, August 30, 2007.

63. Wright, Dixon, and Thompson, *Fauna of the National Parks of the United States.* See the National Park Service's faunal series, http://www.nps.gov/history/history/online_books/series/fauna.htm (accessed March 4, 2011).

64. Sellars, *Preserving Nature in the National Parks,* 91, 95–101.

65. Hartzog, interview with Mengak, May 12, 1996.

66. Wright, *Wildlife Research and Management in the National Parks,* 24.

67. Sellars, *Preserving Nature in the National Parks,* 165.

68. Ibid., 169.

69. Hartzog, interview with Mengak, May 12, 1996.

70. Sellars, *Preserving Nature in the National Parks,* 170.

71. Ibid., 197–200.

72. Ibid., 200.

73. Leopold, Cain, Cottam, Gabrielson, and Kimball, *Wildlife Management in the National Parks,* 32; Barbee, interview Mengak, December 13, 2007. Barbee said that Leopold told him he was surprised that the report became a "manifesto" of sorts. Had the committee envisioned that, they would have "picked their words more carefully" so that words such as "white man" would not later become so controversial. They never intended it to become what it became, he recalled Leopold saying.

74. Sellars, *Preserving Nature in the National Parks,* 215.

75. Ibid., 220.

76. National Research Council, *Research in the National Parks,* 6, 28–32.

77. Sellars, *Preserving Nature in the National Parks,* 224.

78. Hartzog, interviews with Mengak, August 18, 2006, and January 10, 2008. When asked why Kirwan had said NIH (National Institutes of Health) rather something like the NSF (National Science Foundation), he explained that Kirwan oversaw the NIH, so Hartzog guessed "that was the first thing that popped into his head."

79. Sellars, *Preserving Nature in the National Parks,* 225.

80. Ibid., 344.

81. Ibid., 214–15.

82. Ibid., 225.

83. Qtd. in ibid., 226.

84. Simons, "Science," 607.

85. Hartzog, interview with Mengak, October 8, 2007.

86. Olsen, chart 32, in *Administrative History,* http://www.cr.nps.gov/history/online_books/olsen/images/adhi32.jpg (accessed August 20, 2011).

87. Sellars, *Preserving Nature in the National Parks,* 229. Hartzog did not refute the account (Hartzog, interview with Mengak, August 30, 2007).

88. Hartzog, interview with Mengak, August 30, 2007.

89. Sellars, *Preserving Nature in the National Parks,* 230.

90. Ibid., 230, 345.

91. See Clark and McCool, *Staking Out the Terrain,* 48–64.

92. Sellars, *Preserving Nature in the National Parks,* 240.

93. These are common names for legislative acts that were amended multiple times. For example, the first legislation governing water pollution, called the

Federal Water Pollution Control Act, was enacted in 1948. Commonly called the Clean Water Act, it was later revised by amendments such as the one in 1972 that gave it its shape and laid out ambitious plans for improving water quality. See Copeland, *Clean Water Act*.

94. Hartzog, interview with Mengak, September 1, 2006.

95. See Chase, *Playing God in Yellowstone*, 232–61.

96. Hartzog wanted to abolish the many administrative manuals used by the agency, which he felt stifled decision making. He replaced them with three slim administrative policy manuals for natural, historical, and recreational areas that he reportedly drafted evenings in his office. The first draft appeared in 1967 and was followed by revisions in 1968 and 1970. See U.S. Department of the Interior, National Park Service, *Administrative Policies for Natural Areas of the National Park System*.

97. Shortly after the hearings, Hartzog instructed Yellowstone's superintendent John McLaughlin to "stop shooting and start shipping." It was not long before the governor called the park and begged them to stop, as the ranchers were loudly complaining. Hartzog told Jack Anderson, who had replaced McLaughlin, to keep shipping until the governor wrote a letter to that effect, which "really threw everything into a tizzy." Eventually, the governor did (Hartzog, interview with Mengak, August 30, 2007).

98. Sellars, *Preserving Nature in the National Parks*, 246–49.

99. See Baker and Reeser, *Goat Management Problems in Hawaii Volcanoes National Park*.

100. Hartzog, interview with Mengak, July 8, 1999.

101. Qtd. in Sellars, *Preserving Nature in the National Parks*, 260.

102. Leopold, Cain, Cottam, Gabrielson, and Kimball, "Policies of Park Management," in *Wildlife Management in the National Parks*, http://www.cr.nps.gov/history/online_books/leopold/leopold5.htm (accessed August 20, 2011).

103. Qtd. in Sellars, *Preserving Nature in the National Parks*, 260.

104. Ibid., 258–61.

105. Ibid., 252; Chase, *Playing God in Yellowstone*, 173–94; Craighead and Craighead, "Grizzly Bear-Man Relationships in Yellowstone National Park." The grizzlies in Yellowstone slowly rebounded from a low of some two hundred animals in 1982.

106. Leopold, Cain, Cottam, Gabrielson, and Kimball, "The Concept of Park Management" and "Methods of Habitat Management," in *Wildlife Management in the National Parks*, http://www.cr.nps.gov/history/online_books/leopold/leopold3.htm and http://www.cr.nps.gov/history/online_books/leopold/leopold6.htm (accessed August 20, 2011).

107. Hartzog, interview with Mengak, July 28, 1999.

108. See the 1968 edition of the National Park Service's *Administrative Policies for Natural Areas of the National Park*.

109. See Rothman, *A Test of Adversity and Strength*.

110. Allen and Leopold, *A Review and Recommendations Relative to the NPS Science Program*; National Park Service, *State of the Parks—1980*; National Parks and Conservation Association, *Research in the Parks*; National Parks and Conservation Association, *National Parks*; National Research Council, *Science*

and the National Parks; National Park Service, *National Parks for the Twenty-first Century*; National Parks Science Committee, *National Park Service Science in the 21st Century*.

111. Hartzog, interview with Mengak, January 14, 2008.
112. Reed, interview with Mengak, September 11, 2000.
113. Hartzog, interview with Mengak, January 14, 2008.
114. Hartzog, interview with Mengak, May 11, 1996.

Chapter Ten

1. Hartzog, *Battling for the National Parks*, 239–48.
2. Hartzog, interview with McDonnell, 2007, 85–86.
3. Thoreau Institute, "History of the National Park Service," http://www.ti.org/npshist.html#RTFToC3 (accessed March 4, 2011).
4. Frome, "Let's Put the Public Back in Public Lands."
5. Reed, interview with Mengak, September 11, 2000.
6. Hartzog, interview with Mengak, March 23, 1996.
7. "Morton Backs Hartzog in Parks Controversy," 55–56.
8. Hartzog, *Battling for the National Parks*, 233–38.
9. Ibid., 241.
10. Ed Winge to Hartzog, August 11, 1972, and Frank Masland to Hartzog, October 6, 1972, in Hartzog Papers, series 2, box 13, folder 93.
11. Haldeman, *Ends of Power*, 172.
12. Blair, "Eight Are Dismissed from High Posts by Interior Chief."
13. Hartzog, interview with Mengak, August 10, 1996.
14. Hartzog, *Battling for the National Parks*, 247.
15. Hartzog, interview with Mengak, March 23, 1996.
16. Blair, "White House Aid New Parks Chief."
17. Hartzog, interview with Mengak, October 6, 2006.
18. Walker to Hartzog, December 14, 1972, in Hartzog Papers, series 2, box 111, folder 1363.
19. Hartzog to Walker, December 15, 1972, in Hartzog Papers, series 2, box 111, folder 1363. Walker failed to follow Hartzog's parting advice, and as Nixon became mired in Watergate, Walker found himself the center of his own scandal. Awarding a large campground reservation contract to a personal friend ill equipped to handle the volume of on-line requests for reservations, Walker faced an uproar among angry campers and pointed questions from Congress. Five months after a disgraced Richard Nixon left in August 8, 1974, Walker resigned.
20. Hughes and Bullard, "George Hartzog Honored at Gala Retirement Party."
21. Blair, "Eight Are Dismissed from High Posts by Interior Chief."
22. Hartzog to Rockefeller, December 1972, in Hartzog Papers, series 4, box 83, folder 1042; Rockefeller to Hartzog, May 19, 1981, in Hartzog Papers, series 4, box 4, folder 35. Hartzog provided legal counsel for Rockefeller until 1981.
23. Hartzog, interview with Mengak, August 18, 2006.
24. Hartzog, interview with Mengak, July 7, 1997.
25. Ibid.

26. Hartzog, draft notes of book, Hartzog Papers, series 3, box 1, folder 1.

27. Hartzog, "When the NPS Wakes Up," draft of May 9, 1989, speech to NPS superintendents conference, in Hartzog Papers, series 4, box 14, folder 133.

28. "No former employee may knowingly make, with the intent to influence, any communication to or appearance before an employee of the United States on behalf of any other person (except the United States) in connection with a particular matter involving a specific party or parties, in which he participated personally and substantially as an employee, and in which the United States is a party or has a direct and substantial interest."

29. Andrew Normandeau, Ragan and Mason, to John C. Keeney, February 13, 1975, in Hartzog Papers, series 4, box 2, folder 13. Bernard Meyer, a former solicitor for the National Park Service who subsequently went to work for Ragan and Mason, was also investigated.

30. Hodge, "2 Ex-Interior Aides Probed by Justice."

31. Tom Zito and Milton Coleman, "FBI Probing Visitor Center Contracts"; Hartzog, testimony, March 3, 1977, in Hartzog Papers, series 4, box 2, folder 12.

32. Harzog, interview with Sherwood, November 8, 1989; Hartzog, interview with Mengak, May 12, 1996. He recalled that during his first Christmas as director he received many packages from concessionaires. "I packed everything in our yellow station wagon and my wife delivered it to the Salvation Army." He sent thank you notes saying the Salvation Army enjoyed their donation and at the next meeting he asked them not to send gifts in the future.

33. Everhardt to Hartzog, August 1975, in Hartzog Papers, series 4, box 2, folder 15.

34. Parker to Hartzog, May 12, 1977, in Hartzog Papers, series 4, box 2, folder 12.

35. Sherwood, "George B. Hartzog, Jr.," 152–53; Hartzog, testimony, March 30, 1977, in Hartzog Papers, series 4, box 2, folder 12.

36. Hartzog credited the McCarthy hearings with showing him the importance of record keeping. One of McCarthy's targets was the Methodist bishop G. Bromley Oxnam. Oxnam kept such detailed notes of every phone call, meeting, and trip that allegations against him were dropped. Hartzog resolved to do the same, and soon the habit became ingrained. One FBI agent investigating Hartzog remarked that he had "never seen anything like this in his life" (Sherwood, "George B. Hartzog, Jr.," 152).

37. Hartzog, draft of *Battling for the National Parks*, in Hartzog Papers, series 3, box 1, folder 1.

38. Alternate titles for his book included "The Skirmish Line," "Take It Now, Warts and All," "Politics Establish Parks," "Play Hard Ball," "Last Clear Chance," and "An Inheritance at Risk" (Hartzog Papers, series 3, box 1, folder 1).

39. Hartzog, correspondence with Mengak, March 24, 2003.

40. Hartzog, interview with Mengak, August 18, 2006.

41. Hartzog, "Summary of Career Highlights."

42. Hartzog, interview with Mengak, August 18, 2006; Hartzog, "Summary of Career Highlights."

43. See the Hartzog Fund, Department of Parks, Recreation, and Tourism Management, Clemson University, http://www.hehd.clemson.edu/prtm/Hartzog/Hartzog_Fund.php (accessed March 4, 2011).

44. Wright, interview with Mengak, December 11, 2008.

45. Hartzog III, interview with Mengak, January 19, 2009; Wright, interview with Mengak, December 11, 2008.

46. George III recalled that each night his father gathered the family for Bible reading and prayer. The imagine of this "dominant and domineering" man getting down on his knees by the rocking chair each night to lift the family up in prayer left an indelible image.

Chapter Eleven

1. Utley, interview with Mengak, March 31, 1999.

2. Frome, *Regreening the National Parks*, 69–70.

3. Reed, interview with Mengak, September 11, 2000.

4. Everhart, "A Swashbuckler Among the Bureaucrats," 11, 13.

5. Hartzog, interview with Mengak, November 4, 2000.

6. Hartzog, interview with Mengak, May 11, 1996.

7. Utley, interview with Mengak, March 31, 1999.

8. Boyd Evison to Hartzog, December 4, 1970, in Hartzog Papers, series 2, box 23, folder 162C.

9. Udall, introduction, xiii.

10. Brown, e-mail correspondence with Mengak, March 3, 2003.

11. Ibid.

12. Evison to Hartzog, December 4, 1970, in Hartzog Papers, series 2, box 23, folder 162C.

13. McPhee, "Ranger," 52.

14. Everhart, e-mail correspondence with Mengak, August 2002; Mintzmyer, interview with Mengak, October 23, 2000; Utley, interview with Mengak, March 31, 1999; Chapman, interview with Mengak, May 2, 1997.

15. Utley, interview with Mengak, March 31, 1999; Mintzmyer, interview with Mengak, September 6, 2000; Brown, e-mail correspondence with Mengak, March 3, 2003; Foresta, *America's National Parks and Their Keepers*, 59–91.

16. Utley, interview with Mengak, March 31, 1999.

17. Hartzog, interview with Mengak, July 8, 1997.

18. Stanton, interview with Mengak, October 1, 2000.

19. Ibid.

20. "NPS Mourns the Passing of Former Director George B. Hartzog, Jr.," 1.

21. Ibid., 9.

22. National Park Service, "Volunteer," http://www.nps.gov/volunteer (accessed July 22, 2009).

23. Hartzog, interview with Mengak, March 23, 1996.

24. Brown, e-mail correspondence with Mengak, March 26, 2003.

25. Udall to Hartzog, no date, handwritten notes at the bottom of book pages sent by Udall to Hartzog. Udall writes, "Geo—I've always had reservations regarding Mather. This helps explain why I rate you, not he, as the best this century"; Utley, foreword, Hartzog, interview with McDonnell, 2007.

26. "NPS Mourns the Passing of Former Director George B. Hartzog, Jr.," 9.

Selected Bibliography

Archival Collections

Hartzog Directorate Collection. National Park Service Collection, RG 30. Harpers Ferry Center, Harpers Ferry, WV.

George B. Hartzog Jr. Papers. Special Collections. Clemson University, Clemson, SC, Mss74.

National Park Women. National Park Service History Collection, RG 21. Harper's Ferry Center, Harpers Ferry, WV.

Books and Articles

Albright, Horace M. (as told to Robert Cahn). *The Birth of the National Park Service*. Salt Lake City, UT: Howe Brothers, 1985.

———. *Origins of National Park Service Administration of Historic Sites*. Philadelphia: Eastern National Park and Monument Association, 1971.

Albright, Horace M., Russell E. Dickenson, and William Penn Mott Jr. *The National Park Service: The Story Behind the Scenery*. Las Vegas, NV: KC Publications, 1987.

Albright, Horace M., and Marian Albright Schenck. *Creating the National Park Service: The Missing Years*. Norman: University of Oklahoma Press, 1999.

Anderson, Martin. *The Federal Bulldozer*. New York: McGraw-Hill, 1967.

Banner, Lois. *Women in Modern Times: A Brief History*. New York: Harcourt Brace Jovanovich, 1974.

Bearss, Edwin C. "Arno B. Cammerer." In *National Park Service: The First 75 Years*, ed. William H. Sontag. Philadelphia: Eastern National Park and Monument Association, 1990. http://www.nps.gov/history/history/online_books/sontag/cammerer.htm.

Berry, Mary Clay. *The Alaska Pipeline: The Politics of Oil and Native Land Claims*. Bloomington: Indiana University Press, 1975.

"Bible Says Gravel Effective Despite Pentagon Papers Row." *Fairbanks Daily News*, August 10, 1971.

Black, Lydia T. *Russians in Alaska, 1731–1867*. Fairbanks: University of Alaska Press, 2004.

Blair, William M. "Eight Are Dismissed from High Posts by Interior Chief." *New York Times*, December 7, 1972.

———. "White House Aid New Parks Chief." *New York Times*, December 14, 1972.

———. "Park Service Due for Big Changes." *New York Times*, October 17, 1963.

Bird, Caroline. *Invisible Scar*. New York: Longman, 1966.

Branch, Taylor. *Parting the Waters: America in the Kings Years, 1954–1963.* New York: Simon and Schuster, 1988.

Brower, David. "A New Decade and a Last Chance: How Bold Shall We Be?" *Sierra Club Bulletin* 45 (January 1960): 3–4.

Butcher, Russell D. *Guide to National Parks: Alaska Region.* Guildford, CT: Globe Pequot Press, 1999.

Cahn, Robert. *The Fight to Save Wild Alaska.* Washington, D.C.: Audubon Society, 1982.

———. "How National Park Plan Slipped Away." *Christian Science Monitor,* January 23, 1969, 1–4.

Chafe, William H. *The Paradox of Change: American Women in the 20th Century.* New York: Oxford University Press, 1991.

Chase, Alston. *Playing God in Yellowstone.* New York: Atlantic Monthly Press, 1986.

Clark, Jeanne Nienaber, and Daniel C. McCool. *Staking Out the Terrain: Power and Performance Among Natural Resource Agencies.* Albany: State University of New York Press, 1996.

Committee on Women's Employment and Related Social Issues, *Women's Work, Men's Work: Sex Segregation on the Job.* Washington, D.C.: National Academy Press, 1986.

Connally, Eugenia Horstman. "d-2: Saving Our Last Frontier." *National Parks* 55 (March 1981): 5–8.

Craighead, John J., and Frank C. Craighead Jr., "Grizzly Bear-Man Relationships in Yellowstone National Park." *Bioscience* 21 (August 1971): 845–57.

Dallek, Robert. *Lone Star Rising: Lyndon Johnson and His Times, 1908–1960.* New York: Oxford University Press, 1991.

Daugherty, John. "John D. Rockefeller, Jr." In *National Park Service: The First 75 Years,* ed. William H. Sontag. Philadelphia: Eastern National Park and Monument Association, 1990. http://www.nps.gov/history/history/online_books/sontag/rockefeller.htm.

Devine, Robert A., ed. *Vietnam, the Environment, and Science.* Vol. 2 of *The Johnson Years.* Lawrence: University Press of Kansas, 1987.

Dilsaver, Lary, ed. *America's National Park System: The Critical Documents.* Lanham, MD: Rowman and Littlefield, 1994.

Doll, Maurice. "Women Don't Mind Park Service Limits." *Denver Post,* July 14, 1972.

Douglas, Paul. *In the Fullness of Time.* New York: Harcourt Brace Jovanovich, 1972.

Duscha, Julius. "How the Alaska Act Was Won." *Living Wilderness* 44 (Spring 1981): 4–9.

Elder, Glen H., Jr. *Children of the Great Depression: Social Change in Life Experience.* Chicago: University of Chicago Press, 1974.

Elliot, Gary. *Alan Bible and the Politics of the New West.* Reno: University of Nevada Press, 1994.

Engel, J. Ronald. *Sacred Sands: The Struggle for Community in the Indiana Dunes.* Middletown, CT: Wesleyan University Press, 1983.

Everhart, William C. *The National Park Service.* Boulder, CO: Westview Press, 1983.

———. "A Swashbuckler Among the Bureaucrats." *Arrowhead: The Newsletter of the Employees and Alumni of the National Park Service* 15 (Summer 2008): 1, 9.

———. *Take Down Flag and Feed Horses.* Urbana: University of Illinois Press, 1998.

"Five Versions: Why LBJ Changed His Mind on the Parks." *Washington (D.C.) Evening Star*, January 27, 1969.

Foresta, Ronald A. *America's National Parks and Their Keepers*. Washington, D.C.: Resources for the Future, 1984.

Fox, Stephen. *The American Conservation Movement: John Muir and His Legacy*. Madison: University of Wisconsin Press, 1981.

French, Jere Stuart. "The Decline and Deterioration of the American City Park." In *Reflections on the Recreation and Park Movement: A Book of Readings*, ed. David Gray and Donald A. Pelegrino, 225–29. Dubuque, IA: William C. Brown, 1973.

Friedan, Betty. *The Feminine Mystique*. New York: Dell, 1963.

Frome, Michael. "Let's Put the Public Back in Public Lands." *Field and Stream* (October 1971): 42, 140–41.

———. *Regreening the National Parks*. Tucson: University of Arizona Press, 1992.

Gibbons, Steve. "National Natural Landmarks Program: 'On-hold' . . . but Holding Its Own," *Natural Resource Review* 1996, 29. http://www.nature.nps.gov/YearInReview/yr_rvw96/yir1996.pdf.

Gilliam, Harold. "Parks Are for People to Have Fun In." *San Francisco Sunday Examiner and Chronicle*, October 15, 1967.

Glass, James A. *The Beginnings of a New National Historic Preservation Program, 1957–1969*. Nashville, TN: American Association for State and Local History, 1990.

Gould, Lewis. "Lady Bird Johnson and Beautification." In *Vietnam, the Environment, and Science*, ed. Robert A. Devine, 150–80. Vol. 2 of *The Johnson Years*. Lawrence: University Press of Kansas, 1987.

Gray, David E., and Donald A. Pelegrino, eds. *Reflections on the Recreation and Park Movement: A Book of Readings*. Dubuque, IA: William C. Brown, 1973.

Haldeman, H. R. *Ends of Power*. New York: Times Books, 1978.

Harper, Paul, and Joann R. Krieg, eds. *John F. Kennedy: The Promise Revisited*. New York: Greenwood, 1988.

Harrison, Cynthia. *On Account of Sex: The Politics of Women's Issues, 1945–1968*. Berkeley: University of California Press, 1988.

Hartman, Susan M. *From Margin to Mainstream: American Women and Politics since 1960*. New York: Knopf, 1989.

Hartzog, George B., Jr. *Battling for the National Parks*. Mt. Kisco, NY: Moyer Bell, 1988.

———. "Summary of Achievements of George B. Hartzog, Jr. as Director of the National Park Service, 1964–1972." Unpublished, 2006.

———. "Summary of Career Highlights." Unpublished, May 4, 1998.

Hodge, Paul. "2 Ex-Interior Aides Probed by Justice." *Washington Post*, August 3, 1975, B1, B4.

Hughes, Daniel S., and Jean Bullard. "George Hartzog Honored at Gala Retirement Party." *National Park Service Newsletter*, January 1973.

Ise, John. *Our National Park Policy: A Critical History*. Baltimore, MD: Johns Hopkins Press, 1961.

Jacobs, Jane. *Death and the Life of Great American Cities*. New York: Random House, 1961.

Kaufman, Polly Welts. *National Parks and the Woman's Voice: A History*. Albuquerque: University of New Mexico Press, 1996.

Kearns, Doris. *Lyndon Johnson and the American Dream*. New York: St. Martin's, 1991.

Keller, Robert H., and Michael F. Turek. *American Indians and the National Parks*. Tucson: University of Arizona Press, 1998.

Kessler-Harris, Alice. *Out to Work: A History of America's Wage-Earning Women*. New York: Oxford University Press, 1982.

Kwandrans, Paula. "Is FOST Dead?" *U.S. Department of the Interior National Park Service Newsletter*, November 27, 1969.

Larrabee, Donald R. "How Udall's Park Plans Collapsed: Two Stubborn Men and 6 Million Acres." *Anchorage Daily Times*, February 5, 1969.

Lee, Ronald F. *Family Tree of the National Park System*. Philadelphia: Eastern National Park and Monument Association, 1972.

Levy, Peter B. *The Civil Rights Movement*. Westport, CT: Greenwood, 1998.

———, ed. *100 Key Documents in American Democracy*. Westport, CT: Greenwood, 1994.

McCloskey, Michael. "What the Wilderness Act Accomplished in Protection of Roadless Areas Within the National Park System." *Journal of Environmental Law and Litigation* 10 (Spring 1995): 455–72.

McElvaine, Robert S. *The Great Depression: America, 1929–1941*. New York City: Time Books, 1984.

McPhee, John. *Coming into the Country*. New York: Farrar, Straus, and Giroux, 1976.

———. "George Hartzog: Ranger." *New Yorker*, September 11, 1971, 45–88.

Mengak, Kathy K. "Hartzog and Udall Reminisce." *Courier: The National Park Service Newsletter* 31 (May 1986): 14.

Mitchell, Donald Craig. *Sold American: The Story of Alaska Natives and Their Land, 1867–1959*. Hanover, NH: University of New England Press, 1997.

"Morton Backs Hartzog in Parks Controversy." *Parks and Recreation*, September 1972, 55–56.

Nash, Roderick. *Wilderness and the American Mind*. 3rd. ed. New Haven, CT: Yale University Press, 1982.

National Parks and Conservation Association. *National Parks: From Vignettes to a Global View*. Washington, D.C.: National Parks and Conservation Association, 1989.

———. *Research in the Parks: An Assessment of Needs*. Vol. 2 of *Investing in Park Futures: A Blueprint for Tomorrow*. Washington, D.C.: National Parks and Conservation Association, 1989.

National Research Council. *Research in the Parks: A Report by the Advisory Committee to the National Park Service on Research*. Washington, D.C.: National Academy Press, 1963.

———. *Science and the National Parks*. Washington, D.C.: National Academy Press, 1992.

Neuman, Loretta. "Golden Gate, Gateway: First Urban NRA's." *National Park Courier*, January 1973: 1–2.

"NPS Mourns the Passing of Former Director George B. Hartzog, Jr." *Arrowhead: The Newsletter of the Employees and Alumni Association of the National Park Service* 15 (Summer 2008): 1, 9.

O'Reilly, Kenneth. *Nixon's Piano: Presidents and Racial Politics from Washington to Clinton*. New York: Free Press, 1995.

Park, Sharon C. "Dr. Ernest Allen Connally." *Cultural Resource Management* 23 (July 2000): 23.

Potter, Jean C. *Alaska Under Arms*. New York: Macmillan, 1942.

Quinn, Michael, and Jim Petterson. "A Grand Effort in the Grand Canyon." *Bats* 15 (Fall 1997): 4–7. http://www.batcon.org/index.php/media-and-info/bats-archives.html?task=viewArticle&magArticleID=820.

Reisner, Marc. *Cadillac Desert: The American West and Its Disappearing Water*. New York: Penguin, 1993.

Rettie, Dwight Fay. *Our National Park System: Caring for America's Greatest Natural and Historic Treasures*. Urbana: University of Illinois Press, 1995.

Rothman, Hal K. *America's National Monuments: The Politics of Preservation*. Lawrence: University Press of Kansas, 1989.

Runte, Alfred. *National Parks: The American Experience*. 2nd ed. Lincoln: University of Nebraska Press, 1987.

———. *Yosemite: The Embattled Wilderness*. Lincoln: University of Nebraska Press, 1990.

Schullery, Paul. *Searching for Yellowstone: Ecology and the Last Wilderness*. New York: Houghton Mifflin, 1997.

Sealander, Judith. "John F. Kennedy's Presidential Commission on the Status of Women: A Dividing Line." In *John F. Kennedy: The Promise Revisited*, ed. Paul Harper and Joann R. Krieg, 253–56. New York: Greenwood Press, 1988.

Sellars, Richard W. *Preserving Nature in the National Parks: A History*. New Haven, CT: Yale University Press, 1997.

Shafer, Craig L. "The National Landmark Program: A Progress Report," *Park Science* 20 (Spring 2000): 11–13.

Shankland, Robert. *Steve Mather of the National Parks*. 3rd ed. New York: Knopf, 1976.

Sherwood, Frank. "George B. Hartzog, Jr.: Protector of the Parks." In *Exemplary Public Administrators: Character and Leadership in Government*, ed. Terry Cooper and N. Dale Wright, 139–65. San Francisco: Jossey-Bass, 1992.

Simons, Howard. "Science: Sense and Nonsense." *Bioscience* 16 (September 1966): 607–8.

Small, Melvin. *The Presidency of Richard Nixon*. Lawrence: University Press of Kansas, 1999.

Sontag, William H., ed., *National Park Service: The First 75 Years*. Philadelphia: Eastern National Park and Monument Association, 1990. http://www.nps.gov/history/history/online_books/sontag/sontagt.htm.

Student Conservation Association. "Our History." http://www.thesca.org/about/history.

Swain, Donald C. *Wilderness Defender: Horace M. Albright and Conservation*. Chicago: University of Chicago Press, 1970.

Udall, Stewart L. Introduction. In *Battling for the National Parks* by George B. Hartzog Jr., xi–xvii. Mt. Kisco, NY: Moyer Bell, 1988.

———. *The Quiet Crisis*. New York: Holt, Rinehart and Winston, 1963.

———. *The Quiet Crisis and the Next Generation*. Salt Lake City, UT: Peregrine Smith, 1988.

Utley, Robert. "What Were They Thinking? The NHPA 40 Years Ago Today." National Trust for Historic Preservation Conference, Pittsburgh, PA, November 2, 2006.

Von Eckardt, Wolf. "Washington's Chance for Splendor." *Harper's Magazine*, September 1963, 54–64, 97.

Wayburn, Edgar. *Your Land and Mine: Evolution of a Conservationist.* Berkeley, CA: Sierra Club Books, 2004.

Weisner, Brad. "The Value of Historical Research." *Parks and Recreation* 30 (February 1994): 30–40.

Wicker, Tom. *One of Us: Richard Nixon and the American Dream.* New York: Random House, 1991.

Wirth, Conrad L. *Parks, Politics, and the People.* Norman: University of Oklahoma Press, 1980.

Woodbury, Richard B. "John Otis Brew, 1906–1988." *American Antiquity* 55 (July 1990): 452–59.

Wright, Gerald. *Wildlife Research and Management in the National Parks.* Urbana: University of Illinois Press, 1992.

Zito, Tom, and Milton Coleman. "FBI Probing Visitor Center Contracts." *Washington Post*, November 11, 1976, A1, sec. 2.

Government Documents

Allen, Durwood L., and A. Starker Leopold. *A Review and Recommendations Relative to the NPS Science Program.* Memorandum report to director. Washington, D.C.: Department of the Interior, National Park Service, 1977.

Baker, James K., and Donald W. Reeser. *Goat Management Problems in Hawaii Volcanoes National Park: A History, Analysis, and Management Plan.* Natural Resources Report 2. Washington, D.C.: Department of the Interior, National Park Service, 1972.

Binkley, Cameron. *Science, Politics, and the "Big Dig": A History of the Southeast Archeological Center and the Development of Cultural Resources in the Southeast.* Washington, D.C.: Department of the Interior, National Park Service, Cultural Resources Southeast Region, 2007.

Capps, Michael. "Eero Saarinen—Architect with a Vision." Jefferson National Expansion Memorial website, National Park Service. http://www.nps.gov/jeff/planyourvisit/architect.htm.

———. *Kennesaw Mountain National Battlefield Park: An Administrative History.* Atlanta, GA: Department of the Interior, National Park Service, Southeast Regional Office, 1994. http://www.nps.gov/history/history/online_books/kemo/adhi/adhit.htm.

Cockrell, Ron. *A Signature of Time and Eternity: The Administrative History of Indiana Dunes National Lakeshore, Indiana.* Omaha, NE: Department of the Interior, National Park Service, Midwest Regional Office, 1988.

Copeland, Claudia. *Clean Water Act: A Summary of the Law.* Congressional Research Service, Library of Congress, April 23, 2010. http://www.cnie.org/nle/crsreports/10May/RL30030.pdf.

Floyd, Myron. *Race, Ethnicity, and Use of the National Park System*. Social Science Research Review Series 1.2. Washington, D.C.: Department of the Interior, National Park Service, 1999.

House Committee on Interior and Insular Affairs. *To Provide for the Establishment of the Gateway National Seashore in the States of New York and New Jersey, and for Other Purposes*. 92nd Congress, 1st session, July 19. Washington, D.C.: Ward and Paul, 1971.

Karamanski, Theodore J. *A Nationalized Lakeshore: The Creation and Administration of Sleeping Bear Dunes National Lakeshore*. Omaha, NE: Department of the Interior, National Park Service, Midwest Regional Office, 2000.

Lane, Franklin K., "Secretary Lane's Letter on National Park Management, May 13, 1918." In *America's National Park System: The Critical Documents*, ed. Lary Dilsaver, 49–52. Lanham, MD: Rowman and Littlefield, 1994.

Leopold, A. Starker, Stanley A. Cain, Clarence M. Cottam, Ira N. Gabrielson, and Thomas L. Kimball. *Wildlife Management in the National Parks*. Washington, D.C.: Department of the Interior, National Park Service, 1963. http://www.cr.nps.gov/history/online_books/leopold/leopold.htm.

Lerner, William. *Statistical Abstract of the United States*. 94th ed. Washington, D.C.: U.S. Department of Commerce, 1973.

Louter, David. *Contested Terrain: North Cascades National Park Service Complex, an Administrative History*. Seattle, WA: Department of the Interior, National Park Service, Columbia Cascades Support Office, 1998. http://www.nps.gov/history/history/online_books/noca/adhi/contents.htm.

Mackintosh, Barry. *Assateague Island National Seashore: An Administrative History*. Washington, D.C.: Department of the Interior, National Park Service, History Division, 1982. http://www.nps.gov/history/history/online_books/asis/adhit.htm.

———. *The Historic Sites Survey and National Historic Landmarks Program: A History*. Washington, D.C.: Department of the Interior, National Park Service, History Division, 1985.

———. *Interpretation in the National Park Service: A Historical Perspective*. Washington, D.C.: Department of the Interior, National Park Service, History Division, 1986. http://www.cr.nps.gov/history/online_books/mackintosh2/index.htm.

———. *The National Historic Preservation Act and the National Park Service: A History*. Washington, D.C.: Department of the Interior, National Park Service, History Division, 1986.

———. *The National Parks: Shaping the System*. Washington, D.C.: Department of the Interior, National Park Service, 1984.

———. "Revising the Mission." In *National Park Service: The First 75 Years*, ed. William H. Sontag. Philadelphia, PA: Eastern National Park and Monument Association, 1990. http://www.nps.gov/history/history/online_books/sontag/sontag5.htm.

McChristian, Douglas C. *Ranchers to Rangers: An Administrative History of Grant-Kohrs Ranch*. Deer Lodge, MT: Department of the Interior, National Park Service, Rocky Mountain Cluster, 1977. http://www.nps.gov/grko/parkmgmt/upload/adhi1.pdf.

Merritt, Jane T. *Administrative History: Fort Vancouver National Historic Site*. Seattle, WA: Department of the Interior, National Park Service, Cultural Resources

Division, Pacific Northwest Region, 1993. http://www.nps.gov/history/history/online_books/fova/adhi/index.htm.

National Parks Science Committee. *National Park Service Science in the 21st Century: Recommendations Concerning Future Directions for Science and Scientific Resource Management.* Washington, D.C.: National Park Service, 2004.

Olsen, Russ. *Administrative History: Organizational Structures of the National Park Service, 1917 to 1985.* Atlanta, GA: Department of the Interior, National Park Service, Southeast Regional Office, 1985. http://www.cr.nps.gov/history/online_books/olsen/adhi.htm.

Outdoor Recreation Resources Review Commission. *Outdoor Recreation for America.* Washington, D.C.: GPO, 1962.

Paige, John C. *The Civilian Conservation Corps and the National Park Service, 1933–1942: An Administrative History.* Washington, D.C.: Department of the Interior, National Park Service, 1985.

Rothman, Hal K. *A Test of Adversity and Strength: Wildland Fire in the National Park System.* Washington, D.C.: Department of the Interior, National Park Service, 2005.

Rothman, Hal K., and Daniel J. Holder. *The Park That Makes Its Own Weather: An Administrative History of Golden Gate National Recreation Area.* San Francisco, CA: Department of the Interior, National Park Service, 2002.

Senate Committee on Interior and Insular Affairs. *Establishment of Gateway National Recreation Area in the States of New York and New Jersey.* 92nd Congress, 1st session, May 12. Washington, D.C.: Alderson Reporting Company, 1971.

Siehl, George. *Alternative Strategies for Providing Urban Parks.* Major Issues and Study Briefs of the Congressional Research Service. Washington, D.C.: Library of Congress, 1977.

Tilden, Freeman. *Who Am I? Reflections on the Meaning of Parks on the Occasion of the Nation's Bicentennial.* Washington, D.C.: Department of the Interior, National Park Service, 1975.

U.S. Department of the Agriculture, Fish and Wildlife Service. *To Have and To Hold: Alaska's Migratory Birds.* Washington, D.C.: GPO, 1971.

U.S. Department of the Interior, National Park Service. *Administrative Policies for Natural Areas of the National Park System: Compilation of the Administrative Policies for the National Parks and Monuments of Scientific Significance (Natural Area Category).* Washington, D.C.: GPO, 1968.

———. *Administrative Policies for Natural Areas of the National Park System: Compilation of the Administrative Policies for the National Parks and Monuments of Scientific Significance (Natural Area Category).* Rev. ed. Washington, D.C.: Department of the Interior, National Park Service, 1970.

———. *Historic Listing of National Park Officials.* Washington, D.C.: Department of the Interior, National Park Service, 1991.

———. *National Parks for the Twenty-first Century: The Vail Agenda.* Washington, D.C.: Department of the Interior, National Park Service, 1993.

———. *State of the Parks—1980: A Report to the Congress.* Washington, D.C.: Department of the Interior, National Park Service, 1980.

———. *State of the Parks: A Report to the Congress on a Service Strategy for Prevention and Mitigation of Natural and Cultural Resource Management Problems.* Washington, D.C.: Department of the Interior, National Park Service, 1981.

U. S. Riot Commission. *Report of the National Advisory Commission on Civil Disorders.* Washington, D.C.: GPO, 1968.

Unrau, Harlan D., and G. Frank Williss. *Administrative History: Expansion of the National Park Service in the 1930s.* Denver, CO: Department of the Interior, National Park Service, Denver Service Center, 1983. http://www.cr.nps.gov/history/online_books/unrau-williss/adhic.htm.

Williss, G. Frank. *"Do Things Right the First Time": The National Parks and the Alaska National Interest Lands Conservation Act of 1980.* Rev. ed. Anchorage: Department of the Interior, National Park Service, Alaska Regional Office, 2005.

Wright, George M., and Joseph S. Dixon, and Ben H. Thompson. *Fauna of the National Parks of the United States: A Preliminary Survey of Faunal Relations in National Parks.* Washington, D.C.: Department of the Interior, National Park Service, 1933.

Interviews and Correspondence

Barbee, Robert. Taped phone interview with Kathy Mengak, December 13, 2007.

Belous, Bob. Oral history interview with Bill Schneider, October 8, 1991. Project Jukebox, University of Alaska Fairbanks, H91–22–23. http://jukebox.uaf.edu/YUCH/htm/bobbel.htm.

Bowen, Doris Osmundson. Taped phone interview and e-mail correspondence with Kathy Mengak, July 26–27, 1999.

Brown, William. Taped phone interview and e-mail correspondence with Kathy Mengak, June 13, 2001, March 3, 2003, March 26, 2003.

Chapman, Howard. Taped phone interview and e-mail correspondence with Kathy Mengak, May 2, 1997, September–November 1997, and October 23, 2000.

Colby-Ghiatis, Terry. E-mail correspondence with Kathy Mengak, March 16, 2001.

Davis, Gentry. Taped phone interview with Kathy Mengak, October 19, 2000.

Everhart, William. Oral history interview with Robert Moore, October 25, 1994. Jefferson National Expansion Memorial Oral History Project. http://www.nps.gov/jeff/historyculture/oralhistory.htm.

Everhart, William, with George B. Hartzog. Taped interview with Kathy Mengak, March 26, 1996, May 11, 1996, August 10, 1996, July 7–8, 1997, July 30, 1998, June 8, 1999, July 28, 1999, and September 8, 2001. Taped phone interview with Kathy Mengak, April 25, 2005.

Grove, Jesse. E-mail correspondence with Kathy Mengak, September 20, 2000.

Gwaltney, William W. Taped phone interview with Kathy Mengak, August 31, 2000.

Hagood, Reginald (Flip). Taped phone interview with Kathy Mengak, August 31, 2000.

Hartzog, George B., Jr. Interview with Frank Sherwood, November 8, 1989. Hartzog Papers, series 4, box 8, folder 71.

———. Oral history interview with Amelia Fry, April 14, 1965. Hartzog Directorate Collection, appendices, sec. 3.

———. Oral history interview with Charles Hosmer, August 5, 1981. Hartzog Directorate Collection, appendices, sec. 4.

———. Oral history interview with Janet McDonnell, September 7, 2006. Draft copy.

———. Oral history interview with Janet McDonnell, 2007. Department of the Interior, National Park Service. http://www.nps.gov/history/history/online_books/director/hartzog.pdf.

———. Taped interviews and phone interviews with Kathy Mengak, 1996–2008.

Hartzog, George B., III. Taped phone interview with Kathy Mengak, January 19, 2009.

Hartzog, Helen. Taped interview with Kathy Mengak, July 28, 1999.

Hutchinson, Ira J. Taped phone interview with Kathy Mengak, August 4, 2000.

Knight, Betty. Taped phone interview with Kathy Mengak, October 10, 2000.

Lusignan, Ronald R. E-mail correspondence with Kathy Mengak, September 4, 2008.

Mackintosh, Barry. E-mail correspondence with Kathy Mengak, February 17 and 24, December 29, 1999.

Mintzmyer, Lorraine. Taped phone interview and e-mail correspondence with Kathy Mengak, September 6, 2000, and October 23, 2000.

Moore, Robert. Interview with Kathy Mengak, October 25, 1994.

Neal, John D., Phone conversation with Kathy Mengak, November 20, 2000.

Norris, Frank. E-mail correspondence with Kathy Mengak, September 26, 2006, and September 10, 2010.

Reed, Nathaniel P. E-mail correspondence with Mengak, August 28, 2000.

———. Taped phone interview with Kathy Mengak, September 11, 2000.

Shaw, Phyllis P. Taped phone interview with Kathy Mengak, May 10, 1999.

Stanton, Robert G. E-mail correspondence with Kathy Mengak, October 20, 2004.

———. Taped phone interview with Kathy Mengak, October 1, 2000.

Swem, Ted. Oral history interview with Bill Schneider, October 10, 1991, and July 6, 1993. Project Jukebox, University of Alaska Fairbanks, H93–15–26, H93–15–27, H93–15–28, and H93–15–29. http://jukebox.uaf.edu/WRST/swem/tesw.html.

———. Taped phone interview with Kathy Mengak, September 16, 2005.

Szarka, Frederick. E-mail correspondence with Kathy Mengak, March 19, 2001.

Udall, Stewart L. Oral history interview with Joe B. Frantz, April 18, May 16, July 29, October 31, and December 16, 1969. Lyndon Baines Johnson Library Oral History Collection, LBJ Library, University of Texas. http://www.lbjlib.utexas.edu/johnson/archives.hom/oralhistory.hom/UDALL/Udall.asp.

———. Taped phone interview with Kathy Mengak, September 19, 2005.

Utley, Robert M. E-mail correspondence with Kathy Mengak, 1999–2011.

———. Interview with S. Herbert Evison, May 17, 1973. Technical Information Center, Denver Service Center, National Park Service.

———. Interview with Richard W. Sellars and Melody Webb, September 24–December 27, 1985. Department of the Interior, National Park Service, Southwest Cultural Resources Center, Professional Papers 16. http://www.nps.gov/history/history/online_books/utley/utley.htm.

Wright, Brett. Phone interview with Kathy Mengak, December 11, 2008.

Index

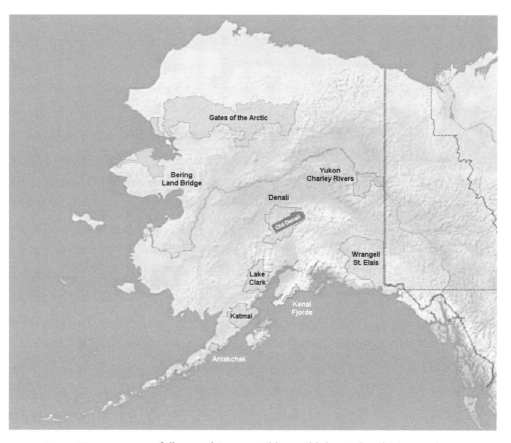

Map 2: Hartzog successfully urged Senator Bible to add the vital 17(d)(2) amendment to the Alaska Native Claims Settlement Act of 1971, which in part recognized the importance of protecting national interest parklands for all Americans. A long and bitter battle ultimately resulted in the Alaska National Interest Lands Conservation Act of 1980 and in the creation of parks that doubled the size of the National Park System. Courtesy of the National Park Service. http://www.nps.gov/state/ak/index.htm, modified by Bob King.